Baseball's Wildest Season

ALSO BY WILLIAM J. RYCZEK
AND FROM McFARLAND

*The Sixties in the News: How an Era Unfolded
in American Newspapers, 1959–1973* (2021)

*Dr. Strangeglove: The Life and Times
of All-Star Slugger Dick Stuart* (2021)

*Baseball on the Brink: The Crisis of 1968* (2017)

*Connecticut Gridiron: Football Minor Leaguers
of the 1960s and 1970s* (2014)

*Base Ball Founders: The Clubs, Players and Cities of the Northeast
That Established the Game* (edited by Peter Morris, William J. Ryczek,
Jan Finkel, Leonard Levin and Richard Malatzky, 2013)

*Base Ball Pioneers, 1850–1870: The Clubs and Players Who Spread
the Sport Nationwide* (edited by Peter Morris, William J. Ryczek,
Jan Finkel, Leonard Levin and Richard Malatzky, 2012)

*Crash of the Titans: The Early Years of the New York Jets
and the AFL* (revised edition, 2009)

*Baseball's First Inning: A History
of the National Pastime Through the Civil War* (2009)

*The Yankees in the Early 1960s* (2008)

*The Amazin' Mets, 1962–1969* (2008)

*When Johnny Came Sliding Home:
The Post–Civil War Baseball Boom, 1865–1870*
(1998; paperback 2006)

*Blackguards and Red Stockings: A History of Baseball's
National Association, 1871–1875,* (1992;
revised edition, paperback 2016)

# Baseball's Wildest Season

*Three Leagues, Thirty-Four Teams and the Chaos of 1884*

William J. Ryczek

McFarland & Company, Inc., Publishers
*Jefferson, North Carolina*

Library of Congress Cataloguing-in-Publication Data

Names: Ryczek, William J., 1953– author.
Title: Baseball's wildest season : three leagues, thirty-four teams and the chaos of 1884 / William J. Ryczek.
Description: Jefferson, North Carolina : McFarland & Company, Inc., Publishers, 2023 | Includes bibliographical references and index.
Identifiers: LCCN 2023002377 | ISBN 9781476691145 (paperback : acid free paper) ∞
ISBN 9781476649252 (ebook)
Subjects: LCSH: Baseball—United States—History—19th century. | Union Association (Baseball league) | American Association (Baseball league : 1882-1891) | National League of Professional Baseball Clubs.
Classification: LCC GV863.A1 R9293 2023 | DDC 796.35709097309/034—dc23/eng/20230207
LC record available at https://lccn.loc.gov/2023002377

British Library cataloguing data are available

ISBN (print) 978-1-4766-9114-5
ISBN (ebook) 978-1-4766-4925-2

© 2023 William J. Ryczek. All rights reserved

*No part of this book may be reproduced or transmitted in any form or by any means, electronic or mechanical, including photocopying or recording, or by any information storage and retrieval system, without permission in writing from the publisher.*

Front cover image: © Miriam Doerr Martin Frommherz/Shutterstock

Printed in the United States of America

*McFarland & Company, Inc., Publishers
Box 611, Jefferson, North Carolina 28640
www.mcfarlandpub.com*

To the memory of Frederick Ivor-Campbell,
historian, writer, and friend,
whose long-ago article on the 1884 season
sparked my interest in the topic

# Acknowledgments

For several of my books, I have experienced the good fortune of having one person who played an invaluable role in helping to create the final product. In this case, it was David Nemec, a prolific author and gifted writer who may know more about 1880s baseball than anyone alive today. He was kind enough to read every word of my draft and made many, many terrific suggestions, coming up with some gems that I would never have found on my own. I can't thank him enough.

My good friend Doron (Duke) Goldman read certain sections of the manuscript and, as always, had a number of excellent suggestions, pointing me to additional sources that helped me expand some ideas.

Research for this book began in the mid-1990s, when it was necessary to visit libraries and scroll through microfilm reels, and ended in the third decade of the 21st century, when research consists of sitting in front of a home computer and accessing newspapers from around the world. Those who help with the process have become increasingly anonymous, and I would like to thank all those who made the digital age possible. For those of us who've been researching baseball history for more than four decades, the transformation is miraculous. The amount of available information has exploded, and I'm not sure how we found anything thirty years ago. Much of the available information is the work product of the Society for American Baseball Research, including numerous mini-biographies of major league players that provide wonderful background for several of the actors in the drama that was the 1884 season.

Finally, I want to thank my fellow members of SABR, especially those of Connecticut's Smoky Joe Wood Chapter. They provide consistent encouragement, a forum for discussion, and a sounding board for ideas. But best of all, many have become good friends in ways that transcend our mutual love of baseball history.

# Contents

| | |
|---|---|
| *Acknowledgments* | vi |
| *Introduction: Prologue to Chaos* | 1 |
| 1. "More money is made and expenses are less than is generally supposed" | 7 |
| 2. The Game | 11 |
| 3. The Players | 21 |
| 4. "The blacklist shackle" | 33 |
| 5. The Magnates | 39 |
| 6. "More famous for his quaintness and eccentricity than his managerial skill" | 47 |
| 7. "There are few men in any business who should be clothed with this authority" | 63 |
| 8. The Drunks | 77 |
| 9. "There will be no more foolishness this year": National League Preview | 91 |
| 10. "Too many—it is going to weaken us": American Association Preview | 102 |
| 11. The Wreckers: Union Association Preview | 119 |
| 12. "He said he'd pitch his arm off to win the flag": National League Season | 131 |
| 13. "The Metropolitan Club is a strong one": American Association Season | 150 |
| 14. "To keep a correct record of the Union Association is worse than solving a Chinese puzzle": Union Association Season | 169 |
| 15. The Pitchers | 183 |
| 16. "Shadows of their former selves" | 190 |

| | |
|---|---|
| 17. The Others | 203 |
| 18. "Champions of the world" | 213 |
| 19. "On the Ragged Edge" | 217 |
| *Appendix A: Rules of the Brooklyn American Association Club* | 233 |
| *Appendix B: The Lake Front Battleground* | 234 |
| *Appendix C: Players Active in Multiple Leagues* | 237 |
| *Chapter Notes* | 239 |
| *Bibliography* | 255 |
| *Index* | 259 |

# Introduction: Prologue to Chaos

The year 1884 was the fourteenth of major league baseball,[1] and it would seem as though the men in charge should have been getting better at it. There had been bumps, bruises, and instructive lessons along the way, and a perceptive, attentive man might have learned how to avoid the type of problems that plagued baseball in its early years. But in 1884, the lessons were forgotten and enthusiasm got the better of good sense.

Baseball's governance had been largely an exercise in trial and error, huffing and puffing a half-step behind the game's evolution. The first organization to oversee the sport was the National Association of Base Ball Players, formed in 1857. At that time, there were just a handful of clubs, all of which were amateur organizations located in New York City and its immediate vicinity. Most were more social club than competitive sporting organization.

In the years following the Civil War, baseball mushroomed and by 1870 there were hundreds of organized clubs, many located far from New York and a few of which were composed of professional players. The latter were *very* competitive, and it became apparent that the parochial NA was not equipped to govern such a diverse group. Each club had equal voting power, which left the handful of professional clubs at the mercy of the far more numerous amateurs, who had a different agenda.

The 1870 season was rife with disputes, and when it ended with multiple teams claiming the national championship, it was clear that things had to change. The amateurs' solution was to prohibit professionalism, but that horse was long since out of the barn. The professionals had a different solution, which was to form their own league, the National Association of Professional Base Ball Players.

The new organization, consisting of nine teams, vowed to find a more equitable way of determining a champion. Under the old method, with no fixed schedule, champions could retain their throne by simply refusing to play a strong challenger. For several years, the New York and Brooklyn clubs used that dodge to keep the title away from Chicago, Cincinnati, and Philadelphia.

The NAPBBP thought it had established a clear path to the championship, but they were mistaken, and the 1871 pennant race was a confused muddle. One club folded, there were forfeits and ineligible players, and no one seemed to know whether the champion was supposed to be the team that won the most games, the most series, the highest percentage of games, or some combination thereof. In the end, the Athletics of Philadelphia were declared professional baseball's first champions.

During the next four seasons, the Boston Red Stockings, under the leadership of the estimable Harry Wright, dominated the league, winning the pennant each year and climaxing their run with a 71–8 record in 1875. But off the field there was a myriad

1

of problems. Contract jumping, gambling, and rumors of thrown games plagued the Association throughout its existence, and the league's nominal ten-dollar admission fee attracted weak organizations that couldn't survive the season.

Everything came apart in 1875. Four clubs folded before the season was over, and suspicious play gave rise to rumors that gamblers were fixing games; on one occasion it was alleged that two competing teams were each trying to throw the game to the other. In July, four of the Red Stockings' best players, in clear violation of the rules, signed contracts to play for Chicago in 1876. The National Association had reached the end of the road.

For years, the NA was regarded as an embarrassment. Alfred Spink, in his 1911 epic history of baseball, which meandered along for about 500 pages, devoted approximately two inches on a single page to America's first professional sports league. He titled it "The Purifying of the Sport" and made it clear that purification was due to the end of the NA.[2]

The National Association of Professional Base Ball Players was aptly named, for it was operated principally for the benefit of the players. There were no owners as they exist today. Most clubs were established for civic pride and backed by groups of local boosters, as in the old amateur days when members' dues covered expenses. Early professional business models were essentially the same, except that dues-paying members hired more skilled men to play. There was little expectation of profit and the reward for being a stockholder was a season ticket and bragging rights. If gate revenue plus dues covered expenses, it had been a successful year.

Some NA clubs operated as cooperatives, a form of socialism under which players were compensated by dividing the gate receipts rather than receiving salaries. While today's players' union often asks for a share of baseball's revenue, players in 19th-century cooperative nines, who got 100 percent of the profits, didn't fare too well. The coops were the least stable franchises and most didn't last even a full season.

The stock organizations didn't do much better. Most teams that reported profits would have lost money without contributions from members, which were included as revenue. National Association baseball was not a money-making proposition, but there was a man in Chicago who thought that, with better management, professional baseball could be a profitable endeavor.

Chicago was a late bloomer among American cities. During the early 19th century, while Boston, New York, and Philadelphia were bursting with people, money, and culture, Chicago was a sparsely populated western backwater. Even the western cities of Cincinnati and Cleveland, with their bustling industry, dwarfed Chicago in stature. During the 1840s and 1850s, however, Chicago began to grow. The Civil War brought prosperity, and by its conclusion, the city was wealthy and burning with ambition.

Any city with ambition needed a baseball team, and in late 1869 a group of prominent citizens formed a club known as the White Stockings. A year earlier, Harry Wright's Cincinnati Red Stockings had demonstrated what a well-compensated team of professionals could accomplish, sweeping through the 1869 season without a loss. Chicago wanted to follow suit, importing several high-priced eastern players who they hoped would make the city proud.

Unfortunately, the White Stockings did not have a leader with the organizational skills of Wright, and although the club won most of its games, the citizens of Chicago were disappointed that it was not the best in the country. For a young city with an inferiority complex, only first place would do, and the fans and press reacted badly to every defeat.

## Introduction: Prologue to Chaos

The White Stockings joined the professional NA in 1871 and led the league for a good part of the summer. In early October, however, the devastating Chicago fire ended all hopes of a championship. For the next two years, Chicago did not field a major league team, but in 1874, the White Stockings paid their ten dollars and re-entered the National Association under the leadership of Norman Gassette and local coal merchant William Hulbert. The club finished with a lackluster 28–31 record in its first year and was on its way to an equally disappointing 30–37 mark the following season when Hulbert stunned the baseball world by signing four members of the championship Red Stockings.

The rules of the National Association prohibited players from signing for a subsequent season before the current playing schedule ended but it had been done before and the NA did nothing. It was unlikely they would do more this time than bluster and unleash a few salvos of righteous indignation, but Hulbert had bigger ideas than just protecting his investment; he wanted to give baseball a structure under which an ambitious man could make some money.

In February 1876, Hulbert assembled representatives of the stronger NA clubs and convinced them to form a new entity, which they called the National League of Professional Base Ball Clubs. Minimum population requirements and an increase in the admission fee from ten to one hundred dollars would eliminate fly-by-night nines. Other regulations gave the clubs more power and the players less.

Only eight teams began the new League's first season, down significantly from the thirteen that had begun the 1875 campaign. Despite Hulbert's high hopes, the new National League was far from an instant success. In its first year, attendance was 31 percent lower than in 1875 and only Hulbert's Chicago club turned a profit.[3] At the end of the season, the Mutuals and Athletics, two of pro baseball's oldest teams in two of America's largest cities, were expelled for failing to complete their schedules. In the old NA that wouldn't have been a problem, but Hulbert was not about to repeat the NA experience, even if it meant losing Philadelphia and New York.

The following year brought an even greater calamity. There had been many rumors of skullduggery in the old NA, but none had been proven. In only the second year of its existence, the National League was wracked by a scandal in Louisville that involved bribes, throwing games, and complete confessions by three of the accused. Hulbert expelled the four guilty players for life. He meant business.

Business didn't mean profits; in 1877 all NL teams lost money. Louisville, beset by scandal and unpaid salaries, dropped out of the League. Hartford and St. Louis, burdened by financial problems, also folded their tents. Milwaukee, Indianapolis, and Providence joined holdovers Chicago, Boston, and Cincinnati in a teetering six-team format that was beginning to look like the old National Association, only smaller.

For the remainder of the decade, the NL struggled, gaining and losing teams each year. By 1878, only Cincinnati, Boston, and Chicago remained of the eight teams that began play just two seasons earlier. In 1879 Indianapolis and Milwaukee folded and new franchises were established in Troy, Syracuse, Cleveland, and Buffalo.

Syracuse didn't make it through the season and was replaced by Worcester the following year. Although Hulbert billed his circuit the "National" League, it included minor cities like Worcester, Troy, Providence, and Buffalo, and was absent from New York, Philadelphia, and St. Louis. When he formed the NL, Hulbert decreed that no team would be allowed in the league unless if came from a city with a population of at least 75,000, but he had to waive the requirement to admit Troy and Worcester.[4]

During the late 1870s, the National League called itself the only "major" league, but not only did it lack representation in America's largest cities—it was missing many of the best baseball players in America. The International Association, a loose conglomeration of professional clubs, began operation in 1877; after its two Canadian entries folded, the name was changed to the National Association. Many players who played in the majors before and after played for Association clubs, either because they were closer to home or because it was more remunerative. National League teams frequently played exhibitions against non-league clubs, and they often lost—37 times in 1876 and 72 the following year.

In 1877, NL champion Boston lost 13 games to non-league teams. The International Association champion Tecumseh club beat Chicago on several occasions and the Lowell Club was 9–5 against NL competition.[5]

Although there was a lot of talent in the new National Association, it was plagued by the biggest problem of its old namesake—a plethora of financially unstable clubs. The key to winning the NA championship was surviving the season, for the champion was not necessarily the best team, but the last one standing.

Eighteen eighty-two saw the demise of Hulbert from heart disease at 49 and the birth of a second major league, the American Association. The seeds of the new Association were planted at a September 1881 Philadelphia meeting between 28-year-old Horace Phillips, a swashbuckling entrepreneur known as "Hustling Horace," and journalist Oliver Perry Caylor of Cincinnati. Phillips had invited a number of baseball men to the meeting, but Caylor, who was well-regarded in baseball circles, was the only one who came. The next morning, Hustling Horace, with his gift for promotion, sent telegrams to everyone who hadn't come informing each of them that they were the only one missing. A new league called the American Association had been established, and they were welcome to join.

Phillips and Caylor called on Al Pratt, a former player and a fixture in Pittsburgh baseball, for guidance, and Pratt suggested they contact Pittsburgh businessman Denny McKnight. McKnight was interested in their proposal and hosted a meeting on October 10, attended by twelve men, including John Day of the Metropolitans of New York and Chris Von der Ahe of the St. Louis Brown Stockings, two of the strongest independent teams in the country.

The group met again in Cincinnati on November 2, with representatives from St. Louis, Columbus, New York, Brooklyn, Louisville, Pittsburgh, Cincinnati, Boston, and Philadelphia in attendance. These cities had two things in common. They were among the largest cities in the United States and none of them had a major league team. When the 1882 season began, five of them had just one thing in common, for they were members of the new American Association. When Brooklyn couldn't get a team together, Baltimore took its place. McKnight was elected president.

The National League had changed what it didn't like about the old National Association and the American Association changed what it didn't like about the National League, particularly Hulbert's stern moralistic dictates. The AA would allow Sunday ball and permit the sale of liquor on its grounds. General admission tickets, which cost 50 cents in the NL, would be 25 cents in the AA.

The new league needed players and was initially more accommodating than the NL, offering generous salaries and agreeing to give released players a half month's salary, not much of a gesture today but a major concession in those days. Fortunately, with only eight National League teams, there was a lot of talent available. The AA didn't need to poach many players; only 19 of the 113 men who played in the first AA season were in the NL in 1881 or 1882.

The NL tried to ignore the AA. It prohibited its clubs from playing exhibitions against AA teams, which would have been very popular, since fans wanted to see the leagues compete against each other. The two leagues had a few skirmishes over players, but they were resolved in reasonably amicable fashion. Six teams started and finished the Association's first season, a major accomplishment for any 19th-century league and, even more surprising, all made a profit. Shockingly, with only six teams to the NL's eight, AA attendance was almost double that of the NL (804,000 to 404,000).[6]

Once the NL realized that the AA was not going away, it decided that cooperation was better than competition. Hulbert's successor, Abraham Mills, wanted peace, which would end the salary war and pave the way for lucrative exhibition games.

Committees from the NL and AA met on February 17, 1883, at the Fifth Avenue Hotel in New York City, along with a representative of the brand-new Northwestern League. Mills, who was an attorney, was the architect of the peace agreement, under which the three leagues agreed to cooperate with each other and respect each other's contracts. An Arbitration Committee was established to resolve disputes. On March 5, at its annual meeting, the NL authorized Mills to sign the agreement, and the AA owners approved it on March 12. The one-year "war" was over and the AA became the NL's partner.

The American Association had a good run. Because it was absorbed into the NL in 1892, most modern fans consider the AA a failed league. But half of the clubs that comprised the National League for the first half of the 20th century (Brooklyn, St. Louis, Cincinnati, and Pittsburgh) started as members of the American Association.

The AA's success in New York and Philadelphia forced the NL to follow. In the fall of 1882, the League created openings by expelling the Troy franchise, which had committed no sin other than failing to draw fans (attendance in their final season was just 26,000), and Worcester, which had drawn but 11,000. In 1883, for the first time since the Mutuals and Athletics were expelled in 1876, the NL had teams in New York and Philadelphia.

Each league fielded eight teams in 1883, with the Athletics of Philadelphia capturing the AA title after an exciting tussle with St. Louis, and the Boston club, known as the Beaneaters, taking the National League flag. Despite the newfound amity between the two organizations, there was no post-season playoff. One of the major achievements of the first season of peace was that every major league club completed its schedule, something that rarely occurred in prior years.

The AA again outdrew the NL (1,005,000 to 611,000) and combined attendance increased by about 50 percent. Further, exhibition games between NL and AA teams proved immensely popular. In New York and Philadelphia, the inter-league series for city supremacy were far more popular than league games.

"Not since the old-time gatherings of a dozen years ago," reported the *New York Clipper*, "when the rivalry between the Brooklyn Atlantics and Philadelphia Athletics was at its highest has there been seen such a vast assemblage of spectators at a baseball match in Philadelphia as crowded the grounds to excess on April 14, on the occasion of the first game of the series for the State championship between the Philadelphia League Club's team and the Athletic Club of the American Association."[7]

The lean days of the late 1870s were over. It was estimated that 45,000 attended the six games of the series, which were evenly divided between the two teams. The deciding contests would take place after the regular season. Enthusiasm was equally strong in New York, where former president Grant attended the opening game of the National League club.

Everything seemed rosy, and Wright and Ditson's *1884 Union Association Base Ball Guide* proclaimed, "The season of 1883 was, beyond doubt, the most successful that our national game has ever experienced ... the most glorious ever known in the history of the game."[8]

The increase in attendance and profits was bound to attract competition. In St. Louis, a wealthy young baseball enthusiast named Henry V. Lucas drew up plans to form a third major league, one that would not observe the rules the NL and AA had agreed upon. Minor circuits like the Northwestern League and Eastern League talked about expansion and perhaps dreamed that someday they would achieve major league status.

The euphoria of 1883 was followed by the chaos of 1884. The next eight chapters describe the state of the game that year and introduce the various members of the cast, followed by a summary of the action on the field in each of the three major leagues. There was also a lot happening beyond the confines of the National League, American Association, and Union Association, and the hectic activity of the minor leagues is worthy of its own chapter, as is the activity of women, blacks, and others little noticed by the mainstream media. The bloody aftermath of the 1884 season and prospects for 1885 are laid out in the final chapter.

It wasn't a pretty sight, and many thought the future of baseball was in jeopardy. "There was a time," said the *Chicago Tribune* in August 1884, "when base-ball might fairly be called the National game, but that was before the era of professional players and clubs, which are organized solely for the purpose of making what money is to be had ... the facts are beginning to come out, and from the disclosures already made it is probable that the close of the present season will witness the death of professional base-ball."[9]

"The game of base ball, as an exhibition," added the *Detroit Free Press*, "is gradually losing its interest ... the competition between the players; the broken engagements in the very midst of the season; the apparent impossibility of any set of rules or contracts to bind the players; the lack of interest in those places whose local club is losing; the riotous mobs that have tried to lynch the umpire in two or three recent New York games, appear to be hastening the present system to an inglorious breakup."[10]

Eighteen eighty-four just might be the most unusual season in the history of major league baseball. It wasn't like the doldrums of the late 1870s; it was more like the confusion of the old National Association. As teams folded and entire leagues collapsed, it appeared to many that America had reached the limit of its love for the sport.

The *Saint Paul Globe* said, "[B]ase ball has been entirely over done this year." After extolling the virtues of the game, the paper concluded, "like many good things, people can get too much of it, and they undoubtedly have."[11] It was time to retrench.

# 1

# "More money is made and expenses are less than is generally supposed"

In 1884, the United States had a population of just over 50 million, spread unevenly throughout 38 states, nine territories, and the District of Alaska. Most Americans lived in the northeast quadrant of the country, approximately 25 percent of them in New York, Pennsylvania, and Ohio, with New York's more than five million inhabitants accounting for over 10 percent of Americans. Eight states, primarily in the West, had total populations of less than 100,000, the least populous being Idaho with just 33,000 people.

New York, with a population of 1.2 million, was the largest city in the United States, and adjacent Brooklyn was an independent metropolis with another 567,000 residents. Philadelphia and Chicago were the only other cities with populations of more than 500,000.

Since major league baseball was played in major population centers, it was concentrated almost exclusively in the northeast. Louisville was the only team south of the Mason-Dixon line and Chicago and St. Louis formed the western boundary. There were 234,000 San Franciscans, enough to support a major league franchise, but how would the other teams get there?

When William Hulbert formed the National League, he wanted to eliminate "one-horse towns" by establishing a minimum population of 75,000 for NL cities. But it was not until Troy and Worcester were replaced by New York and Philadelphia in 1883 that the league met that requirement.

When the 1884 season began, all NL teams and 10 of the 12 AA clubs, as seen in the table on the following page, were at or above Hulbert's 75,000 minimum. Altoona was the only outlier in the UA, but as the latter league's teams failed, they were forced to replace Chicago, Philadelphia, and Pittsburgh with Kansas City, Wilmington, and St. Paul. When Washington failed, the AA went to the well for Richmond, which had a population of just 64,000.

The prosperity of baseball is greatly dependent on the state of the United States economy, and the game's fortunes tend to ebb and flow with the financial state of the country. Baseball's first major growth spurt was fueled by the post–Civil War economic boom. Wartime profits provided the capital to satisfy pent-up demand and business thrived. Europe furnished the United States with workers and consumers and when Europeans realized the economic potential of North America, large amounts of capital flowed across the Atlantic.

| National League | | American Association | | Union Association | |
|---|---|---|---|---|---|
| New York | 1,206,000 | New York | 1,206,000 | Philadelphia | 847,000 |
| Philadelphia | 847,000 | Philadelphia | 847,000 | Chicago | 503,000 |
| Chicago | 503,000 | Brooklyn | 567,000 | Boston | 363,000 |
| Boston | 363,000 | St. Louis | 351,000 | St. Louis | 351,000 |
| Cleveland | 160,000 | Baltimore | 332,000 | Baltimore | 332,000 |
| Buffalo | 155,000 | Cincinnati | 255,000 | Cincinnati | 255,000 |
| Detroit | 116,000 | Pittsburgh | 156,000 | Pittsburgh | 156,000 |
| Providence | 105,000 | Washington | 147,000 | Washington | 147,000 |
| **Total** | 3,455,000 | Louisville | 124,000 | Milwaukee | 116,000 |
| **Average** | 431,875 | Indianapolis | 75,000 | Kansas City | 56,000 |
| | | Richmond | 64,000 | Wilmington | 42,000 |
| | | Columbus | 52,000 | St. Paul | 41,000 |
| | | Toledo | 50,000 | Altoona | 20,000 |
| | | **Total** | 4,226,000 | **Total** | 3,229,000 |
| | | **Average** | 325,076 | **Average** | 248,380 |

NOTE: The Pittsburgh population does not include Allegheny, which was an independent city with 79,000 inhabitants.

Much of the capital was used to expand the rail system. One of the favorite activities of Civil War troops was tearing up track but when peace came the lines were repaired and many new routes added. From 1865 through 1873, the number of miles of railroad track doubled, bringing goods and residents to newly-opened western lands. Production of just about everything increased, and with the European economy suffering from the effects of the Franco-Prussian War, foreign markets absorbed whatever wasn't consumed domestically. Importing people and capital and exporting goods is a winning combination, and the only cautionary aspect of the American economy was a troubling inflation that had begun during the war.[1]

Baseball was a major beneficiary of the thriving economy. Prior to the Civil War, the sport had been popular only in greater New York City, but after the war it spread across the northeast. Prosperous businessmen contributed capital to pay salaries to professional players and consumers with disposable income paid admission fees to watch them play. By 1870, baseball was firmly established as America's national game.

The post war boom collapsed in September 1873, when the failure of the banking house of Jay Cooke signaled the onset of an economic slump that plagued the United States for the remainder of the decade. Cooke had grown famous and wealthy selling bonds to finance the Civil War, but his post-war investment in the troubled Northern Pacific Railroad over-extended him. In 19th-century terms, Jay Cooke and Company suspended payment. In today's parlance, they had a liquidity crisis. In any era, they were broke.

The Cooke collapse was one of many, and soon the economy was in deep recession. While statistics from the era are not particularly reliable, it was estimated that unemployment doubled from 1873 to 1877.[2] Over a two-year period, approximately 18,000 businesses failed.[3]

Major league baseball suffered along with the rest of the country. Entertainment is a discretionary expense, and in the latter half of the 1870s, there wasn't a lot of discretionary income. There were some people in New York and Philadelphia with a lot of money, but the National League didn't have a team in either city.

In 1877, NL teams drew a total of just 204,694 fans, about 60,000 less than the old NA drew in 1871. The champion Boston club led the league in attendance with 55,000, Chicago was second with 46,000, and no other team drew more than 30,000. With a 60-game schedule, that meant that the other four teams averaged less than 1,000 fans per game.

In 1879, six years after the Cooke failure, industrial output and agricultural prices remained depressed. As the European economy recovered from its early decade slump and its agricultural production increased, the balance of trade turned against the United States. With improved investment prospects in Europe and less opportunity in America, the flow of capital across the Atlantic Ocean began to reverse course and flow eastward.

In 1880, the U.S. economy began to revive. Immigration increased and many easterners migrated to the vast open spaces of the west, where there was an almost unlimited supply of cheap land and economic opportunity for the enterprising. In 1881, unemployment decreased to pre-recession levels and the number of business failures dropped precipitously. By the following year, the country was enjoying a new prosperity and the government was generating a surplus large enough to create agitation for a reduction of tariffs and internal taxes.[4]

It was no coincidence that baseball attendance soared in the early '80s:

| 1880 | 256,428 | 1882* | 804,388 |
| 1881 | 301,236 | 1883* | 1,616,154 |

*includes American Association

The return of major league ball to New York, Philadelphia, and St. Louis contributed greatly to the increased patronage. In 1883, 305,000 and 243,000 fans watched AA games in Philadelphia and St. Louis, respectively. Professional baseball was finally beginning to look like William Hulbert hoped it would when he founded the National League.

With capitalist ownership, a revived economy, and competition tempered by the National Agreement, the profit potential of baseball was greater than ever. "More money is made," said *Sporting Life* at the end of the 1883 season, "and expenses are less than is generally supposed."[5] *Sporting Life* claimed that the 1883 season was the most prosperous in history and estimated the profits of American Association teams as follows[6]:

| Philadelphia | $65,000[7] |
| St. Louis | 40,000 |
| Cincinnati | 35,000 |
| Baltimore | 30,000 |
| Metropolitans | 5,000 |
| Columbus | 5,000 |
| Allegheny | 2,000[8] |
| Louisville | (1,000) |

The impressive income of the champion Philadelphia club showed how far the game had come from the days of the National Association, when contributions and dues from stockholders were generally required just to cover expenses. Even Baltimore, which finished a distant last, pocketed a nice profit.[9]

Chicago was believed to have made the most money of any NL team, with Boston right behind them. But no one could be sure about Boston because when the club held its annual meeting on December 19, no financial report was given, ostensibly due to the illness of the treasurer. *Sporting Life* claimed the real reason for the lack of a report was that management didn't want the shareholders to know how much money the team had made. Not only was the treasurer absent; the meeting, originally scheduled to take place at 7:30 in the evening, was moved to 11:00 in the morning, when most investors were at work.[10] A group of dissident shareholders tried to organize a special meeting in order to force financial disclosure, but management refused.

Chicago and Boston had strong teams in 1883 and their financial success was no surprise. But even Philadelphia's National League club, which had a pitiful 17–81 record, managed to clear $10,000,[11] which reinforced the importance of having franchises in New York and Philadelphia. Cleveland was said to have made a profit of $20,000. Buffalo, hampered by cold and rainy northern weather, reported a loss of about $200.[12]

The strong financial results created an aura of optimism among National League clubs as the 1884 season dawned. For only the second time in its history, the League began the season with the same teams that started the prior one. During the previous eight years, the league had 18 different franchises; Chicago and Boston were the only ones that remained from the inaugural season of 1876.[13]

Amid the optimism was a disquieting omen—the economy was losing steam. The early 1880s had been good, but by 1884, warning signs began to appear on the horizon. Government revenue declined and domestic production outstripped demand. The heavy debt load of the railroads, one of America's largest industries, put them under great financial pressure. Several lines were controlled by financier Jay Gould, a reckless deal-maker who was much more adept at stock manipulation than railroad operations. While Gould always seemed to prosper, his shareholders and debt holders rarely did, and in a down economy they were in peril.

The downturn of 1884 was nothing like those of 1873 and 1893, but a Wall Street crash in May and a general decline in business activity reversed the economic gains of recent years. Although not reaching the levels of the late 1870s, unemployment and business failures increased. The investment firm Grant and Ward, in which the son of former president Ulysses S. Grant was a partner, crashed in spectacular fashion. But there was no depression, and the situation probably wouldn't have been disastrous for baseball if they maintained the status quo. But the optimism created by the success of the early '80s led to expansion, and expanding into a declining economy is a recipe for disaster. But that is exactly what baseball did in 1884.

# 2

# The Game

Basketball hadn't been invented in 1884. College football was becoming popular, but if a modern fan were to watch an 1884 football game, they would have trouble understanding what was happening. The baseball played in 1884 had changed a lot since the 1850s, but it was not all that different from the game that would be played for the next century and a modern fan would have little difficulty following the action. Other than moving the pitcher back a few feet and other minor changes, the baseball of 1884 was clearly recognizable as the game played today.[1]

The quality of play had improved greatly since the early days and would continue to get better each decade. Pitching and hitting are adversarial, and batting averages won't increase if pitchers improve at the same rate as hitters. Fielding is man against baseball and therefore the most noticeable and measurable increase in baseball skill was in fielding. Pioneer players were about equally likely to catch or miss a ball, and even after the advent of professionalism, it wasn't unusual for teams to commit ten or more errors in a game. Of the 2,659 runs scored in 1871 National Association games, only 1,055 (40 percent) were earned runs. In the 1884 National League, 2,662 of 5,026 runs (53 percent) were earned, much better than in 1871 but well below 2019, when 92 percent of all NL runs were earned. By current standards, there were a lot of errors committed in 1884, and the difference between a good fielder and a bad one was far more glaring than it is today. The second basemen for the champion Providence Grays committed 56 errors, while those of the New York club were guilty of 110.[2]

The 1885 *Spalding Guide* claimed that players exhibited "almost perfect fielding"[3] during the 1884 season. By today's standards it was abysmal, as the best fielding percentage in the NL was Boston's .922. Six of the nine NL clubs posted averages of less than .900 and the average fielding mark for NL shortstops was .864. Not a single UA team had a fielding average above .900.

One reason fielding was better than it had been but not as good as it would be was the players' equipment. Catchers, who absorbed the most physical punishment, began experimenting with gloves in the late 1860s, and by 1884 virtually every catcher wore two gloves—a larger, more heavily padded version on one hand and a smaller, lighter one on their throwing hand. Many fielders wore gloves, but some would rely on their bare hands for another decade. The gloves were nothing like today's; they were used more for padding than as a tool designed for catching the ball.

A major difference between early baseball and that of the 1880s was the grounds on which the games were played. When baseball first became popular, it was played on any large, open, relatively level surface. When the concept of charging admission fees began, it created a need for fields that had enough seating to accommodate paying spectators and fences to keep out non-paying freeloaders. The first such facility was Brooklyn's Union Grounds, constructed by William Cammeyer in 1862, which hosted baseball in the summer and skating in the winter. Similar facilities were built over the next two decades and by 1884, accommodations had become much more accommodating, although they were still just wooden stands surrounding a field that was often uneven and sometimes un-groomed.

Most parks (stadium is a bit too lofty a word to describe 19th-century ball yards) had relatively limited capacity, and when overflow crowds gathered (usually on holidays) they spilled out onto the field. On such occasions, ropes were used to hold the spectators back, and ground rules usually decreed that any ball hit into the crowd was a double. On busy days, outfielders often had company, either excess fans or horse carriages, which were frequently allowed to park on the field. The St. Louis Browns' park had a beer garden in right field. Any ball hit into the garden was live but had to be returned to the pitcher (the man in the box, not the beer container) before a play could be made on a runner.

Batted balls rarely left the park, for the outfield fences (other than in Chicago) were a comfortable distance from home plate. Most home runs were of the inside-the-park variety, so larger parks, where the ball could roll great distances, were actually more conducive to home runs. The vast open spaces of 19th-century outfields put a premium on speed, both to cover the outfield expanses and to run out long hits.

Buffalo opened a new facility, called Olympic Park, in 1884, and the city's residents dutifully described it as the best ball grounds in the country. When the National League held a meeting in Buffalo in March, the magnates toured the new facility and, being polite guests, enthusiastically agreed that it was the finest park in the United States. Most delegates confined themselves to platitudes, but John Day of New York was more expressive if less sensitive. "The player who could not glorify himself amidst such fine surroundings," Day said, "deserved to be clubbed."[4]

The new grounds could seat 1,000 more people than the old one, and special accommodations were available to attract coveted female spectators, who were often admitted free when accompanied by a paying male. Women had their own toilet-room and seating section, the latter featuring 250 comfortable arm chairs and a prohibition against smoking. Other new parks likewise appealed to the cultured female; the Cincinnati grounds had a theater-like lobby and sliding doors. In 1884, Providence became the final NL team to offer seat cushions for spectators.

All cities liked to boast of a large number of women at their games, for ladies gave baseball respectability, lifting it above crude attractions like prize fighting and horse racing. The presence of women was expected to civilize male spectators and the opportunity to make the acquaintance of a comely lady might boost male attendance. An ad in the *St. Louis Post-Dispatch* one day read, "Will young lady with lady friend at base-ball park yesterday, who left at commencement of last inning and noticed a young gent sitting in center of grandstand and looked between crowd and bowed to gent please send ad to P.3 this office?"[5]

Even if the owner of P.3 didn't connect with the mysterious woman of his dreams, he could still have a good time at the ball park. Pre-game musical concerts were common, especially on opening day or before big games. Detroit produced a fireworks display on the Fourth of July. A female aeronaut took to the sky in a balloon prior to a UA game at Cincinnati, which also hosted Professor Carlos Martinez, the Spanish strong man.

During the game, vendors roamed the stands selling a variety of food, drink, and cigars, sometimes to the annoyance of the less hungry or thirsty spectators. "[I]f the refreshment boys would cry 'good cigars' and 'ham and cheese sandwiches' less frequently," wrote the *Richmond Dispatch*, "it would meet with the approval of the crowd in attendance. It they would make their rounds once every 15 minutes, it would be much better."[6] Liquor was prohibited in NL parks but sold in virtually all AA facilities. UA practices varied.

Although there was no radio or television coverage, fans that couldn't make it to the park could follow the results by telegraph. Inning by inning scores were usually posted outside local newspaper offices and in restaurants and bars that catered to the sporting crowd. On the day of big games, crowds gathered in the street to see each inning's result chalked on the board. Some parks also had scoreboards that posted out-of-town scores, as is done in modern stadiums.

While the presence of ladies was coveted, that of gamblers was not. The 1885 *Spalding Guide* boasted that baseball was the only professional sport without gambling, but that was disingenuous. Gambling was an acknowledged part of horse racing and boxing, was present in almost every sport and game of chance, and was nearly impossible to eliminate. "There was some talk of interfering with the pool selling on the games in this city [Chicago]," said one paper, "but it is not likely that anything of the kind will be done. The authorities might just as well put a stop to stock and oil speculations as to the pool business on baseball games."[7]

The one thing clubs *could* police was wagering on their grounds. Gambling was banned at all Union Association parks. Although there was a sign at New York's Polo Grounds prohibiting gambling, the stands were filled with men making a mockery of the prohibition. There was even more action downtown, at Broadway and Fulton Street, where a high stakes gambler was reputed to have lost $4,000 on one baseball bet.

The ubiquitous presence of gambling led to rumors. After Metropolitan pitcher Jack Lynch, one of the best hurlers in the AA, was hit hard one day, a newspaper reported that Lynch had been entertained by gamblers the previous evening and they slipped drugs into his drinks. The story was a fabrication, and the paper printed a retraction and apologized to Lynch.

Some practices that were common in those days would be viewed harshly today. When the 1883 Athletics found themselves engaged in a torrid pennant race with St. Louis, Philadelphia owner Lew Simmons promised each Pittsburgh player a $25 raincoat if they beat the Browns. They lost. St. Louis owner Chris Von der Ahe upped the ante by promising each Louisville player a $50 suit of clothes if they beat the Athletics four straight times. The best Louisville could do was two in a row.

The race came down to the final week, with the Athletics needing a win against Louisville to clinch the pennant. Louisville, behind star pitcher Guy Hecker, won the first game. After the final out, Simmons raced up to Louisville president Henry Pank and shouted, "I will give you $1,000 cash to put a man we can hit in there tomorrow."[8] Perhaps he was kidding.

Pank didn't take the bait and sent Hecker to the box again. With the winning runs on base and Philadelphia's Ed Rowen at bat, Simmons ran out and promised him $500 if he got a hit. In the end, everything worked out and the Athletics won 7–6 in 10 innings to bring home the flag. And it hadn't cost Simmons anything.

Baseball teams had become busier and much more mobile since 1850. An interclub match was a rarity in baseball's early days and all games took place close to home. The Excelsior Club of Brooklyn took baseball's first road trip in 1860 and by the end of the decade the most active teams were taking long, extended tours and playing 50–60 games per season. During the NA's first season in 1871, teams played between 19 and 33 league games, plus numerous exhibitions. The schedule gradually increased and in the final season of the NA, the Boston Red Stockings played 79 regular season games. In 1884, the championship schedule exceeded 100 games for the first time. Including exhibitions, most teams had a workload approaching today's 162-game slate.

The expanded 1884 schedule and the increased number of teams meant more travel than ever before. The *Cincinnati Enquirer* estimated the miles that each NL and AA club would have to travel and concluded that Brooklyn and the Metropolitans of the AA, with 8,564 and 8,497 miles, respectively, would spend the most time on the rails. Buffalo of the NL, with 5,516, would travel the least.[9]

The completion of the transcontinental railroad in 1869 cut long distance travel time dramatically, but it still took nearly seven days to get from New York to San Francisco. That assumed no delays or breakdowns, and no one like Jesse James lurking along the track. In 1876, an express train made the journey in the remarkable time of 83 hours, but that was a speed trial, not typical travel. Trains were theoretically capable of reaching speeds of 60 miles per hour, but due to the poor condition of many stretches of track, they hardly ever did. That meant that it took a long time to get from one league city to the next. Teams sometimes missed their train and had to forfeit[10] and games were frequently terminated early to allow one of the teams to catch their train.

Travel was not only slow; it was arduous. "It is anything but pleasant," wrote New York's John Montgomery Ward, "to travel as we do. We play every day, with just enough time between dates to reach the next city. The ride is usually made by night; and, what with the loss of sleep and the fatigue of the games, we lose all appreciation of the interesting and the beautiful. I am often so worn out in body and mind that my sensibilities are dulled."[11] Sanitary conditions and hygiene were not what they are today and some players became ill from food or drink consumed while traveling. Sick and worn-down players generally did not do well, and most nines fared much worse on the road than they did at home, not just due to unfriendly crowds, but because they were fatigued or ill.[12]

Once a team left home, it generally kept going, for it made little sense to make several return trips. The schedule consisted of long trips followed by lengthy stretches at home and in one-team cities, home fans had no games for several weeks at a time. In cities with two major league teams, the extended absence of one team was a golden opportunity for the other.

In the National League, all eastern teams went west in tandem, after which the western clubs came east. In 1884, eastern clubs ended their home schedules in mid–September and spent the rest of the season on the road. Buffalo was on the road for the first three weeks of the season, not a bad idea given the chilly Buffalo springs. The schedule committee tried to avoid cold May weather, but that wasn't easy since nearly all major league cities were in the northeast or upper Midwest. Detroit visited every NL city before playing its home opener June 2, more than a month after the season began. In July, when the weather was warmer, the Wolverines had a 19-game homestand.

Without television commercials and other modern-day delays, games were generally concluded in about two hours and anything much longer was considered tedious.

On August 14, Kansas City and Cincinnati took just 1:20 to complete nine innings. Most games began in the late afternoon, usually three or four o'clock, and since there was no daylight savings time, late-season games were often called due to darkness. Sometimes starting times were moved up to enable one team to catch a train, which waited for no one, not even major league baseball teams. In a testimony to the rapid play of the era, two hours was considered sufficient time to get the visitors to the station on time, and they usually made it.

Doubleheaders were rare. Cleveland finished its 1884 season with a doubleheader in which one game followed the other, and Indianapolis did the same in early October, but that was very unusual. Doubleheaders were usually limited to Decoration Day and the Fourth of July, with one game played in the morning and the other in the afternoon. Separate admissions were charged and the afternoon game generally drew a much larger crowd.

The 1884 doubleheader had some unusual variations. In mid–June, New York played its first game in Boston in the morning and the second in the afternoon in Providence. Philadelphia played at Boston in the afternoon. The morning game between New York and Boston lasted 12 innings, and New York manager James Price wanted to forfeit so his team wouldn't miss its train. Captain John Ward wouldn't hear of it and ended the game by scoring the winning run.

Holiday doubleheaders were lucrative events, and schedulers were careful to split the home dates equally. Teams on the road for Decoration Day were generally home on the Fourth of July.[13] The UA, which normally gave visiting teams a $75 guaranty, split the proceeds for holiday games. On Decoration Day 1884, when Boston hosted New York, the crowd for the afternoon game began gathering as soon as the morning affair was over. The club kept selling tickets, even when they had sold far more than the park could safely hold. They reported the sale of 14,000 tickets, but reporters estimated that there were about 18,000 people present. When they realized there was no seating, many fans began scaling the walls and flooding the field, overwhelming the inadequate police force.

The field was cleared with difficulty and the game finally commenced at 4:15. It was interrupted several times when scuffles erupted among the crowd or batted balls disappeared into the mass of spectators. Boston made a lot of money that day, but the ugly scene generated a lot of criticism.

A similar incident took place in Philadelphia, where 12,000 people crowded into a space designed to accommodate far fewer. The spectators surged onto the field, leaving only about fifty feet of open grass behind the bases. At a July Fourth doubleheader in Baltimore, fans who were turned away perched on "surrounding house-tops, telegraph poles, the steeple of No 6 Engine House, fences and other points of vantage overlooking Union Park."[14] About one hundred people climbed on top of a shed, putting so much weight on it that it collapsed.

All games, of course, were played under natural sunlight, although in 1884 there was talk that the Chicago White Stockings were planning to play an exhibition game at night, with illumination provided by fifty electric lights brought in from Boston. Unfortunately, it never came to fruition.

With multiple teams in several cities, scheduling was a bit dicey. As a rule, the NL and AA tried to avoid playing on the same day in the same city, while making sure there was a competing game wherever the UA played. When the National League schedule was released, Philadelphia owner Al Reach was distressed, for there were more than 20 dates when his club was in direct competition with the AA champion Athletics. He moved some games on his own to eliminate the conflicts. In mid–June, there were three games in Boston in a single day—New York versus Boston in the morning and New York versus Philadelphia plus a Union Association match between Boston and Washington in the afternoon.

The most controversial scheduling issue of the mid–1880s was whether to play on Sunday. Most workers toiled six days per week and Sunday was the only day on which they were off while the sun was shining brightly enough to play baseball. Therefore, Sunday games almost always drew well. In 1884, with fierce competition throughout the baseball world, Sunday ball was a matter of survival for several clubs.

The problem was that 19th-century America was deeply immersed in religion. Nearly everyone was a member of some denomination, and when public figures gave speeches, they routinely invoked God, thanked God, and gave praise to God. Science left a lot of things unexplained in those days, and it fell to religion to provide the answers. Further, 19th-century life was physically grueling, and the promise of an idyllic afterlife made the painful present more tolerable. Religion was a big part of 19th-century life, and Sunday was the day most denominations held sacred as a day of rest, which was carefully defined and excluded nearly everything pleasurable. Baseball was pleasurable and many people felt strongly that it should not be played on Sunday.[15]

Old Puritans, who were prevalent in the East, had a strict interpretation of Sabbath prohibitions while European immigrants, many of whom lived in the West, believed it was a day for recreation and fun, which included sporting activities. Democrats were more likely than Republicans to favor Sunday ball, as were members of the working class. The American Association actively sought the patronage of the working man, and since his best opportunity to watch baseball was on the sacred Sabbath, the AA inaugurated Sunday ball—the first Sunday game in major league history took place May 7, 1882.

The National League, under the leadership of prim William Hulbert, had always prohibited Sunday ball, a ban that continued until 1892. When discussing Hulbert's rowdy club's reluctance to play on the Sabbath, the *Pittsburgh Dispatch* commented sarcastically, "The Chicagos crook the elbow and swear in seven different languages, but they won't play ball on Sunday."[16]

Many other clubs seemed inclined to play on Sunday if they could get away with it. The UA permitted it, although Boston and Altoona refused to participate.[17] The Northwestern League allowed Sunday games, but some teams chose not to challenge local custom. Some players, referred to as Sabbatarians, refused to play on Sundays.[18]

The 1884 season was peppered with battles over baseball on the Sabbath and when a Sunday game was announced, there was nearly always speculation that it would be halted by the authorities. Sometimes nothing happened, but on other occasions local bluenoses intervened and attempted to stop the game. The effort was often thwarted by fans, who'd paid their money and wanted to see a ballgame. Sometimes the players were arrested, although that usually happened after the game was over. The battle then moved to the courthouse, where the result was nominal fines.

A conflict arose when eastern teams, which generally eschewed Sunday play, were asked to play on Sunday in western cities. When Virginia entered the AA in August, they reluctantly played those games that were already scheduled but said they wouldn't take the field on Sundays in 1885.

The issue was not just the desecration of the Sabbath. Sunday games drew large crowds, which was remunerative to the clubs but potentially disruptive to non-baseball fans, many of whom claimed that the working-class people who attended Sunday games were undesirables.

"The Sunday games," said Chet Webster of Indianapolis, "collect all the snide gamblers, who would else be playing poker in hidden places, all the shoulder hitters,[19] to whom Sunday is a dull day; in fact all the vicious elements of the city into one mass. Then if vice is collected into a mass it is dangerous and obscene. Then the boys and young men from the farms in the neighborhood come to town and learn their first lessons in vice and lawbreaking. And when the game is over the saloons are crowded."[20]

Apparently, the churches weren't as crowded. "The season of the year is here," one paper said, "when St. Louis citizens on Sunday toss up a penny to decide if they will take in church or the base ball matches. A great many of them have provided themselves with pennies with heads on both sides."[21]

Some members of the St. Louis clergy were in favor of Sunday games because they provided wholesome entertainment and an alternative to saloons. Many people thought Sunday crowds made the city safer. In Chicago, where the UA club played on Sunday, theaters initiated Sunday performances, which soon became the most popular shows. That didn't raise a lot of hackles, but when the Chicago Driving Park announced its intention to hold Sunday horse races, the clergy thought that was going too far.

When it came to baseball on the Sabbath, Indianapolis was a divided city. The ball club and many fans wanted it while the Methodists opposed it. The *Indianapolis News* was an avid opponent and, after a Sunday game took place, protested by refusing to report any of the club's games for the rest of the season. In addition, they published several editorials critical of the team and of city officials for not taking action.

The Indianapolis club secured a ground outside the city limits which they thought was beyond the reach of the city's blue laws. The first Sunday game was uneventful, despite the fact that the team was prepared for arrests and ready to post bonds. There was plenty of money available for bonds, since the crowd of more than 4,000 was the largest ever in the city (or near the city).

When a grand jury was instructed to return indictments against the team, it refused. But the City Council wasn't ready to concede, and after a May game the players were arrested. The city attorney said there was no jurisdiction, the State Attorney General backed him up, and the council decided not to push the issue.

Sunday ball in Ohio was a mixed bag. Cleveland was in the NL and didn't play on Sunday. Toledo wouldn't allow it. In Cincinnati several players were arrested when they tried to play on Sunday but after a hung jury returned no verdict, the games were allowed to go on. Columbus was a battlefield.

Columbus had laws regarding Sunday activity but they were not always enforced. In September 1882, an ordinance that would have specifically prohibited Sunday baseball was voted down 12–11, an indication of the deep division in local opinion. As a compromise, the team promised not to sell liquor on Sundays. It also made certain that all City Council members were issued free season passes.

Apparently, the Council couldn't be bought, for in May 1883 it passed a law prohibiting Sunday baseball. But when protestors claimed the ordinance would put an end to major league baseball in Columbus, it was repealed. Sunday games continued, with excellent attendance, although spectators were urged not to show too much enthusiasm, lest it be thought they were unduly enjoying themselves on the Sabbath.

Complicating the matter was the fact that Columbus president H.T. Chittenden opposed Sunday ball. He was in a somewhat compromised position, since he was an executive of the local horse railway company that brought fans to the park on Sundays. Chittenden volunteered to contribute to a fund that would make good the economic loss to the club if Sunday games were discontinued, but they went on despite the president's opposition.

The game of Sunday, May 18, attracted a crowd of nearly 6,000, which in turn attracted the attention of the Law and Order League and its president, Raymond Burr. On June 22, in the midst of another sinful encounter between Columbus and Brooklyn, the Law and Order League made its move. As the teams changed sides to begin the sixth inning, three constables walked onto the field with warrants for the arrest of Columbus manager Gus Schmelz and several players. It being Sunday, there was a large crowd, and they didn't appreciate the interruption. If opponents of Sunday baseball were correct in their assertion that those who went to games on the Sabbath were ruffians, the three constables were in for a hard time. Many fans climbed down from the stands and insisted that the intruders leave and let the game continue.

In addition to the fans milling around them, the constables had a second problem. Apparently, they weren't baseball fans and couldn't recognize the men whose names were on the warrants. No one was willing to help them and they stood uncertainly in the middle of the field, unsure of who to serve. Finally, after a 20-minute delay, the constables agreed to let the teams finish the game if they would consent to being served afterwards.

Raymond Burr protested. He wanted the men served then and there, but the constables were not about to take on 3,000 impatient fans. They sat on the Columbus bench until Brooklyn's manager protested that their presence violated the rules. Then the three men were escorted to the directors' box, jeered and hooted all the while.

After the game, the players were brought in front of a judge and posted $100 bonds. The penalty for their crime, if convicted, was a $100 fine and/or six months in jail. That seemed a bit harsh; there were several 1884 ballplayers that probably deserved to be in jail, but not for playing ball on Sunday.

The next day, president Chittenden, four Columbus directors, three Brooklyn players, and six members of the Columbus team were arrested on warrants sworn by the Law and Order League. Chittenden, who was an attorney, demanded an immediate trial, but his request was denied, leading to an angry exchange with the prosecutor.

The Columbus directors were upset because they thought they had an agreement with Burr and his group. Since the immediate cancellation of all Sunday games would require the AA to revise its schedule, the club had asked for time. They thought the L & O League had agreed, but the more aggressive members thought the team was stalling and obtained the warrants.

The baseball team retaliated by taking out warrants for the arrest of the officers of the streetcar company for bringing fans to the grounds on Sunday and pointed out that Columbus saloons were open on the Sabbath. They noted that Burr was an assistant postmaster who required some of his men to work on Sunday. If citizens realized that a Sunday shutdown would take away streetcars and liquor, perhaps they would leave the baseball team alone.

When the players went to court, they were found guilty of violating the Sunday laws and fined. Many baseball fans attended the hearing and expressed strong disapproval of the verdict. The club contemplated the revenue that would be lost without Sunday ball and wondered whether they could play and pay a fine, which would be a good financial bargain. Columbus was allowed to play the following Sunday, with the understanding that it would be the last time, and a crowd of nearly 4,000 watched without interruption.

When Columbus began to struggle financially, they announced their intention to resume playing on Sundays, which led to Chittenden's resignation. The first Sunday game, against the Alleghenies on September 7, proceeded peacefully with no interference from the Law and Order League.

Not every issue was as contentious as Sunday games, but even the baseball itself was an object of controversy. The NL and AA used the Spalding and Beach balls, respectively, while the UA, looking to create excitement, used the livelier Wright and Ditson ball, which was expected to produce more offense but was rougher on the hands of catchers and fielders.

In today's game, the ball is changed virtually any time it touches a surface other than the pitcher's hand or the catcher's glove. In 1884, many games were completed with a single ball; when it was hit outside the grounds, someone went to retrieve it while everyone waited. In New York, they gave young boys free admission if they returned balls hit out of the field, but the youngsters soon realized that admission to the game was 25 cents while the ball was worth $1.50 and began running off with them. Some teams kept a second ball on hand, which they used while the first was being retrieved, but other teams just waited.

Playing with only one ball affected the course of the game, for baseballs were stitched by hand, and as the innings went by, they became softer and didn't travel as far. In 1884, a coin flip determined which team had the choice of batting first or last[22] and some captains elected to bat first to get a shot at the ball while it was most resilient. The team that held a lead wanted to keep playing with the same ball, especially if it was the worse for wear, while the team trying to catch up wanted a new ball.

During a UA game between St. Louis and the Nationals, the latter wanted to replace the ball, which was badly beaten up. When Henry Boyle of St. Louis hit a foul over the fence, third baseman Jerry McCormick jumped over and pretended to look for it, while Washington captain Phil Baker called for the umpire to throw in a new ball. When McCormick continued to poke around, St. Louis captain Fred Dunlap climbed over the fence, found the ball and insisted it be put back in play. When the umpire agreed, Baker pulled his team off the field and forfeited the game.

Perhaps the most controversial 1884 incident involving a baseball took place in an exhibition game between the Baltimore UA team and Portsmouth, Virginia, in the latter city. Portsmouth suspected that Baltimore was using a lively ball when they batted and a slipping in a dead one when Portsmouth took its turn. While Portsmouth was at bat, they asked umpire Dave Sullivan to check the ball. Baltimore gave him the lively one, while they attempted to conceal the dead ball by passing it from one Baltimore player to another. Eventually, it ended up under the shirt of left fielder Emmett Seery. A number of angry Portsmouth fans had seen Seery hide the ball, and they went up to him and lifted up his shirt, causing the ball to fall to the ground. The fans grabbed the ball and the Baltimore players made a beeline for their waiting boat, pursued by a horde of hooting Virginians. Baltimore president Al Henderson was right in the middle of things and it was reported that he was punched during the mad rush to the boat.

Despite the incriminating evidence, Baltimore denied switching balls and despite several reports to the contrary, Henderson denied that he had been punched. He said that when the ball became soft his players took it upon themselves to substitute a more vibrant one, bypassing the umpire. The incident was soon forgotten, as was the Baltimore team when it folded not long afterward.

The game of 1884 had many unique nuances. But the most interesting thing about baseball in any era is the players, who create the drama, win and lose the games, and who were more numerous in 1884 than ever before.

# 3

# The Players

By 1884, America had celebrated its hundredth birthday. A century is an exceptionally long life span for an individual, but a relatively brief one for a nation. The United States was a young country and its people were young. The average life expectancy in the 1880s was just over 40 years, a statistic greatly impacted by the high level of infant and childhood mortality. Anyone who survived until the age of 20 could expect to live to about 60. Most didn't live much beyond 60, and in 1880, there were just 1.7 million Americans (3.4 percent of the population) over the age of 65, compared to 16 percent in 2020.[1]

The major league baseball players of 1884 were also young, with an average age of 25.1, more than three years younger than the players of 2020. There was not much variation by league; the AA was the oldest at 25.5 and the fledgling UA the youngest at 24.8. The oldest major league team was the Metropolitans, who won the American Association championship with a veteran squad that averaged 27.4 years of age. The youngest was Harry Wright's Philadelphia National League team, with an average age of just 23.6. Although people tended to marry young in the 19th century, many baseball players were single. When John Richmond of Columbus wed late in 1884, he became one of only two married players on the team.

The life of a 19th-century baseball player was hard, and most didn't last long. Baseball was a young man's game, and the typical athlete was played out by the time he reached his 30s. In 1884, the vast majority of players were between 20 and 29 years of age:

|       | *NL* | *AA* | *UA* | *Total* | *%* |
|-------|------|------|------|---------|-------|
| <20   | 7    | 8    | 24   | 39      | 5.28% |
| 20–29 | 143  | 237  | 227  | 617     | 83.49% |
| 30–39 | 15   | 30   | 35   | 80      | 10.82% |
| 40+   | 1    | 0    | 2    | 3       | 0.41% |
| Total | 166  | 275  | 298  | 739     |       |

NOTE: The statistics are by team, and those who played with more than one team are counted in the statistics of each.

The UA had more players in the older and younger buckets, for they were new and had to take chances on athletes the established leagues left behind. Overall, the youngest players were 17 and the oldest was 41-year-old first baseman Joe Start of Providence. Another veteran, 39-year-old Ned Cuthbert, had the distinction of playing in the first season of the National Association, National League, American Association, and Union Association.

It was just 13 years since the first major league season in 1871, but only 15 players who'd participated in that first season were still active (see Appendix C). And some of them had been absent from the major league scene for several years before returning for a brief appearance during an 1884 season that featured a great demand for players, even old ones. More than 31 percent of the players (nearly 39 percent in the UA) who appeared during the 1884 season never played another major league game before or after. The next year, when things settled down, only 7.4 percent of all players made single-season cameos.

Nearly all the top pitchers of 1884 were in their 20s, with Hoss Radbourn, the year's best, being a relatively old 29. The top five winners in the NL ranged in age from 23 to 29, those in the AA were 25–28, and the UA's top five were 26–32. Thirty-two-year-old George Bradley was the only one of the 15 over the age of 30.

Pitchers were almost exclusively right-handed. Over the first 11 years of major league baseball (1871–1881) only 5.6 percent of all innings were pitched by those who threw from the port side.[2] In 1874 and 1876, not a single inning was thrown by a lefty. Left-hander Bobby Mitchell pitched for a number of teams in the early years of the National League, but the first prominent left-hander was John Lee Richmond, who hurled major league baseball's first perfect game. Richmond won 32 games for Worcester in 1880, but was just 75–100 during a career that ended somewhat prematurely due to a heavy workload (he pitched nearly 1,500 innings during his three peak seasons) and an education that allowed him to pursue post-baseball careers in medicine and teaching.

There were 456 National League games in 1884 and consequently 912 starting pitchers. More than 83 percent of the games were started by pitchers who were known to be right-handed, 12 percent by pitchers whose dominant arm was unknown, and only 4.5 percent were started by men who were known to throw left-handed. Fred (Dupee) Shaw of Detroit had 28 of those starts and no other left-hander had more than 6. Shaw and Ed Morris of the Columbus AA team, who won 34 games, were the only really good left-handed pitchers of 1884.

It was not until the 20th century that managers realized that left-handed throwers were at a disadvantage in the infield and behind the plate, and there were lefties at all positions in 1884. Jack Clements, one of the great left-handed catchers of all time, made his debut in 1884 with Philadelphia of the Union Association.

Nineteenth-century players were much smaller than current day performers; very few were over six feet tall and the average was about 5'8". There were numerous references to Louis (Jumbo) Schoeneck of Chicago's UA team being as tall as 6'6" but Retrosheet lists him at 6'2" and 223 pounds, which was jumbo for the era but nothing unusual today.

The players of 1884 were versatile. Most could play a number of positions, including pitcher. In 1884, Mike Kelly, one of baseball's biggest stars, played 63 games in the outfield, 28 as a catcher, 12 at shortstop, 10 at third base, two at first base and two as a pitcher. Non-pitchers often took to the box, usually to finish one-sided games, but occasionally they started when no regular was available. During his career, Kelly pitched 12 times in relief, hurling a total of 45 innings. During the 1884 season, Chicago's Kelly, Cap Anson, Ned Williamson, and Fred Pfeffer all took turns in the pitchers' box.

Rosters were limited and, in order to conserve traveling expenses, only the bare minimum went on road trips. Sometimes, a player was sent home in mid-trip to cut expenses. Teams didn't need much of a bench because prior to 1889, a player could not be removed from a game except for a disabling injury.

The definition of "disabling" was different in 1884 than it is in the 21st century. Players who felt a slight tightness in their quad weren't injured. No one had ever heard of an oblique. Life was difficult in the 19th century, and playing with pain was both expected and admired. A banged-up player was sometimes left in the game and moved to a less strenuous position (generally the outfield). Players were knocked unconscious and revived, sometimes with whiskey, and resumed playing. If a catcher's left hand was useless, they tried to continue using just their right hand.

There was great incentive to continue playing, since an injury often meant no pay. A star player was usually carried on the payroll while injured, but those who were replaceable were replaced and their pay was cut off. They might also have to pay their own medical expenses. When Jim Keenan of Indianapolis broke his thumb, his manager told him to play or his salary would be discontinued. It wasn't an empty threat, for the Athletics stopped paying Jack O'Brien when he contracted pneumonia.

Detroit's Joe Farrell continued to play despite a feeling of malaise and an arm that was a hideous shade of black and blue. "Farrell," a reporter wrote, "who has been doing some wretched work of late, was worse than ever. He has become fat and sluggish and his play is about as animated as is the spectacle of an elephant eating hay."[3] A few days later, Farrell disclosed that he had been suffering from malaria.

If a player was totally incapable of continuing, a substitute could take his place. Sometimes it was a reserve who was slightly less injured than the man he replaced. On one occasion, Tommy Burns, still suffering from the aftereffects of malaria, had to be sent in. Traveling teams often found themselves short-handed and filled out the lineup by hiring a local amateur for a day or two. Several one-game major leaguers listed in baseball encyclopedias were emergency replacements.

The typical 19th-century baseball player had little education, many not progressing beyond grade school. As teenagers, most worked at menial jobs and played amateur or semi-pro baseball in their off hours. Before he became a professional ball player, Kelly worked in a silk mill for three dollars a week hauling buckets of coal.

A few players were educated, including William Vinton, who pitched for Philadelphia's National League club in 1884 and 1885. The son of a minister, Vinton attended Andover and Yale and did not report to Philadelphia until the 1884 school year was over. He left in mid-September when classes resumed. John Montgomery Ward of the New York Gothams was perhaps the most educated major leaguer. After being expelled from Penn State, Ward resumed his education during his playing days, earned law and philosophy degrees, and eventually became a sharp thorn in the side of baseball owners.

Even after they became professionals, the more industrious players held jobs during the off-season, both to supplement their income and to prepare for life after baseball. Kelly and Arlie Latham played on the stage and John Munce of the Wilmington Quicksteps was a song and dance man. After his playing days, Bill Geer carved out a lengthy career as a forger than earned him several prison sentences, but most players had more mundane off-season occupations.

Charlie Eden of the Alleghenies was a conductor on the rail line between Cincinnati and Indianapolis and Charley Bastian was a furniture maker. Louisville's George Latham was a streetcar conductor in Philadelphia for $60 a month. Burly Dave Orr of the Mets was a stone mason. Other players were saloonkeepers, railroad workers, factory workers, and drove milk wagons or hacks. Government employment was common for those who played in Washington.

California natives, and many non–Californians, went west to play with professional teams during the winter. Each year, there was at least one southern barnstorming tour, usually including a visit to New Orleans, which had a rich baseball tradition. These tours never seemed to go well. Receipts were invariably less than anticipated and alcohol consumption much greater than expected. That didn't stop the planning of new tours the following winter.

Some players used their baseball earnings to get started in business. Al Spalding, George Wright, and Al Reach, star players from the old National Association, built prosperous sporting goods concerns. Will White, star pitcher of the Cincinnati club, owned a tea and grocery shop and a drug store.

Of the players who took part in the 1884 season, the most successful businessman was Frank Olin, who played for Washington and Toledo of the American Association.[4] After graduating from Cornell in 1886, Olin began a career in engineering, and in 1889 he formed W.W. Olin company, which designed and built powder plants. The company prospered and Olin got his big break during World War I, when he was awarded contracts to supply ammunition for the French and American armies. Olin ran his company until just before the Second World War, when he turned it over to his son. John Olin continued expanding the operation, which became Olin-Matheson Chemical Corporation and eventually Olin Corporation, one of the Fortune 500 firms.

Although professional ballplayers earned much more than the typical laborer, many were impecunious, and the press liked to point to those who squandered their money. "In brief," said the *Kansas City Times*, "it is turkey and ice cream in the summer and a free lunch route in the winter."[5] Cap Anson, perhaps the best player of the 19th century, made a series of bad investments that left him destitute after his career ended. The same was true of star second baseman Fred Dunlap.

The idea that players sat around drinking beer all winter and had to be whipped into shape in March wasn't completely accurate. Some did, but after the start of the new year, many worked out regularly in gymnasiums to prepare for the season. Bill Gleason of St. Louis even had a gym in his home.

While no teams went to Florida or Arizona for spring training, many northern clubs ventured to more temperate climates, like Washington or Baltimore, where they could play exhibitions against local clubs. In 1884, Detroit went to the Washington area to train and then went on a barnstorming tour through Pennsylvania and New Jersey. With no radio or television, these country tours were the only opportunity rural fans had to see big league players. The two-fold purpose of southern training junkets was to get the players in shape and generate revenue; sometimes the latter goal resulted in too much activity and some teams were worn down before the season even started.

The players of 1884 were a diverse group in many ways. Some were educated while others were not. Early players were nearly all from big cities, but by 1884, small town boys were beginning to make their mark. Players from old amateur teams like the Knickerbockers and Excelsiors had patrician sounding names, but as professionalism took hold, European immigrants began to infiltrate major league lineups. Many were of Irish descent, and the latter part of the 19th century was what historian Jerry Casway called The Emerald Age of Baseball.[6] Between 1876 and 1884, about 40 percent of all players coming to the major leagues had Irish surnames.

Until 1884, diversity did not include black players. There are two myths that have been perpetuated regarding baseball's integration, similar to the myths of baseball's creation. The first, comparable to the Abner Doubleday story, is that Jackie Robinson broke the color line in 1947. That's just wrong. Robinson reintegrated the major leagues after 62 years of segregation; the true pioneers were Moses Fleetwood (Fleet) Walker and his brother Welday, who played for Toledo of the American Association in 1884.[7]

The second racial myth is similar to the theory that Alexander Cartwright invented baseball. The Doubleday story is mere fanciful imagination, but Cartwright was actually involved in the early days of baseball, albeit briefly. The Cartwright-like racial myth is that Adrian (Cap) Anson was the man who ended the career of Fleet Walker and established the color line that kept blacks out of the major leagues until 1947. Like Cartwright, Anson was on the scene and, like Cartwright, he is often assigned a more prominent role than he actually played.

Cap Anson was one of the dominant figures of 19th-century baseball, the star player and manager of the Chicago team that won five pennants in seven years. Anson was a large, powerful man well-suited for athletics, but his natural gifts did not include great intellectual capacity. He was not a complex man or a deep thinker. "The element of poetry was left largely out of my make-up,"[8] he wrote in his autobiography. Cap was a simple man who liked baseball, billiards, and Mrs. Anson.

A more objective observer, Anson's biographer David Fleitz, wrote, "Anson was honest to the core, and so fiercely independent that he refused to accept charity even in his darkest financial hours. He was also a racist, a bully, and a martinet...."[9]

There is no question that Anson was a racist. Most people of his era were, and Anson took a back seat to no one in his low opinion of African Americans and his willingness to express it in public. Black mascot Clarence Duval accompanied the White Stockings on their world tour during the winter of 1888–89, and Anson, in his autobiography, made many disparaging and embarrassing comments about him, referring to Duval on one occasion as a "no account nigger."[10]

Blacks weren't the only people Anson didn't like; he was an equal opportunity bigot who was really only fond of people who were a lot like Adrian Constantine Anson. When Anson was a child, he lived in an area that contained many Native Americans and later confessed that he was afraid of them and worried they might kill him. He found it distasteful when the Irish began to dominate baseball. When describing his trip to England during the 1874 baseball tour, Anson wrote disparagingly of the British.

On the 1888–89 world tour, Anson noted that Egyptian women wore veils, "a fact for which we probably had reason to be devoutly grateful, as there was nothing in their shapeless figures to indicate any hidden beauty."[11] Then he took a few gratuitous digs at "John Chinaman." One of the biggest problems with foreigners, Anson concluded, was that most of them didn't speak English.

Anson's first encounter with Fleet Walker came on August 10, 1883, when his Chicago club stopped in Toledo to play an exhibition against the local Northwestern League team. Walker was on the Toledo roster, but Anson and Chicago president Albert Spalding informed the home team they would not take the field if he was in the lineup.

At first it appeared there would be no trouble, for Walker, suffering from an injured hand, was expected to spend the game on the bench. That wasn't good enough for Anson, who said he wouldn't even allow Walker on the premises. When Anson bullied

**While Cap Anson has often been blamed for instituting baseball's color line, an early 20th-century team he controlled frequently played against black clubs. He is pictured here with Rube Foster, founder of the Negro National League (National Baseball Hall of Fame Library, Cooperstown, N.Y.).**

and blustered, he only made Toledo manager Charlie Morton angry. Morton decided that not only was Walker staying, but he was also going to play right field, sore hand and all.

Anson didn't pull his team off the field. That would have meant walking away from a share of the gate receipts, and Anson's twisted principles had a price. "We'll play this here game," he said, "but we won't play never no more with the nigger in."[12] The following spring, Chicago arranged an exhibition game with Toledo and got Morton to agree that Walker would not play. The game was eventually cancelled.

Four years later, Chicago played an exhibition against Newark, which featured the African American battery of Walker and pitcher George Stovey. Walker was again injured, but Anson refused to play if Stovey pitched. Newark manager Charlie Hackett had less spine than Charlie Morton and apparently didn't want to risk the gate. He kept Stovey out of the game. The next year, when Walker played for Syracuse, Anson again refused to put his team on the field unless Walker was held out of the game.

For these incidents, it is often claimed that Anson was responsible for drawing the color line in professional baseball. But despite his renown, the Chicago captain did not have the power to segregate baseball. When he protested Walker's presence in Toledo, Chicago president Al Spalding supported him. Had Spalding ordered Anson to play against Newark or Syracuse, he undoubtedly would have, his personal bias notwithstanding. Baseball continued to exclude blacks long after Anson was dead and, as it had been in Anson's time, segregation was a team effort. Many blame Commissioner Kennesaw Mountain Landis, another racist, for baseball's lack of progress, but that is also

The 1883 Toledo Baseball Club, champions of the Northwestern League. Catcher Fleet Walker stands at the center of the back row. When Toledo joined the American Association for the 1884 season, Walker became the first black major leaguer (National Baseball Hall of Fame Library, Cooperstown, N.Y.).

a simplification. But at least Landis was the commissioner. Anson was only a playing manager with no authority to ban anyone.

In 1907, after his major league career ended, Anson formed a semi-pro team that competed in the Chicago City League. Over the next couple of years, Anson's Colts played a number of games against the Leland Giants, a black team featuring pitcher Rube Foster, later founder of the Negro National League.

Anson had sole authority over his club, and the decision to play a black team was his alone. Had he mellowed over the years? Was Spalding the one who didn't want to play against blacks? Were the Leland Giants less of a threat than a black individual playing in a white league? Was the lure of large gate receipts sufficient to overcome his racial bias? We'll never know, but the possibilities add to the mystery and reinforce the supposition that Anson did not keep blacks out of major league baseball.

The ban on black players at all levels of organized ball was essentially complete by the end of the 1880s and finalized by the end of the century. The year the movement gained momentum (1887) was one in which several black players had exceptional seasons, weakening the notion of black inferiority and awakening white players to the idea that if more blacks were allowed in the game, there would be fewer jobs left for them. Some players were completely opposed to associating with blacks on moral grounds, while others were concerned about losing their job. Self-interest is an even stronger motivation than racial condescension, and it created a durable system of exclusion. Self-interest was also evident in the 1887 International Association vote that prohibited contracts with black players. The four clubs that opposed the ban employed black players while the six who supported the ban did not.

In 1884, before the ban took effect, Moses Fleetwood Walker became the first black man to play in the major leagues. Although his race was noted, Walker's debut had none of the fanfare or divisiveness that greeted Jackie Robinson in 1947. When Walker played his first game at Louisville on May 1, *Sporting Life* described the game in just three sentences. The third read, "Toledo, however, suffered greatly through the errors of Walker, who made three terrible throws."[13] The *Clipper*'s only reference to Walker was likewise to his poor throwing.

Walker, like Robinson, was an educated, well-spoken young man who played piano and was a fluent writer. Born in Mount Pleasant, Ohio, in 1857, he was the son of a well-known mulatto physician, also named Moses, one of the first black men to practice medicine in Ohio. There was undoubtedly some white blood in Walker's heritage, which gave him, under the mores of the time, an elevated status among American blacks. Mount Pleasant was a somewhat progressive town, at least by the standards of the time, as was Steubenville, Ohio, where Fleet and Welday graduated from an integrated high school.

Fleet entered Oberlin College (which admitted both blacks and women) in 1878[14] and later became a law student at the University of Michigan, playing baseball at both schools. Fleet was not much of a hitter, but he was a very skilled defensive catcher.

Prior to the 1883 season, the Peoria Club proposed that the Northwestern League ban black players, but the motion was voted down. Walker signed with Toledo shortly afterward. When the *New York Clipper* announced his signing, it made no mention of his race, perhaps because the writer was unaware Walker was black. He played with Toledo in 1883 and when the club was admitted to the American Association the following year, Fleet Walker went with them.

A southern city like Louisville was probably not the best place for Walker to make his debut, and while his race may not have been mentioned in the national media, it did not go unnoticed in Kentucky. One local paper's headline after Louisville's win was "The Negro Catcher's Disastrous Errors."[15] After giving the score, the *Louisville Commercial* added, "Those are the magic figures that tell the story, and 'twas all on account of a coon."[16]

Walker had never played in Louisville before, but he'd been there. In 1881, he visited the city with the White Sewing Machine team from Cleveland, but remained on the bench after Louisville threatened to walk off the field if he played. When the team's other catcher was injured, the Cleveland manager tried to substitute Walker, but the clamor was so great that he backed down. One spectator, offended by Walker's mere presence on the bench, assaulted him. No one assaulted Walker during the 1884 opener, but the Louisville fans rode him hard all game long, which may have contributed to his subpar play.[17]

Another factor that made it difficult for Walker to catch effectively was his relationship with Toledo's star pitcher, Tony Mullane. They didn't work well together, and some said Walker, who generally caught bare-handed, was not strong enough to handle Mullane's powerful delivery. Tony set them straight. The problem, he said, was that even though Walker was the best catcher he'd ever had, he objected to being caught by a black man. The idea of Walker flashing him signals and, in effect, giving him orders, was unacceptable; he ignored Walker's signs and threw whatever pitch he felt like throwing.

Walker eventually stopped giving signs and just stooped behind the plate and prepared for anything. Fortunately, Walker had no problems with Toledo's other regular pitcher, Hank O'Day, a man perhaps most remembered for his role as an umpire in the famed Fred Merkle game of 1908 and as the only umpire to eject Connie Mack from a game.[18]

The 19th century was an insensitive era. In 1887, the *Hamilton Spectator* said, "Walker the coon catcher of the Newarks is laid off with a sore knee. It is insinuated by envious [illegible] that in early life he practiced on hen roosts until he got the art of foul-catching down fine." But Walker's gentlemanly deportment and skillful play made him popular with fans and the press. In response to the *Spectator*'s crude comments, *The Sporting News* replied, "It is a pretty small paper that will publish a paragraph of that kind about a member of a visiting club, and the man who wrote it is without doubt Walker's inferior in education, refinement, and manliness."[19] "Walker, the colored catcher of the Toledoes," said *Sporting Life*, "is a favorite wherever he goes. He does brilliant work in a modest, unassuming way."[20]

Some saw Walker as a novelty that might attract fans, especially black fans. The *Washington Post* predicted, "This afternoon the Washingtons will meet the celebrated Toledo team with their famous battery, Tony Mullane and Walker. The latter is a colored man, and no doubt many will attend the game to see 'our colored brother' in a new role."[21]

Virginia was admitted to the American Association in August 1884, the first major league club from a state that had been part of the Confederacy and the last until the Braves moved to Atlanta in 1966. When Toledo visited Richmond for the first time in September, manager Morton received a letter signed by several Richmond men that read, in part, "We the undersigned do hereby warn you not to put up Walker, the negro catcher, the evenings that you play in Richmond, as we could mention the names of 75 determined men who have sworn to mob Walker if he comes on the ground in a suit.... We only write this to prevent much bloodshed, as you alone can prevent."[22] The warning was unnecessary, for by the time Toledo got to Richmond Walker had been released. Like most catchers, he'd been beaten up during the season, suffering a broken rib in July and then a shoulder injury. In 1884, with no disabled list, injured players, white or black, were given their release. Walker returned to Ohio and got a job with the U.S. Postal Service.

Earlier in the season, when Toledo was struck by a rash of injuries, they signed Fleet's younger brother Welday, who was playing for the University of Michigan. When he made his debut July 15, Welday became the second black major leaguer, with even less fanfare that that which accompanied his brother's first game. He played just five games, and when the injured players returned, Welday was released.

Toledo withdrew from the American Association after the 1884 season and Fleet Walker's big-league career came to an end. Like his unheralded entrance, Walker's departure received little attention, and few realized it would be more than 60 years before another black man would appear in a major league game. In 1889, Walker was the last black in the International League until Robinson played for Montreal in 1946. As Walker's biographer David Zang wrote, "So though he did not know it at the time, when Fleet Walker had left the University of Michigan to become a professional baseball player, he was positioned on the swell of a small wave. He rode it a very brief time before it broke, and the undertow began to carry him, and other blacks, back toward where they had been."[23]

Fleet Walker's life after baseball was very eventful. He was arrested and charged with murder after killing a man named Patrick "Curly" Murray in 1891 but was acquitted on the grounds that he acted in self-defense. He was not so lucky when, as a postal employee, he was arrested for stealing checks; Walker was convicted and sentenced to a year in prison.

Early in the 20th century, Fleet became an advocate for black emigration to Africa and wrote a book on the subject called *Our Home Colony*. He and Welday also published a newspaper (*The Equator*) that covered similar topics. Despite his legal problems, Walker was well-regarded in his sphere and the final years of his post-baseball career were spent as the proprietor of a well-known opera house in Cadiz, Ohio.[24] He died in 1924.

Baseball's color line was nebulous, and there were some major leaguers who appeared to be a little on the dark side. Among them was a Mexican catcher named Sandy Nava. Nava was actually born in San Francisco to Josefa Simental, a woman of Mexican origin. Shortly after his birth, Josefa moved her family back to Mexico, but they returned to San Francisco around 1865.

The date of Nava's birth is disputed and the identity of his natural father is uncertain. Most sources give his year of birth as 1850, but historian Brian McKenna found evidence that he was actually born a decade later. At birth, the child was named Vincent Simental, but when his mother married a white man named Irwin, young Vincent assumed his surname. When he first began playing baseball, he was known as Sandy Irwin, but when he joined the Providence Grays in 1882, he was called Vincent Nava, which eventually became Sandy Nava. For the first Mexican-American major leaguer to be known as Vincent Irwin would be perplexing. Sandy Nava sounded much better.

Sandy Irwin began playing baseball and cricket in California in the late 1870s. Since there were a lot of Spaniards in California, he didn't stand out, and his Caucasian surname made it easier for him to assimilate. He was a valued commodity because, like Fleet Walker, he was an excellent defensive catcher who could handle hard-throwing California pitchers like Jim Whitney and Charley Sweeney, who were notoriously difficult to catch.

During the winter of 1881–82, an entourage of major league players traveled to California for a series of exhibition games. The traveling party included Providence third baseman Jerry Denny, who'd played with Nava (as he was then known) in California, and Grays pitcher John Montgomery Ward. Denny convinced Ward to let Nava catch him. After the young Mexican handled 25 chances without an error, Ward persuaded Providence manager Harry Wright to sign him.

Nava was described at various times as Mexican, Cuban, Indian, Portuguese, black, and mulatto. Racial identity is fluid, and it was not clear what Nava might be or on which side of baseball's nebulous color line he might fall. If a Hispanic player's bloodlines were believed to be European rather than African, he could play. After all, Spain is in Europe, as are England, Ireland, and Germany, whose natives were readily admitted to the major leagues. Nava's background was so murky that a case could be made for just about any lineage. His defensive skill and toughness behind the plate (he often played without a mask) made Harry Wright certain that Nava was of Spanish descent.

Nava was usually identified as a Spaniard (not a Mexican) and there is no indication that anyone, not even Cap Anson, objected to his presence on a major league diamond. He made his NL debut on May 5, 1882, becoming the first Mexican-American and second Hispanic to play in the major leagues.[25]

In 1882–83, Nava played just 57 games and batted only .223, but he was sound defensively and courageous behind the plate, playing through numerous injuries, including a broken finger. Nava suffered from the twin curses of many 19th-century catchers—he couldn't hit (he had a lifetime average of .177 and managed just 11 hits in 105 at bats in 1884) and he was frequently injured. He also had a testy relationship with the Grays' management, once being fined the substantial sum of $100 for "conduct prejudicial to the interests of the association."[26]

Before the 1884 season, Nava was offered $2,800 to sign with St. Louis of the UA, a tribute to the importance of a good defensive catcher, even one who couldn't hit. Nava chose to remain with Providence and played a fair amount early in the season, often working with his old California teammate Sweeney. But when Sweeney jumped to St. Louis in mid-season, the pitching burden fell on Hoss Radbourn, and Radbourn preferred pitching to Barney Gilligan. Nava became a forgotten man. Henry Lucas of St. Louis came calling again, offering him $500 to finish the season catching Sweeney. "Sweeney says come," reported one paper. "Nava said 'No come.'"[27] He did not play in the World Series and probably didn't even go to New York with the Grays. After the season, he requested and received his release.

Baltimore's American Association club signed "the little Dago Nava"[28] and he played a few games with them in 1885 and 1886, before settling down to live the rest of his life in Baltimore. He worked as an upholsterer, never married, and died in 1906 at the age of 46.[29]

Perhaps the most talented African American player of the 19th century, who would be elected to the Hall of Fame in 2022, wasn't playing in the major leagues in 1884. Bud Fowler would never play in the major leagues—and everyone knew why. "He is one of the best general players in the country," it was said in 1885, "and if he had a white face would be playing with the best of them."[30]

Fowler, whose given name was John Jackson, was born in Fort Plain, New York, in 1858 and moved to Cooperstown, that most hallowed of baseball locales, at the age of two. He was introduced to baseball in Cooperstown and by 1878 was pitching for a white semi-pro club in Chelsea, Massachusetts. Early in the season, Fowler defeated the Boston NL club 2–1, throwing a three-hitter. A win over a major league club was bound to attract attention, and Fowler was soon engaged by the Live Oak club of Lynn, Massachusetts. The Live Oaks played in the International Association, making Fowler the first African American to play in an organized professional league, although to call the IA organized is a bit of a stretch.

Fowler played with some all-black teams, but for most of his first ten years in baseball, he was on integrated teams, integrated only because he was on them. Although he was allowed to play on white teams, Fowler was not always welcomed; in 1881 several of his teammates on the Maple Leafs of Guelph, Canada, most of whom were from the United States, objected to playing with a black man and he was forced to leave.

Perhaps the sorriest episode of Fowler's long career occurred in 1887, a watershed year for black participation in organized baseball, when he and another black man, pitcher William Renfroe, starred for the Binghamton Bingos of the International Association. Although Fowler was batting .350, some of the white players didn't like the idea of having blacks on the team and on June 27, two of them quit in protest. Nine players signed a petition demanding that the two blacks be released and on June 30, management complied. "Coons Gone," said the *Binghamton Leader*.[31]

After obtaining his release, Fowler wrote a very gracious letter stating that he was leaving Binghamton because of an offer he'd received from the Cuban Giants (which he had not). He thanked the directors for their courteous treatment and the fans for the manner in which they had supported him (he'd recently won a prize for having the best batting average during a homestand[32]). Fowler did not thank his teammates.

The following year, Fowler was signed by a team in Lafayette, Indiana, under the mistaken presumption that he was white. When he arrived and the manager learned that he was not, he was released. In 1889, he was the only black player on the Findlay, Ohio, team until the white players demanded he be released.

During his early years in professional ball, Fowler was primarily a pitcher, but like most pitchers of his era, he threw an ungodly number of innings and damaged his arm. He spent most of his later career at second base. Fowler often served as captain and/or manager of his club and was a very ambitious and active baseball entrepreneur. Bud was apolitical and went out of his way not to antagonize anyone.

He knew how the game was played, on and off the field, and as a promoter learned to cater to white audiences, often emphasizing black stereotypes. In 1883, Fowler was part of a group that unsuccessfully attempted to form a black professional league.

The life of a black player was dangerous. Other players often went out of their way to injure them, and Fowler, like fellow infielder Frank Grant, usually wore shin guards in the field. With Stillwater of the Northwestern League in 1884, he was badly spiked in a play at home plate, an injury that might have been intentionally inflicted.

Like Fleet Walker, Fowler did his best to be gracious, but after his bitter experience in Binghamton, he became more aggressive in fighting racial discrimination. He began to complain when he was treated poorly, and in 1890 in Iowa, sued for discrimination when he was not allowed to eat in a hotel dining room.[33]

When injuries and age ended his active career, Fowler became involved in the management of the Findlay Colored Western Giants, the Page Fence Giants, the Muncie Londons, and other teams. He organized several tours, but his attempts at more spectacular excursions, including junkets to the West Coast, Hawaii, and England, did not come to fruition. When he was not playing baseball, Fowler was a barber, often opening up a shop in the city where he was playing.

It was no accident that 1884 was the high point of major league baseball's integration, with the Walker brothers and Sandy Nava in the majors and Bud Fowler in the Northwestern League. There were so many teams and such a demand for players that some managers were willing to go beyond traditional boundaries. Catching was probably the most difficult position to fill, and Fleet Walker and Sandy Nava were both skilled catchers. By 1885 the labor crisis passed; there were far fewer teams and the supply of players was more equal to the demand. That meant a return to the old status quo, which would be the standard for more than half a century.

# 4

# "The blacklist shackle"

"The reserve clause was the central financial concept of Gilded Age baseball," wrote historian Rob Bauer, "the lynchpin holding the entire system together."[1] And what gave the reserve rule[2] its absolute power was the infamous blacklist, which had a noble origin but evolved into one of the most brutal weapons ever wielded by baseball owners against players.

One of William Hulbert's primary goals when he established the National League was to rehabilitate the image of professional baseball, which had been badly tarnished by the shenanigans that took place in the National Association. One of the biggest shortcomings of the NA had been the fact that teams persisted in engaging players with tainted reputations, including some who had almost certainly been involved in dishonest play.

The method Hulbert chose to eliminate shady characters was a blacklist, an odious classification that not only prohibited a man from playing on an NL team; it prohibited NL teams from playing a team that employed a blacklisted player. It wasn't hard to land on a blacklist; any team could unilaterally put a player on it. The National League and American Association each had blacklists, and after their 1883 agreement each honored the other's list. Even the Union Association, supposedly formed to counter player abuse, had its own blacklist, although the NL and AA didn't recognize it.

Banning disreputable players was a big step in the right direction, but the problem with the blacklist was that it was used much too frequently for reasons that had nothing to do with dishonesty. Its roster included anyone Hulbert didn't think was good for the National League, which covered a great deal of questionable territory.

The blacklist was used to ban the four culprits in the Louisville scandal of 1877, which was good, but it was also employed to discipline players who had problems with alcohol, contract disputes with their clubs, or refused to play if they weren't paid. In 1884, Springfield wanted to blacklist William Murphy for taking a six-dollar advance and then not signing a contract. Two Northwestern League players were blacklisted for asking for the return of fines they'd paid. Sam Wise of Harrisburg was banned for leaving his team after receiving a telegram that his mother was dying. In mid–October 1884, Al Spalding was said to have told all his players to come in the following Monday to sign 1885 contracts or be blacklisted. That was bad.[3]

Blacklisted players had little recourse. NL players could appeal suspensions, but the appeal was heard by the league's directors, who represented the clubs that had imposed the suspension. Further, each appellant had to post a $200 bond to cover expenses, a cost that was beyond the capacity of most players.

When the AA was formed in 1882, its clubs wanted to sign players who'd been blacklisted by the NL for any reason other than dishonest play. Hulbert sent a stern letter to AA president McKnight warning him that the NL would refuse to have anything to do with his teams if they signed *any* blacklisted players. McKnight ignored the warning and the two leagues were thereby deprived of lucrative exhibition games.

Henry Chadwick, one of the most outspoken advocates of discipline for dishonest players, was appalled at the liberal use of the blacklist, which he thought should only be employed only to eliminate fraudulent play. Fellow journalist O.P. Caylor of Cincinnati agreed. "It is hardly probable that the cause of base ball with the public," he wrote, "will be subserved or bettered by taking up the blacklist shackle every time a player gets a little unruly."[4]

Perhaps the most egregious use of the blacklist involved outfielder Charley Jones. Jones, born Benjamin Wesley Rippay in 1852, was a strapping six feet tall and nearly 200 pounds, a large man for his era. He first came to the major leagues with the ill-fated Keokuk club in 1875 and joined Cincinnati when it entered the NL in 1876. After three years with Cincinnati, he went to Boston in 1879 and led the league with nine home runs and 62 RBI. The nine homers were the most ever in a major league season.

After the 1879 season, Jones asked Boston to release him so he could go back to Cincinnati, where he made his home. Boston president Arthur Soden refused and said that if Jones didn't play with Boston he would be placed on the blacklist. Jones reluctantly agreed to play for the Red Caps.

In June 1880, Jones became the first major leaguer to hit two home runs in one inning, but then he began to have problems. In July, he was "given permission by the Bostons to 'lay off' with loss of pay, on account of careless and indifferent playing."[5] He was soon reinstated, but in early September, he was fined $100 for indifferent play and insubordination and suspended again. The *Clipper* noted that "as usual there are two sides to the story."[6] Jones' side was that Boston owed him $378 in salary, which he demanded while the club was in Cleveland. The 1880s were dangerous times, and club officials didn't carry a lot of money when

Slugging outfielder Charley Jones was banned by the National League in one of most glaring abuses of the blacklist (National Baseball Hall of Fame Library, Cooperstown, N.Y.).

they travelled. If payday came while a team was on the road, the standard practice was to wait until returning home to disburse the money. When Boston manager Harry Wright refused Jones' request for payment, he left the team and went home to Cincinnati.

Shortly after arriving home, Jones received a letter from Boston secretary Frederick Long informing him that he had been expelled for leaving the team without permission. Long said he believed Jones was angling to get released, as he had the previous winter, so he could play in Cincinnati. Jones sent a letter to NL secretary Nick Young announcing his intention to appeal and hired an attorney to sue the Boston club.[7]

During the winter of 1880, after Cincinnati lost its NL franchise, Jones wanted to sign with Cleveland, but the league wouldn't reinstate him. On March 8, 1881, the NL adopted a resolution stating that "any complaint made by a player or any grievances by players shall never be made excepting when the club to which such player or players belong is at home."[8] The wording of the resolution was so precisely directed at Jones' case that there was no mistaking its intent, but *ex post facto* law would carry no weight if Jones followed through on his threat to sue. At the same time, the NL ruled that since Jones had not filed an appeal prior to the annual meeting, he had forfeited his right.

On May 14, 1881, Jones brought suit in Cleveland Common Pleas Court for the $378 in salary. Boston did not appear and Jones was granted a default judgment for the full amount, backed by an order of garnishment for any money payable to the Boston Club. His problem was that the judgment was effective only in Ohio.

The next time Boston came to Cleveland to play the League nine, Jones' attorney filed an attachment against the club's baggage, but Harry Wright successfully argued that the baggage belonged to the players and not the club. Boston's share of the gate receipts, however, totaling $272, was impounded.[9] Jones continued to be a thorn in Boston's side, attaching the proceeds of the Boston-Cleveland game on June 24. In December, Boston filed suit to recover the total of $568.55.

During the summer, Jones played with the Columbia Club of Cincinnati, which on June 5 went to Louisville to play the Eclipse Club. For playing against a team that included the blacklisted Jones, the Eclipse Club was banned from playing exhibitions against National League clubs. Jones also played with the Buckeyes of Cincinnati and a second local club. Other teams were leery of playing them, fearing the same fate as the Eclipse.

When Cincinnati was admitted to the AA for the 1882 season, they signed Jones, even though he remained on the NL blacklist. At that point, the AA and NL had not yet made peace, and the AA was open to signing all but dishonest players. The AA urged the NL to reinstate Jones and the *Clipper* agreed, stating, "The circumstances of the case … are not discreditable to Jones, and do not reflect upon his character as a player or as an honorable man. It would be only just for the League to reinstate him."[10]

When the League met in December, it voted to keep Jones on the blacklist, based upon his failure to file a timely appeal. The Cincinnati club then decided they didn't want to risk employing him and Jones sued them for breach of contract. The club's defense was that the contract was conditional on the NL removing him from the blacklist. The case went to trial and a jury ruled against Jones, who lost again on appeal.

By that time, Jones had signed two contracts, one with the Cincinnati club and the other with Philadelphia's NL club, the latter contingent on his reinstatement by the NL. At the League convention on March 5, 1883, Jones was reinstated, ending a two-and-a-half year odyssey. He didn't play with Philadelphia, however, returning his advance money and signing with his hometown team in Cincinnati. Jones had lost none of his skills during his long layoff and batted .294, with ten home runs (second to Harry Stovey's 14) and a league-leading 80 RBI. He continued playing major league ball through 1888.

The professional baseball contract was a one-way agreement, non-negotiable and filled with onerous provisions. There were a lot of rules for the players and not many for the clubs. The Columbus team ended the 1884 season on the road and the team refused to pay train fares back to Columbus. Baltimore's UA club also left their men to find their own way home. Players were frequently required to pay for their uniforms and traveling expenses when the team was on the road. When they weren't playing, substitutes were required to collect tickets at the gate and help out wherever needed.

There were a few college men in the professional ranks, but there were many more whose education ended in the fourth or fifth grade. They were in no position to negotiate with the experienced businessmen who operated baseball clubs. Some were illiterate and made their mark on a contract rather than signing it, mostly likely having no idea what was in it.

There were, of course, no player agents in 1884, but Samuel Morton, secretary of the Northwestern League and head salesman for Al Spalding's sporting goods business, established a brokerage to connect players with teams. Morton's business was short-lived however, for when he began including the Union Association in his dealings, NL president Mills told him to close up shop and threatened to strip him of his NWL title if he persisted.

Players were eager to sign one-way contracts because they needed the money. One of the most important aspects of their contract negotiations was the amount of the advance they could obtain on their salary. Most teams paid advances, but they didn't like it, since some players had a habit of collecting the money and then reneging on the contract.

From time to time, teams took a stand. Prior to the 1884 season, Buffalo boasted that it was the only major league team that hadn't paid any advances. Philadelphia made the same claim and said its players weren't happy about it. Cincinnati's AA team, on the other hand, had advanced $6,000.

Most agreed that advances were not a good thing for the club or the player. Clubs had to put up money for players who might not fulfill their contracts while the players locked themselves into a cycle of taking advances, running short, and taking more advances until there were no more contracts.

While blacklisting was the sledgehammer, fines were the annoying pinpricks. They were arbitrary, usually unjust, and sometimes exorbitant. Players were often fined for poor play. A Terre Haute player named Van Dyke was fined $10 for leaving to get married without obtaining permission. "If discipline and rigid enforcement of the rules can make a base ball club win," said one paper, "The Terre Hautes ought to be champions of the world."[11] Fines were often imposed when a player was due back salary, with the fine conveniently offsetting the amount owed.

At the end of the 1884 season, the *Detroit Free Press* urged managers to levy more fines to get players to perform up to their abilities. They praised Cap Anson, who they said was the toughest manager in the business and didn't hesitate to take money from his players. More managers should be like him, the *Free Press* said, ignoring the fact that the White Stockings finished well down in the race and were perhaps the most undisciplined nine in the league.

The player was bound in perpetuity but could be released at any time. While trades and player sales were theoretically forbidden, a team could pay another team to release a player with the understanding they would sign with the team paying for the release. There were risks to that practice, as we shall see, but it was a new development which, said the *New York Clipper,* reduced the players to a "mere herd of base ball cattle."[12]

Once he'd signed with a team governed by the National Agreement, the only way a player could regain his freedom was to obtain an honorable release. The most likely reason for teams to release a player was poor performance, and some players were suspected of doing so intentionally. At least one player was suspected of drinking to excess to obtain a release.

Some players had to be clever just to get money owed them. George Pinkney and Bill Sweeney, who played with Peoria in 1883, signed with the club for 1884 just to get their past due salary. When they got it, they signed elsewhere.

Courts were not generally helpful. During the 1883 season, the Anthracite Club of Pottsville, Pennsylvania, ran out of money, leaving them between a rock and a hard place. They couldn't pay their players, who took them to court under the Pennsylvania Wages Act. The judge ruled that the definition of "laborer" did not apply to baseball players and that the law was not applicable.

Henry Overbeck had a better result. Overbeck was released by St. Louis in June 1883 after playing just four games and going hitless in 14 at bats. The following winter, he filed a suit seeking $625, the remainder of his salary for the year. Overbeck's attorney Newton Crane said he "hope[d] to make this case a test of the question whether base ball contracts are jug-handled affairs, conferring extraordinary powers on the clubs, or arrangements drawn up and signed by two parties, both of whom are equal in law and justice."[13]

The *St. Louis Post-Dispatch,* which was friendly to Browns owner Chris Von der Ahe, ridiculed the claim, saying Overbeck was an incompetent player who was only signed as a favor. They called him a tool of others and described the case as "a specimen of the petty annoyance—for it is nothing else—to which business men are submitted...."[14]

Much to the surprise of baseball magnates, the case turned out to be much more than a petty annoyance and, had it served as precedent, could have changed the future of the game. Despite testimony from several baseball men, including St. Louis manager Ted Sullivan, that Overbeck was a poor player, the jury returned a verdict in his favor. Von der Ahe appealed, based upon the fact that the contract (Overbeck had actually signed two different contracts) gave him the right to release Overbeck with ten days-notice. The verdict stood, one of the few victories achieved by players during the 1880s.[15]

The biggest victory for the owners was the reserve rule. During the dark days of the late 1870s, with revenue declining, teams failing, and most teams losing money, National League owners looked for a way to control expenses, the largest of which was player salaries. The primary cause of escalating salaries was teams bidding against each other to obtain the services of the best players.

Since the beginning of professional baseball, players had signed contracts, almost always for one year, and when the contract ended, they were free to sign with any team for the following year. The outstanding exception was the Boston team, which signed some of its players to multi-year contracts to keep its championship team intact. The core of the Boston nine stayed together for several years, but after the 1878 season, star shortstop George Wright, who'd been with Boston since it was organized in 1871, decided to sign with Providence.

Something more was needed, and in 1879 the owners instituted the reserve rule, under which they could retain exclusive negotiating rights to five players. Credit for the reserve rule is generally accorded to Arthur Soden of Boston, who'd been cuckolded by Providence in the Wright affair, but it was popular across the board.

By 1883, the reserve rule had been expanded to include nearly the entire roster, and the rival American Association endorsed it. NL and AA teams were required to offer reserved players a minimum salary of $1,000, those in the Eastern League $800, and those in the Northwestern League at least $750. It didn't matter what the player's salary had been the previous year. If the offer met the minimum, even if it represented a severe cut, the player had to sign or risk blacklisting. If a player chose not to accept a contract offer, he was in limbo, as the club had no obligation to release him. A few players, including Jim O'Rourke, signed contracts that prohibited them from being reserved, but it was rare.

The reserve rule was very unpopular with players and many sportswriters believed the provision unfair and urged that it be eliminated. There were continuous rumors, particularly after the advent of the Union Association, that it was going to be terminated. They were correct, but it would be nearly a century before their prediction was realized.

The success of the reserve rule led major league executives to look for additional ways to control salaries. There were several proposals to classify players by ability and pay them fixed salaries based upon their classifications. Early classification plans failed to gain traction, for NL president A.G. Mills was against them, but the battle wasn't over.

Still, owners held the upper hand. The *St. Louis Post-Dispatch,* said, "League players long ago made up their minds to put up with whatever was dished out to them…." The AA, which had initially been pro-player, had begun acting in lock-step with the NL and the players' only hope was the new UA. "The Union Association may not be a success," the *Post-Dispatch* concluded, "but another will follow on its heels if the reserve is persisted in and graded salaries will make matters more complicated than ever."[16]

The advent of the UA gave the players a brief moment of power and with the explosion in the number of major league teams, demand caused salaries to increase significantly. By the end of the year, the situation returned to normal and management regained control. They'd learned a lesson and wouldn't relinquish their power again without a long fight.

# 5

# The Magnates

There were no magnates in the old National Association. The majority of those involved in the management of NA teams were sportsmen, local movers and shakers who just loved baseball. They didn't expect to make money; they just wanted to have a successful team and enjoy the season ticket that came with ownership. William Cammeyer of the Mutuals was a profit-incented man, but his primary interest was earning rental fees as the proprietor of Brooklyn's Union Grounds. Team ownership was typically spread over many shareholders, since it was better to parcel out the pain. If there was a profit, it would also be spread thinly, so no one had an overwhelming incentive to generate one. The main goal was to keep the team in the field without having to shell out additional money. If there was a surplus, it was usually rolled over to the following year.

Things began to change when William Hulbert formed the National League in 1876. Hulbert had as much civic pride as the next man, but he was a capitalist who thought that professional baseball could be a profitable endeavor if operated honestly and efficiently. Hulbert did not succeed at first and although most NL teams lost money in the early years, the structure of ownership was changing. The mass of stockholders was replaced by small groups, or in some cases a single individual, who owned a majority of the shares.

The profit potential of the sport began to attract men who viewed baseball as a business rather than a hobby. They took management seriously, and making money was equally important as winning games. By 1884, perhaps the shrewdest and most powerful of the new baseball magnates was Hulbert's protégé Albert G. Spalding. Spalding was well-suited for the role; his biographer, Peter Levine, wrote that "A.G.'s flamboyant personality, insatiable ego, and knowledge of baseball marked him as the chief promoter, spokesman, and enforcer of the league's position on all matters regarding the professional game."[1]

Spalding's story has been told many times. He was the best pitcher in the old National Association, winning 204 games and losing just 53 for Boston over five years before he and three teammates jumped to Chicago for the 1876 season. Spalding played just two seasons in Chicago before retiring from active play at the age of 27. He never learned to throw a curve ball, which was becoming a standard weapon in every hurler's arsenal. When Spalding gave up five runs in one inning without retiring a batter and suffered the further indignity of being hit in the chest with a line drive, he decided he could no longer pitch effectively and moved to first base. He was a good hitter and could have played longer, but during his tenure with the White Stockings, Spalding established a thriving sporting goods business in partnership with his brother. Walter Spalding was a former banker and a good administrator, while Albert was the marketer with connections in the sporting world and growing influence in major league baseball. By 1878, the Spalding baseball had become the official ball of the National League.

Spalding's firm also made baseball gloves, which were beginning to come into general use during the late 1870s. Spalding never wore a glove during his NA years, adhering to the general sentiment that it was "unmanly." Even though catchers absorbed terrific punishment and infielders got their hands battered, the concept of wearing any type of protective equipment was slow to take hold. There were no rules prohibiting the use of gloves, masks, or chest protectors, but peer pressure kept most players bare-handed, bare-faced, bare-chested, and perpetually beaten up.

To Albert Spalding, there was nothing more manly than making money, and when his firm began manufacturing baseball gloves, he started wearing one. Since everyone knew Al Spalding was a man's man, other players began to believe they could protect themselves without being emasculated. Soon, Spalding was selling masks, chest protectors, and other unmanly pieces of baseball equipment.[2]

After Hulbert's death in 1882, Spalding assumed the presidency of the Chicago club and purchased part of the team from Hulbert's widow. A.G. Mills succeeded Hulbert as president of the National League. Spalding and Mills, who'd also been involved with the White Stockings, had a close relationship, and the former wielded significant influence in League circles. When trouble arose, Spalding was the man his colleagues turned to. Rival leagues popped up in 1882, 1884, and 1890, and in each case, Spalding led the NL war party that fought the newcomers. They took down the Union Association in 1884 and the Players' League in 1890, while the battle with the American Association took a little longer. The two leagues cooperated in the battles against the UA and PL, but after the NL stole some of the AA's best franchises, the two leagues merged in 1892. While the transaction was referred to as a merger and the amalgamated league was officially called the National League and American Association, the latter half of the name was quickly abandoned in common usage. Albert Spalding won again.

While Spalding was a former star player turned businessman, New York's John Day was primarily a businessman, although he'd played a little amateur ball. Day, a Connecticut native, operated a cigar-making business in partnership with his brother-in-law Charles Abbey.[3] They established an office in New York City and did well enough for Day to move into a Fifth Avenue mansion. He became involved with Tammany Hall politics and began playing baseball, organizing and pitching for amateur teams.

Sportswriter William Rankin introduced Day to Jim Mutrie, who'd managed and played for teams in several Massachusetts cities. Mutrie had learned a lot about promotion, and suggested to Day that with Day's money and his marketing and recruiting ability, they could organize a top flight team.

Day formed the Metropolitan Exhibition Company, whose Metropolitans debuted in September 1880. In 1881 and 1882, they played as many games as any major league team and their schedule was almost as competitive. Day and Mutrie had use of the Polo Grounds, and virtually every National League club that came east stopped there, for they could make more money playing exhibitions in New York than they could playing league games in Worcester or Troy. In 1881, the team played 151 games against a mix of college, amateur, and professional teams. Sixty of the Mets games were against National League teams, and they won 18 of them, not a bad showing.

The following year, the Mets decided against joining the AA but were even more active, playing a total of 162 games and posting a 29–45 record against NL teams. In

1883, after turning down an offer to join the National League, Day entered his team in the American Association. That gave the AA teams in New York and Philadelphia and forced the NL to follow suit. The NL New York club, called the Gothams, was also owned by Day's Metropolitan Exhibition Company.

Unlike many owners, Day was respected and well-liked by his players and was offered the presidency of the Players' League in 1890, which he declined. The new league was to prove Day's downfall, as the competition crippled his club and he had to be bailed out by his fellow owners. Shortly thereafter, his tobacco business, hampered by foreign competition, began to lose money and Day faded from the baseball scene.

Spalding and Day had played baseball and knew the game. Chris Von der Ahe, owner of the St. Louis Brown Stockings, knew virtually nothing about baseball when he got involved in the game and many thought that when he left the game decades later, he still knew nothing about baseball.

Finding the real Chris Von der Ahe is difficult, first because his life was so chaotic and second, because so many stories about him are either fanciful or stereotypical. Ed Achorn wrote, "He struck some observers as the quintessential cartoon of a German immigrant: moon-faced and strawberry-nosed, with twinkling eyes, a bushy mustache, and an emerging pot belly that pushed on the vest of his loud checkered three-piece suit."[4] Von der Ahe wasn't a suave, dignified executive in the mold of Albert Spalding. His clothes were flashy and his manner bombastic. Chris was noisy.

Like Latino players of the 1950s and 1960s, the Browns owner was quoted in phonetic and heavily-accented English that made him appear to be a buffoon. But Von der Ahe was not stupid. He had been successful in the grocery and saloon businesses, and his Browns won four successive pennants in the 1880s. His greatest weakness was his massive ego and a thirst for attention that caused him to ignore sound advice and often embark on a foolhardy, ill-advised course. Like George Steinbrenner and other owners who'd been successful in business, Von der Ahe thought he knew more about baseball than the managers he hired and, like Steinbrenner, he often acted impulsively, with disastrous results.

Von der Ahe was born in Westphalia and came to St. Louis in 1867 at age 19 to avoid conscription in the Prussian army. He obtained a job as a grocery clerk, married Emma Hoffman in 1870, and within a couple of years had assembled a business conglomerate consisting of a boarding house, delicatessen, saloon, and beer garden. Any St. Louis business involving beer had potential, for the city had a large German population that loved its lager, and Von der Ahe began to accumulate some capital. His annual revenue was estimated at $75,000.

The Grand Avenue Grounds were across the street from his saloon and the young immigrant couldn't help noticing that people who attended baseball games liked to drink beer. In 1876, Von der Ahe became a director of the Grand Avenue Base Ball Club, and made the acquaintance of Al Spink, whose brother Billy was a leading St. Louis sportswriter, and Ned Cuthbert, veteran manager of the St. Louis baseball club. Cuthbert tended bar for Von der Ahe and urged him to try to get the concession to sell beer at the ballpark. He was successful and provided the beer for all games at the Grand Avenue Grounds, including those of the National League Brown Stockings.

After the NL club gave up its franchise, Von der Ahe became involved in financing a new version of the Browns. After the 1881 season generated a profit of $25,000, he bought out his partners for $1,800 and became the sole owner. Von der Ahe invested nearly all his savings in the Browns and made massive renovations to the ballpark. "If not for the support extended in the early 1880s by Chris Von der Ahe," said historian Jon Cash, "major-league baseball probably would have died in St. Louis and might have indeed come to an end throughout the nation."[5] Von der Ahe was so enthusiastic about the Browns' prospects that, prior to the 1884 season, he sold most of his other business interests in order to concentrate on baseball.

Von der Ahe was rebuffed in his attempt to join the National League and when the American Association was formed for the 1882 season, the Browns were one of its original teams. The league became an instant financial success, and Von der Ahe, who reportedly made $50,000 that year, was one of the first owners to perceive that baseball was not merely sport, but entertainment. Sportsman's Park was not just a baseball field; it was, in today's parlance, a venue.

There was a beer garden in right field. Vendors roamed the stands selling beer and whiskey. A phone line communicated out-of-town scores. Bicycle races attracted fans but tore up the baseball turf. There was a Civil War re-enactment titled "The Bombardment of Fort Sumter," a Wild West Show featuring Buffalo Bill Cody and Sitting Bull, and a water attraction called "Shoot the Chutes." Von der Ahe put in electric lights for evening dancing and staged elaborate fireworks displays. He led his team up Sullivan Avenue as they marched to the ballpark each day, and when the game was over, they all went to Chris' saloon.

Von der Ahe was disappointed by his team's fifth place finish in 1882 and dismissed Cuthbert as manager. His young first baseman, Charlie Comiskey, suggested that Von der Ahe hire his old friend Ted Sullivan.[6] Sullivan overhauled the St. Louis roster and, with his eye for talent, retained only the best of the holdovers—Comiskey, Bill Gleason, and Jumbo McGinnis. He brought in new players and built the roster that would eventually win four consecutive pennants.

Sullivan and Von der Ahe clashed and the former quit late in the 1883 season. Von der Ahe replaced him with Comiskey, who was a good fit for the Browns, for he was as combative and rough around the edges as they were, but just a little smarter. Comiskey rivaled Cap Anson as an umpire baiter, which Von der Ahe liked, for he thought it entertained the fans.

Unlike Sullivan, Comiskey was adept at dealing with Von der Ahe. "To placate his boss," wrote J. Thomas Hetrick, "Comiskey became expert at listening sympathetically to Chris's tirades. When the Browns' President issued Comiskey daily instructions, the manager did the opposite. When Von der Ahe was criticized by the Association, newsmen, or players, Comiskey deflected the remarks onto himself."[7] He was the buffer between the owner and the players, a role Sullivan had been unable to fill.

Von der Ahe was sometimes unfairly maligned, but he brought most of his trouble on himself. While he was ahead of his time in understanding that baseball was entertainment, he didn't always execute well—or perhaps like so many who are ahead of their time, the world wasn't ready for him. His many initiatives created a huge pile of debt, which eventually sunk him.

The personal life of the Browns' owner was even more chaotic than his baseball activities. Although Von der Ahe had been married since he was 18, he didn't allow his marriage to hinder his love life. His wife learned to tolerate his affairs and Chris made little effort to keep them secret. Eventually, his wife lost her patience and on one occasion supposedly attacked Von der Ahe and a female companion when they rode by her house in a carriage.

Emma's patience ran out for good when Von der Ahe hired an attractive 22-year-old maid named Anna Kaiser. On January 19, 1895, she filed for divorce, which was granted. The trial was an interesting one, for Mrs. Von der Ahe's testimony included titillating details about her husband's philandering.

In September 1896, Von der Ahe married Della Wells, one of the women mentioned in the divorce hearings. The new marriage encountered problems almost immediately, for Von der Ahe had secretly proposed to his young housekeeper Anna and having the two women under the same roof was bound to lead to trouble. They were suspicious of each other and reportedly came to blows on one occasion.

When Anna was informed by Browns secretary Benjamin Muckenfuss that her fiancé had married Wells, she was heartbroken, but not so heartbroken that she couldn't sell her story to the *St. Louis Post-Dispatch* and sue Von der Ahe for breach of promise. She received a settlement reported at $3,000, and it wasn't long before the Browns' owner was available to fulfill his broken promise. Della had been primarily interested in Von der Ahe's money, and when she realized he no longer had any, she lost interest. After they divorced, Von der Ahe and Anna were married. He was 47 and she was 24.

When the Browns were winning championships and making money, Von der Ahe was the toast of St. Louis and a vital force in American Association affairs. By the 1890s, the Browns were neither winning nor making money, and Von der Ahe was continuously involved in scandal and lawsuits.[8] Charley Comiskey and his mitigating influence were long gone, and the Browns went through a number of managers without success. Von der Ahe had never been a good judge of talent, but when he had Ted Sullivan and Comiskey to override his bad judgment, the Browns prospered. Without them, they suffered.

In 1898, the financial difficulties became overwhelming and the Browns were placed in receivership. Von der Ahe sued the National League (the Browns had been merged into the NL in 1891) but was unsuccessful. His final years in baseball were filled with lawsuits, a jailing,[9] a kidnapping, and an incident in which he beat and shot a black man. After he left the game, Von der Ahe lived on the charity of others, telling stories of the glory days to anyone who'd listen. Anna sued for divorce in 1902, but never pressed the suit to a final conclusion. Von der Ahe died in 1913 of dropsy and cirrhosis of the liver.

The Buffalo team didn't have a dynamic celebrity as president. "[T]he local management," a Buffalo paper noted, "does not boast a Spaulding [*sic*], Soden, Harry Wright, or even a Bancroft...."[10] It had Josiah Jewett, 41, a business executive from a prominent local family whose ancestors arrived in America in 1638.[11] Josiah's father, Sherman S. Jewett, was a wealthy stove manufacturer who sent Josiah to Yale, from which he graduated in 1863. That was in the midst of the Civil War, but people like Josiah Jewett didn't have to become soldiers if they didn't choose to. After graduation, while Union men were falling at Gettysburg and Vicksburg, young Jewett toured Europe and the Far East, where his most dangerous encounters were with snooty waiters. When he returned, he joined his father's company and became very active in civic affairs. In addition to serving as president of the Bisons, he was president of Columbia National Bank and was actively involved in numerous cultural organizations and events. Jewett ran for mayor of Buffalo in 1884 but lost.

Jewett was never a major voice in National League circles, but when Abraham Mills announced his intention to retire as league president after the 1884 season, he was one of those mentioned as a potential successor. His tenure as a magnate ended when he sold the Buffalo franchise to Detroit in 1885.

The principal Boston owners were Arthur Soden, owner of a roofing business, shoe factory owner J.B. Billings, and William Conant, who dealt in women's hoop skirts. The three men were often referred to as the Triumvirate, but Soden was clearly their leader.

There are many stories about Arthur Soden's legendary frugality and venality, most of which are true. "He had a near singlemindedness," wrote Brian McKenna, "when it came to the bottom line. He saw baseball as a business, pure and simple.... Controlling costs and expanding revenues were his priorities."[12]

Soden's father was a businessman, but he died when Soden was just a year old, and the young man was forced to make his own way in the world. After serving in the Civil War, he founded Chapman and Soden Company, a roofing and material supply business located in downtown Boston. Despite claims that he cared nothing for baseball other than the business aspects, Soden was actually quite enthusiastic about the game. He played amateur ball for many years and accompanied the Boston Red Stockings when they visited England in 1874, even playing a game in center field. As owner, he attended virtually every game.

Soden purchased $45 worth of stock in the Boston Club and when the old owners sold out, he became president. When Soden took over in 1877, economy was needed, for the team was in sorry financial straits. He immediately began to cut expenses, and since most expenses involved his players, they became unhappy. Salaries were reduced 20 percent from 1877 to 1880 and players were required to pay many of their own expenses, including the purchase and cleaning of their uniforms. The players' wives had to pay full price for tickets and press accommodations were eliminated. The team traveled in the cheapest possible manner and Soden even offered a bonus for players who could make their shoelaces last two years.

Prior to 1879, each player became a free agent when his contract ended, and the disgruntled ones could move on. No players were more disgruntled than those on the Boston nine, but Soden, who'd been using multi-year contracts to retain his players, had an even better idea. It was the infamous reserve rule, which was first instituted in 1879 and became his lasting legacy. With the reserve rule in effect, Soden could offer one-year contracts without the risk of losing players.

Soden was not the only baseball owner to cut costs and treat his players poorly; he just did it with more enthusiasm. The Boston franchise became profitable in 1881, and sportswriter Tim Murnane estimated that the club made at least $300,000 during the 1880s. That earned Soden more enemies, as he infuriated the smaller shareholders by refusing to divulge the club's finances and by voting himself and his two partners generous salaries.

Soden ran the Boston franchise until he sold it in 1906. When William Hulbert died in 1882, he served as interim president of the National League, and over the years he became a powerful force in League affairs, serving as a director for 30 years. From time to time, he helped prop up troubled franchises with loans. Soden is best remembered for his devotion to the bottom line but, to his credit, he was also known for his integrity. He was cheap but honest.

Philadelphia's AA entry was also managed by a "Triumvirate," consisting of Charley Mason, Lew Simmons, and Billy Sharsig. Mason was a former major league player who, when the Athletics found themselves short-handed one day in 1883, shucked his coat and went to right field, a unique role for a major league owner. Mason was responsible for player procurement and field operations.

Simmons and Sharsig handled the financial and marketing functions. Simmons was a former minstrel performer, a banjo-playing end man, who gave up the stage once he realized the profit potential of professional baseball. As might be expected of a show business performer, he was an affable sort who always had a good story and was generally well-liked by his fellow magnates. Although he wasn't in Mason's league, he knew baseball, he'd played some baseball, and was an enthusiastic fan until the end of his life.

Sharsig, who had the longest executive career of the three, played for a number of Philadelphia semi-pro teams in the late '70s. By 1880, he'd raised enough money from his family to become partners with Horace Phillips in the Athletics.

Mason, Sharsig, the ubiquitous Phillips, and player Chick Fulmer were the original partners in the Athletics' franchise. Simmons put up $200 in gold (per his account), or borrowed $16,000 (according to another story) and replaced Phillips, and Fulmer eventually left to continue his playing career elsewhere.

Mason recalled that on game days the three partners gathered and counted the gate receipts, piling the coins up into three stacks. When they determined that the stacks were equal, each partner scooped up his share and left. In 1882, it was said that the total of the three piles at the end of the season was $15,000. The next year it approximated $50,000, making the Athletics one of the most profitable teams in the history of professional baseball.

Who was the Arthur Soden of the Philadelphia Triumvirate? Jerrold Casway, who penned a biographical sketch of Sharsig, wrote, "Without deprecating Mason and Simmons, Billy Sharsig remained the central figure in the Athletics' organization."[13] Michael McAvoy, who wrote a sketch of Simmons, called him "the most visible and active of the triumvirate."[14] Tim Hagerty, who profiled Mason, said he was "the baseball expert among the Triumvirate."[15] It sounds like a team effort.

The American Association gained a leader when the Brooklyn Club entered the league in 1884. Small in stature, 40-year-old Charles Byrne[16] was erudite and educated. A graduate of St. Francis Xavier College who'd also taken classes in law, he had the business savvy to succeed in New York's real estate market. Intelligence alone doesn't make for business success, and Byrne's intellect was complemented by honesty, a calm temperament, and a suave, persuasive manner. He was a cultured man who loved theater and opera and was a fastidious dresser. Said one writer, "Charley Byrne would be immaculate if there was a frost in Hades."[17]

Charley Byrne was not Arthur Soden. He had good relationships with most of his players, taking them to social events and encouraging them to be financially prudent. Byrne was also concerned with the Brooklyn fans; he was an early proponent of Ladies Day and one of the first to issue rain checks when a game was washed out. In addition, Byrne worried about baseball's image and tried to curb the unruliness that permeated the sport during the 1880s.

As a new owner, Byrne was not a powerful figure in the 1884 American Association. As he became more experienced, his influence grew. He was a prominent candidate for the AA presidency in 1885, but was not selected. In 1890, Byrne transferred his club to the National League and became a member of the NL board of directors. He was a leader in the fight against the Players' League but in the end, Byrne made peace with the rival

Brooklyn franchise, making Brotherhood leader John Ward his manager. He continued to run the Brooklyn club until his death in January 1898.

Phillies owner Al Reach was an old baseball man. A native of London, Reach came to New York at a young age and was an infielder for the champion Eckford Club of 1862 and 1863. He left the Eckfords to play for the Athletics of Philadelphia and was for a long time considered the first professional player, although later evidence indicates there were sub rosa professionals before Reach. He was a member of the Athletic team that won the first NA title in 1871, but by that time he was in his 30s. For the next few years, Reach played infrequently before retiring completely in 1875.

Like Al Spalding and the Wright brothers, Reach entered the sporting goods business (he later sold his business to Spalding, who retained the Reach name). By 1883, he had a contract to supply the American Association with its baseballs and publish its annual guide. Reach's business made him a wealthy man and when the National League wanted to return to Philadelphia in 1883, president Mills approached him about backing the new team. He agreed, but the first season was a disastrous one on the field. The Phillies finished last with a dreadful 17–81 record while the cross-town Athletics won the AA championship.

Being a baseball magnate was a new occupation, and the men who filled the role were as diverse as their players. There were eccentrics like Chris Von der Ahe, shrewd hard-headed businessmen like Spalding and Soden, irascible men like Detroit's William Thompson, whose exploits are described elsewhere, and financially sound but benevolent owners like Day and Byrne.

At the beginning of the 1884 season there were 28 major league teams and by its end there were a few new ones, which meant there were a lot of new executives on the major league scene. Henry Lucas was a hybrid, an owner and the driving force behind his league. Others were men with money who would have less money by October. Some were men without money who didn't last the season. Each, in his own way, would help shape the bizarre season of 1884.

# 6

# "More famous for his quaintness and eccentricity than his managerial skill"

Harry Wright was both field captain and business manager of the 1869 Cincinnati Red Stockings, and no one had ever filled either position better. On the diamond, Wright was responsible for numerous strategic innovations and off the field he was a shrewd negotiator and financial manager who arranged games and terms, made travel arrangements, and signed players. But Harry Wright was a man of exceptional talents. Few men combined his knowledge of on-field strategy with the business acumen required to run a professional baseball team.

By the time the National League was established, field captain and club management duties were generally segregated, but having one man focused solely on finances had not resulted in pecuniary success. Very few National League teams were profitable in the 1870s, and outside the league insolvency and disbandment were common occurrences. The *Clipper* laid the blame for most failures on poor management. Managing a baseball team, Henry Chadwick explained, was not like managing other types of business; it required special skills.

"A feature of the season's management," the *Clipper* stated following the 1877 season, "was the failure of the experiment of supposing that, because a man was wealthy and flourishing, sharp in commercial dealings, and shrewd in business enterprises, he was fully competent to run a professional nine successfully."[1] One of Chadwick's biggest complaints was managers who interfered with the field captain's prerogatives on lineups and game strategy.

The qualities required of a good manager, he said, were, "First—honesty; second—a man of financial ability; third—a good judge of character; fourth—a man having some consideration for those in his employ, as regards their moral and social welfare; and fifth and lastly, he should be pretty well posted in the control of small parties of individuals as a leader or head man."[2] Perhaps one reason for the deficiency in talent, Chadwick hinted, was money. "The folly of paying an outfielder $2,500 a season," he wrote, "and a club manager $1,200 was very conspicuous in 1877."[3]

The main goal of the manager was to ensure that the club's revenue exceeded its expenses. The first determinant of a positive bottom line is a healthy top line, and good managers prided themselves on their ability to schedule as many games as possible. A day spent in idleness was a day of expenses with nothing to show for them.

By 1884, there were a number of men, most of them former players, who were making a career of managing professional teams. Among the most renowned were Dan O'Leary, Horace Phillips, Frank Bancroft, Jim Mutrie, and Ted Sullivan.

O'Leary and Phillips were unusual characters, energetic types affectionately referred to as Hustling Dan O'Leary and Hustling Horace Phillips. They were a new breed among baseball managers, the antithesis of Harry Wright, who was never referred to as Hustling Harry. Calling someone a hustler can be a compliment if it refers to energy and innovation, or an insult if it means being a man of questionable ethics and a perpetrator of scams. For O'Leary and Phillips, the nickname was meant both ways.

O'Leary and Phillips were baseball men, but they were first and foremost hucksters who promoted anything they thought would put money in their pockets, including roller rinks, theatrical troupes, and comedy acts. They were not concerned with the reputation of baseball and frequently became embroiled in the kind of controversies that could only bring ill to the game.

O'Leary, who was 27 years old[4] in 1884, played just 45 games during his five-year major league career, thirty-two of them during talent-starved 1884.[5] Some of O'Leary's exploits were legendary, and it is difficult to separate legend from fact, for many amazing, not quite believable tales came directly from the high-octane lips of Hustling Dan. There was the daring but probably fictional story of the time he inspired his team to win by telling them he'd bet the entire payroll on them, and the time he lambasted the clubhouse attendant in front of the team's owner for bringing him a bucket of beer rather than the milk he claimed he'd sent him for. O'Leary got a lot of mileage out of the latter story; it appeared in print many times over the years.

Even the story of O'Leary's introduction to baseball is shrouded in mystery. For years it was believed he first became involved in the sport when he came to Chicago in 1871 with the Detroit Fire Company to fight the Great Fire, but historian Paul Browne doubts the veracity of that story. In any event, by 1876, Dan was playing with the Cass Club of Detroit. The following year, he was elected captain, but the Cass Club didn't last. Dan then joined the ill-fated Browns of Minneapolis, who failed in August.

The 1878 season was an active one for O'Leary. He played in the New England mill towns of Lynn, Manchester, and Lowell, twice with the latter club. In 1879, O'Leary was relatively stable, spending most of the season with Springfield and playing well enough to earn a two-game trial with Providence of the National League. The following season he appeared briefly with Boston and Detroit, but played a total of just five games.

O'Leary established his reputation as a manager with the Indianapolis club in 1883. Indianapolis was an independent team, but O'Leary's persuasive powers lured a number of future major leaguers to the Indiana city and the team did quite well, setting a blistering pace late in the season.[6]

There was another side to O'Leary—one that liked to drink. In June 1883, celebrating his team's big upset win over the AA Metropolitans, O'Leary was arrested for drunkenness, use of profanity, and resisting an officer. Some of the Indianapolis directors wanted to suspend him, but in the wake of the great victory they settled on a $100 fine and a warning.

When Indianapolis joined the expanded American Association in 1884, O'Leary became a somewhat unlikely major league manager. In its analysis of the season's skippers, *Sporting Life* said, "Dan O'Leary, of Indianapolis, is more famous for his quaintness and eccentricity than for managerial skill...."[7] Another paper was more charitable. "Among professionals," it said, "he is known as big-hearted Dan O'Leary. He is a shrewd business man, and in his hands the financial matters of a club with which he is connected are not likely to suffer. He possesses executive powers to a marked degree."[8]

O'Leary was in trouble long before the season even began. He'd displayed his typical energy and done an excellent job of promoting the team, but his loose tongue, probably further loosened by alcohol, caused him to curse one of the directors. That and an insulting telegram to the board resulted in his summary dismissal in early January.

Dan was devastated and pleaded with the directors to take him back. While he was a braggart, a drunk, and a liar, O'Leary was likeable and charming, and it wasn't long before a majority of the directors signed a petition requesting reconsideration of the dismissal. The press, which liked him, called his firing unjust. "Dan," said one journal, "is one of the most impulsive of mortals and in warm moments is apt to say things he is afterwards very sorry for. This is a failing which those who know the man make full allowance for and after all the fault is a trifling one to men whose skin is not especially thin."[9] Just ten days after his firing, O'Leary was reinstated.

It wasn't long before he was in trouble again, for asking for a contract guaranteeing he would manage the club all year, regardless of his performance. While such an agreement is customary today, it was highly irregular in 1884, and the directors refused. In fact, they told O'Leary that when he paid the $158 he owed the club, he would be released. If he did not pay it, he would be blacklisted.

O'Leary claimed the debt was offset by money the club owed him for his share of the 1883 profits, and told anyone who would listen how he had been the savior of Indianapolis baseball. "[T]hey actually thought I was a fit subject for a lunatic asylum in persisting in my endeavors to organize a club and put it on a paying basis," he said.[10] Dan claimed he had received a number of offers following his successful season and perhaps he was angling to obtain his release so he could accept one of them. With Dan O'Leary, who knew?

When the directors suspended him for the unpaid debt, O'Leary retaliated by refusing to release his correspondence concerning the club's business affairs and games he had arranged. Indianapolis put him on the blacklist, brought in James H. Gifford to replace him, and asked all other clubs to inform them of any games they had scheduled with O'Leary.

Dan wasn't out of work for long, quickly signing a contract (supposedly for $3,000 per year) to manage Cincinnati's Union Association team.[11] Despite his problems in Indianapolis, the Hoosiers' treasurer and secretary told the baseball people of Cincinnati he was sorry things had ended badly for O'Leary in that city and that he was an "excellent manager and a hard worker."[12] After he got the job with Cincinnati, O'Leary went to Indianapolis and offered to pay the $158 he owed them, but by signing with the UA, he had cooked his goose. They refused to remove his name from the blacklist and he left the meeting in disgust.

Dan had a rough summer in Cincinnati. He was ill early in the season, and after he recovered, he contracted malaria, which sidelined him for an extended period. In May, he was hit in the eye with a line drive. Management suspected he was betting on games and were upset that he drank with the team. One of the reasons Dan was always popular with his players was that he allowed them to drink as much as they wanted.

O'Leary was released in mid–June, despite his team's 20–15 record. In August, he paid Indianapolis the money he owed them and was removed from the blacklist. There were rumors that he would soon be managing Indianapolis again. That did not come to pass, and by September he was managing in Evansville, where he had operated a roller rink the previous winter. It is a tribute to O'Leary's persuasive charm that, in the manner of Billy Martin in the next century, he was always able to find employment after so many untoward incidents.

In December 1884, after his tumultuous season, *Sporting Life* noted O'Leary's "harmless eccentricities" that "made him a character in the baseball world.... Dan's failings are his own, but are connected with the bottle.... The fellow is lucky and always 'lights' on his feet between his laughable escapades. He drank himself out of the management of the Indianapolis Club, repeated the feat at Cincinnati, and once again 'caught on' at Evansville, getting a good team together."[13]

O'Leary's life after 1884 was more of the same. "Dan O'Leary is as yet without an engagement for next season," a paper reported late that year. "He will, however, cast an anchor to the windward before long, and turn up smiling on the right side by the time the grass on the diamonds begins to sprout."[14]

Dan bounced from town to town managing a number of teams, most of which failed. In 1886, he raised money for a team in Elmira and hired a very impressive group of players, including some former major leaguers.[15] O'Leary was never content with simple situations, and in late April he acquired the Scranton franchise in the newly-formed Pennsylvania State Association. He didn't, however, sign any players for his new team. Scranton fans thought the Elmira club had relocated to Scranton and those in Elmira thought their team was filling in temporarily until O'Leary could hire a new team for Scranton. He explained to his Elmira backers that the players had to be signed to Scranton contracts so they would be protected as part of a league. Signing players was expensive, and if O'Leary could stock two teams with a total of nine players, he was going to do so as long as he could get away with it.

The charade was maintained for most of the summer, while the people of Elmira kept waiting hopefully for the team to play another home game. The nine became known not as Elmira or Scranton but as the "O'Learys" or "O'Leary's Indians." As always, Dan got into trouble with management and there were mutual accusations of bad faith. Finally, on July 24, he ran out of money, his landlord seized the team's assets, and that was the end of the Scranton/Elmira/O'Leary nine.

Dan left unpaid debts in Elmira, for which he was arrested in New York City in late August. He handed over forty dollars, his watch, and his overcoat and hustled out of town. That was a typical season for Hustling Dan O'Leary. He ruffled feathers and lived on the edge wherever he went, but in the end, he was always forgiven. After all, he was Dan O'Leary.

Around 1887, O'Leary left baseball and became a police reporter, operating the O'Leary News Bureau. He reported the news somewhat more truthfully than he told stories about his own exploits, and stayed in the business for 35 years, until his death in 1922. Even in his later years, he couldn't be completely honest, frequently telling people that his habitual wearing of a carnation had inspired president McKinley to do the same.

Legendary sportscaster/fantasist Bill Stern told his 20th-century listeners a remarkable tale that occurred in 1871. When the Chicago White Stockings played an exhibition in an obscure Wisconsin town, Stern related breathlessly, over a background of dramatic organ accompaniment, the Chicago captain hit a home run that cleared the fence, broke the window of a nearby house, knocked over a lantern, and started a fire that killed 1,100 people. When the team returned to Chicago they learned, in a remarkable coincidence, that their city had been destroyed by an even more disastrous fire the same day. And even more remarkable, the man who hit the home run was Dan O'Leary, son of the infamous Mrs. O'Leary whose cow started the Chicago blaze.

Who knows whether O'Leary himself started the story, or if the tale was just a figment of Stern's fertile imagination? In any event, Dan got a fleeting moment of fame with 20th-century sports fans.

O'Leary was sometimes referred to as Hustling Dan, but Horace Phillips was almost *always* called Hustling Horace, perhaps because of the better alliteration—maybe O'Leary should have been called Drunken Dan. In the case of Phillips, the description was not only alliterative but accurate;

They don't make them like "Hustling Horace" Phillips any more, for which many people say, "Thank God!" Phillips was a charming individual of questionable character who served as manager for numerous 19th-century clubs (courtesy Justin McKinney).

he was always on the move, always one step ahead of trouble, and always in search of the next opportunity. During the summer, he played a little baseball, managed baseball teams, and sometimes served as umpire or talent scout, and during the winter he fronted for theatrical troupes and other entertainment ensembles.

Phillips was good looking and persuasive, with a lifelong propensity for trouble and, like O'Leary, he possessed the charm to wiggle out of it, pick himself up, dust off his pants, and proceed to the next adventure. "The handsome, smooth-talking Phillips," wrote Roy Kerr, "possessed superior skills of communication and persuasion, and he was expert at manipulating the media of his day—newspapers—to suit his own purposes."[16]

Phillips was born in Salem, Ohio, in 1853, but started his baseball career in Philadelphia, where he was a player of marginal ability. Horace began the 1877 season as assistant manager and secretary of a newly-organized Philadelphia club, but soon he was in Hornell, New York, as manager of an International Association team.

Hornell, with a population of just 1,895 in 1880, was an unlikely place to locate a professional baseball team. Not only was it tiny, but it was also not near any population centers, with the nearest cities, Binghamton and Rochester, 120 and 75 miles distant. But if anyone could make a go of it under such unpropitious circumstances, it was Horace Phillips. Recruiting was his long suit, and he wasn't squeamish about approaching players under contract with other clubs. Phillips used his many contacts to get leads and closed the deal with his convincing manner. He persuaded a number of skilled players to come to the little New York town, including future NL star second baseman Fred Dunlap, and put together a very competitive team.

For teams like Hornell, survival constituted a successful season, and Phillips' club made it through the summer without running out of money. He remained in town for the winter and partnered with one of the Hornell stockholders to open a laundry. He married a local girl, Jessie Kellinger, early the following year and appeared to be putting down roots. Putting down roots, however, was not in Phillips' DNA, and in any event, managing a team in tiny Hornell was a tenuous occupation.

By late July 1878, Phillips and the board of directors were denying rumors that they were on the "ragged edge."[17] Less than a month later, they announced that the club would play the rest of its games in Bath, New York, which had a usable field, a train station, and supposedly some eager fans. With a population of more than 7,000, the city was much larger than Hornell.

Bath proved no more remunerative than Hornell, and a week later, on August 22, the club officially disbanded, despite a fine record of 44-28-2. "The desertion of Manager Phillips is given as the immediate reason," reported the *Clipper*, "but the primary cause was a lack of support."[18]

Phillips, who had accurately deciphered the handwriting on the wall, had absconded about 120 miles to the southeast, where he finished the season as manager of the Crickets of Binghamton. As always, Phillips assembled an impressive array of talent, including future major league pitching stars John Montgomery Ward and Jim Whitney.

Managing failed teams in out-of-the-way places like Hornell and Bath didn't seem like stepping stones to the major leagues but somehow Phillips got hired to manage the Troy club when it entered the National League in 1879.

Phillips' promotional skills would be tested in Troy, which was bigger than Hornell, but with just 57,000 residents, a bit small for the National League. Small market teams faced the same problems in the 19th century that they do in the 21st. They needed good players, but had difficulty generating sufficient revenue to pay good players. A team without money needed a manager with an abundance of charm and the ability to discover diamonds in the rough. Hustling Horace Phillips was that man.

Phillips' other great talent was his ability to generate publicity, a skill honed by his experience in theatrical promotion. He sent pictures of his players to the towns and cities in which the team was to appear. He gave his players catchy nicknames. He took out ads in local papers and sent people into the streets with handbills promoting the games. He wrote long letters to *Sporting Life* detailing his activities, promoting his team, or explaining his side of the many controversies in which he found himself.

"Either one of the above pair," said one paper, referring to Phillips and O'Leary, "could go to Egypt, Honolulu or some other out of the way post and inside of a week organize a good baseball team and have the populace worked up to a high pitch of excitement over the game."[19]

One of the most important jobs of the manager was to schedule as many games as possible. Independent teams had to book all of their games, and National League teams played just 60 games as late as 1878. That left a lot of open dates to be filled with exhibitions, and managers like O'Leary and Phillips were skilled both at finding opponents and negotiating favorable financial terms. When venturing to the hinterlands, it was important to get a minimum guarantee that would at least cover traveling expenses.

Phillips and O'Leary were tough negotiators, and *Sporting Life* speculated that when they were scheduling games against each other, "It must have been something in the nature of a picnic to see Dan and the 'Hustler' squabbling about the terms."[20]

Like most fast-talking hucksters, Phillips was not very good at managing men over a long period of time. In 1879, Troy played miserably under his leadership, winning just 12 of 46 games, and he was jettisoned in favor of Bob Ferguson in August. Ferguson, a notorious bully and autocrat, was no better at managing men, but he could play third base, saving one precious salary.

Phillips was not called "Hustling Horace" for nothing, and it wasn't long after leaving Troy that he surfaced in Baltimore, where he quickly incurred the ire of the Athletic Club of Philadelphia by stealing two of their players and spreading a rumor they had disbanded, which cost them playing dates.

Following the season, Phillips accompanied Cap Anson's White Stockings to California to serve as umpire, and supposedly was going to remain there and play in San Francisco the following summer. A subsequent rumor had him organizing a team in Philadelphia. But in March, Phillips sent a letter to the *Clipper* stating that he was going to manage a team in Baltimore. He listed the names of a number of players he wanted to sign and asked that they send him their terms.

Phillips was officially named manager of the Baltimore team March 31 and by the time the season began he was already causing trouble, breaking engagements with Yale University and the Boston and Worcester NL clubs. On June 28, the Baltimore team disbanded in the wake of a financial disaster and Phillips was on the move once more, taking several of his players to Rochester and forming a team backed by a patent medicine manufacturer. The nine was called the Hop Bitters to promote the company's product.

At the beginning of August, Phillips absconded again. Normally, he popped up somewhere almost immediately, but this time he did not. "Nothing has been heard from the late manager of the Rochester Club," the *Clipper* reported in mid–August.[21] Phillips was finally located in Chicago, working as a hotel clerk. The reason he was not in baseball was that when he left Rochester, he took the remainder of the team's money.

The following April, Phillips returned to Rochester and confessed judgment in the amount of $1,463, and a month later he was managing the Athletic Club of Philadelphia. After the season ended, he began raising money for a Philadelphia club and in September 1881, Phillips arranged a meeting with Oliver P. Caylor to discuss the possibility of forming a new league. He did most of the talking while Caylor listened quietly.[22]

Caylor was a deliberate man with the discipline to see the ambitious scheme through to fruition. Phillips was a man of action who didn't always follow through and his checkered past made him more of a liability than an asset to a league with big aspirations. When the American Association became a reality, Phillips found himself on the outside looking in. He was released as manager of the Philadelphia team and replaced by the triumvirate of Billy Sharsig, Charley Mason, and Charley Fulmer. Phillips said he was going to work with Al Reach to form a second Philadelphia team, which he hoped would be admitted to the AA in place of the Sharshig/Mason/Fulmer club.

At its November meeting, the AA declined to accept Phillips' team, relegating it to the League Alliance, a loose aggregation playing under the auspices of the National

League. Before the 1882 season began, Phillips resigned as manager to promote non-baseball events such as lacrosse, football, and polo.

By July, Hustling Horace had several lines in the water. He was attempting to organize an Indianapolis team he planned to enter in the AA in 1883. He took a job as an AA umpire and was also signing players for the St. Louis club.

Three months later, Phillips was in Columbus, Ohio, trying to organize yet another club. His past caught up with him in Columbus, as reports filtered in that he had been less than honest in some of his prior engagements. The shareholders decided to investigate, for they planned to apply for admission to the AA and were afraid they wouldn't be accepted with Phillips as manager. "Leading base ball men seem to be afraid of him," said a local paper. "Why they are opposed to him is best understood by themselves and Mr. Phillips and his friends."[23] Phillips claimed the allegations were the result of personal differences and convinced the people of Columbus he was clean enough to manage the team, which was admitted to the AA for the 1883 season.

Rumors dogged Phillips throughout the season, including an accusation of taking kickbacks from players to keep them on the roster. The players produced a letter of support, denying there were morale problems or that they had paid money to Phillips. That kept the wolves at bay for a time, but the club's poor play led to calls for Phillips' dismissal.

In June, when Phillips brought his team to Philadelphia, he was arrested for nonpayment of an 1882 bill of $91 at the Great Western Hotel. He paid the money and was released.[24] After hearing rumors that Horace was pocketing gate receipts, the club sent vice president Frank Failing on an Eastern trip to keep an eye on Phillips and the finances. Because of his reputation, Phillips had been hired under the condition that he not handle any money, but the finances had become convoluted and no one was sure how much money had changed hands. Several stockholders signed a petition calling for Phillips' removal.

One of Phillips' greatest talents was an ability to put his team on the field almost every day, and he managed to book 156 games in 1883, which generated a small reported surplus for the year. Despite all the suspicions, it was tempting to retain a manager who could turn a profit. Phillips offered to manage the team in 1884 for $1,800, but the directors demurred. They told him to come up with a lower number but that too was declined by a resounding 46–11 vote. Although nothing had been proven, there were too many murky, unresolved issues. Phillips was angry, claiming he'd been promised that if he turned a profit he would return for the following season at an increase in salary.

In early December, Phillips was in St. Louis trying to get a job as business manager for a theatrical company, but by mid-month *Sporting Life* reported, "Horace Phillips is still lingering under the shadows of the big bridge across the Mississippi. Micawber-like he is 'waiting for something to turn up' but as yet the fates are against him."[25] Within a week, something turned up and he signed as manager of Grand Rapids of the Northwestern League.

Phillips came east looking for players and placed an ad in *Sporting Life,* from which he said he received over 60 applications. By the first week in January, he was able to report that he had filled his roster, and that the stockholders intended to raise $15,000 for operating expenses. With his usual energy, he began scheduling games, and by mid–April, his club had only two or three open dates through the end of the season. "The fine Italian hand of Hustling Horace is already visible," said one paper, "in the management of the club. It is saft [sic] to bet there will be a balance in the treasury at the close of the season."²⁶ And hopefully Horace would leave it there.

Although it would seem that Phillips had his hands full trying to get up a team in Grand Rapids, he found time to insert himself into the middle of the AA's attempt to get pitcher George Bradley to break his UA contract (see Chapter 11). Ironically, the caper placed him in cahoots with Charley Fulmer, who'd helped squeeze him out of the AA, and against fellow huckster Dan O'Leary.

Under Phillips' leadership, Grand Rapids got off to a terrific start, but nothing went right in the NWL in 1884, and by the end of June, Grand Rapids was in financial difficulty.²⁷ They had a 48-13 record when they received notice in mid–August that they would need to post a $500 bond to remain in the league. Two hours later, a second telegram informed them they had been dropped from the NWL. The Grand Rapids players and their manager found themselves unemployed but, as *Sporting Life* observed, "Hustling Horace Phillips never gets left. He didn't lose anything by the disbandment of the Grand Rapids Club, and has already secured another berth—the management of the Allegheny Club."²⁸ Philips also reportedly earned a few dollars for arranging the transfer of several Grand Rapids players to Detroit.

Phillips managed the Allegheny Club through 1889 with mixed results. In 1886, he led the team to an 80-57 record, but overall they posted a 244-296 mark. The Alleghenies had a 28-43 record in 1889 when Hustling Horace's baseball career came to an abrupt end.

Horace, feeling the pressure of his team's poor record, began to exhibit behavior that was strange even for him. At the suggestion of the Allegheny president, he took a two-week leave of absence. When he returned, Phillips began negotiating transactions to sell several of his players. After managing the game on July 24, he checked into the Girard House in Philadelphia and told the desk clerk he was worth millions, owned all the baseball teams in the country, and was looking for investments. He also said he managed the Girard House and that he would make the clerk his partner.

The clerk thanked him, sent him to his room, and called a doctor. When the doctor arrived, he diagnosed "acute paresis or softening of the brain"²⁹ and sent Phillips to Kirkbride's Asylum. He was later transferred to Dr. Jones' private hospital in Merchantville, New Jersey, but from that point, the trail turned cold. For years, Phillips' final years remained a mystery, until SABR historian and sleuth Peter Morris learned that he died February 26, 1896, in the Philadelphia Hospital for the Insane.³⁰

Following Phillips' career is exhausting. He was always on the move, and perhaps the stability of settling down in Pittsburgh drove him over the brink, for he'd never been in one place nearly as long as he stayed with the Alleghenies. What is perhaps most remarkable about Phillips is that even after the numerous scrapes in which he was involved over the years—accusations of misappropriating funds, stealing players, and skipping out on hotel bills—he was always able to find another job. News traveled much slower in the 19th century, and Phillips somehow stayed one jump ahead of his past. His glib tongue gained access, and his energy and ability to keep a team in action impressed his employers. He and O'Leary are the best examples of the somewhat shady hustlers of 19th-century baseball.

Frank Bancroft and Jim Mutrie were promoters of a different breed, possessing the aggressiveness and hustle of Phillips and O'Leary without being burdened by their fatal flaws. Bancroft, 38 years old in 1884, was a Civil War veteran who enlisted as a musician in the 8th New Hampshire Infantry in 1861. Since he was only 15, he used the alias Henry Coulter. Although wounded in action, Bancroft served through the end of the war in the Invalid Corps and the Veteran Reserve Corps.[31]

Bancroft began his baseball career pitching for an amateur club in his hometown of Worcester, Massachusetts. He then organized a team in New Bedford, where he ran the Bancroft House Hotel, and managed it in 1877 and 1878; in the latter season Bancroft's team played a record 130 games. One of his players was shortstop Jim Mutrie.

In 1879, the club in Worcester, which was located about 70 miles from New Bedford, noticed Bancroft's success and asked him to manage their team. He worked the Worcester nine hard; they played 125 games in his first season. As he had in New Bedford, Bancroft turned a profit in the small Massachusetts town, and when Worcester entered the National League for the 1880 season, he was retained as manager.

Unlike the slick Horace Phillips, Bancroft established a reputation for honest dealing and gained the respect of his fellow managers. In 1880, he took his club to Yale for an exhibition and when the game was rained out, Bancroft asked only that his team's travel expenses be reimbursed, rather than demanding his guaranty, as most managers did.

Although he was honest, reputable, and sober, Bancroft was like Phillips and O'Leary in many ways. He was good at filling up a schedule. He was good at advertising and promotion and attending to detail, like coordinating with the railroads to see that there were enough cars available to ferry spectators to his games. He was good at acquiring talent, and established a reputation for luring players away from other teams, even if they happened to be under contract.

Bancroft was also not above a little gamesmanship. One day when he was managing Cleveland, he was scheduled to play Providence, but his two best players, Fred Dunlap and Jim McCormick, were injured. When a slight drizzle ensued, Bancroft ordered the groundskeeper to flood the grounds with a fire hose. When Grays manager Harry Wright arrived on the scene, he found the field drenched from what had appeared to be only a few raindrops. Bancroft told Wright they would have to postpone the game. "Oh, these are the queerest grounds you ever saw," he told the Providence manager. "They are flooded over every time it rains."[32]

Following the 1879 season, Bancroft took a group of players to Cuba, the first time Americans had played baseball on the island. He encountered a problem as soon as he arrived, as his hosts wouldn't let him charge admission fees. A number of Cuban baseball fans and businesses came to his rescue by contributing funds voluntarily, and the games went on. Financially, however, the trip was a washout and as a goodwill tour it fell short. A correspondent reported that the singing of American national songs was "very distasteful to the hundreds of Spanish soldiers roaming about the streets, and who show in every conceivable way but that of actual violence their hatred of Americans."[33]

Bancroft's Worcester team posted a mediocre mark of 40–43 in its first NL season, but it got through the season without touching the initial capital of $4,500 and made a profit of more than $1,000.[34] That made Bancroft a valuable commodity and he received several attractive offers.

During the winter, while weighing his options, Bancroft kept busy by re-acquiring the lease on the Bancroft House, completely renovating it, and operating it until it was time to leave for pre-season practice. Bancroft first agreed to manage Buffalo, but changed his mind when he got a better offer from Detroit. While Buffalo protested futilely, Bancroft prepared the Wolverines for their first NL season. To give them a boost, he took a couple of the best Worcester players with him.

Detroit got off to a fast start, but faded and finished fourth with a 41–43 record, not bad for a first-year team. Bancroft was an efficient financial manager, and by mid-season the *Clipper* reported, "The Detroit Club is in a flourishing financial condition, and the stockholders are not likely to have any deficit to make up at the close of the season. The cost of the erection of the grandstands at Recreation Park, besides all the running expenses, including salaries, have been paid out of the gate receipts, and there is still a handsome balance in the club's treasury."[35]

When the National League schedule ended, Bancroft kept his men playing for another month to generate additional revenue and when the ledgers were balanced there was a reported $12,000 in the coffers. In its annual analysis of club management, the *Clipper,* which was usually critical, said, "For a first season in the League, Detroit did wonders."

Over the winter, Bancroft announced that he was going to retire from baseball and devote his attention to managing his hotel, but when spring arrived, he was back in Detroit. In early July, he had his team in first place, but they faded and finished sixth. Part of the reason for the fade, it was rumored, was that the directors were interfering with Bancroft's management.

Bancroft was unhappy and because of his reputation for being able to turn a profit, he was in demand, coveted by both Baltimore and Cleveland. He signed with the latter club and, during the winter, sold his interest in the Bancroft House to devote more time to baseball.

As he had in Detroit, Bancroft took a Cleveland team that began the season without fanfare and put them in the midst of the pennant race. They sat briefly in first place in mid–July before finishing fourth with a 55–42 record, seven and a half games behind Boston. Thanks to Bancroft's energy and initiative, the club played a total of 153 games and the financial results were good.

One of the most difficult jobs of any manager in the 1880s was keeping his nine sober, and Bancroft used a clever dodge to keep the Cleveland team on the straight and narrow. When he suspected his boys had been drinking too much, he went to the local telegraph office and claimed to have received a message from the Cleveland president that he would be there the next day. That usually caused the team to behave better, after which Bancroft would say he received a second telegram stating, "Could not get there. Will be along tomorrow."[36]

Despite their success, there were rumors that there would be no Cleveland team in 1884. With the situation uncertain, Bancroft began looking at options. When Harry Wright left Providence to join Al Reach in Philadelphia, Bancroft agreed to take his place. His wife had died just before the start of the 1883 season, and his son was living with Bancroft's sister in New Bedford, just 30 miles from Providence.

*Sporting Life* opined, "Even if Providence does not win the championship under Bancroft, she will certainly make money."[37] "Bancroft's forte is in picking a good team, placing a man at their head, and then letting the latter run the nine while he looks after the finances. While [Harry] Wright thinks of nothing but the discipline of his team, Bancroft thinks of nothing but the dollars and cents."[38]

Having sold his hotel, Bancroft occupied himself during the winter by managing a New Bedford roller rink and added to his income by winning $260 in a lottery. But while he prospered financially, Bancroft's winter, like the previous one, was marked by personal tragedy, this time the death of his father. Bancroft himself had a narrow escape. In January, he booked passage on the *City of Columbus,* but cancelled due to pressing business appointments. It was a fateful decision, for the ship went down with great loss of life.

Bancroft, managing his fourth team in five years, had a great opportunity. He had probably the most talented roster he'd ever assembled and while Providence wasn't the largest city in the National League, it gave Bancroft access to the big eastern cities. He began aggressively booking exhibition games, and after looking at the Grays' ambitious schedule, which gave them not a single day off through July 9, one paper noted, "They evidently want money, not fame."[39]

In the event, Bancroft led his team to more fame than money, capturing the NL title, which led to an historic October encounter with the manager of the New York Metropolitans, James Mutrie. Like Bancroft, Mutrie was a Massachusetts native, born in Chelsea in 1851.[40] He recalled playing baseball on the Boston Common for the entertainment of Civil War soldiers but, like Dan O'Leary's, Mutrie's recollections did not always hold up under investigation. He acquired the nickname "Truthful James" or "Truthful Jeems," in sarcastic appreciation of the fact that his tales were sometimes fanciful.[41] Like O'Leary, Mutrie had a weakness for the bottle, which sometimes landed him in trouble.

Mutrie began playing baseball in 1875 with an amateur team in Chelsea, Massachusetts, and later that season moved to the Androscoggin Club of Lewiston, Maine. He was with Fall River in 1876 and 1877 and New Bedford (under Bancroft) the following season, where he served as captain and operated a cigar store. While he often received praise for his fielding at shortstop, Mutrie's batting was weak.

In addition to his baseball activity, Mutrie participated in one of the most popular sports of the late 19th century—pedestrianism. For some reason, postwar America became enthralled by lengthy walking races in which men either circled an indoor track continuously for days on end or set forth on lengthy

JAMES MUTRIE.

"Truthful Jeems" was the manager of the American Association champion Metropolitan nine. He arranged the first World Series with Providence manager Frank Bancroft and saw his team swept in three straight games (National Baseball Hall of Fame Library, Cooperstown, N.Y.).

journeys by road. Competitors covered hundreds of miles in masochistic endurance contests on which substantial amounts of money were wagered. In early 1879, Mutrie took part in a 100-mile competition with a gentleman appropriately named Walker, the champion pedestrian of Bristol County, Massachusetts. A few months later, the *Clipper* reported that Mutrie planned to retire from baseball after the season to pursue a career as a professional pedestrian.

Before the 1879 season began, however, Mutrie was engaged to manage the Lowell team, replacing Bancroft, but before managing a game, he followed Bancroft to Worcester as captain. That year, Mutrie's last as a regular player, was divided between Worcester, Brockton, and New Bedford.

The following year, Mutrie managed a team from Brockton, which also played several games in New Bedford. In June there were rumors the team would disband due to financial difficulties. "The Cambridge-Brockton game…" said the *Clipper*, "was advertised as the 'farewell game' of the local club, owing to the fact that the manager had not been seen for a week, and was a little behind on salaries. Manager Mutrie arrived, however, at noon that day and said he'd made arrangements to move the club to Springfield, to be known as the Springfields or the Brockton-Springfields."[42] When the team was unable to prosper in Brockton, New Bedford, or Springfield, Mutrie disbanded it, got hold of a bicycle, and rode to New York, believing that his baseball future lie in the big city.

In New York, Mutrie, as stated earlier, was introduced to John Day by William Rankin and convinced Day to provide the financial support for a new club. Day persuaded James Gordon Bennett, son of the founder of the *New York Herald*, to lease him a parcel of land located at Fifth Avenue and 110th Street, previously used by Bennett and his friends to play polo. Day constructed a baseball field on the site and called it the Polo Grounds.

With financial backing and a playing field in America's largest city, Mutrie began signing players for a team he called the Metropolitans. Playing outside of any organized league, the Mets were open to all comers, and the prospect of playing in New York enticed nearly all major league teams to schedule a game with Mutrie's nine. By not affiliating with either the NL or AA, he was able to play exhibitions with teams from both leagues.

After the AA and NL consummated the National Agreement, there was no longer a need to maintain an independent status, and Day entered teams in both the National League and American Association for the 1883 season. Mutrie managed the AA club, while veteran catcher John Clapp ran the NL nine. Clapp had the best talent, but a year later Mutrie had a champion, taking his Mets to the World Series against Bancroft's Providence Grays.

Irish immigrant Timothy "Ted" Sullivan was one of the most remarkable figures of 19th-century baseball. He wasn't much of a player; his major league career consisted of just three games with Kansas City of the Union Association.[43] He was a big-league manager four times, but never completed a full season. He served briefly as an umpire in 1880 and 1887 but showed no particular aptitude for the position.[44] Ted Sullivan made his mark as an organizer and talent scout. Al Spink called him "the best judge of a ballplayer in America"[45] and historian David Nemec described him as "a scout who knew how to judge talent, if not always how to use it when he assumed his other familiar baseball role as manager."[46]

Sullivan was a typical baseball entrepreneur—a man of immense energy, great personal charm, a wide array of talents, a gift for gab, and a penchant for exaggeration. Like so many early baseball entrepreneurs, he was always on the move. Whenever something interesting happened in baseball, it seemed as though Sullivan was there. He knew everyone and everyone knew him. And while eccentrics like O'Leary and Phillips flamed out early, Sullivan had staying power; his career lasted well into the 20th century.

Ted Sullivan was born in Ireland in 1851,[47] immigrated to the U.S. at the age of 10, and by 1865 was living in Milwaukee. He attended school there and in St. Mary's, Kansas, where he met 15-year-old Charlie Comiskey. In 1876, he signed Comiskey to play third base for a Milwaukee semi-pro team he managed.

In 1878, Sullivan managed and played for the Dubuque Rabbits, and the following season he entered the Rabbits in the Northwestern League, which he helped establish. The 1879 Rabbits were a powerhouse and included Comiskey at first base, future pitching star Charles Radbourn at second, and Bill and Jack Gleason, both of whom would have long major league careers, at short and third. To gather such talent in a small midwestern town was a tribute to Sullivan's scouting and recruiting abilities.[48] His knack for attracting capital was evidenced by the fact that financial support for the Rabbits came from two prominent politicians.[49] Unfortunately, the league collapsed before the end of the season, but the champion Dubuque club played on, scheduling exhibitions against other independent teams.

When the St. Louis Browns entered the AA in 1882, they were managed by veteran Ned Cuthbert, who displeased Browns president Chris Von der Ahe by finishing fifth. In 1883, Von der Ahe hired Sullivan, a marriage of two strong-willed men that was pre-destined to end in divorce. The two constantly got on each other's nerves. Ted loved dialect humor and irritated Von der Ahe by making fun of his speech. Von der Ahe continually interfered with Sullivan's managing, telling him who should pitch and fining players for poor performance.[50]

It would take a thick-skinned and forgiving manager to work in St. Louis, and Ted Sullivan was not that man. "Ted is a good fellow," *The Sporting News* wrote a few years later, "but he never forgets an injury, and in consequence has led a very rocky life."[51] There were a lot of injuries to forget in 1883, and not merely hurt feelings. Two of Sullivan's players, Fred Lewis and Pat Deasley, got drunk and physically assaulted him during a road trip.

On August 29, the Browns were losing badly to the Metropolitans and Von der Ahe sent a message from the stands ordering Sullivan to replace pitcher Jumbo McGinnis with ace Tony Mullane. Mullane had pitched a lot recently, and Sullivan felt that a day of rest would be better than putting him into a game that was probably lost anyway. He ignored Von der Ahe's advice.

That evening, the angry Von der Ahe conducted a surprise bed check. Since the hard-drinking Browns were in New York, it wasn't surprising that he found very few of them at the hotel. When he discovered that most of the team was out on the town, Von der Ahe lit into Sullivan for not keeping a closer watch. A row ensued and shortly afterward Sullivan resigned.[52]

Sullivan made a verbal agreement to manage the Richmond club of the Eastern League for the 1884 season, but when Henry Lucas offered him the St. Louis job, Sullivan asked the Virginians to release him. He acknowledged (according to the Virginians' version) that he had a valid contract and said that if he was not released, he would honor it.

When the release wasn't granted, Sullivan had second thoughts, for the St. Louis offer was reportedly $1,000 per year higher than the Richmond deal, and he decided to breach the contract. As always, Ted had a ready excuse. His friends, he said, had been so insistent that he go to St. Louis and outdo Von der Ahe that he couldn't turn his back on them. Sullivan was blacklisted but that was no hinderance in the Union Association.

Almost any manager could have won with the talent Lucas assembled, and Sullivan rode his thoroughbred to a commanding lead. But as in 1883, trouble ensued, this time a dispute between Sullivan and the players, and he was on the move once more.

Sullivan soon reappeared as manager of the new Kansas City UA club, quite a comedown from the league-leading St. Louis nine. Kansas City finished with a terrible 16–63 record, but Sullivan performed the miracle of bringing an awful club in a struggling league home with a profit. Financial reporting from that era is often vague, but Kansas City drew fairly well despite their sorry record, and the fact that the club had enough money to finish the season is a testimony to Sullivan's financial and promotional ability.

Ted Sullivan was one of the most remarkable figures of 19th-century baseball. He formed teams, he formed leagues, he found talent, he told stories, and by the 20th century, he became one of the grand old men of baseball (National Baseball Hall of Fame Library, Cooperstown, N.Y.).

When there was no Union Association in 1885, Sullivan formed his own league. The Western League had no pretensions to major league status but it had teams in big cities like Cleveland, Toledo, Milwaukee, Kansas City, and Indianapolis. In June 1888, Sullivan became manager of the Washington NL club, and remained there for the rest of the season. That was his last turn as a major league manager; his lifetime record was a mediocre 139–133.

Sullivan's managerial record was not the defining aspect of his career; it was his energy, his involvement in nearly every aspect of the game, and his larger-than-life personality that created his legacy. His touch was everywhere. In 1895, Sullivan organized the Texas League and operated the Dallas Steers, its most successful franchise. When he left and the league failed, he returned to establish a second version of the Texas League in 1902. He was involved in some fashion with formation of the Atlantic League, the Southern League, the Virginia State League, the South Atlantic League, the Virginia–North Carolina League and the Southwestern Base Ball League. At baseball's 1911 winter meetings, Sullivan was introduced as the "Father of Minor League Baseball" and compared to Father Henry Chadwick for his role in bringing the sport to the West.

Ted promoted himself well during his long life. In 1903 he wrote a book called *Humorous Stories of the Ball Field* and in 1907 authored the uncomfortable *Negro Stories of the South*. Sullivan didn't acquire the scorn Cap Anson earned from his racism because Sullivan's was ostensibly humorous rather than mean. A number of his stories involved black dialect, foolish black behavior, and blatant scorn. But it was all in good fun.

"Wherever Ted Sullivan lights," said *The Sporting News*, "he can always tell the natives a story they have never heard before."[53] One reason Sullivan could tell stories that were never heard before was that most of them weren't exactly true, such as the one about the black laundress who could tell the quality of a team by the amount of time it took her to get the dirt out of their uniforms. The laundress conveniently had a deacon husband who was banned from his church for ten years for betting and losing his bible on a baseball game.

Sullivan traveled extensively, accompanying the Giants and White Sox when they toured Europe during the winter of 1913–14 and delivering a series of paid lectures when he returned. He promoted baseball in Mexico and Cuba and made friends wherever he went with his stories and his charm. "He is such a fine mimic and master of dialect," said *The Sporting News*, "that he can pass muster anywhere as Sam'l of Posen, as a British bagman, as a French coutier, a Scotch piper, a veteran Canuck, or a down-east Yankee."[54]

During the 20th century, Sullivan scouted for his old friend Comiskey, as well as the Senators, Reds, and Yankees. He signed star catcher Johnny Kling, Dummy Hoy, Chick Gandil, and Buck Weaver, the last two best known as members of the infamous Black Sox.

By the 1920s, Sullivan was one of the grand old men of baseball, compared with Harry Wright as one of the great talent evaluators of all time. Ted was knowledgeable about the early history of baseball and often contributed columns to *The Sporting News* on various aspects of the game. He is little remembered today, but in his time, he was one of the great men of baseball.

The baseball manager needed promotional and scouting ability, which O'Leary and Phillips had in abundance, and sound judgment and business sense, in which both were lacking. Perhaps the greatest attribute of the successful manager was an ability to land on their feet, for they were frequently swept off them. Sullivan, Bancroft, and Mutrie had just about all those qualities, which enabled them to have lengthy careers, while Phillips drifted into insanity and O'Leary into the world of police reporting. But in 1884, Hustling Horace and Hustling Dan were at their peak, which made the baseball world just a bit more exciting.

# 7

# "There are few men in any business who should be clothed with this authority"

"Who is that young man walking on the other side of the street? He must be some fugitive from justice. See the nervous, haunted expression of his countenance. 'Oh, no; he's no criminal. You're mistaken. Poor fellow, he's a base ball umpire....'"[1]

From baseball's earliest days, when the position of umpire was one held in high esteem, respect for the man charged with enforcing the rules had plummeted dramatically, and by the 1880s the umpire's job was downright dangerous. He was abused, sometimes physically, by fans, managers, players, and the press. He was not well-supported, modestly compensated, and required to travel long distances in an era when travel was arduous and unpleasant.

"In these modern base ball days," one paper wrote, "the umpire has raised the worm to a higher plane by sheer force of comparison. He is generally understood to be the most abused and the longest suffering of all created things. There is not one bright spot in the gloomy, friendless career of the umpire."[2]

Another paper printed a hypothetical story of a man on trial for murder. When he explained that the victim was an umpire who made a bad call, the judge replied, "Oh, I beg your pardon. You are discharged, sir. The clerk will enter the costs against the late umpire's estate."[3]

In the early days of baseball, the umpire was usually a non-playing member of one of the competing clubs or a member of another club. Umpiring was not considered a profession, and during the 1860s, there was scarcely an umpire who was not also a player—often a well-known player. Bob Ferguson had an excellent reputation as an umpire, and others like Dick Pearce filled the position capably.

The two main criteria for an umpire were knowledge of the rules and impartiality. Many early arbiters were lacking in the first requirement, especially since the rules were frequently changing and dissemination of information was slow. Bias was another issue, since the umpire was often connected with one of the competing teams. Umpires were selected by the mutual decision of the two clubs, which led to problems when there was no consensus, usually because one team believed the umpire recommended by its opponents would be biased.

Baseball became major league in 1871, but its umpires did not. Ferguson, Billy McLean, and Theodore Bomeisler were probably the best National Association umpires, but the quality of umpiring was very uneven, and there were many unfortunate episodes. One of the impediments to attracting good umpires was the fact that they weren't paid. The idea of paying umpires would have been ridiculous during the amateur era, when baseball was mostly played for sport, and baseball was slow to catch on to the fact that if players were paid for their skills, the men who interpreted and enforced the rules should also be paid professionals.

Everyone complained about umpires but no one in authority seemed inclined to do anything about the situation. William Hulbert tried to make baseball more business-like and reputable when he formed the National League, but the quality of umpiring didn't seem to be one of his priorities.

One thing that made umpiring difficult was the fact that there was only one umpire per game and he was invariably positioned behind the plate. Later, John Kelly, who was one of the better umpires, experimented with the idea of standing behind the pitcher in order to get a better look at plays on the bases and in the field, and a few other umpires tried it from time to time. For the most part, however, they remained anchored behind the plate, one of the worst places to see anything but balls and strikes.

There are often several things happening simultaneously during a baseball game, and it was impossible for one man to see if a ball was fair or foul while watching to ensure that runners touched their bases and no fielders interfered with them. With only one umpire, it was easy to get away with chicanery, and fielders tripped baserunners, grabbed them, and knocked them down. When they missed a play, umpires sometimes took testimony from players, which they were not supposed to do, and from fans, which was allowed.

For the 1877 season, the National League appointed three umpires from each league city, with one to be selected by lot for each game. That didn't work well, and after the season, the *Clipper* commented, "[O]ne of the most difficult problems connected with the national game is this self same matter of selecting impartial and experienced men to act as umpires in matches."[4]

Eighteen seventy-seven was the year of the Louisville scandal and other shady occurrences, which put umpires under the microscope. They, like players, could be the target of gamblers looking to determine the outcome of games. Umpire Dan Devinney claimed he had been approached by gamblers, but little effort was made to investigate, perhaps because the League was concerned with what it might find.

In 1878, the International Association required each team to designate from three to five men to serve as umpire for their home games. The visiting club selected one of them, with his fee to be paid by the home team. The IA also prohibited umpires from taking testimony from fans.

That didn't work either. Some of the umpires weren't familiar with the rules, others had bad judgment, and too many IA games were forfeited when a team walked off the field in protest of an umpire's call. In an October 1878 exhibition game between Springfield and Providence, umpire Norton got so fed up with the abuse he was taking that he left in the middle of the game. After a half-hour delay, a player from the Holyoke Club was recruited from the stands to finish the contest.

For the 1879 NL season, the captains of each team were to agree on an umpire, and if they could not, they were to decide the matter with the toss of a coin. Yet, in June, the *Clipper* observed, "The abuse of umpires is being carried on this season, and almost to the same disgraceful extent as it was last."[5] Two Chicago umpires resigned after being raked over the coals in the local papers. "[U]nless this newspaper abuse of umpires is at once put a stop to," one writer said, "the business of umpiring will assuredly be driven into the hands of regular professional umpires; and when that time comes we may say goodbye to professional contests."[6]

When the American Association was formed in 1882, however, it did just that, becoming the first league to hire its own umpires, pay their salaries ($140 per month), and assign them to games. They selected former players Joe Simmons, Tom Carey, and Mike Walsh, but within a couple of weeks, Carey was involved in a dispute and quit, and Walsh's ability was called into question on several occasions.

In 1884, Brooklyn posted a set of ground rules including a provision that all players and fans must be courteous to umpires, even when they disagreed with his decisions. The action was roundly praised, but it was ineffective, as umpires were as abused in Brooklyn as they were elsewhere. When General William T. Sherman umpired a game between two military teams, many sportswriters commented sarcastically that he would be the perfect umpire, since he would be feared by the players.

Although he was frequently critical of bad umpiring, Henry Chadwick said he "always had and always would sustain the umpires except when they did as Dick Higham did (see below)."[7] "The umpire stands alone and defenseless," he wrote on another occasion, "as one man against thousands, and to vent one's personal spite by abusive comments on such errors [of judgment] is cowardly in the extreme."[8] Finally, Chadwick summarized, in a lengthy article titled, "Has an Umpire Any Rights Entitled to Respect?" "The evil has grown to such an extent, that unless put a stop to it threatens the very life of professional ball playing."[9]

Despite its criticism, the *Clipper* advocated continuing with the existing system and ridiculed the suggestion of adding a second umpire. "Our correspondent does not seem to be aware," Chadwick scoffed, "that this cumbrous contrivance of two umpires was abolished a quarter of a century ago."[10]

Others wanted to change the system and some of their suggestions were very futuristic. *Sporting Life* said, "The necessity of discovering among the lost arts an automatic, never-failing, level-headed umpiring machine grows more apparent every day."[11] Anticipating instant replay, a man from Washington suggested, "that an arrangement be constructed to take instantaneous views of the ball as it passes over the plate, which could be thrown on a screen so that the spectators might see if the umpire calls balls and strikes with good judgment."[12]

Nineteenth-century technology was not up to the task, and the path taken to improve umpiring was to craft the rules so that minimal judgment was required on the umpire's part, and to provide more guidance. All three major leagues held meetings prior to the 1884 season to instruct their umpires on the rules and try to avoid the problems of previous years. In the AA, umpires were required to swear before a magistrate to uphold the rules and put forth their best efforts. The UA sent its western umpires to work games in the east and vice versa in an attempt to eliminate bias. Still, in July 1884, the AA felt it necessary to caution its men "to umpire games according to the established rules and not as interpreted by them."[13]

National League umpires were at the center of two controversies in 1882. The first incident occurred on May 27 and involved two veterans, umpire Dick Pearce, a great player with the champion Atlantics in the 1850s and 1860s, and Boston third baseman Ezra Sutton. Sutton claimed that Troy pitcher Tim Keefe had committed a balk, but Pearce had not seen it and would not call it. When Sutton showered Pearce with verbal abuse, the umpire fined him, after which Sutton threatened to punch Pearce. Pearce told Sutton to meet him after the game if that was what he wanted. Sutton took up the challenge, and when the two men met, Sutton punched Pearce in the face. Pearce was restrained before he could retaliate, and filed a complaint with the League office. If Sutton was found guilty of the offense, to which numerous witnesses could testify, he could be expelled from the League.

Sutton was not one of baseball's troublemakers and he was remorseful. He found Pearce outside his hotel later that day, apologized, and said he had acted in the heat of the moment, even though the punch was landed long after the balk incident. Pearce accepted the apology, withdrew the complaint, and life went on.

No apology could absolve Richard Higham. Higham *was* one of the bad guys in baseball, and the fact that he was chosen as an umpire was a serious indictment of the system. Higham had a good pedigree, born in England to a respected cricket professional, and was a good player in the old National Association and the NL, posting a lifetime batting average of .307. But he always seemed to be immersed in controversy, moving from team to team under suspicious circumstances and being frequently suspected of dishonest play. After a game he umpired in 1872, he openly boasted of his partisan decisions.

In 1882, Wolverine president William Thompson felt that Higham's biased umpiring was directly responsible for several of his team's losses. He came into possession of a number of letters, signed "Dick," including one addressed to a gambler named James Todd, containing a code as to whether Todd should bet on Detroit or its opponent. Freeman Brown, manager of the Worcester Club, also testified at a League meeting that he had seen Higham in the company of gamblers when he was in Worcester.

Higham denied the charge and claimed he was not the author of the letters, but four handwriting experts identified the writing as his. After examining the evidence, the League voted on June 24 to expel Higham for life, the only umpire ever banished from major league baseball for dishonesty.

In the *New York Clipper* of July 1, 1882, it was stated that "Higham has many friends who refuse to believe him guilty." He also had a descendant who believed him innocent, or at least not guilty. The late Harry Higham, an attorney and baseball historian, wrote an article[14] analyzing the case from a legal perspective and claimed there was insufficient evidence to ban Richard for life. As an attorney, he established reasonable doubt and made a plausible case that Higham might have been found not guilty in a court of law, but did not make a strong case that he did not do what he was accused of doing. Larry Gerlach, SABR's foremost authority on the history of umpiring, also didn't believe Higham had a fair hearing, but stopped short of declaring him innocent of wrongdoing.

There were, of course, some good umpires. McLean was highly regarded, as was the capable John Kelly, who stayed with the profession through 1897 and acquired the nickname Honest John Kelly. After praising another umpire and comparing him to Kelly, the *Columbus Times* concluded, "But then there is but one Kelly."[15] The mustachioed arbiter was born in October 1856 and was just 25 years old when he became a major league umpire in 1882. He'd played briefly in the majors and began umpiring college games in 1879, while still harboring dreams of being a big-league player. He never left umpiring, however, and for many years switched back and forth between the NL and AA. In 1884, he was with the latter.

The hard-drinking Kelly had the toughness required of a 19th-century umpire; he was not intimidated by a hostile crowd or aggressive kickers like Cap Anson and Charlie Comiskey.[16] He was so well-respected that he was chosen to work the first World Series game ever played.

At the end of each season, the *Clipper* wrote articles on the state of the game, and each year they spoke of the need to improve the umpiring. In November 1882, however, the *Clipper* stated, "Never have we seen better umpiring in the professional baseball arena than that which characterized the work done in the position by a minority of the umpires of 1882."[17] That was faint praise, but it was a step in the right direction.

The *Boston Globe,* examining the situation in January 1884, didn't think much progress had been made. "There will be little doubt," it said, "that the league will make a much better choice of umpires for next season than it did in 1883. In any event it cannot do worse.... Generally the applications come from broken-down players, and, as a whole, this class has been shown to be corrupt, intemperate and unfit for the position."[18] Detroit's Thompson said the League's umpires were, "broken down by dissolute (drink), vicious habits of life; [they] are a lot of tramps."[19]

Umpiring in 1884 was as chaotic as it had been in previous seasons and turnover was heavy. Despite the fact that the National League had just eight teams, which meant four games at a time and therefore four umpires, 20 different men officiated NL games. The League was a paragon of stability, however, when compared to the 42 men who umpired AA games and the 33 who handled UA contests. The only umpires to work more than 100 games were Billy McLean, Stewart Decker, John Kelly, and John Valentine. Three new AA umps, disgusted with the abuse they had received, quit abruptly at the end of July.

Union Association umpires could be removed if four teams objected to their work or if two clubs certified they had appeared on the field while intoxicated. Dave Sullivan worked 88 UA games, Dan Devinney 57, and no other man had more than 40. Devinney, an NL veteran, took a hiatus from the UA in mid-season to umpire a number of AA games. Young Blake Mapledorum, considered by many the best umpire in the UA, quit in June without explanation. By the end of July, Sullivan was the only original UA ump still active.

The number of umpires is deceptive, for several of them filled in for just a single game, and many were players from one of the competing clubs who were pressed into service when the regular umpire didn't show up. Half of the 20 NL umpires had one-game cameos, as did 18 in the AA and 10 in the UA. Several others worked just two or three games.

A lot of men wanted to be umpires—there were 150 applicants for four Eastern League positions—for the salary was not bad. American Association umps made $1,000 for the season plus expenses. In the Union Association, they received $140 per month plus expenses of up to $3 per day, while substitutes were paid $10 per game.[20] In the Northwestern and Eastern Leagues, umpires earned $100 per month plus traveling expenses.[21] If an umpire missed a game for any reason, the substitute's pay was deducted from his salary. In addition, umpires were subject to fines for failing to submit required reports or for other transgressions.

The minor leagues, with their lower pay scales, had trouble finding competent umpires. "The Northwestern League umpires," reported *Sporting Life*, "are incompetent, judging from the criticisms of the press in that section."[22] "There is a general kick against the umpiring in the Northwestern League. Three clubs have protested against

[Frederick] Gunkle,[23] and George Frank came near being killed by a Terre Haute mob who did not like his decisions."[24]

There were numerous occasions on which teams left the field and forfeited the game due to their dissatisfaction with an umpire's decision. On August 11 in Chicago, the White Stockings had a runner on first base when Mike Kelly hit a grounder to second. Buffalo second baseman Hardy Richardson went to tag runner George Gore, who put a bear hug on Richardson to prevent him from making what would have been an easy double play. Umpire Stewart Decker called both men out and Cap Anson erupted. When Decker refused to change his decision, Anson pulled his team off the diamond and allowed the umpire to award the game to the Bisons. Anson was technically correct, since the rules didn't call for a double play, but Decker enforced a provision of the rules that, in his opinion, allowed him to use his judgment to determine that the illegal act prevented a double play. That didn't make the Chicago fans very happy, since they paid to see a ballgame, not a forfeit. In order to appease them, the White Stockings asked Buffalo to immediately play off a previously postponed game, which was scheduled for Thursday, three days hence. They refused to do so unless they were paid $200 to play an exhibition on Thursday. Al Spalding was called to the grounds, agreed to the demand, and the postponed game was commenced. In the event, the second game wound up in a tie that was called due to darkness, and had to be replayed Thursday. Buffalo therefore didn't get their $200.

UA umpires were nattily attired in blue yacht cloth suits, topped off with straw hats adorned with a broad black ribbon with the word "Umpire." The AA adopted a similar jacket and black cap in July, while NL umps wore gray suits with straw hats. Since the mid–1870s, umpires had used ball-strike indicators to keep track of the count. Most wore a mask that provided some protection but sometimes caused injury when the wires were broken by a foul tip or wild pitch and driven into their face.

Umpires came from a variety of backgrounds. NWL umpire Young was a schoolteacher, Stewart Decker was a law student, George Seward a saloon keeper, and Terrence Connell a police sergeant.[25] Most were relatively young men who had been players and might be active players again. The Cincinnati *Enquirer* commented, "when a man has made a failure as a ballplayer he attempts to obtain either the position of umpire or manager."[26] Some played and umpired at the same time. During a series in August 1884, in the absence of the regular umpire, Wes Curry alternated between pitching for the Virginia club and umpiring. On one of the days Curry pitched, Brooklyn pitcher Adonis Terry served as umpire.

Although the pay wasn't bad, the life of an umpire was a hard and dangerous one.[27] "If the official umpires don't earn their salaries," said *Sporting Life*, "there is not a class of men on the face of the globe that do."[28] Baltimore was a particularly rough town. *Sporting Life* said, "This city has long been considered as a terror to umpires. To honestly officiate in that capacity before a Baltimore audience requires a stock of moral courage which is commendable in any person and possessed by few."[29] "The addition of a Gatling gun and a company of militia would make these grounds comparatively safe," said the *Cincinnati Enquirer*.[30]

On June 2, Charley Daniels was supposed to work a game in Baltimore, but he had been abused so badly on previous occasions that he sat in the stands and refused to go on the field. After the teams waited 45 minutes, they decided to play an exhibition with manager Bill Barnie as umpire. After an inning and a half had been played, Daniels got a telegram from the AA office instructing him to take the field. He did and the game was started over.

On June 12, after umpire Jack Brennan called Baltimore Oriole Joe Sommer out at third on a close play in the tenth inning of a 13-inning game against Louisville, several spectators climbed the fences, charged onto the field, and attempted to get at Brennan. One of them drew a pistol, but thanks to the police and the strident efforts of Barnie, Brennan was spared from harm and although it took half an hour to clear the field, the game resumed. Louisville didn't want to continue, but Brennan courageously ordered the game to go on.

After darkness put an end to the game with the score 4–4, Brennan was not so lucky. As he left the field, fans began chasing him, and this time they were quicker than the handful of police protecting him, landing a few blows to his face and head before Brennan, a small man, was able to sprint to the safety of the clubhouse, surrounded by a phalanx of Baltimore players who told the fans Brennan's call had been correct. After reaching cover, Brennan said he never wanted to work a game in Baltimore again. "Brennan is badly scared," said one paper. "It is doubtful if he will umpire again."[31]

Barnie and most papers agreed that Brennan made the right call, and *Sporting Life* stated that the incident "relegates Baltimore back to the unenviable name she had borne for years, but which by good conduct in the early part of the season had in great part been obliterated."[32]

The Baltimore managers had been criticized earlier in the season for getting rid of the deputy sheriff at the park when the fee was raised from $2 to $5 per day, but Barnie indicated that although there were no city policemen at the park, there were four county policemen, two magistrates, and 13 private guards. He said the perpetrator of the assault was a man named George Braden, who had been arrested and would be prosecuted.

Barnie also had a double line of barbed wire fence installed to keep the fans where they belonged, but told Brennan it would be wise if he never set foot in Baltimore again. Brennan continued to officiate AA games and after one series in Louisville it was claimed that he ruled against Baltimore intentionally in order to get back at them for the earlier incident. Who could have blamed him?

Baltimore wasn't the only city in which umpires were treated badly. In July, *Sporting Life* noted sarcastically that "A whole week has passed and no umpire has been mobbed."[33] In September, Billy Quinn was charged by a Louisville crowd after one of his decisions went against the home team. It took 50 policemen and impassioned speeches by both managers to defuse the situation. On another occasion, Toledo catcher Tug Arundel filed his own protest, stepping aside as one of Tony Mullane's pitches approached and intentionally allowing it to hit Quinn. Some owners and managers, particularly Chris Von der Ahe, thought that a little umpire abuse made the game more fun for fans.

The press did nothing to calm the situation. "An umpire is an autocrat," said *Sporting Life*, "and from the time he enters the field until he leaves it he has absolute power to do pretty much as he pleases. There are few men in any business who should be clothed with this authority, and it is especially dangerous and apt to be abused when conferred upon men comparatively unintelligent."[34]

The *Cleveland Leader* rated National League umpires as follows: "Decker is very good, unquestionably the best of the lot, but McLean, Burns and Van Court have no business behind the bat. The latter is honest but incapable, Burns has no judgement whatever, and McLean evidently cannot see the ball at all."[35]

Kansas City papers had a vendetta against George Seward and continuously accused him of bias, drunkenness, and gross stupidity. "Seward Still Stealing," read a headline in the *Kansas City Times*.[36] Earlier, the paper suggested getting a photo of umpire Dan Devinney so that young boys could throw rocks at it. The *Columbus Dispatch* wryly commented on one occasion, "[Umpire John] Dyler was sick yesterday, and consequently the Cincinnati's were a man short."[37]

When the St. Louis Maroons beat Cincinnati, the local *Enquirer* placed the blame squarely on the shoulders of "Dan Devinney, an alleged umpire." The paper tried to be fair with umpires, it insisted, and didn't quibble with small errors. "It is not often it is called upon to criticize such an exhibition of incompetency as was given in yesterday's contest. Mr. Devinney's work was rank … he is entirely unfit for the position."[38]

Remarkably, umpire John Burns was allowed to work games in which his brother Tom played for Chicago. Apparently, he showed his brother's team no favoritism, for after one Buffalo-Chicago game, a Buffalo paper said, "The umpiring of Burns was rank, but impartial in its rankness…."[39]

Some umpires attempted to take matters into their own hands, with disappointing results. After Washington's *Sunday Herald* excoriated the work of UA umpire Al Jennings, Jennings went to the newspaper's office and confronted sports editor J.H. Doyle. He asked Doyle who had written the article, and Doyle replied that he had and that it represented his true opinion of Jennings' work.

When Doyle saw Jennings' hand resting on his hip in what he considered a threatening manner, he grabbed a brickbat. An employee named Fitzgerald seized Jennings by the throat and a second employee named Collins brought a paste bucket down upon the head of the unfortunate umpire, who made his escape slightly the worse for wear.

During an Eastern League game in early June between Virginia and the Domestic Club, William Hoover called a Virginia runner safe at the plate, which brought Stephen Dan, treasurer of the Domestic Club, running onto the field to protest. Hoover punched him and the police rushed in to prevent a riot. Hoover was suspended and the Domestics said they would never let him officiate another of their games.[40]

In July, Jack Brennan encountered more trouble from the Orioles, although this time it involved players rather than fans. When he found Brennan's calls objectionable, Baltimore catcher Sam Trott threatened to punch him, and after the game Barnie called him "a damn thief," although he did not threaten to punch him.[41]

Brennan's call in Baltimore that had nearly cost him his life earned him no friends in Louisville. In July, a notice in the *Commercial* warned, "It is to be hoped that Umpire Brennan will do his duty impartially today. A Louisville crowd once aroused is not easily conciliated. This is merely a timely suggestion."[42]

As a reward for his tribulations, Brennan was summoned to a meeting of the AA Board of Directors on July 19 and informed that he had been suspended. "Umpire Brennan," said *Sporting Life*, "is probably the most unfortunate man in the world, and during his short but checkered career as an umpire he has had more trouble and has effected more narrow escapes than all of the other umpires in the country combined. A mob thirsting for gore recently ran him off the ball grounds in Baltimore, and in Louisville, Pittsburg and other cities, he has more than once been in imminent danger of going to the hotel with his scalp missing. All this has occurred in face of the fact that Brennan has manifestly desired on all occasions to do equal justice in giving his decisions.… It simply seems that he is pursued by the demons of ill luck [and a few enraged Baltimore fans]."[43]

Eventually, Brennan was dismissed, for reasons that were unclear, for he appeared to be no worse than most other umpires. "Brennan, the incompetent," gloated the *Police Gazette*, "has at last met his just due, and has been fired bodily by the American Association. This is the insignificant little snipe who informed the New York spectators (way back in May) that he was running the game, and would have the first man who said anything to him thrown out of the grounds."[44]

Apparently, Brennan was a glutton for punishment, for at the end of the season he was working games in Indianapolis and Toledo, where his work was favorably received. He continued to umpire in the minor leagues for many years, and was hired by the NL in 1899. In the first series of the season, disgusted with the abuse he was taking from Cleveland manager Patsy Tebeau, Brennan, while Tebeau was attempting to steal second, mocked him by sliding into the base from the opposite side, then getting up and making an elaborate show of dusting himself off with his whisk broom. NL president Nick Young wasn't amused and sent him to the Western League. Brennan moved on to the Montana State League, where he antagonized the Helena owner by refusing to take a bribe. He continued to officiate almost until his death in 1910.

Eastern League ump Bill Hague, a former major league infielder, was so fed up he simply walked off the job in Reading, leaving the city without an umpire. He didn't send in a resignation; he simply said he was "sick," possibly of the abuse he took at every stop. When the league sent for a substitute, no one answered the call. Finally, Howard Chandler of Philadelphia was sent to Reading, but he was nervous, did a poor job, and immediately quit.

EL secretary Diddlebock called on Hague in Philadelphia and, finding him in excellent health, ordered him back to Reading. Hague refused and asked for his salary and expenses. Diddlebock claimed the expense vouchers were not in proper order and refused to pay them, which resulted in Hague filing a protest and announcing that he was going to return to active play with the Oil City Club.

One of the best umpires was Billy McLean, 49, who'd worked in the old National Association. McLean, a former boxer who taught sparring and general athletic skills at his Philadelphia gym,[45] was also a walker, not the type who competed in pedestrian contests, just a man who liked to walk long distances. He claimed to have covered as many as 128 miles in a day, which seems impossible, but McLean was known to have put in some prodigious hikes. He said he walked the 44 miles from Boston to Providence to umpire a game and later walked back to Boston to be ready to officiate the next day.

Although McLean was a very good umpire, he had a temper. In May 1884, he became enraged by an abusive Philadelphia crowd and threw a bat at some spectators, hitting one in the forehead and knocking his hat off. McLean was arrested after the game, but released when the injured party was convinced not to press charges. McLean apologized, said he had snapped under pressure, and all was forgiven.

McLean was generally well-received in Boston, but it took just a few calls against the home team to turn Bostonians against him. A man named Allen wrote him, saying "If you ever step your foot upon the Boston base ball grounds again, you do so at your peril." McLean never backed down from anyone. "Sir," he replied, "you are a coward. If you are not, write and inform me where you can be found, for in that case I shall certainly find you when I go to Boston again."[46]

By late July, McLean had had enough. "You fellows can talk all you're a mind to," he told a reporter, "but none of you have as hard a time as we poor umpires. We get it from all sides. The papers give it to us, the players kick and the audiences howl.... The catchers and pitchers of these League teams are tricky as mules—particularly those of the Chicago and Boston teams, while Providence is something terrible.... Well, some of the boys, particularly those of the Chicago and Providence teams, willfully violate that rule [the one that required them to stand behind the line in front of the bench] and make fun of us ... such catchers as Nava and Buck Ewing are in the habit of taking a ball from away out and quickly bringing it down in front of them as though it had come straight across the bag, and kicking when we call a ball on them."[47] Apparently, catchers were "framing" pitches over a hundred years ago.

Billy said he planned to quit after the season and it would take more than $2,000 to convince him to come back after the tribulations he'd endured. In addition to suffering abuse from the players, fans, and press, he'd lost a diamond in New York, had his watch destroyed in Chicago, and been laid low with heat prostration several times. His dignity was ruffled when he slipped and fell in the mud on one occasion and again when he collided with massive Dan Brouthers and was knocked silly.

McLean named Philadelphia as the worst city for umpires, followed by New York, Buffalo, and Cleveland.[48] He thought the Detroit crowds were fair. Although fans in Chicago and Providence treated umpires a little better, the players on those teams, especially Anson and his Chicago kickers, were tougher.[49]

It was interesting that McLean selected Philadelphia as the worst city, for the National League club in Philadelphia was managed by Harry Wright, one of most respectful men in baseball. Harry didn't kick and one day, while sitting in the stands, he admonished some fans who were abusing the umpire and got them to stop. But one man wasn't enough to silence Philadelphia.

McLean did not leave umpiring, but he worked very few games thereafter, just 22 in 1885 and a total of six games in 1889 and 1890. His departure was a shame, for he was one of the best umpires in the major leagues.

Stewart Decker, a law student who used his summer income to pay his tuition, was considered one of the better NL arbiters, but even he couldn't escape criticism. "Decker manifests the same faults," said the *Buffalo Commercial*, "that he did when here last. His hearing is defective, he is too slow, and does not cover enough ground."[50] "Decker is rapidly demonstrating," said the *Chicago Tribune*, "how many different kinds of an idiot it is possible for an umpire to be."[51]

O.P. Caylor, noting the abuse heaped on umpires, wrote sarcastically, "Maybe a balloon anchored several hundred feet above the diamond would be a handy place for [the umpire]. Then he would be out of reach of beer glasses, and if he made a mistake he could cut the cables and sail away out of danger, thus doing away with a strong police escort."[52]

Eugene Van Court of San Francisco, who worked the NL circuit, was one of the most controversial umpires. He was a veteran, having played for 18 years and umpired for five. Van Court was a small man with a booming voice who was known for his emphatic calls and elaborate mannerisms. "[H]is yells and calls," said the *Buffalo Times*, "take the soda cracker right off the baker's shelf. He has as many mannerisms and motions to his hands as [actor] Lawrence Barrett."[53]

Van Court's work was often praised, but like all the others, he came in for his share of criticism. "His judgement," said the *Buffalo Morning Express*, "on pitched balls ... seems fairly open to comment, but his exhibition in this respect has passed the stage when fair minded observers are justified in complaining. In fact it is so wretched as to be worthy only of ridicule. Occasions to question the motive of the young gentleman from the Pacific slope need not be sought for. He is deserving of the warmest sympathy in his infirmity. That he may find a remedy is the wish of every devotee of this part who is acquainted with Secretary Young."[54] The *Chicago Tribune* was just as cruel. "The umpiring of Van Court," it wrote, "was exasperating in its rankness and on his idiotic decision on a play at second base New York made its only earned run."[55]

Van Court said he had been warned about Anson, and told that he couldn't let the Chicago manager intimidate him. Although Anson towered over the tiny umpire, Van Court generally held his own.

Al Spalding denied that Chicago was hard on umpires. In an interview with *The Mirror of American Sports,* the White Stocking president said that Boston was the toughest place for a visiting club to win. The crowd was hostile and the newspapers warned umpires not to be intimidated by Anson. For that reason, Spalding said, they were hesitant to make any calls favoring the visitors. "Boston is the last city in the world," he concluded, "that ought to say anything about unfairness on the ball field."[56]

What about Chicago's notorious reputation for cheating? Oh, Spalding admitted, they sometimes cut bases or took advantage of umpires, but the temptation was great and he had always been against such tactics. Besides, everyone did it. "No, no," he said, "base ball will not suffer from the tricks that are done openly and above board." "These statements," said the *Boston Globe*, "are so weak that they need no comment."[57]

Because of his histrionics, Van Court received a lot of press coverage. It wasn't all bad, and many were surprised when he was dismissed in August. He returned to San Francisco and never umpired another major league game.

Former player Ferguson Malone was one of the worst umpires. Teams complained about him all season and afterward, the *Boston Courier* said, "[L]et us hope, in the juster [sic] dispensation of the coming age, the power to appoint and control umpires shall never again be intrusted [sic] to the incompetent hands that dropped Malone among us."[58]

Malone had one of his worst days in Boston during a game with the White Stockings. Whenever he made a call against Boston, captain John Morrill ran to the plate to protest. That wasn't bad, for Morrill was a gentleman. When a call went against Chicago, Anson came running in from first and Mike Kelly from third. Neither was a gentleman, and they blistered and hectored poor Malone, while Morrill usually arrived on the scene to look out for his interests and see that Malone wasn't bullied by Anson. It wasn't long afterward that Malone resigned his position and, as the *Boston Globe* pointed out, "It is pleasanter to resign than be removed."[59]

Another problematic ump was 24-year-old E.A. Griffith, who owed his appointment to Brooklyn president Charles Byrne. "A youth named Griffiths [sic]," the *Times* noted, "made a desperate attempt to umpire the game, but he convinced both players and spectators that he knew nothing about umpiring."[60] "[Griffith's] umpiring," said the *Baltimore Sun,* "was the poorest witnessed on the grounds this season, and that is saying a great deal. He looks like a boy and umpires like one."[61] After the 1884 season, he never umpired in the major leagues again.

Julius Reeder, known as "Icicle," worked just one game. "He is a big man with a little voice," observed the *St. Louis Post-Dispatch*, "and he was unmercifully guyed. He will no doubt retire on the laurels already won. The last heard from him was, 'If the Lord will forgive me this time I'll never umpire another game.'"[62]

Nineteenth-century travel was unreliable, and on several occasions, umpires failed to arrive by game time. Once, Seward got confused by the time zones and showed up an hour late. If there was no umpire on the scene at game time, the contest either became an exhibition or a substitute player from one of the teams was pressed into service, often with predictably bad results. Most gave an honest effort, but occasionally the player gave all close calls, and some not-so-close calls, to his own team.[63]

On one occasion, when it appeared that Baltimore manager Billy Barnie, filling in as umpire, was making calls favoring his own team, the opposing Alleghenies insisted he step down. He agreed and was replaced by Baltimore catcher Bill Traffley, who didn't satisfy the home crowd any better. After a controversial call precipitated a major row, Traffley awarded a forfeit to his own team.

In August, there was a riot at the Polo Grounds when Boston captain Jack Burdock, a notorious umpire-baiter, bullied Boston reserve catcher Tom Gunning, filling in as umpire, into calling the game due to darkness, even though there was plenty of daylight left. Gunning escaped the angry crowd in the company of nine policemen and Burdock snuck out the back door.

Sometimes things got very confusing. On July 6, Dave Sullivan, scheduled to work the Cincinnati-Baltimore UA game, was feeling unwell and lay down around noon to take a pre-game nap. He overslept and when he didn't show up at game time, the two clubs commenced an exhibition. Sullivan arrived fifteen minutes later and insisted that the regular game begin. When Cincinnati refused, he ordered Baltimore pitcher Bill Sweeney to pitch, and when Sweeney threw nine pitches to an unoccupied home plate, Sullivan declared Baltimore the winner by forfeit.

The two teams then resumed the exhibition game, which was what Cincinnati wanted. If the game were a regularly scheduled one, they were entitled to a $75 guaranty. For an exhibition, they received half the proceeds, and the crowd of 3,000 was an unusually good one for the UA. Since there was no rule covering the tardiness of an umpire, the situation dropped into limbo.

In September, John Gaffney, a new NL umpire, called a New York-Buffalo game due to darkness when New York captain John Ward thought there was sufficient daylight to continue playing. When they ran into each other in the rotunda of the Genesee House that evening, Ward called Gaffney a lousy umpire and Gaffney called Ward a lousy player. That enraged Ward, who took a swing at Gaffney and landed two blows, opening a deep cut over the umpire's eye. When he saw the damage he'd inflicted, Ward apologized profusely and accompanied Gaffney to the surgeon. Although Gaffney umpired the following day, his mask re-opened the wound every time he put it on, so he went home to Worcester to recuperate and sat out the rest of the season. The League took no action against Ward.[64]

On October 10, not long after Ward's attack on Gaffney, Dude Esterbrook of the New York Metropolitans attacked umpire John Kelly. Esterbrook, rather than arguing directly in the face of an umpire, liked to direct his acerbic comments to no one in particular, in order to avoid being ejected. Kelly tired of Esterbrook's gambit and challenged him. The two men met after the game and unlike Gaffney, Kelly, who had done some boxing, fought back. Esterbrook, one of the best boxers in the Staten Island Athletic Club, emerged with a black eye. Apparently feeling that Kelly had extracted sufficient revenge, the AA took no action against the Metropolitan player.

Both Esterbrook and Ward were severely criticized in the press, the *Brooklyn Eagle* stating, "Ward, of the League Club of New York, and Esterbrook, of the Metropolitans, are apparently ambitious of being regarded as toughs of the professional fraternity." They called Ward's attack on Gaffney "cowardly" and said the two had forfeited their claim to be gentlemen.[65]

Umpiring was a dangerous way to make a living. Not only were the men in the blue yacht suits attacked by fans, pilloried in the press, and assaulted by players, they were knocked unconscious by foul tips, felled by heat exhaustion, and accidentally flattened by players. Dan Devinney suffered a gash over his right eye when a foul ball broke the wire of his mask and drove it into his face. AA ump John Dyler was hit in the groin and sidelined for an extended period.

In 1883, AA ump Bob McNichol lost his voice after he was hit in the throat by a foul tip and communicated by sign language for the rest of the game. When his problems continued the following day, Columbus manager Horace Phillips announced his calls for him. McNichol did not return for the 1884 season.

The most serious injury of 1884 was suffered by 44-year-old UA umpire Patrick Dutton at Wilmington in early September. Dutton, an Irish immigrant and former Connecticut League umpire who'd joined the UA staff in July, had his jaw broken by a foul tip off the bat of Jack Glasscock. Dutton fell backwards, hit his head on the ground, and lost consciousness. When his dislocated jaw pressed against his windpipe and blood began pouring from his mouth, Abraham E. Frantz, a 25-year-old physician who happened to be in attendance, came to the rescue. With Dutton's life hanging in the balance, Frantz yanked his jaw back into place, clearing the passage. After 30 minutes, Dutton regained consciousness and was given a bracing shot of liquor. The players were so shaken they called the game. Although worse for wear, Dutton recovered and was back on the field six days later. He worked three more games, the last of his major league career.

NWL umpire Charles Cushman was seriously injured at Fort Wayne when hit by a rock thrown by a 14-year-old he'd ejected from the park earlier. After another incident, *Sporting Life* said, "Fort Wayne is the worst city in the Northwest for the abuse of umpires and the miserable little journalistic botches that they call *newspapers* there are mainly responsible for this state of affair."[66]

Needless to say, some umpires turned to drink. Before the season even began, UA ump John Kelly (not "Honest John" Kelly) was fired after going on a prolonged bender. The *Toledo Bee* claimed that AA umpire George Seward was drunk when he worked a Toledo-Metropolitan game on July 7. Foghorn Bradley was dismissed by the Eastern League for drunkenness, although he was taken back to replace William Hoover after the latter was suspended for hitting the treasurer of the Domestic Club. Apparently, a drunk was preferable to a brawler. With decent umpires at a premium, league presidents couldn't afford to be picky.

In July, Charles Daniels[67] and Seward were released by the AA for alleged drunkenness, and the league instructed its secretary to "call the attention of umpires to the fact that several of the late umpires have been dismissed for indulging too strongly in intoxicating drinks and for other ungentlemanly conduct, tending to bring the corps of our umpires into disrepute."[68]

On September 20, with the Union Association in disarray and most of its clubs in financial distress, it dismissed all of its umpires and appointed men in each league city to handle the games. The discharged umpires claimed they had not been paid, and in December the UA levied an assessment on each of its teams to make good the arrearage.

The Eastern League also failed to pay its umpires, and Wes Curry, owed $150 plus expenses, announced his intention to appeal to the Arbitration Committee. When Abraham Mills informed Curry that the Arbitration Committee had no authority in the matter, he threatened to sue the Eastern League president.

After the 1884 season, *Sporting Life* summarized the sorry state of umpiring. "Virtually the umpires of the American staff of 1884 ran the Association's rule to suit themselves.[69] Then, too, they were so amenable to club influences in their work of interpreting the rules of the game that it was impossible for them to discharge their duties with that thorough impartiality of judgment so essential to successful umpiring."[70] The *Spalding Guide*, which generally had only good things to say about the NL, expressed disappointment in the quality of its umpiring. "[O]nly a minority of the occupants of the position of umpire on the League staff," it said, "show[ed] themselves competent to discharge the onerous duties required of them."[71]

Another paper added, "Next year, something must be done in this umpire business … the appointment of such incapables—not to say worse—as have mangled and distorted the rules during the last half of the season, since Daniels and other good men were fired bodily, because of the objections of some sore heads."[72]

Despite the fact that there were a few good men among them, it was obvious that professional baseball had an umpire problem. They would continue to have one so long as they allowed their men to be abused, beaten, and run out of town whenever someone thought they'd been wronged. Although everyone agreed there was a problem, it would be several years before they found a solution.

# 8

# The Drunks

"Leary was tried in two games," the *New York Clipper* reported in December 1881, "but whatever skill he might have possessed when in good form, his incapacity in other respects rendered his engagement alike by the Mets and Detroit Club failures."[1]

That pretty much summed up the career of Jack Leary. When he made his first appearance with the Mets, the *Clipper* noted, "Leary at one time ranked as one of the most effective of pitchers, but he became careless in his habits and lost much of his skill in consequence."[2]

"Becoming careless in one's habits" and experiencing "incapacity in other respects" were a journalist's obtuse way of saying that Jack Leary was a drunk, one of many alcoholics in 19th-century baseball. Alcohol abuse was as severe a problem in the 1880s as recreational drug use in the 1970s and 1980s and performance enhancing drugs at the turn of the 21st century.

Copious consumption of alcohol was an American tradition that dated to the colonial era.[3] The most popular drink in those days was rum, which gave way to whiskey and other distilled spirits by the late 18th and early 19th centuries. By that time, Americans were moving to the fertile lands of the West, which were bursting with those amber waves of grain immortalized in song. The best way to preserve the value of those amber waves while they were shipped to market was to distill them. The return to the farmers and distillers was good and, because of its abundance, the price to the consumer was cheap.

In 1830, the average American adult drank 37 gallons of alcoholic beverages annually. Drinking was part of nearly every American pastime, including political campaigning, where each candidate was expected to provide alcoholic refreshment to prospective voters, and at work, where laborers were often given whiskey breaks rather than the current day coffee break. Just about everyone drank, and many drank to great excess.

Moderate alcohol use wasn't necessarily a bad idea, for in many cases distilled whiskey was more healthful than brackish, disease-laden water drawn from polluted streams. "If God had intended man to drink water," said Benjamin Franklin, "He would not have made him with an elbow capable of raising a wine glass."[4]

Through the early 20th century, physicians prescribed alcohol as a treatment for numerous ailments. While most Americans thought the moderate—as defined in 19th-century America—consumption of alcohol was harmless or perhaps even beneficial, the effects of overindulgence were impossible to ignore. Dr. Benjamin Rush, one of the leading physicians of the late 18th century and a pioneer of American psychiatry, wrote a pamphlet called *An Inquiry into the Effects of Spirituous Liquors* in 1784, pointing out the dangers of excessive alcohol consumption and expressing the belief that alcoholism was a medical problem rather than a behavioral flaw.[5]

Over the next century, there were many attempts to find a cure, including the establishment of a Home for the Fallen in Boston in 1857 and the New York State Inebriate Asylum in Binghamton, New York, founded in 1864. The Salvation Army opened the Water Street Mission in New York in 1872.

During the 1870s, Ribbon Reform Clubs were formed throughout the United States. The Reform Clubs were a forerunner of Alcoholics Anonymous; their members wore a colored ribbon to identify themselves and express their solidarity with others in similar situations. Problems provide opportunity for profit, and many enterprising men were ready to cure alcoholism for a price. in 1879, Dr. Leslie Keeley declared, "Drunkenness is a disease and I can cure it." He opened more than 120 for-profit Keeley Institutes throughout the United States and established the Keeley League, with the slogan, "The Law Must Recognize a Leading Fact: Medical Not Penal Treatment Reforms the Drunkard."[6]

By the 1880s, American taste had shifted from distilled spirits to beer, and the average American's annual consumption of 21 gallons of alcohol included 18 gallons of beer. The temperance movement had grown by that time and many Americans abstained completely from alcohol. Therefore, those who did drink consumed far more than 18 gallons of beer. The saloon, especially for immigrants, was often the center of a neighborhood's social life, and what would one do at the saloon but drink beer?

The profile of a problem drinker was very similar to that of a professional ballplayer. The typical heavy drinker was a 21-year-old male, more likely to live in an urban area, and more likely to be Irish. There was less drunkenness in Jewish, Italian, and French cultures, where wine was more popular. Ballplayers were young, generally lived in big cities, and there were many more Irish than Jews, Italians, or Frenchmen. Baseball was a manly sport, and players who could down large quantities of beer or whiskey confirmed their manliness.

There were many reasons for heavy drinking. Some are timeless, such as family habits, body chemistry, and social pressures, but there were more reasons to get really drunk in the 19th century than there are today. Drinking is a way to cope with pressure, and 19th-century life was filled with anxiety. Antibiotics were unknown and death often resulted from diseases easily cured today. Children were particularly vulnerable, and childhood mortality rates in 1880 were 214.8 per thousand (compared to 5.7 per thousand in 2000).[7] Many people who were not dead lived with chronic pain, including pitchers who threw more than 500 innings a year and catchers who stood behind the bat with minimal protection. There was no social safety net, and poverty was everywhere. There were no therapists or life coaches, but there was alcohol, and plenty of it.

Drinking remained a serious problem in baseball during the 20th century, but players were rarely drunk during a game. They were in the 1880s; one day in 1883, Wilmington's Bert Dorr passed out on the field.[8] Alcohol was considered a stimulant, and some players thought they played better after a swig or two. But as one journal pointed out, "The ball player that can score the winning run when having rum for an opponent has not yet been born."[9]

One thing 19th-century managers did not have to worry about was recreational drugs.[10] Although Native Americans used cannabis at the time white men first came to the continent, the latter never acquired the habit. Opium, which was prevalent in some Asian cultures, was heavily prescribed as a pain killer, but it was rarely used for kicks. W.J. Rorabaugh, in his book *The Alcoholic Republic,* stated that the tendency of opium and marijuana to make the user passive and complacent was inconsistent with the vim and drive of mid-19th-century America.[11]

For the most part, Americans stuck with alcohol as their drug of choice. And choice is an appropriate word to describe the prevailing American attitude toward addiction. "In the nineteenth century," wrote Rorabaugh, "it was widely accepted that people drank because they were undisciplined, ungodly, or degenerate."[12] Jack Leary was an alcoholic during an era when the solution was self-control, which he clearly did not have.

Born in 1857 in New Haven, Connecticut, Leary played briefly with the Tecumsehs of London, Ontario in 1876. He next surfaced in Manchester, New Hampshire, in 1879, with a club that played in the loosely-organized National Association, where a team's life expectancy was well short of the 40 years expected for humans. Sure enough, the Manchesters disbanded in July, but not before expelling Leary and his catcher, Ed Rowen, for bad behavior. The reason for the disbandment was a lack of patronage but, as the *Clipper* pointed out, "the management also [was] having no end of trouble with Leary this season."[13]

Manchester's expulsion of Leary, which rendered him ineligible to play for any other team in the National League or National Association, would not take effect until it was acted upon by the Association's Judiciary Committee, which was not noted for its promptness. In the meantime, Leary signed with Rochester and defeated the National League Buffalo Bisons in an exhibition game in his debut. At the end of the season he went to California, where he played with the Bay City Club.

On March 21, Bay City suffered a bad defeat to the Athletics before a large crowd of 4,000, much to the dismay of gamblers who had bet heavily on the favored home team. They were disgusted with Leary, who pitched in an intoxicated state and was hit very hard. He was suspended, but reinstated upon payment of a $150 fine. It was not long, however, before Leary got in trouble again and was expelled, along with three teammates, including Rowen, who'd followed him to California.

Leary gradually wandered eastward during the summer of 1880, playing in Nevada and Topeka, Kansas. On August 21, he made his major league debut with Boston, but was removed from the box after three innings in which he surrendered five runs on eight hits. Boston released him after the game, but he'd shown enough ability in California to attract interest from Detroit, preparing for its first season in the National League.

Leary spurned the Detroit offer to play with an independent club in New York, but soon jumped his contract to join the Metropolitans as their change pitcher, which earned him an injunction from the angry New York nine. It wasn't long before Leary was on the move again, leaving the Mets to go to Detroit, where he hadn't wanted to go earlier. The Mets were as unhappy as the New York club had been, and when they played an exhibition against Detroit, Leary was not allowed to pitch. His status with Detroit was legal, however, for the Mets had neglected to register his contract with the National League.

Leary's tenure with Detroit was longer than his time in Boston, but not by much. He appeared in three games, losing his only two starts. The reason given for his quick release was that he had been drinking too much. By June 24, Leary was back with New York and by August, he was pitching for Albany. In about a season and a half, he pitched for Bay City, Nevada, Wichita, Boston, New York, the Metropolitans, Detroit, New York again, and Albany. Given the slower transportation of the era and the distance between San Francisco and Albany, it was quite a feat. His continual wanderings were a function of his unreliable behavior and the forgiving nature of baseball managers, always willing to overlook a flaw to sign a talented player.

In the same 1881 issue in which the *Clipper* hinted at Leary's problems with the bottle, it reported that he had signed a contract with the Allegheny Club of Pittsburgh for the 1882 season. The Alleghenies were a member of the newly-organized American Association, whose teams needed players, sober or not.

Leary surprised his new teammates by working hard and keeping himself in good condition early in the season. It wasn't long, however, before his old problem surfaced, and on May 15, when the club was in East Liverpool, Ohio, for an exhibition game, he was suspended for being "indisposed" and cursing at manager Al Pratt.

Shortly thereafter, the stockholders reinstated Leary. He spent most of the season in Pittsburgh, playing 60 games at third base and the outfield. By the end of the season, however, he was pitching for Baltimore of the AA, winning two games and losing one while posting a fine 1.04 ERA.

In 1883, Leary signed with Louisville, but was suspended in May for drinking too heavily. He denied the charge and the club reinstated him. After playing 40 games, he was released and signed with Baltimore again, playing a few games at the end of the year.

After five years of professional baseball, Leary had a record of constant movement and frequent suspensions and expulsions for drunkenness. But in 1884 the demand for players was greater than ever, and when the season began, he was a third baseman and change pitcher for the Altoona Mountain Citys of the new Union Association. Bothered by a sore arm, he pitched poorly. When Altoona failed in May, Leary moved on to Terre Haute, where after just three days he was fined $25 for "monkeying." Monkeying was not defined but, since it was Jack Leary, there is a good chance that alcohol was involved. He was released in late June when the financially-strapped team needed to trim expenses.

From Terre Haute, Leary went to Chicago of the Union Association, where he teamed up with Frank McLaughlin, another prodigious drinker. Nothing good could come of that liaison. "Jack Leary is now with the Chicago Unions," wrote a reporter. "He will play there just as long as they can keep him out of reach of a distillery or brewery, and no longer." Apparently, they couldn't, for the *Cincinnati Enquirer* soon reported, "Jack Leary and Frank McLaughlin, two of the most talented 'boozers' in the base-ball profession, after creating a corner in the whiskey market during their short stay with the Chicago Unions, are once more open for engagements."[14]

The Union Association rid itself of Leary, but there were plenty like him, and when Wilmington joined the association later that summer, it included pitcher Edward ("The Only") Nolan,[15] who had a track record nearly as erratic as Leary's. Nolan was born in Canada the same year as Leary, but grew up in Paterson, New Jersey, which in the mid-'70s was a breeding ground for future big leaguers. Nolan began playing with the city's Keystone Club in 1873, where his teammates included future major league stars Jim McCormick and Mike Kelly, and first came to prominence as an 18-year-old pitcher for the Buckeye Club of Columbus, Ohio, in 1876.[16] Nolan's most notable attribute was the speed of his delivery, but he also had a good curve and screwball.

In 1877 with Indianapolis, Nolan enjoyed the best season of his career and it was then that he became known as the "Only" Nolan. Indianapolis was an independent club, but frequently played exhibitions against National League teams and Nolan's $2,500 salary was higher than that of most major leaguers. The team made a southern pre-season tour, where Nolan dominated a series of weaker teams. In New Orleans, he pitched a no-hitter against the Robert E. Lee Club, striking out 22, and during the first five games of the tour, which took the team to Dallas, Galveston, and New Orleans, Indianapolis won by a combined score of 160–0, as Nolan did not yield a single run.

It was one thing to pitch a no-hitter against the Robert E. Lee Club, but when the season began, Nolan showed that he could beat National League teams as well. Indianapolis played 121 games, one of the highest totals of any professional club, and Nolan did about 90 percent of the pitching, playing in 108 games overall. The biggest challenge for a team with a swift pitcher like Nolan was finding someone who could catch him, and in Indianapolis Nolan teamed with Frank Flint, one of the finest defensive catchers in baseball, who later starred with the pennant-winning Chicago teams of the 1880s.

"[W]e have a word to say about Nolan and his pitching," the *Clipper* commented late in the season. "In consequence of the success of the club, this player has achieved a notoriety as the pitcher of the day. That he has speed, the 'curve,' etc., there is no doubt; but had he not had the unqualified support behind the bat that Flint has given him, not a third of the victories scored by the Indianapolis nine would have been recorded."[17]

Included among the Indianapolis wins were 14 against National League clubs, including five over Louisville which, but for the duplicity of four of their players, would probably have won the pennant. For the season, Indianapolis posted 32 shutouts and in 20 other games they allowed just one run; opponents batted just .170 against Nolan. He pitched a no-hitter against his old club, the Buckeyes of Columbus, and on April 26 he shut out Syracuse in both ends of a doubleheader.

Encouraged by their success against major league competition, Indianapolis entered the National League in 1878. When they were an independent team, a victory over a major league team was a pleasant surprise, but a National League team was expected to win on a regular basis, and Indianapolis did not. They finished fifth in a six-team league with a 24–36 mark and folded after the season. After his scintillating pitching of 1877, Nolan was a disappointment, finishing with a 13–22 record, and while his 2.57 ERA is impressive by today's standards, the league ERA that year was 2.30.

In addition to the decline in his pitching, Nolan was involved in some unsavory conduct. In June, he was suspended under suspicion of crooked play in a game against Providence, but nothing was proven and he was quickly reinstated. In mid–August, he said his brother was seriously ill and left the team, supposedly to rush to his brother's bedside. Instead, Nolan rushed to the nearest bar and embarked on a prolonged bender, possibly involving a woman, who was quite possibly a prostitute. Indianapolis expelled Nolan for misrepresentation, lying, and absence from duty. In December, he applied to the League for reinstatement but was denied.

Ineligible to play in the National League, and with his options limited since all clubs subject to the National Agreement were prohibited from playing against any club he belonged to, Nolan, like Leary, went to California. He pitched fairly well, but without Flint behind the plate he wasn't the same pitcher he'd been in 1877.

In the fall of 1879, Chicago planned to make a post season trip to the West Coast, which presented a problem, since the California clubs had all played against Nolan and consequently Chicago was prohibited from playing them. Therefore, in October, Nolan was reinstated by the League, on the premise that he had never been involved in dishonest play.

Despite his newly-legal status, Nolan stayed in California in 1880, and did not pitch particularly well. Still, he had a reputation, and Cleveland signed him for the 1881 season, hopeful that with capable veteran John Clapp as his catcher, he would recapture the magic he'd had with Flint.

Nolan pitched a two-hitter in his Cleveland debut, but finished the season with a lackluster 8–14 record. In September, he was again placed upon the NL blacklist for "dissipation and general insubordination," following an incident in which Nolan and two teammates missed a game after an escapade in New York.[18] With his baseball career in limbo, Nolan returned to Paterson and tended bar, not the best occupation for a man with a weakness for alcohol.

Nolan was signed by the Allegheny club for the 1883 season. His arm hurt and he lost all seven of his decisions. In May, manager Al Pratt, who apparently hadn't learned his lesson with Leary the previous year, found him drunk and fined him ten dollars. Nolan was so enraged by the fine he got even drunker, which earned him a $100 fine and a suspension. The suspension was supposed to cover the 1883 and 1884 seasons, but after paying the fine, Nolan was reinstated after an absence of about a week. The Alleghenies had a weakness in the pitching box and needed Nolan, who apologized and pledged to stay on the wagon.

In his first game after the reinstatement, Nolan pitched well and lost 3–2. In his next start, he was knocked out of the box in the fifth inning in a game the Alleghenies lost 25–10, which resulted in his release. Nolan had started drinking again, and while Pratt might be willing to tolerate a drunk, he didn't need one who pitched as badly as Nolan was pitching.

At the end of the 1883 season, Nolan was only 27, but it seemed as though he'd been around forever. He'd been pitching since 1873 and had been a star since 1876. He'd played all across the country and done almost everything, including many things he shouldn't have done. Nolan, who'd known Wilmington manager Joe Simmons since 1875, signed with the Eastern League Quicksteps for the 1884 season. Wilmington was not a major league club, but in 1884 baseball was fluid, and before the end of the season Nolan, without leaving Wilmington, was back in the majors.

The season began promisingly for Nolan and he became a fan favorite in the Delaware city. It was reported in late June that "the 'Only' Nolan's reformation appears to be lasting. So far he has behaved most excellently and is pitching finely for the Wilmingtons."[19] The good pitching didn't last, and after Wilmington entered the Union Association late in the season, Nolan was just 1–4.

Nolan's major league career ended after a few games for Philadelphia the next year and by 1887, at the age of just 30, he was completely out of baseball. The man who ten years earlier had seemed as though he might be the best pitcher in the history of baseball had produced only one outstanding year and finished his major league career with a record of just 23–52.

Nolan's drinking undoubtedly contributed to his physical decline and the periodic bans it earned him caused him to be absent from the majors during his prime years. But alcohol was not the only factor that caused Nolan to flame out early. He pitched a phenomenal number of innings in 1877, possibly 800 or 900, and on some occasions, it was reported that he was removed from a game because his arm was sore. But as soon as he could function again, he was back in the box.

Indianapolis played 121 games that year because they were a good draw, and Nolan was the reason. They only had one or possibly two games at each stop, and fans wanted to see the club's phenomenal pitcher. Did Nolan drink because his arm hurt? Possibly.

After his baseball career, he seemingly gained control of his life, spending several years as a police officer in his home town of Paterson. It's doubtful he could have done that if he'd been a dysfunctional alcoholic.

Leary and Nolan had promising careers ruined by alcoholism. Pete Browning of Louisville carved out an excellent career despite a lifelong problem with alcohol. Browning was known to occasionally show up drunk for a game and seemed to hit as well drunk as sober. ("I can't hit the ball until I hit the bottle," he once said.[20])

Many alcoholic players pledged to reform, but Browning made no secret of his fondness for liquor and his intention to keep on imbibing. He was good at it. One writer marveled, "The man's recuperative powers are wonderful.... Other baseball players have dissipated as much in a given time as Pete, but I know of no one who has kept it up as steadily for eight regular baseball years and can yet play a good game."[21] One must wonder if, had he stayed sober, Browning could have been one of the great hitters of all time.

Philadelphia native Frank Flint, known as Silver for his blond hair, was Nolan's catcher during his fabulous 1877 season. While Nolan's drinking cost him a promising career, Flint's put him in an early grave. Trouble seemed to find Flint and it located him soon after he joined the Chicago White Stockings. When the team visited Indianapolis for an exhibition game, he and George Shaffer were confronted by a constable seeking to collect past due debts.

Captain Anson unleashed a profane blast at the constable and he and a local official bullied the man, providing a distraction while Flint and Shaffer were hustled to the train that was to carry the club to Cincinnati. Anson was arrested and taken to the police station, but by that time Flint and Shaffer had made their escape. Anson was released on bail, which he forfeited and left for Cincinnati.

When the train returned through Indianapolis, police came on board looking for the two men, but Anson was too clever to put them in harm's way. The police mission was not a total loss, however, for infielder Joe Quest *was* on board, and he was served with an unpaid bill for $5 due to the Indianapolis club. President Hulbert paid the $5 and all was well. It was just another day in the life of an 1879 major league team.

In 1883, a man from Florida wrote to Spalding stating that Flint had not repaid a loan and threatening to take the story to the papers if he didn't get satisfaction. Spalding pressured Flint to pay the debt and the story remained hidden.

Flint played with Chicago through 1889, helping them to four NL titles, before retiring at age 34, badly broken up from too many foul tips and wild pitches. He frequently played in pain and in 1884 was able to play in just 73 of 113 games; on some occasions when he did play, his hands were so sore he had to leave midway through the game. "Those hands were a sight to behold," wrote Anson, "and if there is a worse pair to-day in the United States, or a pair that are as bad, I should certainly like to have a look at them. His fingers were bent and twisted out of all shape and looked more like the knotted and gnarled branches of a scrub oak than anything else I can think of."[22]

After leaving baseball, Flint's life unraveled. In 1890, his wife sued him for divorce. "I will say nothing at all," Mrs. Flint told a reporter. "Frank is a good fellow and I'm not going to say one word against him. Besides, I do not wish this matter made public. That is all that has kept me from taking the step I have long ago." However, the reporter added, "Mrs. Flint further said that Frank had been spending too much time lately in saloons."[23]

At the end of Flint's playing career, his hands were gnarled and twisted and his wallet was empty, the former from the effects of catching Nolan, Fred Goldsmith, and Larry Corcoran, and the latter from years of drinking, improvidence, and generosity to a host of friends. After his wife divorced him, Flint sank deeper into alcoholism and his body completely broke down.

In late 1891, Flint's ex-wife ran into him on the street and, shocked at his physical decline, took him into her home and cared for him. As one journal said after his death, "His athletic form had shrunk away, and the only thing that remained of the ball player familiar to his old acquaintances was his blond mustache."[24] Flint lingered and wasted away, unable to eat solid food for the final month of his life, and died January 14, 1892, at the age of 37. His ex-wife died of consumption soon after.

Flint's funeral was attended by many old teammates, one of whom, Billy Sunday, by then an evangelist, performed the service. Anson stood before the casket and wept. The White Stockings of the 1880s partied hard and, in addition to Flint, Mike Kelly and Ned Williamson died at 36 and Larry Corcoran passed at 32. George Gore, known for his intemperate habits, managed to live until 1933, when he died at age 79.

The second baseman for Richmond of the American Association in 1884 was Frank Larkin, also known as Terry Larkin.[25] Larkin began his career as a pitcher and for three years, beginning in 1877, was one of the better pitchers in the National League, first with Hartford and then with Chicago. Bob Ferguson was the Hartford manager in 1877, and when he went to Chicago following Hartford's disbandment, he took Larkin with him.

Larkin was a good pitcher with an excellent curve ball, and Ferguson, a hard driving manager, pitched him in nearly every game. In 1877 he started 56 of Hartford's 61 games and completed 55 of them. The following year, he again started 56 of 61 contests, and this time he finished them all, throwing 506 innings. In 1879, he pitched 513 innings, despite a sore arm that disabled him for a good portion of the season.

Following the 1878 season, the *Clipper* commented, "The difficulty in the case of Larkin in the Chicago nine—we do not refer to peculiar habits, but simply to pitching skill—was that he did not have the catching support necessary."[26] The "peculiar habits" referred to by the *Clipper* were indeed strange. Among them was a belief that Larkin would win if he played "The Rocky Road to Dublin" on the banjo before each game or if his teammates threw three pebbles into the spot his toe had worn in the pitchers' box. Although Larkin had complete faith in these rituals, they worked 89 times and failed 80 times during his career.

During a workout prior to the 1879 season, Larkin was knocked unconscious by a line drive off the bat of Cap Anson. There was no awareness of traumatic brain injury at that time, and when a man regained consciousness, he was recovered. "Those who know Terry, however," said one report, "say that the ball left a dent in the side of his head as though it had crushed the skull, and that he was never the quiet, gentlemanly fellow afterward."[27]

Despite posting a 31–23 record in 1879, Larkin was released at the end of the season; his arm was shot. He pitched a few games with Troy the following year, but was ineffective. He played the infield for the minor league Brooklyn Atlantics in 1881 and for the Metropolitans the following season.

In April of 1883, Larkin was under contract to play for Baltimore of the American Association, but suffered an attack of malaria and was unable to practice. By the end of the month, malaria was the least of Larkin's problems. On April 24, while heavily intoxicated, he shot his wife Kate in the face when she confronted him about his drinking, wounded a policeman who rushed to the scene, and cut his own throat in a suicide attempt. The following day, while being held in jail, Larkin attempted to kill himself again by bashing his head against a steam register.

Both Larkin and his wife survived, and since she refused to press charges, he was released. He did not play baseball that season, and for the next several months he was drunk most of the time, ending up in jail sporadically. By July 30, Kate had apparently run out of patience, for Larkin was arrested on her complaint that he had beaten her. She said she was afraid he was going to kill her. While in custody, Larkin again tried to kill himself by jumping head first off his bed onto an iron grate. With Kate now willing to testify, he was sentenced to six months in the Kings County Penitentiary.

Larkin was released just before the end of the year and went on another rampage, stabbing Kate and his father, chasing three police officers with a gun and again attempting to end his own life by cutting his throat. He was sent to prison once more but was released in January. His father took him in and gave him an overcoat, which Larkin promptly pawned and used the money to buy a gun. He went out, got drunk and returned to his parents' home at 4:00 a.m., threatening to shoot them and anyone else who crossed his path. The police were called and Larkin went to prison once more.

Larkin had not played baseball in 1883 for two reasons. First, he was frequently in jail and second, he had been suspended by Baltimore for the 1883 and 1884 seasons. But by May 1884, Larkin had been released from prison and signed with Allentown. "Terry Larkin, the 'terror' has served out his penitentiary term," *Sporting Life* reported, "and is at liberty once more. He was present at the ball grounds in New York and Brooklyn last week. He was very subdued, and has promised reformation."[28]

A month later, when Larkin was with Richmond, the *Clipper* noted approvingly, "Larkin and Nolan have been making a good record of late by their temperate habits. Keep it up, young men."[29] Larkin became a favorite of the Richmond fans, who organized a benefit game for him. "I return my sincere thanks," Larkin wrote, "to the people of Richmond and also the press for their kindness towards me while in this city, and I can safely say that in my ten years' experience on the diamond field I have never played before a more gentlemanly and appreciative audiences than those of Richmond."[30] Unfortunately, Larkin's revival didn't last, and he committed suicide in 1894, while institutionalized for a gun incident.

Other stories had a happy ending, at least in the short run. The 1884 Union Association club in Baltimore had a battery of Sweeneys, pitcher Bill and catcher Rooney. Bill was a reliable performer, but Rooney was a persistent tribulation to his managers due to his drinking and addiction to poker. A Brooklyn boy, he spent some time in California before coming to the major leagues with Baltimore in 1883. At the end of the season, he was suspended along with Larkin. Rooney wasn't a violent drunk like Larkin, and many wanted to see him reform and do well. In January, *Sporting Life* said, "Some Union Association club should give Sweeney, blacklisted for drunkenness, a chance. He is a most remarkable catcher, and if given another opportunity may break himself of his failing."[31]

A week later, the journal saw its wish realized when Sweeney was signed by Baltimore, which the *Clipper* said was like giving "a plank to a drowning man." They wished Rooney well and stated that no one would be happier to see him turn his life around than former manager Billy Barnie.[32]

Sweeney was one of the few who was able to conquer his demons, at least for the 1884 season. In December, he said he had not taken a drink in several months and intended to remain on the wagon. It's unclear whether Sweeney stuck to his promise, for he left the major leagues in 1885 and, despite numerous efforts, was never able to get another big-league job. It's quite possible he backslid, for he was arrested a couple of times and did a stretch in prison for petty theft before disappearing from sight just before 1900.

Other cases had a very bad ending. Jim McElroy, who went on a bender after one game with Wilmington, died of a morphine overdose at the age of 26. Catcher Frank Ringo committed suicide by means of morphine in 1889 at the age of 28. That same year Lew (Blower) Brown, who'd struggled with alcohol during his career, died at 30 after an accident and complications from an amputation.

On September 27, 1884, the *New York Times* reported the death of 26-year-old James Egan in the New Haven County Jail. Egan was an ambidextrous pitcher, a native of Derby, Connecticut, who began his career in nearby Waterbury. He pitched for Troy of the National League in 1882 and for Brooklyn in 1883, when the latter club was a member of the Interstate Association. Egan was expelled from the Brooklyn team for excessive drinking and went back to Waterbury to play for local clubs. "But his old habits asserted themselves," the *Times* reported, and one night in Waterbury, while drunk, he went to a circus with some friends and was arrested along with Maurice Brick, a pitcher for the Monitor Club of Waterbury, for stealing $50 and a gold watch from a man named Thomas Thoomwin. Egan was sentenced to a year in prison, but died in jail of "brain fever."[33] "Let his disgraceful death within prison walls," wrote the *Spalding Guide*, "point the moral of his wretched folly, as Devlin's death in low poverty did that of the results of dishonesty on the ball field."[34]

Club managers were well aware of the dangers of alcoholism. "[I]n the 1880s," wrote Dr. Rob Bauer, "a player's perceived sobriety level was usually the second most important consideration teams had when deciding whether to sign a new man, trailing only the talent of the player."[35]

The AA that stood for American Association might have meant Alcoholics Anonymous, for the players in the circuit, known as The Beer and Whiskey League, consumed plenty of both. Controlling alcoholism was so important to a club's performance that, prior to the 1884 season, the *Critic* of St. Louis felt the need to analyze each AA club not just for its offense and defense, but for its consumption of alcohol.

"We know nothing about the conduct of the members of the Athletic Club when at home," wrote the *Critic*, "but when they were here they drank neither whiskey nor beer, and when they went on the field it was with bright eyes and clear heads. The 'Mets' while here also deported themselves well. The Cincinnati was the model nine in this respect, and the Louisville while here always acted like good sober fellows. As much can be said for the Columbus. The Allegheny and the Baltimores, however, devoted much of their time to the shrine of Bacchus. As to the St. Louis team, last year they were a mixed lot. Half of the regular army drank moderately, a third eschewed liquor altogether, while the remainder drank to excess. If the teams of last year were graded according to their capacity for getting away with liquor, they would hold respectively the following positions: Allegheny, Baltimore, Metropolitan, St. Louis, Athletic, Louisville, Columbus, and Cincinnati. These positions are given upon our personal observations of the men composing the different teams."[36]

## 8. The Drunks

The Alleghenies were called, "the most talented collection of boozers in the country."[37] Leary and Nolan had both passed through Pittsburgh, and both had been suspended for drinking. In 1884, each Allegheny player was offered a $500 bonus if he could get through the season without drinking, which did not appear to be a major financial gamble.[38]

Even before the season began, there were disquieting reports from Pittsburgh. In late March, the *Cincinnati Enquirer* reported that a group of Allegheny players "tried to drink up Pittsburgh's stock of mountain dew, and made a fairly good job of it. Denny [McKnight] should muzzle several of his men and allow them to drink nothing but Ohio River water."[39]

Baltimore was also known as a haven for drinkers, for manager Billy Barnie seemed to think he could rehabilitate troubled players and get the best out of them. The Orioles were, like the Oakland Raiders of the NFL, a haven for problem children. Baltimore captain Tom York was determined that things would be different in 1884 and said he would "stand nothing in the way of bumming and drinking."[40] Louisville likewise instituted a comprehensive set of rules intended to curb the abuses of the previous season. Every Eclipse player was required to be in bed by eleven o'clock unless they had a good excuse. A good excuse was not defined.

As for the National League, the Providence players were so incorrigible, the *Critic* said, that even honorable old Harry Wright couldn't control them.[41] Bauer crowned his own champion, which conflicted with the opinion of the *Critic*, stating that "Of all the teams in 1880s baseball, the Athletics probably lushed the hardest and most consistently and often did so in plain view of the public."[42]

"[T]he bummer and lusher," wrote O.P. Caylor, "should be eliminated from the ranks of the League and American Association."[43] Desperate for talent, Caylor said, too many teams signed men with a history of drunkenness, without considering that "negligent, dissipated and indifferent men are of no use or service to a nine."[44] The *Spalding Guide* called drunkenness "the most conspicuous evil that was connected with professional ballplaying in 1884."[45] The only reason alcohol abuse didn't hurt teams more, Bauer wrote, was that the habits of their opponents were just as bad.[46]

Despite all the good intentions, the 1884 season was no better than previous years. In June, *Sporting Life* reported, "The American Club ranks are again suffering from the evil of drunkenness among their players, two signal defeats having been sustained in the Metropolitan district entirely from this cause, while a visiting western team lost games recently from the same trouble."[47] In late September, a report said, "Since [the Athletics] have started on their Western trip they have maintained a continuous debauch, there being not a single exception on the team."[48] When Bill Sharsig of the Athletics denied the report, the paper retorted, "A match held near the open mouth of several of the players would have caused a conflagration such as Cincinnati has never witnessed."[49]

The Athletics had gotten rid of one of their worst abusers when pitcher Enoch (Jersey) Bakely jumped to the Keystones of the UA. One day in February 1884, Bakely and a man named Michael Scarlett refused to pay for their drinks at John Hart's Philadelphia saloon. Scarlett threw a pitcher (a glass container—not Jersey Bakely) at Hart's head and ran off, while Hart hit Bakely on the head with a club. Bakely was taken to the hospital with a serious head wound but Hart was not charged. The departure of Bakely was offset by the acquisition of shortstop Sadie Houck, who'd been released by Detroit for drinking too much.

St. Louis had an equally bad reputation. The Browns' Tom Mansell's 1883 season ended prematurely when he fell down an elevator shaft in a Cincinnati hotel, but perhaps the team's most outrageous offender was catcher Thomas (Pat) Deasley. Deasley had a reputation in St. Louis for beating up black women, which didn't seem to upset anyone, but in May 1884 he made the mistake of assaulting the honor of a white woman in Indianapolis, and the police were much less forgiving. Inebriated, he approached two women on the street and grabbed one of them (Anita Kerr) by the arm. She believed he was just trying to keep his balance and thought nothing of it. When he grabbed the second woman (Mrs. Stenhauer) and said he wanted to talk to her, the two women ran into a nearby millinery store. Deasley followed to—he claimed—tell them he meant no harm, but a policeman arrived and he was arrested. When neither woman deigned to file a complaint, he escaped with a reprimand and a $10 fine.[50]

After he engaged in a drunken fight in Toledo with teammates Joe Quest and Tom Dolan, Deasley's wife joined the club in the hope that she could keep an eye on her husband. In July, after being fined for drunkenness and insubordination, Deasley went before a judge and swore an oath to abstain from alcohol and managed to stay out of serious trouble for the remainder of the season.[51]

Deasley, like most 19th-century catchers, was frequently injured, and probably suffered multiple concussions; perhaps the blows to his head affected his behavior. Peter Morris, in *Catcher,* devoted an entire chapter to the supposition that several 19th-century catchers suffered permanent brain damage. Tug Arundel ended his life in an insane asylum and Harry Decker had a bizarre, erratic life after baseball.[52]

At the end of the 1884 season, St. Louis released Deasley for a payment of $400, which most thought was a good move. "[T]he bad, reliable, and insubordinate element has been gotten rid of and the team will be one of the best behaved and best disciplined in the baseball arena," said one paper.[53]

Powerful left-handed hitting St. Louis outfielder Fred Lewis was another habitual offender. Lewis hit .301 for the Browns in 1883 after he was acquired from Philadelphia in mid-season. He was available because he was trouble. The Browns suspended him for drinking that year but reinstated him because they were involved in a tight pennant race and needed his bat.[54]

When the hard-drinking Baltimore club visited St. Louis, there was bound to be trouble. In July 1884, after a Baltimore-St. Louis game, Gid Gardner, Bob Emslie, and Hardy Henderson[55] of Baltimore and Lewis and Tip O'Neil of St. Louis met up at the Lindell Hotel for a night on the town. About an hour later, they were in a St. Louis bordello operated by a woman named Maude Allen. When one of the girls made a remark O'Neill found offensive, he hurled a spittoon at her. It missed and hit the wall, but the contents spilled on her and a brawl broke out. When they learned the police were on the way, Emslie and O'Neill had enough of their wits about them to get away. Lewis and Henderson were arrested and while he was in the police wagon, Lewis became so violent he had to be clubbed into submission. Gardner returned to the team's hotel to plead with Barnie to get Henderson released. Instead, Barnie suspended Gardner. Eventually, Barnie relented, bailed Henderson out, and fined him $150.

Everyone knew Gardner was trouble. Before the 1884 season started, the *Baltimore Sun* warned "Gardner is a good player, except on off days."[56] But they didn't think that should stop Baltimore from signing him. "Of course, Gardner is 'off' sometimes, but he is too good a batter and thrower to be dropped, and supposedly there is no way out of the dilemma."[57] There was, of course, a way out, but in 1884, with good players at a premium, Baltimore was not willing to take it, despite the warnings of *Sporting Life*, which said, "It is to be hoped that both these incorrigible fellows, Gardner and Lewis, will be kept where they belong, out of the profession on which they in the past have brought so much disgrace; both having seen the inside of a cell more than once."[58]

One night in June 1884, an intoxicated Gardner went to the house of Effie Jones, a woman, as described in delicate 19th-century fashion "with whom he was intimate."[59] Apparently, Effie wasn't in the mood to be intimate that evening, and Gardner beat her, demolished her furniture, and beat up a second woman who came to her aid.

Gardner was arrested and hauled off to jail. The following day, his friends visited Jones and got her to withdraw the charges, and after paying court costs and a $25 fine, Gardner was released. He was fined by Baltimore and suspended without pay, and just a few days later, was involved in the incident with Lewis and Henderson.

After the St. Louis debacle, the Baltimore players urged Barnie to reinstate the penitent Gardner, and he did. When Baltimore finally gave up on him late in the season, they replaced him with Lew Dickerson, who was as deeply immersed in alcoholism as Gardner. Banned by the AA, Gardner soon found work in the UA, and was removed from the AA blacklist in October. He returned to Baltimore in 1885 and later played in the National League.

It had been quite a season in St. Louis. "I will give $3,000," Von der Ahe told the Athletics' Lon Knight, "for a manager and he won't have to do a d__n thing but keep the gang sober."[60] A Cincinnati paper remarked sarcastically, "Strange but true. Another week has rolled by, and up to eleven o'clock last night the wires have brought no news about the St. Louis American players sand-bagging anyone, or taking a ride in a patrol wagon. What's the matter? Have the saloon keepers of the Mound City rung in a new brand of whiskey, or has Chris Von der Ahe and Manager Jimmy put a muzzle on the boozers?"[61]

The *Cincinnati Enquirer* suggested a solution. "The management of the St. Louis Americans would do the profession a service did they but lock up the two tans, Lewis and Deasley, in a room by themselves and let them fight it out like Kilkenny cats. They would be certain to do a good job of it, and the less that was left of the pair, the better."[62]

Lewis' hitting ability (he batted .323 in 1884) earned him second, third, and umpteenth chances. After his romp with Henderson, a paper reported, "As was to be expected, by all familiar with Von der Ahe's methods, Fred Lewis has been reinstated."[63] The St. Louis directors, after initially suspending Lewis for the rest of the season, decided that he had been led astray by others and that a fine was more appropriate. Like Deasley, he signed an affidavit in front of a judge pledging to abstain from all intoxicating liquors for the remainder of the season.

In early September, Lewis got in trouble again, attacking a bartender and getting badly whipped in return, although he managed to retaliate by throwing two beer kegs and a box of mineral water through the front window of the bar. Even Von der Ahe had his limits, and this time he released Lewis. In 1884, however, jobs were plentiful; Lewis signed with Henry Lucas' Union Association team for the remainder of the season and played two more years of major league baseball.

Lucas had his own problems with Lewis (Buttercup) Dickerson, a hard-drinking 25-year-old outfielder. Although a diminutive 5'6" and 140 pounds, Dickerson could store a lot of liquor in his small frame. He was one of the reasons the 1883 Alleghenies had a reputation as lushers. In 1884, during a July road trip, Dickerson met up with some old friends, starting drinking heavily and disappeared. He surfaced with Baltimore of the AA and Lucas placed him on the blacklist.

Henry Luff of the Philadelphia UA club had a checkered history dating back to 1875 when, while playing for New Haven of the NA, he was arrested for stealing property from a hotel during a road trip. While in Cincinnati in May 1884, an intoxicated Luff boarded a street car and when the conductor asked for his fare, he drew a knife. The action got Luff arrested and he was fined $25. One reporter joked that when the judge found out Luff was a ballplayer, he suspended his sentence "for fear the other convicts would become contaminated."[64]

There was just as much drinking in the minor leagues, maybe more. With the expanded number of teams in 1884, players were at a premium, and no minor league team could afford to pass up a player just because he liked to tipple. One solution was to locate a club in a town that was dry, making it difficult for the players to find liquor. Milwaukee was not dry, and several players from the Northwestern League club went on a spree one night, played horribly in a loss to Muskegon the following day, and were fined a total of $450. Reading, Pennsylvania, catcher John Grady got drunk, entered a Chinese laundry and assaulted a female employee. When the owner came to her defense, Grady hit him with a bottle.

After the 1884 season, the *Brooklyn Eagle* said, "Next to crookedness comes the evil of drunkenness in the ranks.... Club after club has adopted stringent rules against drunkenness in their teams, which have been enforced for a time, but owing to the frequent condoning of offenses the rules have become almost dead letters … there is but one remedy for this evil and that is total abstinence, from the first day of the season to the last, and for any failure to observe this rule strictly the penalty should be a fine of one hundred dollars for the first offense and expulsion from employment for the whole season for the second. As for the habitual drunkards, they should be driven from the ranks of the fraternity forever, just as Jim Devlin, Al Nichols, Craper [Bill Craver], and others were for their proven dishonesty."[65]

In November 1884, *Sporting Life* wrote, "The old talk about adopting stringent rules for the disciplining of drunken and obstreperous players crops out again. It will amount to nothing more than talk. New rules are not needed. What is needed is a little nerve in managers to enforce them."[66]

Dan O'Leary, who was known to drink a bit himself, had a contrary theory. Dan said, "If a player wants to drink, he will drink, and you can't keep him from it by scoldings and fines. In the evening, I tell my players, 'Now, boys, if you want a drink go and get it and then come back and go to bed' and I never knew them to fail to do it, and they went to bed good-natured, too."[67] If he kept watch on them, O'Leary said, they would go out later and not be in condition to play the next day.

The difficult part of policing drinking was that many of the drunkards were good players when sober, and it was their employers' perpetual hope that they would, despite their failings, contribute to a winning team. There were so many problem cases that to eliminate them all would thin the ranks considerably. Most alcoholics experienced periods of sobriety that created hope they'd changed their ways. But with self-enforced abstinence the only cure, a permanent solution was unlikely. Baseball was to suffer with the alcoholic for more than a century.

# 9

# "There will be no more foolishness this year"
## *National League Preview*

In 1883, Boston's National League club recaptured the glory days of the 1870s. That was the decade when the city's nines ruled the baseball world, capturing six pennants in seven years. From 1872 to 1875, the Red Stockings won four straight National Association pennants before William Hulbert of Chicago stole four of their best players. Hulbert's White Stockings won the pennant in 1876, but Boston rebounded to win the National League title in 1877 and 1878. Then came a four-year drought before a re-tooled club won the NL crown in 1883.

The latest title was somewhat unexpected, for the previous year Boston had finished ten games behind the champion White Stockings. For most of the season, they met expectations, and on September 7, Boston rested in fourth place. Then they won 14 of their last 15 games to surge past Chicago by four games. "It was a general surprise to us last year," said Boston president Arthur Soden, "that the Bostons came off champions."[1]

Soden referred to his club as the "Bostons," as did nearly all newspapers. Current professional sports teams have well-defined nicknames, but that was not true in the 19th century. In 1884, major league baseball teams were usually identified by their city. While current sources refer to teams like the Kansas City Cowboys, the Washington Statesmen, and the Columbus Buckeyes, they were rarely called that in contemporary accounts. The Browns of St. Louis, the Eclipse of Louisville, the Metropolitans of New York, and the Athletics of Philadelphia were the teams most frequently called by their nicknames.

The Boston nine that dominated the National Association was called the Red Stockings. Shortly after joining the NL, the club became known as the Red Caps, and by the time they won the 1883 title, they had become the Beaneaters. But mostly they were called the "Bostons."

The '83 Bostons didn't have a lot of big stars, but they were second in the league in batting and first in home runs. Their 34 homers don't seem like much today, but they were 10 more than the second highest total. More importantly, Boston had two good pitchers, Grasshopper Jim Whitney and Charlie Buffinton. Whitney had been with the Beaneaters since 1881 and Buffinton joined him the following year.

Whitney had a very unusual motion. With no pitching rubber to restrict his movements, he took several hops and steps forward and leapt toward the batter, adding both speed and intimidation. Whitney threw very hard, often too hard for his catcher to handle, and was referred to as the "Human Cannon." The removal of the restriction against

91

overhand pitching would make him even more formidable in 1884, both for opposing hitters and his catchers. The old rule, however, had not hampered Whitney that much, for he was often accused of violating it by raising his arm over his shoulder during his delivery. In 1883, Whitney led the league with 345 strikeouts and posted a record of 37–21 with an ERA of 2.23.

The championship team returned almost intact in 1884. The infield consisted of three solid veterans; the oldest, third baseman Ezra Sutton, 34, participated in major league baseball's first game in 1871 and had been with Boston since 1877. Feisty second baseman Jack Burdock, 32, known as Black Jack for his dark eyes and complexion, had been a major leaguer since 1872 and captain and first baseman John Morrill had been a Boston regular since the first NL season in 1876. Morrill, known as "Honest John," was a respected leader who, in an era of heavy drinking, was known for his sobriety. Other top players included outfielder Joe Hornung, a power-hitting five-year veteran, and catcher Mert Hackett. With the hard-throwing Whitney in the pitcher's box, Hackett's ability to handle his cannon shots was a key to Boston's success.

Chicago's string of three straight pennants had been snapped in 1883, and the two men atop the White Stockings organization, president Albert Spalding and manager Adrian (Cap) Anson, weren't happy about it. William Hulbert had brought Spalding and his Boston teammates to Chicago to establish a dynasty and while Chicago didn't win every year, Boston and Chicago had won seven of the eight NL titles, with only the 1879 Providence team of George Wright interrupting the streak. In Chicago, a second-place finish was unacceptable, and Spalding and Anson were determined to finish first in 1884.

William Hulbert had been known for his moralistic stands, but by 1884, just two years after his death, the White Stockings were somewhat of an embarrassment. Many writers contrasted the good behavior of the Boston club with that of the swashbuckling White Stockings and insinuated that was the reason the former won the pennant.

Baseball's moralists, Henry Chadwick foremost among them, had always insisted that well-behaved players were the best players, a theory called into serious question when Chicago's band of brigands won three straight pennants from 1880 to 1882. On the field, the White Stockings fought with umpires and opponents and ignored the rules when it was to their advantage, and off the field they had a proclivity for liquor and late hours. Everyone knew it. There were rumors that several White Stockings played drunk during the 1885 World Series.

Manager Anson, who was 32 years old in 1884, had been with the White Stockings since 1876 and served as manager since 1879. He liked to gamble and play cards and billiards, and in his younger days was a bit of a hell-raiser, but by 1884 Anson had settled down and stopped drinking.

Anson's greatest vice was bullying umpires. He was a large man with a forceful personality and was often successful in getting his way, for many of the umpires were incompetent and easily swayed. When the White Stockings lost, Anson often blamed the umpires, although *Sporting Life* pointed out that the players' lifestyles probably had something to do with their failure to win more often. Bad behavior was tolerated when Chicago was winning, but when they finished second in 1883, Anson lost his patience. On the dawn of the 1884 season, he promised, "There will be no more foolishness this year, no staying out all night and next day telling me they were looking for a lost locket."[2] Anson said there would be a pool of players waiting in the wings ready to replace any

## 9. "There will be no more foolishness this year"

White Stocking who misbehaved. All it would take was a telegram to call on fresh blood, blood with a lower alcohol level that that of the man being replaced.

The White Stockings were an impressive group of athletes. Spalding was tall and well-built and he liked his players big. Anson was six feet tall and nearly 230 pounds. There was size in his DNA; his father was a husky man and his mother stood five foot, ten and a half and weighed more than 200 pounds. During the winter of 1883–84 Anson got a little bigger. So did several of his players, who reported for spring practice greatly overweight. Slugger Ned Williamson, who always had a problem in that regard, was quite heavy.[3]

If Anson could get his club in shape and keep them sober, the White Stockings would be contenders, for they probably had the best talent in the league. Mike (King) Kelly and Anson were two of the top players of the 19th century, but both had played below their usual standard in 1883. Anson's .308 average was short of his .334 career average, and Kelly's .255 was well below his .308 lifetime mark.

Anson was beginning to get a little older, and although Kelly was only 26, he'd packed a lot of living into those 26 years. The King came from a hardscrabble background and loved the fame he'd acquired as a star baseball player. He was a hard drinker, a flashy dresser, a dynamic personality, and an enthusiastic gambler who loved to frequent the horse track. "Women and wine brought about his downfall,"[4] Anson later wrote. Kelly was one of the highest-salaried men in the game, but he spent freely and was very generous with his friends. Money, Anson said, "slips through Mike's fingers as water slips through the mesh of a fisherman's net."[5] After Kelly's poor season in 1883, there was talk that Anson and Spalding, thinking he was more trouble than he was worth, might get rid of him, but when the 1884 season began, Kelly was still a White Stocking.

The rest of the Chicago team included stars like outfielder George Gore, a strange, eccentric man who also hit the bottle heavily, second baseman Fred Pfeffer, and third baseman Williamson. The latter two comprised half of Chicago's renowned Stonewall Infield, named for the inability of batted balls to get through it. Billy Sunday was a utility outfielder who could run and drink, but couldn't hit. Catcher Frank Flint couldn't hit that well either, but the job of a 19th-century catcher

Frank Flint was a standout defensive catcher for the champion Chicago teams of the 1880s. Known for his toughness, he drank himself into an early grave (National Baseball Hall of Fame Library, Cooperstown, N.Y.).

was principally defense, and behind the plate Flint was one of the best and certainly one of the toughest. One of the reasons Flint wasn't that good a hitter was that his hands were usually beaten to a pulp by mid-season, which made it difficult to grip and swing a bat. He was a rarity among 19th-century catchers, playing almost every game, including a remarkable 176 of 181 in two years in Indianapolis. In his first five seasons in Chicago, Flint missed just 36 games.

In 1883, Chicago's pitching rotation consisted of Fred Goldsmith[6] (25–19) and Larry Corcoran (34–20) a tiny man who stood just 5'3" and weighed only 127 pounds. In early 1884, Corcoran signed with the new Union Association (see Chapter 11), but Spalding soon managed to get him back in the fold. That was fortunate, because Goldsmith was nearing the end of his career. He was only 28, but his arm had logged enough innings to age it well beyond the rest of his body. In 1878, he pitched 682 innings for Tecumseh and another 221 for Springfield for a total of 903 in 101 games.[7] He'd pitched about 800 major league innings the past two years.

There was another problem facing the White Stockings in the months before the 1884 season. The Michigan Central Railroad was attempting to purchase the club's Lake Front Grounds and evict them. Almost through opening day, the White Stockings were not sure they would have a place to play. (See Appendix B.)

New York was another club that was disappointed by its 1883 performance. John Day owned both the New York NL club and the AA Mets, and the National League team was assigned the best players. Their 46–50 sixth place showing had been an unpleasant surprise, a failing Day blamed on manager John Clapp.

During the fall, Day attempted to convince Walter Camp, who'd played baseball at Yale and later became the school's legendary football coach, to manage the New York club, but Camp declined. Day wound up hiring James Price, long-time captain in Company H of the 7th Regiment, a move he would later regret.

New York was the most glamorous city in America, and there were a number of luminaries on the Gotham roster, including future Hall of Famers Mickey Welch, John Montgomery Ward, Buck Ewing, and Roger Connor. An old baseball adage states that the best teams are strong up the middle, and in 1884, no major league was stronger up the middle than the New Yorkers, with Ewing behind the plate, Welch on the mound, Connor at second, and Ward at shortstop.

Ewing was one of the best players of the 19th century, and in 1939 became one of the first from that era to be elected to the Hall of Fame. He could play any position on the diamond and during his career, Ewing caught 636 games, played 253 at first base, 235 in the outfield, 127 at third base, 51 at second, 34 at shortstop and nine (47 innings) as a pitcher. For a catcher, versatility was a necessity, for unless you were Frank Flint, it was nearly impossible to stand up to the punishment of catching day after day.

Ewing could hit (a .303 lifetime average over 18 big league seasons), he could run, and he had a powerful throwing arm. He was a great player in his day whose legacy, like that of so many 19th-century players, is diminished by the current perception of statistics. Ewing was a power hitter who had 71 home runs in 18 seasons. He was, according to Johnny Ward, the best defensive catcher of his era, but his 1884 statistics show 38 passed balls in 80 games. That's horrific by today's standards but pretty good for a man catching with 19th-century equipment. In 1884, a game without a passed ball was an accomplishment. Barney Gilligan of the Providence Grays, who got 59 wins out of Hoss Radbourn, had 46 passed balls in 81 games and Bill Holbert of the Mets, whose defense kept him in the majors despite a woeful bat, had 36 in 59 games. Flint, considered one of the finest catchers in the league, had 639 passed balls in 743 career games.

John Ward was the captain and shortstop of the New York nine. He'd been one of the best pitchers in the major leagues, leading the 1879 Providence Grays to a title with an NL-best 47 wins. His 1880 perfect game was the last in the NL until Jim Bunning threw one in 1964. Like many 19th-century pitchers, Ward could hit, and when his arm went bad, he played the infield or outfield, occasionally throwing left-handed when using his right arm was too painful.

While Chicago and New York wouldn't settle for anything less than a pennant, expectations weren't as great in Providence, where the fans were happy just to have a team. The Grays had always been competitive, winning the pennant in their second season, finishing second the next three seasons, and coming in third in 1883, but attendance had been spotty and finances were always in a precarious state.

**Many considered Buck Ewing the most talented and versatile player of his era. George Wright was the only 19th-century player inducted to the Hall of Fame before Ewing, who was elected by the Veterans Committee in 1939 (National Baseball Hall of Fame Library, Cooperstown, N.Y.).**

The Providence board of directors called a meeting in September 1883, and word spread that they had decided to declare a cash dividend equal to all of the club's assets and end the career of the Providence Grays. The meeting was well-attended and the discussion very spirited. After an emotional exchange, president H.B. Winship and all of the incumbent directors resigned and were replaced by a new slate, which expressed a firm determination to field a team in 1884.[8]

Providence engaged veteran manager Frank Bancroft to run the team and he began aggressively signing players, trying to shore up the weaknesses of the previous year's third-place club. The most glaring shortcoming, said *Sporting Life*, was the lack of a capable second pitcher behind Charles (Hoss) Radbourn, who pitched 632 of the club's 871 innings.

Radbourn had a 48–25 record, but behind him Charlie Sweeney was just 7–7 and Lee Richmond, author of major league baseball's first perfect game, was 3–7. Although Richmond was only 26, his career was over, and that left Radbourn and Sweeney for 1884.

In the other eight positions, Providence had a solid core of experienced veterans, including 41-year-old first baseman Joe Start, one of the steadiest and most dependable players of the 19th century. Start began playing baseball in 1859, when he was just 16 years old and baseball was an amateur sport that consisted of a handful of games each summer. He'd adjusted to the many changes that took place through 1884 and, despite the slower reflexes that come with age, was still a respectable hitter. A left-handed batter and thrower who stood 5'9" and weighed 165 pounds, Start had good power, was a good base runner and, perhaps most noteworthy of all, was known to be thoroughly honest, so trustworthy that his nickname was "Old Reliable." Start fielded his position so well that Bill James named him the first baseman on his Gold Glove team for the 1870s.[9]

Behind the plate, the Grays had strong-armed Barney Gilligan, who joined Providence in 1881 after spending a couple of years with Cleveland. A weak hitter like so many catchers (he had a lifetime batting average of just .207), Gilligan was quick, tough, and the pitchers, especially Radbourn, liked working with him. Despite a reputed $2,500 offer to jump to St. Louis of the Union Association, Gilligan elected to stay in Providence.

In the outfield the Grays had 39-year-old Paul Hines, the only player left from the original 1878 team. Hines, like Start, was a veteran of the old National Association, a contentious man and tough negotiator who often engaged in contract disputes. Hines was totally deaf and blind by the time he died, and he had already lost most of his hearing by 1884. *Sporting Life* reported that he was "so deaf that he cannot hear the umpire call the balls; he depends on the captain of the nine to inform him."[10]

Cleveland, which entered the NL in 1879, had the best season in its history under Frank Bancroft in 1883, leading the league in mid-season and finishing with a 55–42 record. They also made money under Bancroft's astute financial management. Despite their success, Cleveland's prospects of fielding a team in 1884 were questionable, mainly because they weren't assured of a suitable place to play. They'd lost their old location and while there were plenty of open spaces in the city, none had the central location that was essential for success. "The lot of the Cleveland club is not a happy one," *Sporting Life* reported in late October. "It loses both ground and manager."[11] The directors planned to keep looking for both and vowed to have a team in 1884.

Finally, in mid–December, the directors announced that they had obtained a lease on a suitable playing site, a number of players had been signed, and there would be an 1884 season after all. Perhaps the most important signee was pitcher Jim McCormick, who'd been with the club since 1879. McCormick was a workhorse, having pitched a total of 2,668 innings the past five seasons, with a high of 658 in 1880. In 1883, hampered by a serious elbow injury, he pitched a mere 342 frames. "[I]f his arm holds out," said *Sporting Life*, "it is certain that the club will hold its own."[12] In the event that it didn't, the club engaged John Harkins, who had previously signed with Trenton but was awarded to Cleveland.

In Fatty Briody and Doc Bushong, Cleveland had two strong defensive catchers capable of handling McCormick and Harkins. Bushong, a practicing dentist, was yet another light-hitting catcher prized for his defensive skills. He was one of the first to crouch behind the plate rather than stand upright and one of the first to regularly use signs to signal what his pitcher should throw.

The best Cleveland player was shortstop Jack Glasscock, known as Pebbly Jack for his habit of picking up pebbles from the infield. Glasscock was a good hitter, having batted .291 and .287 the previous two seasons, and an excellent fielder who led his league's shortstops in fielding percentage six times. Like McCormick, had been with the team since it entered the NL.

Cleveland had been badly hurt by raids of the Union Association, which pilfered star second baseman Fred Dunlap, ace pitcher Hugh Daily, and outfielder George Shaffer. Cleveland supporters noted that the first two had been disruptive influences, but most admitted they'd rather have Dunlap with all his faults. "He is a crank and disorganizer, but he is, nevertheless, a great ballplayer."[13] In May, when the team got off to a slow start, one reporter commented, "Harmony prevails among the Cleveland players this year. The disturbing elements, Dunlap and Daily, are gone. But less harmony and more batting could be tolerated."[14]

Buffalo had a rich baseball history, dating back to the 1850s, and in 1877 formed the team that would eventually enter the NL. The Bisons won the International Association title in 1878 and posted a 10–7 record against NL teams in exhibition games, indicating they were ready for bigger things. They joined the NL in 1879.[15]

In 1884, Buffalo, like New York, had four eventual Hall of Famers on its roster. A couple of them were older, but both 36-year-old Deacon White, who played third base in 1884, and 33-year-old outfielder Jim O'Rourke had several more productive years ahead of them. White, an angular, odd-looking man, didn't look like a professional athlete, but he was a consistent star for 20 major league seasons, although almost every year he created a little drama by threatening to retire to his farm. "Jim has made this same little speech every winter," said one paper, "for the past thirteen years, and about the time the salary is raised to a figure that meets his views he concludes that the cows, watermelons, turnips and sich can take care of themselves another year anyhow and signs a contract."[16]

The other Hall of Famers, pitcher Jim Galvin, 27, and first baseman Dan Brouthers, 26, were in their prime. Galvin had been with the Bisons since 1878 and won 159 games in his first five major league seasons, including 46 in 1883. In 1888, he would become the first major league pitcher to win 300 games. While Galvin was one of the Bisons' best weapons, they had no one behind him, which would turn out to be a serious problem.

Brouthers began his career as a pitcher but was a full-time first baseman by 1880. He was an average-sized player by today's standards but a very large one for his time at 6'2" and over 200 pounds, a gentle giant with a placid disposition. Like a later slugger, Babe Ruth, he was a big man with an odd body, a large upper half, from which he generated his power, supported by thin legs and small feet. His knees pointed at each other when he stood at the plate, which made him appear less than graceful. Dan's supporters claimed he was a better fielder and base runner than he was generally given credit for, but the frequency with which they defended him leads one to believe there was something to defend.[17]

Big Dan was the best hitter in the league in 1883, leading in average (.374), hits (159), RBI (97), and triples (17). His OPS of .969 was by far the best in the circuit. He'd led the league in homers in 1881 and would do so again in 1886. Of all players whose careers were exclusively in the 19th century,[18] Brouthers ranked first in slugging percentage and OPS. Like other 19th-century sluggers, he is overlooked today because of his modest home run totals. His other career marks, such as hits (he had 2,303) were impacted by the shorter schedule. Had Brouthers played in the era of the 162-game schedule, he would very likely have had more than 3,000 hits, and had he played under 20th-century conditions, he would have had a lot more than 107 home runs.

They used the naked eye rather than a tape measure to determine the length of home runs in those days, but some of Brouthers' best shots, even with the dead ball, were recalled for years afterward. Unlike many sluggers, he was extremely difficult to strike out. In 6,726 career at bats, Brouthers fanned just 201 times. In 1894, he struck out a mere five times in 525 official at bats.[19]

At shortstop, Buffalo had 35-year-old veteran Davy Force, a light hitter but good defender who had played a key role in the formation of the National League. Following the 1874 season, Force signed contracts with both Chicago and the Philadelphia Athletics. The ensuing controversy infuriated Hulbert and created a rift in the old National Association that made it easier for him to topple the tottering old edifice.

Force, who stood just 5'4" and weighed only 130 pounds, had been an excellent hitter in the NA, batting .335 during his five seasons. Once the pitching got faster and Force got older, his offensive skills declined precipitously. In ten NL seasons, he averaged just .211, and dropped as low as .169 in 1880. He'd batted .217 in 1883.

There were not many players active in 1884 who'd taken part in the first major league season of 1871, but the Bisons had three of them: Force, White, and center fielder Dave Eggler, a Brooklyn boy who'd bounced around considerably since beginning his major league career with the New York Mutuals. He'd divided the 1883 season between Buffalo and Baltimore of the AA.

Some teams seemed destined to finish near the bottom of the standings, and Detroit was one of them. Detroit has been a city in decay in recent years, but in the 19th century it was thriving, at one point the fourth largest city in America. A city that big and vibrant needed a major league baseball team, and in 1881, Mayor William G. Thompson, a 38-year-old lawyer and wounded Civil War veteran, headed a group that organized a club and gained admission to the

Dan Brouthers was one of the top sluggers of the 19th century. He had a career batting average of .342 and led his league in batting five times. In 1884 he hit the impressive total of 14 home runs, but finished fifth in the National League. The four men who exceeded his total all played in Chicago, which had a ridiculously short outfield fence. Brouthers was elected to the Hall of Fame in 1945 (National Baseball Hall of Fame Library, Cooperstown, N.Y.).

National League, replacing the Cincinnati franchise. Frank Bancroft agreed to manage the new entry.

The Wolverines played well under Bancroft during their first two NL seasons, but after he left, they plummeted to 40–58 in 1883, finishing ahead of only the woeful Philadelphia club. The poor play hit the Detroit club in the pocketbook, and the Wolverines cleared a grand total of $34.57.

Bancroft's replacement was 39-year-old John Chapman, a man who, like Joe Start, spanned several eras. Chapman was an outfielder for the old champion Atlantics of Brooklyn in the 1860s, where he acquired the nickname "Death to Flying Things" for his ability to catch fly balls. Apparently, Chapman was also death to anything on a plate, for he became quite portly late in his playing career, which ended in 1876. When he visited the office of the *Detroit Free Press,* a reporter said, "At 5 o'clock yesterday afternoon, the hall door leading into THE FREE PRESS editorial rooms swung wide open, but to the workers therein, the hall remained invisible. The door had merely given place to the stalwart, rotund figure of John C. Chapman, Manager of the Detroit Base Ball Club."[20] The article ended by describing the creaking of the stairs when Chapman departed.

After retiring as an active player, Chapman carved out a lengthy career as a manager. He escaped unscathed from the Louisville gambling debacle of 1877, and after a few seasons of bouncing around the bushes, was engaged by Detroit for the 1883 season. One of Chapman's problems in Detroit, and probably the reason Bancroft left, was Thompson. "His best friends," the *Cleveland Herald* said, "never accused Mr. Thompson of conservatism or careful handling of any subject. Whatever he does is done with a rush, be it right or wrong."[21]

When it came to the Wolverines, Thompson was certain he was right, and although Chapman insisted that Thompson had not interfered with his management, few believed him. In January, *Sporting Life* said that Thompson had been a "disturbing element" in 1883 but was reined in by the directors and insisted that in 1884 Chapman would have total control of his team.[22]

Chapman was saddled not just with Thompson but also with a sorry crew of players. "The Detroit team," said *Sporting Life,* "has an able manager in Jack Chapman, but even an able manager cannot pull to the front so weak a team as Detroit seems to be."[23] Chapman did the best he could, cleaning house, bringing in a number of new faces, and disposing of the most disruptive members of the 1883 club. He was optimistic about his youthful nine and said that playing hard was more important than winning, which was a good attitude, since his team didn't win often.

One thing Chapman's club did have was a strong battery, in the person of left-handed pitcher Fred "Dupee" Shaw and catcher Charlie Bennett. Shaw had been signed as an outfielder in 1883, before Chapman realized he was much more valuable as a pitcher. Bennett was a bona fide star who led NL catchers in fielding percentage seven times, during an era where fielding percentage was an important measure of defensive skill. Outfielder Ned Hanlon was a sound defensive center fielder with a good head on his shoulders who later became the manager of the championship Baltimore Orioles teams of the 1890s. Other than those three, there was precious little talent on the Wolverine roster.

If Chapman had a tough job in Detroit, legendary manager Harry Wright faced an even more difficult undertaking in Philadelphia, which won just 17 games in its first National League season. The 1883 team was hastily thrown together when the National

League decided it had to be in Philadelphia, and the roster consisted largely of holdovers from the independent team of 1882. They were overmatched in the NL, but if anyone could mold a winning team, it was Harry Wright, baseball's first great manager and winner of six of the first eight major league pennants. In Philadelphia, even a .500 record would be a miracle.

Signing Wright was a coup. In the late summer of 1883, when he was managing the Providence Grays, Wright had been the subject of intense speculation regarding his 1884 plans. It was said that he was going back to Boston, or perhaps he would manage John Day's New York club for $5,000 and a share of the profits. Or maybe he would manage in Pittsburgh. In the October 15 issue of *Sporting Life*, Wright was rumored going to Pittsburgh, New York, or St. Louis. A week later, it was announced that he would work for Al Reach in Philadelphia, for a reported salary of $3,000 ($2,500 per another account), the scorecard concession, and 25 percent of the team's profits.

Wright left Providence on good terms, and said he went to Philadelphia only because he saw a great benefit to the National League if it had a strong team in such a large city. That would be a challenge, for many of Wright's players were the men who'd won just 17 games the previous year. "Nearly all the men," said *Sporting Life*, "played a listless, indifferent sort of game last year, influenced partly by bad management, by demoralizing influences among the men and by a general feeling of 'it's no use.'"[24] "If Harry Wright can't make the Philadelphia club a good one," it added, "no one can."[25] And perhaps no one could.

Wright started signing as many players as he could, hoping to get quality from quantity. "Harry Wright seems to take in all the unfortunate and stranded players,"[26] said one paper. The best was a 20-year-old youngster from Virginia named Charlie Ferguson, who pitched and played the infield with equal skill.

Wright knew as much about baseball as anyone in the game. He'd developed many of the strategies then in vogue and was the first to train his nine to act in a disciplined manner both on and off the field. He marched his team onto the diamond with military

Harry Wright was baseball's first great manager. He won six of major league baseball's first eight pennants, but by 1884, when he took over the Philadelphia National League club, his best days were behind him. He brought his team home sixth, 45 games behind the pennant winning Providence club he'd managed in 1883 (National Baseball Hall of Fame Library, Cooperstown, N.Y.).

precision; they lined up nine abreast and broke off to assume their positions. Harry didn't argue with umpires when he was a field captain, and he didn't want his captain or players to hector officials like Anson and others did. He couldn't do it himself, for while AA managers were allowed to sit on their team's bench during a game, non-playing NL managers had to sit in the grandstand while the field captain ran the team.

By 1884, many of Harry's values were those of a bygone age. Everyone was cheating, arguing with umpires, and walking off the field if they didn't get their way, and any team that played honestly put themselves at a disadvantage. But for Harry Wright there was no option other than to play straight, even if he was playing in a crooked game. After winning six pennants in seven years, he never won another after 1878.

And so the eight National League teams left the gate for the start of the 1884 season. New York, Boston, and Chicago expected to win the pennant, Providence, Cleveland, and Buffalo hoped for a good showing, and Detroit and Philadelphia just wanted to avoid finishing last. No matter where they finished, each team hoped to make a profit, a difficult task with more major league teams in the field than would appear in any season until 1998. It promised to be an interesting summer.

# 10

## "Too many—it is going to weaken us"
*American Association Preview*

When the American Association made peace with the National League, it was free to prosper, and thus far it had. After starting with six teams in 1882, it grew to eight the following year with its bold move into New York and Philadelphia. Flush with success and eager to keep prospective franchises out of the Union Association, the AA decided to expand to twelve clubs for the 1884 season. The NL and AA both feared the new league, but the NL managed to convince the latter organization to take a more aggressive approach. Two of the most stable UA teams were located in the AA strongholds of St. Louis and Cincinnati and thus the Association took the lead in trying to crowd the new organization out.

"*Sporting Life* is of the opinion," the journal stated in November 1883, "that the admission of twelve clubs would be a mistake, and the number will entail increased traveling expenses.... With increased membership would come a larger proportion of weak clubs, with no drawing power.... Brooklyn is entitled to membership; Indianapolis must be taken in to balance the sections; there the association should stop."[1] When the AA held its annual convention at the Grand Hotel in Cincinnati on December 12 and 13 it did not, as *Sporting Life* recommended, stop with Brooklyn and Indianapolis but also added Toledo and Washington.

Growing the league by 50 percent was a risky proposition. The 1883 expansion had incorporated large cities while the 1884 growth would add teams from less populous cities, which in some cases would have to compete for patronage. If the new teams were too weak, there would be uneven competition, less interesting games, and a lackluster pennant race. The strong clubs would have fewer games in New York and more in Toledo. As if the new entrants didn't have enough obstacles, the league burdened them with a schedule that pitted them against the stronger teams at the start of the season and imposed a system where visiting teams received a fixed guaranty rather than sharing in receipts from games in Philadelphia, New York, and the other large cities.

Brooklyn, Indianapolis, and Toledo were admitted by a unanimous vote, but there were questions regarding the Washington club's finances. John Hollingshead, a longtime fixture in Washington baseball and manager of the new team, was called to testify as to the soundness of the exchequer. "By his assurance on his honor," reported *Sporting Life*, "that the schedule of games would be carried through faithfully, as far as the Washington Club was concerned [Washington] was also admitted."[2] That was a bit weak, but it was good enough for the AA, as it gave them an even twelve teams. "Too many," said Athletics captain Lon Knight. "It is going to weaken us, and will hurt us."[3] Before play even began, there were rumors that four clubs would be dropped after the season, particularly if the strategy of wiping out the UA was successful.

Brooklyn was a good addition. In the fall of 1882, newspaperman George Taylor decided to rejuvenate baseball in Brooklyn, which hadn't had a competitive team in several years. He hired a lawyer named John Brine to help raise the capital. Charles Byrne, a real estate investor who shared office space with Brine and graduated from the same college as Taylor, heard about the plans and became interested. He enlisted his brother-in-law, Joseph Doyle, who operated a New York casino, who in turn recruited Newport casino owner Ferdinand "Gus" Abell.

Byrne became the leader of the group, which secured grounds at Washington Park, located between Fourth and Fifth Avenue and running from Third to Fifth Streets, the site of the Revolutionary War Battle of Brooklyn. They spent $30,000 fixing up the park, placed an ad in the *New York Clipper* seeking players, and by the time the 1883 season began, the grounds were ready and Brooklyn had a team, a nine good enough to win the Inter-State Association pennant.

Brooklyn had a strong team, a good park (additional seats were added when the club joined the AA) and good leadership in the person of Byrne, who would become one of the leading figures in the AA and later the NL. The team's management had been a model of efficiency in 1883, acquiring and improving their grounds and getting a team together in just five weeks. "The success of the Brooklyn Club," the local *Eagle* stated, "is entirely due to the able management."[4] Most of the 1884 Brooklyn players were holdovers from the 1883 club, and the question was whether the best team in the Inter-State Association could be competitive in the American Association.

If the Brooklyn club played well, it could expect strong fan support, for at one time Brooklyn was the hottest baseball city in the United States. During the 1850s and 1860s, most of the top clubs were located in Brooklyn and the city's Union Grounds was the center of baseball activity. After the Mutuals were dismissed from the NL in 1876, the Hartford club played one season at the Union Grounds, but they had not been well-supported. There had been no major league baseball in the city for six years.

The Brooklyn club didn't have any big stars; none of the 1884 club would achieve significant fame. There was a pitcher named William Terry who, because of his good looks, had acquired the nickname "Adonis," but in 1884 he was a 19-year-old rookie whose ability would take time to catch up to his looks. He and Sam Kimber would share the pitching duties. There were a handful of old National Association veterans like John Cassidy, Billy Geer, John Farrow, and Jack Remsen, plus a supporting cast that had steady habits and modest talent.

Indianapolis had tried major league baseball once before. In 1877, they had one of the best independent teams in the country and joined the National League in 1878. The jump was too much for them. The Hoosiers finished fifth in a six-team league and at the end of the season severe financial problems forced them to withdraw. The city had not fielded a major league team since.

In 1883, Indianapolis formed an independent team, managed by the colorful Dan O'Leary, that played 142 games against assorted competition, finishing 95–47, including 11–23 in exhibitions against NL and AA teams. After a slow start, O'Leary began adding players and getting better talent, and his team finished with a flourish. With the problems of 1878 a distant memory, Indianapolis decided to take another run at major league ball. Like Brooklyn, they had a modestly talented roster. The manager was Jim Gifford, a railroad man who'd handled a number of National Association clubs in the late 1870s and early 1880s.

Washington was one of two teams (AA and UA) in a city that could probably support only one, particularly with a competing team in nearby Baltimore. The Washington AA team was backed by the shady Lloyd Moxley, while the UA club was led by Michael Scanlon who was, like Hollingshead, a veteran of the Washington baseball scene. Scanlon had petitioned the AA to admit his club, sending a telegram to the annual meeting stating, "For God's sake, have my club admitted to the Association."[5] Apparently, God wanted Moxley's club instead. If so, it indicated that not even God is infallible, for Scanlon had the organizational skills to lead a team through the treacherous currents of 1884 and probably would have been a better choice.

Moxley was a colorful character in his mid–40s who was heavily involved in the Washington theater scene. One evening nearly 20 years earlier, he was hanging around Ford's Theater and became engaged in conversation with an actor named John Wilkes Booth. When he learned later that evening that Booth had assassinated Abraham Lincoln, Moxley went into hiding for fear that someone had seen him with Booth and would think he had been a conspirator.[6] Fortunately, no one noticed the connection and Moxley re-appeared without incident.

After the war, Moxley pursued a number of endeavors, primarily selling theater costumes and advertising. He constructed a park for sporting events, mostly to sell advertising, and somehow wound up as president of the Washington club.

Despite Hollingsworth's oath of solvency, Moxley was dogged by rumors that his club wouldn't last more than a month into the season. Al Houck, one of Moxley's business partners who was involved in the Baltimore AA franchise, insisted that Moxley was solvent and had more than $100,000 in government bonds.

The persistent rumors made it difficult for Moxley to sign quality players. One paper commented, "Hawkes is the only married man in the Washington (American) team. This is lucky, as the rest of the team can better stand a loss of salary or a walk home over the mountains about June without inconveniencing their families."[7] Hollingshead, who'd given up the government post he'd held for 14 years to manage the club, said he hoped to finish seventh or eighth, a modest aspiration, but given the financial cloud over the club and the mediocre cast Moxley assembled, just finishing might be considered a success.

One of Moxley's problems was that Scanlon's club had acquired a more desirable site. Moxley first tried to solve that problem by getting the owner of the ground to void the lease. When that failed, he tried to purchase a parcel in the middle of the field. That didn't work either and Scanlon began the season with yet another advantage.

The fourth new AA team was the Toledo club that won the 1883 Northwestern League championship. It wasn't long after the end of the season that the city, which had never had a big-league club, developed major league aspirations. The board of directors assessed each stockholder 30 percent of their investment and sought to sell $12,000 in new stock. "The Toledo Club is tired of the Northwestern League," *Sporting Life* reported, "and would like to join the American Association. Slim chance."[8] But when the AA met in December, Toledo was admitted, much to the chagrin of the Northwestern League, which lost its best team.

NWL president Elias Matter said Toledo was in arrears with its dues payments and therefore ineligible to join a league operating under the National Agreement. He appealed to the Arbitration Committee, and when it ruled against him, Matter and his colleagues were bitter. At the annual NWL meeting, a spirited discussion arose as to whether the Toledo club should be awarded the 1883 pennant, since it had withdrawn from the league. It was eventually decided that Toledo would be declared the champion, but the pennant was awarded to Saginaw, which finished second.

Toledo won the championship with an impressive lineup that included a number of former major leaguers. Perhaps the two most interesting players were the catchers, Fleet Walker and James McGuire. Walker was the first African American major leaguer (see Chapter 3), while McGuire, an unknown quantity in 1884, would eventually carve out a memorable niche in baseball history. That year was the first of his 26 major league seasons. The only men to play longer are Cap Anson and Nolan Ryan, with 27.

Toledo's star pitcher was Tony Mullane, a good-looking, talented, and egotistical performer who jumped from team to team and courted trouble his entire career. Mullane was sarcastically referred to as the Count of Macaroni for his foppish dress and as The Apollo of the Box for his good looks. "[O]f all the petrels who stood in a pitcher's box during those years," wrote David Nemec, "few were more gifted and none was stormier than handsome, talented, and versatile Tony Mullane."[9] Mullane had a mean streak and never hesitated to throw at hitters he thought were too close to the plate. When he first came to the major leagues, batters were not awarded first base when hit, which enhanced Mullane's pleasure. In 1884, the 32 he plunked were awarded first base.

A 26-year-old Irish immigrant who came to America as a boy and grew up in Erie, Pennsylvania, Mullane began his baseball career with the Bradford, Pennsylvania, club in 1879. In 1880 and most of the following year he pitched for a team in Akron, Ohio, but in late August, he was signed by Detroit of the NL. Mullane's introduction to the National League was rocky. He was wild, pitched poorly, and after a one-sided 12–6 loss to Worcester on September 23, he was released.

Mullane pitched in New Orleans during the winter and got his first taste of big-league success with Louisville in 1882, finishing second in the AA with 30 wins and posting a 1.88 ERA. His first taste of success spawned his first case of wanderlust. In early August, with almost two months left in the season, it was announced that Mullane would pitch for St. Louis in 1883, despite his having assured Louisville he would remain with the Eclipse. St. Louis had offered him more money and, throughout his stormy career, money usually dictated Mullane's actions.

The Browns got their money's worth out of Mullane, as the big fellow won 35 games while losing just 15. His winter was even more eventful than his summer and after a long, dramatic contractual battle involving the Union Association (see Chapter 11), Mullane wound up with Toledo. He had a tumultuous season, supposedly stealing teammate Sam Barkley's girlfriend and clashing with Walker over signs (see Chapter 3). It was not the kind of harmony that led to a pennant.

Toledo was not expected to contend for the pennant. The defending champions were the Athletics of Philadelphia, winners of the thrilling 1883 race, in which they finished a game ahead of St. Louis. The name Athletics was a storied one in Philadelphia, dating back to the formation of an amateur club in 1860. Within a few years, the amateurs had become professionals and were one of the best teams of the late 1860s. In 1871, they won the first pennant in major league history.

The Athletics were charter members of the National League, but by that time they were a mere shadow of the earlier powerhouses. They finished with a dismal 14–45 record and were dropped from the league for failing to make their final road trip.

There were a number of Philadelphia professional clubs after 1876, but none were members of the National League. Major league teams often played exhibitions against the local clubs, but it wasn't until the AA was formed in 1882 that Philadelphia returned to the major leagues. The next year the National League placed in team in Philadelphia and the city, which had three major league clubs in 1875, would be represented by three (including the UA Keystones) again in 1884.

The Athletics' 1883 pennant had not come easily. Late in the season, their veteran hurler, Bobby Mathews, was hampered by a series of injuries and the team had difficulty finding a replacement. In desperation, they engaged a former Yale pitcher who'd spent the early part of the season in Detroit with mixed results.

The new man, Daniel Albion Jones, became a national sensation, partly because he won five of seven starts but mostly because he had a bizarre pitching motion; he frequently jumped in the air, with both feet off the ground, as he delivered the pitch. His strange delivery made him a celebrity and by the time the season was over, every baseball fan in America knew about "Jumping Jack" Jones.

Jones won the game that clinched the 1883 pennant, but he would not wear a Philadelphia uniform in 1884, for he had returned to Yale and was singing tenor for the glee club.[10] That meant the Athletics would be relying on Mathews as their number one hurler.

Mathews, 32, was a diminutive 5'5" veteran who'd won the first game in major league history in 1871. He was an early practitioner of curve ball pitching and, according to some, was the inventor of the spitball or some variation thereof. Mathews had been one of the top pitchers in the old National Association, winning 131 games during the league's five seasons, third behind Al Spalding and Dick McBride. But after pitching for the Mutuals in 1876, his career went into decline. From 1877 through 1881 he bounced around, pitching with limited success for several major and minor league clubs, and acquiring a reputation as a problem drinker. Suddenly, in 1882, Mathews caught his second wind, winning 19 games for Boston using strategy to compensate for his diminished speed. Despite his injuries, Mathews won 30 games in 1883 and appeared to have regained his old form.

The Athletics' first baseman was Harry Stovey,[11] a native Philadelphian who was one of the great hitters of the 19th century. Stovey began his major league career with Worcester in 1880 and joined Philadelphia in 1883 when Worcester lost its franchise. Over a seven-year period from 1883 to 1889, he led the AA in runs scored four times, in home runs three times, and twice in triples. He was also one of the best base runners in the major leagues. While 19th-century stolen base totals aren't comparable with those from the 20th century, Stovey's were very impressive. During the six years from 1886 through 1891, he stole 446 bases (more than 74 per year) with a high of 97 in 1890. He scored more than 100 runs nine straight years, averaging 127 per season.[12]

Stovey is little remembered today primarily because he, like Dan Brouthers, was a power hitter in an era when the home run was not in vogue. His home run totals are negligible by 21st-century standards but he reached double figures six times in years when some teams didn't reach double figures. He set the major league record with 14 home runs in 1883, was the first to reach 100 career homers and finished his career with 122. Roger Connor had a few more home runs (138) than Stovey, and when Babe Ruth broke the all-time career mark in 1921, it was Connor that he passed, which may have gotten the latter into the Hall of Fame. Stovey tumbled into 19th-century oblivion.

Although the Athletics were the defending champions, they were not favored to repeat. As one baseball insider said, "[I]n the first place, the Athletics have not the strongest nine; in the second place they want a good manager and thirdly there are too many drinkers in the nine."[13]

The city of St. Louis, home of the 1883 AA runner-up, had a spotty major league history.[14] In 1875, there were two Mound City teams in the old NA, and one of them, the Brown Stockings, finished a strong fourth and drew 78,500 fans, by far the best attendance in the league. The second club, the Red Stockings, didn't finish the season.

After their successful 1875 debut, the Brown Stockings became a charter member of the NL and finished third with a 45–19 mark. Attendance in virtually all NL cities dropped dramatically in 1876, and St. Louis drew just 36,000, less than half the previous year's total.

The following season was one of the worst in the long history of the National League. The Louisville scandal rocked the game and in St. Louis, reporter William Spink alleged that Joe Blong and Joe Battin of the Brown Stockings threw a game to Chicago. The Brown Stockings were urged to put them on the blacklist, and although neither was expelled, the episode put a dark stain on St. Louis baseball.[15]

The 1877 St. Louis club, which lost its leading hitter (Lipman Pike) and best pitcher (George Bradley) posted a mediocre 28–32 record and attendance dropped further to 29,000. It was estimated that the club lost $8,000 and at the end of the season, some players had not been paid. The stockholders were unable to raise additional money and under the weight of a mediocre team, insolvency, and scandal, surrendered their NL franchise.

Over the next four years, there were a number of semi-pro teams in St. Louis, and their success led a German saloon keeper and grocer named Chris von der Ahe to get involved in the game; he was president of the franchise that joined the AA in 1882 (see Chapter 5). The Browns were fifth in a six-team league their first year, but their attendance of 135,000

Harry Stovey was the Athletics' best player and one of the best in the American Association. In 1884, he led the league in triples and runs scored. He set a major league mark with 14 home runs in 1883, and when he retired after the 1893 season, his 122 homers were the major league career record (National Baseball Hall of Fame Library, Cooperstown, N.Y.).

was the best in the AA and far more than any St. Louis team had ever drawn. The following year, with the hot pennant race against the Athletics, attendance skyrocketed to 243,000.

The Browns had barely lost the pennant in 1883 and fully expected to win it in 1884. Their manager and first baseman was Charlie Comiskey, who had been discovered by the legendary Ted Sullivan at St. Mary's College. Comiskey's father wanted him to concentrate on his studies and was angry when he chose a career in baseball, but Sullivan was a very persuasive man.

At the beginning of the 1884 season, Comiskey was a good-fielding, light-hitting 24-year-old who had already gained a reputation as a leader of men and scourge of umpires, both requisite qualities for a 19th-century manager. Although he wasn't the first man at his position to play off the bag, Comiskey stationed himself deeper than most and was known for roaming far to his right to field ground balls. That was revolutionary, for in baseball's old days, the first baseman just stood on the bag and caught throws. Comiskey was also a daring baserunner, setting the pace for the aggressive style his team employed with great success throughout the 1880s. The Browns took chances on the bases, they played to win at all costs, and established a reputation for rough play that was unequaled until the Oriole teams of the 1890s.

Comiskey was intelligent and mature, but the reason he was the Browns manager was that he was able to get along with the mercurial Von der Ahe, something Sullivan, his predecessor, had been unable to do. One of the most contentious issues between Von der Ahe and Sullivan was the former's insistence that Sullivan keep a tighter rein on his troublesome players, of whom there were many. Catcher Pat Deasley and outfielder Fred Lewis were involved in the drunken escapades described in Chapter 8. Third baseman Arlie Latham, 24, was not as susceptible to alcohol as Deasley and Lewis, but he was a great womanizer who drove his distraught wife Emma to attempt suicide by drinking chloroform in her hotel room.

Mrs. Latham didn't succeed in killing herself. When a chambermaid entered her room, Emma told her she'd left a note on the dresser. The woman, who may have been illiterate, took the note, which told of Latham's infidelity and her distress, to the desk clerk, who immediately summoned Latham and a doctor. The doctor rushed to the hotel and administered an antidote that saved Emma's life. Latham was less helpful. "[He] acted in a very indifferent and unfeeling manner," one paper reported, "laughing and asking roughly what was the matter.... Latham takes it very coolly, and this afternoon played a better game of ball than he generally does."[16]

Acting badly and playing a good game of ball were what Latham generally did. He worked in a shoe factory as a teenager before getting a short, unimpressive NL trial. When he joined the Browns in 1883, he blossomed and became one of the best players on a very good team. Latham was a solid hitter and one of the fastest men in the major leagues, but his enduring legacy is his brash, obnoxious personality. Players served as base coaches in those days, and Latham became renowned for the show he put on in the third base coaching position, taunting umpires and opposing players and entertaining the fans. He was so effective in that role that when his playing skill faded, he became the first man hired exclusively as a base coach. If anyone objected to his behavior, he was always ready, like most of the Browns, to use his fists.

With Mullane having decamped to Toledo, the pitching was in the hands of Jumbo McGinnis, who'd won 28 games in 1883. Other St. Louis stalwarts included slick-fielding shortstop Bill Gleason, another Sullivan protégé who'd been with the Browns since 1880, and James (Tip) O'Neill, a handsome Canadian whose bad arm would soon end his pitching career and send him to the outfield, where his batting exploits would make him famous.

O'Neill arrived in St. Louis through some typical 19th-century shenanigans. He was under contract to the New York Gothams, who were under common ownership with the AA Metropolitans. Intending to transfer O'Neil to the Mets, John Day gave him his release from the Gothams, but failed to wait the required ten days before signing him to a Mets contract. When the new contract reached the AA office, secretary Jimmy Williams declared it void. Then, in his role as a St. Louis executive, Williams signed O'Neil to a Browns contract.[17]

Although New York is a city in which expectations run very high, no one expected much of the 1884 Metropolitans, who were clearly the less-favored children of owner John Day.[18] The Gothams got the best players and the best field, the Polo Grounds, which made its debut in 1883. The Mets played a few games at the Polo Grounds that year, but had to limit their occupancy to days on which the National League club wasn't using the field. For most of 1884, the Mets were relegated to a sorry, low-lying patch of real estate located on the East River between 107th and 109th Streets. The field was built atop a landfill and smoke from nearby factories wafted across the diamond. Mets Pitcher Jack Lynch said a player could catch malaria by fielding a ground ball.[19] The players hated playing there and relished the days they were allowed to use the Polo Grounds.[20]

Charles Comiskey is best known as the long-time owner of the Chicago White Sox and the man for whom Comiskey Park was named. In the 19th century, he was a good-fielding, light-hitting first baseman and manager of the St. Louis Browns, who won four consecutive American Association pennants (National Baseball Hall of Fame Library, Cooperstown, N.Y.).

The Mets finished fourth in 1883, eleven games behind the Athletics. Since the Gothams finished sixth in the NL, many thought Day should put his best players on one club in order to bring a championship to the city. And they thought the stronger club should be the one in the more prestigious NL. After the 1883 season, there were rumors that several Mets, including pitcher Tim Keefe, catcher Bill Holbert, and infielder Jack

Nelson, would be transferred to the National League franchise. The moves did not take place, much to the relief of Mets manager Jim Mutrie, who had been encouraged by the way his team played in the latter part of 1883.

One of Mutrie's best young prospects was 24-year-old first baseman Dave Orr, a massive 250-pounder who'd played a few games in 1883. In one game against Columbus, Orr hit two home runs and a triple, quite a feat for a team that had just six home runs all year. By the end of May 1884, after he became the first man to hit the ball over the fence of the Mets' new grounds, *Sporting Life* compared Orr to Dan Brouthers, the top power hitter in the National League.[21] While he was a feared slugger, Orr was not a complete player. "He was a left-handed hitter (sic—Orr batted right-handed)," said Ted Sullivan, "and could kill a fastball, but he couldn't run a lick and never covered an inch of ground around first base."[22]

At third base was Thomas (Dude) Esterbrook, a 26-year-old in his fourth major league season. Esterbrook dressed in a fashion befitting his nickname, appearing at an American Association meeting in December 1884 in a sealskin coat, plug hat, and kid gloves. "A Bowery swell and a dude and a crank," they called him.[23] "No wonder the girls can't resist him,"[24] *Sporting Life* remarked. And Esterbrook couldn't resist the girls, supposedly losing his concentration at the sight of a pretty lady in the stands.

By 1884, most managers realized they needed two strong pitchers to work in rotation, and the Mets had a pair of good ones in Jack Lynch and Tim Keefe. Lynch, a heavy-set, jovial man known for his story-telling ability, had been a mediocre 23–24 in his first two major league seasons but was destined for better things in 1884. Keefe, whose 342 wins would get him to the Hall of Fame, began playing baseball as a first baseman in 1874 and two years later played in Androscoggin, Maine, with a shortstop named Jim Mutrie. Keefe wasn't much of a hitter (he batted just .187 during his major league career) and therefore decided to try pitching. In 1881 he threw a no-hitter for Albany in an exhibition game against the NL Troy club, which signed him after Albany disbanded.

Keefe posted losing records in three seasons with a poor Troy team and when they were bounced from the NL after the 1882 season, he was one of several Troy players who went to New York. In his first year with the Mets, with a better team behind him, he was 41–27. Keefe was a gentlemanly, well-respected, well-read, well-spoken man known as Sir Timothy and a strategic pitcher who relied on control and changing speeds. He was so knowledgeable about his craft that he was employed as a college coach and wrote a book on the art of pitching.

Lynch operated a tavern in Harlem in partnership with John Clapp, a former major league catcher and manager. The establishment did well and became a hangout for the New York baseball fraternity.[25] Unlike many players who ran saloons, however, Lynch was not a heavy drinker.

The man behind the bat was just as important as the pitcher, and the Mets were fortunate to have Bill Holbert, whose excellent defensive skills enabled him to last 12 years in the majors despite a career .208 batting average. Holbert still holds the major league record for the most times at bat (2,335) without hitting a home run.[26] He'd begun his major league career with Louisville in 1876, and Charles Chase, one of the directors of that club, loved relating the story of how he discovered Holbert.

Louisville, Chase said, was playing an exhibition game in Pennsylvania mining country, and the local club supplied an umpire who was "one of the most remarkable specimens I ever saw. His clothes were ragged and dirty, his face covered with coal dust, and his brown hair stuck out through the holes in his hat in several places." It was our hero Holbert. When Louisville catcher Charley Snyder was injured, the umpire volunteered to take his place. Everyone laughed, but agreed to let him try. He caught five innings, astonished everyone with his faultless play, and was immediately signed by Louisville.

That was a great story, marred only by the fact it was a complete fabrication. About a week after it appeared in print, Holbert revealed that he was not a hayseed pulled from the stands but had been playing baseball for three years before signing with Louisville, most recently with the Wilmington Quicksteps, one of the best non-major league teams. By 1884, Holbert was a solid veteran, as were many of the Metropolitans, several of whom had been playing for the club since it was an independent team. Although many dismissed the Mets as the poor relations of the Gothams, they thought they could win the pennant.

Clothier Aaron Stern was the primary financial backer of the Cincinnati team, but its mouthpiece was newspaperman Oliver P. Caylor. In 1869, Cincinnati was the center of the baseball world, but Harry Wright's legendary Red Stockings disbanded after the 1870 season and Cincinnati was without a major league team until 1876. The NL Red Stockings generally finished near the bottom of the pack and in 1880, unhappy with the league ban on Sunday baseball and the sale of liquor, Cincinnati challenged the rules and lost its franchise. When the AA was formed and offered both alcohol and baseball on the Sabbath, Cincinnati rejoined the big leagues.

The new club won the first AA title and finished third in 1883, five games behind the Athletics, with a fine record of 61–37. In 1884, however, the Reds faced a formidable off-the-field challenge in their own city from the new Union Association club organized by Justus Thorner. Thorner had been involved with both the NL and AA clubs, but couldn't get along with either group. He sued the AA club for a greater share of the profits, lost, appealed, lost again, and embarked on a crusade to destroy the franchise.

In November 1883, when the AA club went to renew the lease on its grounds, they discovered that Thorner had beaten them to it. He'd signed a new lease and all the improvements the AA team had made now belonged to Thorner's club. To rub even more salt into Caylor's open wound, the Cincinnati Consolidated Street Railway, which owned the parcel, gave the UA team a better deal than Caylor had gotten. With the old grounds unavailable, Caylor tried to secure a site in the rear of Lincoln Park, but found that Thorner had obtained a right of refusal on it.

After a lengthy search, Caylor was finally able to obtain a five-year lease on a parcel on Western Avenue known as the Hulbert Ground. It wasn't the best place to put a ball diamond, since it was far from the center of the city and more difficult to access than the old park. It was also too small, and balls left the field too frequently before additional land was acquired and the park was expanded.

The new ground also needed a lot of work; there were homes, gardens, and a brickyard to be removed, the field had to be cleared, graded and sodded, a grandstand needed to be constructed, and fences had to be erected. The total cost was estimated at $10,000, money that wouldn't have been needed if the club could have retained its old site. The upstart UA club had clearly won the first round.[27]

Caylor was furious. He removed everything he could from the old site, including home plate. The AA team's lease didn't expire until April 1, and when a contractor arrived in March to prepare the field for the UA season, he was turned away and told he could not begin work until April 1. Anything he built before then would be torn down. Thorner told him to start anyway and dare Caylor to do something about it.

The two teams conducted a vicious season-long battle in the newspapers. The *Commercial* supported the AA and the *Enquirer* and *News-Journal* took up the cudgel for the UA. "Carey and Weldon [the respective proprietors of the *Commercial* and *Enquirer*]," reported *Sporting Life*, "are saying all sorts of unpleasant things of each other and the whole thing has degenerated into a bitter personal newspaper quarrel."[28]

Cincinnati's best pitcher was Will White, brother of Hall of Famer Deacon White and the first major leaguer to wear glasses. With his spectacles, frail build, and prematurely white hair, White looked more like the tea merchant he was in the off-season than a major league ballplayer, but he led the AA in victories during each of its first two seasons, with 40 and 43, respectively. He'd also won 43 games for the 1879 Cincinnati NL club. Like most pitchers of that era, White had been worked extremely hard, averaging 544 innings for his first five full seasons, with a high of 680 in 1879. And that doesn't include his work in the numerous exhibitions the team played each summer. During his career, White completed 394 of 402 starts.

Future Hall of Famer Bid McPhee was the Cincinnati second baseman. At 24, McPhee was in his third year in the major leagues and, although he was a good fielder, had shown limited skill at the bat, hitting .228 and .245 in his first two years. Outfielder Charley Jones showed plenty at the bat. He was the major league career leader in home runs with 33 and led the league with 80 RBI in 1883.

Veteran infielder Chick Fulmer, who'd been an original NA player in 1871, had an unusual skill. He took great pride in his ability to don a uniform quickly and won five dollars from teammate Jimmy Peoples by betting him that he could change from civilian clothes to a uniform in two and a quarter minutes. He had a standing bet of fifty dollars for any player who thought he could change clothes faster.

The Cincinnati first baseman was local product John Reilly, who was also a talented artist.[29] The son of a riverboat captain who was killed during the Civil War, Reilly lived with relatives for a while before returning to his mother's Cincinnati home in 1872, when he was 13. The following year he commenced an apprenticeship at Stonebridge Lithographing Company and began to play baseball, starting as a catcher but quickly switching to first base for fear that a hand injury would ruin his budding art career. By the late 1870s, Reilly was pursuing dual careers as an artist with Stonebridge and an amateur baseball player. First base proved the ideal position for the lanky youngster, who had grown to 6'3" and acquired the nickname "Long John."

Reilly played for the Cincinnati NL team in 1880 but did poorly, batting just .206 and driving in only 16 runs in 73 games. He struck out a lot and rarely walked, but played well defensively. It was a rough year, but the most traumatic event of Reilly's rookie season had nothing to do with strikeouts or errors.

After a game in Providence June 10, Reilly made a quick visit to New York and was returning on the steamer *Narragansett* when, during the night, it collided with another vessel. The boat caught fire, water began pouring in, and panic ensued. Reilly scrambled up on deck and saw a man, thinking all was lost, put a revolver to his head and shoot himself. The strapping young ballplayer helped cut the lifeboats free and load people aboard, nearly falling overboard in the process. Then he grabbed a plank and jumped into the water. For about an hour, Reilly floated and paddled along in the darkness until a boat picked him up and took him ashore.

This photo of the 1882 Metropolitans, who played as an independent nine, first appeared in *Harper's Weekly*. Seated, left to right: Thomas Mansell, outfield; Frank Larkin, second base; Jack Nelson, shortstop; John Reilly, first base. Standing, left to right: Jack Lynch, pitcher; Charley Reipschlager, catcher; Tip O'Neil, pitcher; Ed Kennedy, outfield; John Clapp, catcher; John Doyle, pitcher; Frank Hankinson, third base; Steve Brady, outfield (courtesy John Thorn).

While his teammates played in Providence, Reilly sat shivering on a New York dock. In Cincinnati, his death was reported in the *Gazette*. But Reilly, still very much alive, made his way to Providence and was back in the Cincinnati lineup on June 15.

Reilly remained in Cincinnati working as an artist after the city lost its franchise, playing occasionally with amateur teams. In 1882, he was a member of the New York Metropolitans, spending nearly every morning at Stonebridge's New York office and playing ball in the afternoon.

Reilly agreed to play for the Cincinnati AA club in 1883 if Stonebridge would transfer him to their Cincinnati office. When they wouldn't, he signed a contract with the new National League team in New York. Cincinnati claimed it had a valid contract and refused to grant Reilly a release.

The NL and AA were at war, and one of the battles involved the case of John Reilly. In December 1882, the *Clipper* reported, "John Reilly has announced his intention to play with the Metropolitans [sic] this season, preferring expulsion from the American [Association] to expulsion from the League."[30] When the two leagues made peace, Reilly was assigned to Cincinnati.

By 1883 Reilly had refined his offensive skills and had an excellent year for his new club, batting .311 with nine home runs and 79 RBI, the latter figure placing him just one behind Charley Jones for the AA lead. He hit for the cycle twice.

Columbus, a member of the old International Association in 1877, joined the AA in 1883, under the erratic leadership of Hustling Horace Phillips. They finished sixth in an eight-team league with a 32–65 record and chose not to retain Phillips. The directors asked a local newspaper man to help find a replacement, and he mentioned it to one of his foremen. The foreman pointed to one of his workers, Gus Schmelz, and said he knew a lot about baseball and might be a good choice. Schmelz had considered applying for the job but didn't think he'd be chosen because he had no major league experience. The directors decided to hire him anyway, and the Columbus native turned out to be a good choice. He wound up managing 11 seasons in the big leagues.

Columbus didn't have any stars, but they had two good pitchers in left-hander Ed Morris and right-hander Frank Mountain. Morris, who stood just 5'7", was born in Brooklyn, but got most of his baseball experience in San Francisco, where he started as a left-handed catcher. Jerry Denny, a Californian who was responsible for discovering a lot of West Coast talent, was impressed with Morris and convinced him to go east and play with an independent team in Philadelphia.

Morris' best feature as a catcher was his powerful, accurate throwing arm (he acquired the nickname "Cannonball"), and it wasn't long before he was asked to try pitching. By 1883, Morris was pitching regularly and effectively; his primary weakness was a very bad temper.[31]

Mountain pitched for Union College of Schenectady, New York, plus two unimpressive games for Troy in 1880. He joined Detroit in 1881 but didn't last long, finishing the season with a semi-pro team called Haverly's Minstrels, for whom he also sang. The following year he pitched for Worcester of the NL, was briefly loaned to Philadelphia of the AA, and then returned to Worcester to finish the season. When the city lost its NL franchise, Mountain signed with the new Columbus team. He pitched 503 innings in 1883 and was 26–33, but there was no one behind him. The second pitcher was deaf-mute Ed Dundon, who was just 3–16. The combined record of pitchers not named Mountain was 6–32. With the addition of Morris, Columbus had a rotation.

Louisville joined the National League at its inception and the following season the Grays were in first place when, in major league baseball's first major scandal, four of its players fell in with

Long John Reilly was a talented graphic artist who played first base for Cincinnati's American Association club. In 1883, he led the league in home runs and slugging percentage and batted .339 (National Baseball Hall of Fame Library, Cooperstown, N.Y.).

gamblers and sold games. The result was a late season collapse and the end of the NL franchise.

In 1878, the city's best club was a semi-pro team called the Eclipse, whose president was T.W. Reccius, a member of one of Louisville's most prominent baseball families. In its first season, the Eclipse stayed close to home, playing local teams, and claimed the championship of Kentucky with a 23–11–1 record.[32]

The Eclipse became a stock club in 1881 and began paying their players, who included Louisville natives Pete Browning and Fred Pfeffer. The following year they joined the AA and were a respectable 42–38, finishing third in a six-team league. In 1883 they were 54–45 and fifth in an expanded eight-team circuit. The three best players from the 1883 team, pitcher Guy Hecker, Browning, and outfielder William (Chicken) Wolf, returned in 1884.[33]

Browning began playing with the Eclipse in 1877 at the age of 16, and when they entered the AA in 1882, he led the league with a .378 mark, 36 points higher than the next best average. He finished second in 1883 at .338[34] and would complete his major league career with a .341 lifetime batting average.

Browning was 22 years old when the 1884 season began, unmarried—he would remain single his entire life—and illiterate.[35] While hitting came easily to Browning, he had difficulty with nearly every other aspect of life, notably a very serious problem with alcohol.

Many people thought Browning wasn't very good looking and, in that politically incorrect time, they didn't hesitate to say so. The *Cincinnati Enquirer* informed its readers that Browning was "not blessed with a superabundance of personal beauty; in fact, if Pete was entered in a prize contest with this question as an issue against a hyena, the chances are that the animal would have the call in the polls."[36] Browning was an eccentric who stared into the sun to improve his vision, treated his bats almost as treasured human friends, and kept his batting statistics on his shirtsleeves. He never slid, believing he might damage its legs and hurt his batting.

Browning suffered from mastoiditis that rendered him nearly deaf and caused significant pain that was perhaps the reason he consumed so much alcohol. In May 1884, Browning had surgery to remove a painful tumor from his ear.

Hecker, a husky six-footer who weighed 190 pounds, was a 28-year-old native of Youngsville, Pennsylvania.[37] On the 1879 Oil City, Pennsylvania, team, Tony Mullane pitched and Hecker played first base. When Mullane joined Louisville in 1882, he convinced the club to sign Hecker as a change pitcher and first baseman. Although Hecker didn't pitch much that year, he threw a no-hitter against the Allegheny Club late in the season.

Pitchers were expected to hit in the 1880s, and since rosters were limited, a pitcher who hit well enough to play another position was a valuable man. Pitchers who could hit better than almost any other player in the league were *very* valuable, and Hecker hit so well that he actually played more games at first base and the outfield (397) than as a pitcher (336) during his major league career.

In 1883, when Mullane left for St. Louis, Hecker shared the pitching duties with Sam Weaver and had a 28–23 record, starting 52 games and pitching 469 innings. When Weaver jumped to the Keystones of the Union Association for the 1884 season, Hecker became an iron man.

Leech Maskery, Louisville's left fielder, was one of the most admirable men in the

American Association. He didn't drink or smoke, was careful with his finances, and had many intellectual pursuits, including classic English literature, guitar and piano, and painting landscapes in oil.

Maskery was a late bloomer, perhaps because of his many interests, and did not appear in the major leagues until 1882, when he was 28. He was not a strong hitter—the .250 average he posted in 1884 was the highest of his major league career—but he was a good defender.[38]

Veteran manager Billy Barnie faced a difficult task with the Baltimore club that finished 28–68 in 1883. The city's baseball heritage began in 1860 when Brooklyn's famous Excelsior Club paid a visit, and in the late 1860s, Baltimore's Marylands, led by teen-aged pitcher Bobby Mathews, were the best team in the area and possibly the best in the "southern" region. In 1872 and 1873, the Lord Baltimore club was one of the better NA teams, but in 1874 they were reduced to co-op status, lost most of their talent, and finished last.

The 1874 team was the last Baltimore major league club until it was awarded an AA franchise in 1882. After the 1882 and 1883 teams finished last, Providence manager Frank Bancroft looked at the talent on the Baltimore roster and wondered why. It might have been the management, Bancroft surmised, or maybe it was the fact that so many of the players drank heavily.

Barnie, called Bald Billy Barnie for his rapidly receding hairline, was a 31-year-old New York City native who began playing baseball with the Nassau Club of Brooklyn as a 17-year-old in 1870. He worked briefly for a Wall Street firm before leaving to pursue a baseball career full-time, making his major league debut with Hartford of the National Association in 1874.

Barnie played for the NA Keokuk Westerns before they disbanded in 1875 and caught young phenom Edward Nolan in Columbus in 1876. He played in San Francisco in 1879 and 1880, but in 1881, he returned to New York to run the Brooklyn Atlantics. Barnie was never much of a hitter, batting just .171 in his major league career, but he was adept behind the bat and was credited for helping in the development of talented young pitchers Nolan and Jim Whitney. In 1882 Barnie took over the management of the independent Philadelphia Club, and the following year he came to Baltimore.

Despite Baltimore's sorry record, Barnie was well-respected as a field manager and for his ability to handle the business affairs of the club. Because of his integrity, he was often asked to serve as umpire. Barnie was also known as a disciplinarian, which many people thought was just what the undisciplined Baltimore club needed. He promised heavy fines for anyone who drank too much.[39]

The key to success was pitching, and late in the 1883 season, Baltimore acquired Canadian hurler Bob Emslie, who posted a 9–13 record, but with a respectable 3.17 ERA. Besides, a 9–13 record wasn't all that bad for a last place team. Emslie later spent 33 years as a major league umpire and worked the famous Merkle game in 1908. Like Barnie, he lost his hair early, but unlike the Baltimore manager, Emslie tried to disguise his baldness by wearing a wig. Since turn of the century hairpieces were of dubious quality, Emslie fooled no one.

Having Emslie for the full season to team with Hardie Henderson, who started 42 games in 1883, boded well for 1884. Barnie could also count on a number of solid, dependable players like veteran outfielders Tom York and Jim Clinton, third baseman Joe Sommer, and slick-fielding, light-hitting shortstop Jimmy Macullar.[40]

Barnie's biggest challenge wouldn't necessarily come from his AA rivals. It would more likely arise from the Union Association and Eastern League clubs competing for the entertainment dollar of Baltimore fans. Before the start of the season, the Buffalo NL team and the Chicago UA team (controlled by A.H. Henderson, who also owned the Baltimore UA club) came to the city to take advantage of Baltimore's milder climate. The presence of five teams training in the city created a great deal of excitement, but having three throughout the summer would bring more pain than joy.

The final AA team was based in Allegheny, an area now encompassing the northwestern portion of Pittsburgh that was an independent municipality until 1907. Professional baseball had been slower to take hold in western Pennsylvania than in the eastern part of the state, and the 1882 AA nine was the first major league team from the region.

The Alleghenies first formed as an amateur club in 1861 and after a sporadic existence became a semi-professional organization in 1876. Rejected by the National League, they played as an independent organization and posted a record of 39–27–3. With only eight major league clubs, there was a lot of talent left for non-league teams and the 1876 Alleghenies employed future major leaguers Ned Williamson, Joe Quest, Adam Rocap, and Jack Nelson.

The following season, when the NL was reduced to six teams, the Alleghenies were able to assemble an even stronger nine. The 1877 team, which competed in the International Association, included Williamson, Nelson, future Hall of Famer Pud Galvin, and catcher Bill Holbert, whose skill was critical to Galvin's success.

The Alleghenies claimed to have won the 1877 International Association championship and embarked on a lengthy battle of words with the Tecumseh Club of London, Ontario, which was officially awarded the title. The IA was a loosely-organized entity, with no set schedule and a nebulous line separating exhibition games from championship matches. "Much amusement has been created here," wrote the secretary of the Tecumseh Club, "over the charming innocence displayed by the secretary of the Alleghenies in his claim to the championship."[41] The Alleghenies' claim never got beyond amusement and despite their protracted protest, the Tecumsehs retained the title.

Galvin, Williamson, and Nelson left the team after the season, and the 1878 club won just two of 26 games before disbanding June 8. The team was rejuvenated in 1880, but it was a second-rate organization that was little noted outside of the local area.

On October 15, 1881, a new version of the Alleghenies was organized, with Harmar Denny McKnight as president. McKnight was born in Pittsburgh in 1848 (1847 according to some sources), son of a prominent Pittsburgh lawyer and politician and a mother who came from a wealthy family with interests in real estate. He was an 1869 graduate of Lafayette College with a degree in mining and metallurgy who became involved in banking and manufacturing. McKnight helped form the original Allegheny team in 1876 and served for a time as president of the IA. When the AA was formed in the fall of 1881, he became its first president.

The Alleghenies had two big problems, both of which involved liquids. The first was a field that flooded easily, and a rainy spring generally rendered the field unplayable for the first month of the season. The second problem was that their players consumed far too many alcoholic liquids, which led to a third tribulation—the Alleghenies did not play well as a unit. "The Alleghenys [sic] have a strong team," the *Clipper* reported in May 1882, "with good material in it, but it lacks direction and combined action."[42]

Good material and bad intangibles resulted in a mediocre 39–39 record in 1882. The following year brought more troubles when hard-drinking Edward Nolan joined the club. He was released in June, and in August, Billy Taylor, Mike Mansell, and George Creamer were fined and briefly suspended for drunkenness. Manager O.P. Butler clashed with captain Ed Swartwood and was replaced by Joe Battin. This time the talent couldn't make up for the troubled nature of the team and the Alleghenies tumbled to seventh with a 31–67 record.

Allegheny fans were able to tolerate drunks who won at least half the time, but the seventh-place finish tried their patience. At the end of the season, an irate stockholder wrote an anonymous letter to the *Pittsburg Times,* severely criticizing the management of the club, including the decision to reserve so many of the troublemakers who had contributed to the woes of 1883.

On October 10, 1883, the club held a special stockholders' meeting. McKnight began the session by stating that the finances of the club were in a precarious state and appointed a committee to audit the accounts. A stockholder (perhaps the one who'd written the letter) wanted to know why the nine from 1883 had been reserved after such a poor season marked by bad behavior. Potential managers for 1884 were discussed and the stockholders asked about the possibility of hiring Harry Wright, Frank Bancroft, or Chick Fulmer, none of whom was available.

At a second meeting on the 16th, it was announced that the audit showed the club $1,400 in arrears, with no money to make a $1,000 salary payment that was due the next day. Varying factions were vying for control of the club and stockholders were reluctant to contribute any money until they knew who was going to be in charge. With their salaries unpaid, the players claimed they were not bound by the reserve rule. Finally, at a meeting on October 29, a new group of investors agreed to acquire the stock and provide the needed funds. Ten thousand dollars was raised, which was sufficient to pay the arrearages and engage players for 1884. McKnight was chosen as manager.

In order to regain the confidence of their fans, the Alleghenies signed players who acted better and drank less than the disreputable crew from 1883. Unfortunately, the talent they selected was sober but unremarkable, and it was unlikely that the better-behaved 1884 Alleghenies would play much better than the rowdies of the previous year.

Thus constituted, the bottom-heavy AA commenced the 1884 season, burdened with too many teams but buoyed by the optimism that was *de rigueur* at the start of every season. "The American Association," said *Sporting Life,* "is taking on the spirit that was formerly with the National League—that of cooperative working for the common good. In the League, on the contrary, each club seems to be for itself, and with no thought for the welfare of the League."[43] With so many weak sisters, it was incumbent upon the stronger clubs to be altruistic if the Association were to survive, but when survival is at stake, altruism generally takes a back seat. It would be an interesting season.

# 11

# The Wreckers

*Union Association Preview*

Throughout the long history of major league baseball, the adage "two's company while three's a crowd" has been proven correct time and again. The National League was alone from 1876 through 1881 and 1892 through 1900, and neither period was particularly prosperous. It was not loneliness that caused the problem. It was the lingering effects of the Panic of 1873 in the first instance and the Panic of 1893 in the second. There were no other leagues because the poor operating results discouraged potential competitors.

Two-league baseball has generally been prosperous, provided the leagues colluded effectively and avoided salary wars, but years in which there were three major leagues have always been ruinous. The Brotherhood War of 1890 was a financial disaster. The advent of the Federal League in 1914 and 1915 sent salaries soaring and all three leagues lost money.

The first year featuring three major leagues was 1884. The peace treaty between the American Association and National League had been in place for just a year when a third league joined the party and spoiled the fun.

In the fall of 1883, two new organizations announced their intention to begin play in 1884. The first, called the Union League, wanted to become a party to the National Agreement. The second, called the Union Association, planned to operate independently of the NL and AA, and while it would honor existing contracts, the UA planned to sign players who had been reserved by their teams but had not signed contracts.

The Union Association was first conceived by Al Pratt, former major league pitcher who'd been tangentially involved in the formation of the AA. He sent letters to several men, including Tom Pratt (no relation) of Philadelphia, A.H. Henderson, a mattress manufacturer who operated a team in Chicago in 1883, and former major leaguer Warren White of Washington, to see if they were interested in forming a new league. When it did not appear there was sufficient interest, Pratt dropped out.

The others wanted to pursue the idea and made a connection with St. Louis native Henry Van Noye Lucas, who had inherited more than a million dollars from his father ten years earlier.[1] Lucas, a 26-year-old who stood a stocky 5'8" and sported a dapper dark mustache, was connected to the city's elite by his father's money and his marriage to the daughter of a prominent St. Louis businessman; his wife's brother-in-law served as mayor for six years.

The elder Lucas, said to be the wealthiest man in St. Louis, made his money in real estate, but his sons had baseball rather than real estate in their blood. Henry's older brother John played with local teams and was president of the old NA St. Louis Brown Stockings. Henry attended nearly every Browns game in 1882 and 1883 and laid out a baseball field on his large estate, on which he played games with his friends. Young men with large amounts of inherited money tend to spend it on vices, and Lucas' vice was baseball. When he became involved with the UA and announced his intention to sign the NL and AA's biggest stars, owners from the other two leagues wished Lucas had more traditional weaknesses like women or alcohol.

The NL and AA were not about to let Lucas start his new league without opposition, for his attack on the reserve rule was a thrust at the heart of their enterprise. *American Sports* of Chicago stated, "[T]he new Association proposes to adopt the club-wrecking policy and go into the 'cut throat' business helter skelter."[2] For the rest of its existence, the UA was referred to by its enemies as "Wreckers" and chief villain Lucas was called either the "Wrecker" or "Millionaire Lucas."

*American Sports* perused the list of men involved with the new organization and found no one they liked. "The organization savors of the wildcat species all through," it warned. "Nevertheless, a wildcat may scratch around and do considerable mischief when people are off their guard."[3]

The men of the Union Association were called wreckers because they would wreck the sport, they would dilute the talent and, most important, they would wreck the profitability of professional baseball by driving up salaries. The reserve rule had created stability and prosperity, and for nearly a century afterward, executives and many players insisted that baseball could not survive without it. By ignoring the rule, Lucas would be the death of them all.

The two leading national sporting journals were both supportive of the new league. "Surely," the *New York Clipper* wrote in mid–December, "if the American Association could start its organization with six clubs and exist a whole season while ignored by the League—as they did in 1882—the Union Association can do likewise, starting as it will with teams better calculated to draw public patronage than the American clubs were when they started."[4]

Much of the sympathy for the UA was based on the fact that they were fighting the reserve clause, which many considered unjust. The *Clipper* criticized the NL and AA for threatening to blacklist any player who signed with the UA. "There is but one offense for which a player should be forever disbarred," the *Clipper* stated, "from re-entering the professional arena, and that is for proven dishonesty ... the action of the Union clubs is not that of a war upon League or American contracts, but simply upon the reserve-men rule."[5]

The opinions of the *Clipper* were those of veteran writer Henry Chadwick, who had been frozen out of the formation of the NL by William Hulbert and nursed a grudge against Hulbert ever after. He had been very supportive of the AA and now took up the cause of the upstart organization. But while he was supportive, Chadwick sometimes had his doubts. "I do not see for the life of me," he wrote on one occasion, "what the Union Association hopes to exist upon. There are only one or two nines of any strength whatever, and which can make attractive base-ball."[6]

*Sporting Life* was more optimistic. "American Association officials sneer at the new Union Association," it said. "Only two short years ago the National League sneered at the American Association. History will repeat itself, as usual."[7] "The organizing work of the new Union Association shows plainly that old and experienced men are at work and that it can be neither sneered nor frowned down."[8]

But the NL and AA unceasingly sneered and frowned down upon the UA, an attitude some found unbecoming. "[A] most unscrupulous fight has been waged against the clubs composing the Union Association," said one paper. "So relentlessly have they been pursued and so unfair and disreputable have been the methods employed to kill them off that public sympathy has been excited on their behalf ... the end of the season will find O.P. Caylor and his unconscionable colleagues dangling, like many another piratical crew, at their own yard-arm."[9]

Their Herculean efforts notwithstanding, the NL and AA weren't able to prevent Lucas from getting his new venture off the ground. "Despite every effort to discourage the movement," proclaimed Wright and Ditson's Union Association Guide, "the Union Association of Base Ball Clubs has been formed. Its object will be to cater to the public taste, to give the best attainable sport at popular prices, and to foster and encourage our national game."[10] "In case the association lives through one season," Lucas said, "the older associations will be compelled to do business with us in the future."[11] "The national game has achieved such popularity with the masses," he said, "that we can all survive."[12]

The inaugural convention of the new league took place on December 18 at the Bingham House in Philadelphia, a meeting attended by representatives from St. Louis, Chicago, Cincinnati, Philadelphia, Baltimore, and Washington. Lucas was elected president[13] and Tom Pratt, a former star pitcher of the 1860s who'd become a successful businessman, was chosen vice president. Warren White, a third baseman with the Washington NA clubs, was secretary. The directors were Henderson, Justus Thorner, and H.B. Bennett of Washington. Many baseball men, including Harry Wright and Bob Ferguson, roamed the corridors of the Bingham House while the UA leaders conferred, as did some of the most prominent UA signees. Perhaps Lucas wanted to show them off, or maybe he just didn't want them out of his sight, for the NL and AA were desperately trying to get most of them back.

The UA had one of the key ingredients for a fledgling league—deep pockets. Lucas was a millionaire at a time when it meant something and like most millionaires, he kept company with other rich men. His friend Ellis Wainwright, president of the Wainwright Brewing Company, was supposedly worth $2 million, and a third friend, brewer Adolph Busch, was also a man of substance.[14] A.H. Henderson, who was behind the teams in Chicago and Baltimore, had the backing of the Chicago Street Cable Railroad Company.[15] Another capitalist named Dennison was reported to have contributed $40,000 to the UA. Despite all of his wealthy associates, however, it was the money of Henry Lucas that would drive the Union Association.

The UA had a tougher road than the AA faced in 1882, since virtually all major cities were occupied by the two existing leagues and there were far fewer available players than there had been two years earlier. Not only were there two other major leagues; there were more minor leagues, relegating the UA to engaging players who, for the most part, had little or no major league experience.

The only way to attract top talent was to offer big salaries, and the UA began making generous overtures to some of the NL and AA's best players. While Lucas portrayed himself as an instrument through which the players could break the chains of the reserve rule, it appeared that most players were more concerned with the amount of money he was willing to pay them. If they could get more by consenting to be reserved, they would sign with the NL or AA and deal with next year's contract when next year arrived. The main question he was asked, Lucas said, was whether his teams had the financial strength and staying power to pay the large salaries they offered.

One way to assure players they would be paid was to give them a substantial percentage up front, a risky proposition. But the UA had little choice, for players were reluctant to take the risk of being stranded on the blacklist without any money if the UA failed. "[N]o man who has signed with us," said Warren White, "to my knowledge, has been refused ample security for his salary if he so wished."[16] By early December, it was estimated that the UA had as many as 30 men under contract.

Meanwhile, the NL and AA prepared for war. "They [the NL and AA] are both arrayed against us," said White, "and have been and are doing everything in their power to crush us, but we are too strong for them financially, and have too many good ballplayers on our side."[17]

The two older leagues tried to get every minor league to sign on to the National Agreement, which would prohibit their clubs from playing exhibitions against UA teams or even playing on grounds used by UA clubs. Exhibition games were a significant component of the 1884 baseball economic model and by limiting potential opponents, they hoped to starve Lucas of revenue.

The Eastern League (formerly the Union League), which had made a move toward affiliating with the UA, received generous concessions for signing the National Agreement. "It was made up for no other purpose," said one paper, "than to freeze out the new Union Association, and had this new venture never been thought of the officials of the older organizations would have treated all applications for membership and recognition from the small associations as they have always done, with contempt."[18]

The NL and AA signed more players than usual to keep them out of the clutches of the UA. Several clubs established reserve teams in order to tie up more men. The reserves could give the regulars practice before the season began and then serve as a source of replacements. They could also provide motivation for those on the regular roster, who knew that if they faltered or misbehaved, a replacement was only a telegram away. During the season, reserve teams would play when their major league team was on the road, especially if a UA team from the same city was playing at home.

It wasn't long before reserve teams didn't seem like such a good idea. With a record number of major league teams in the field, the last thing the fans needed was more games. Attendance was meager, and it was reported that the Pittsburgh reserves netted two dollars from one game in St. Louis and a total of $42 from the three-game series. The reserve team concept was quickly abandoned; Boston had the only team that lasted through the season, playing to small crowds and losing money. They did contribute a couple of players, catcher Tom Gunning and pitcher John Connor, to the Beaneaters late in the season.

The teams bound by the National Agreement formed a united front under the leadership of Abraham Mills, a corporate attorney who was a vice president of the Otis Elevator Company. In a letter to AA president Denny McKnight, Mills wrote, "[I] do not think it wise to under-estimate the strength of the enemy. We should all exert the utmost vigilance and defeat as far as possible their efforts to entice away our players."[19]

In mid–December, Mills wrote to Northwestern League president Elias Matter about the difficulties created by the UA. "They are certainly giving us a good deal of trouble, and while I do not really think they will live through the season, yet they have plenty of money, are able to do a great deal of damage, and must be fought with determination and vigour."[20] He wrote to the owners looking for information he could use to discredit the Union Association and asked Philadelphia president Al Reach to see if he could obtain some intelligence from the UA meeting at the Bingham House. "As I have no doubt I will soon be in an open fight with this Union Association," he wrote to Arthur Soden, "I want all the ammunition obtainable and I want to answer every allegation made by them, or in their behalf, which can be squarely and fairly met."[21]

At its convention on December 12, the AA declared that any of its clubs that played against a team that defied the National Agreement (those teams being, of course, UA teams) would be expelled, even if the UA team had not signed an AA player. Mills forbade college teams from playing UA nines if they wanted games against National Agreement clubs.

In February, Mills wrote a long letter to John Hadley Doyle, baseball editor of Washington's *Sunday Herald,* in which he set forth a detailed explanation of his position. The National Agreement and the reserve rule, Mills said, were for the protection of both clubs and players and were essential to the continuing success of professional baseball.[22] Territorial restrictions were not monopolistic; they were intended to avoid ruinous competition. Baltimore could not support three clubs, Mills said, nor could Washington support two.

Several UA owners, he pointed out, had tried to gain admission to the NL or AA, and at that time expressed their willingness to adhere to the existing rules. It was only when they were rejected that they decided the rules were unacceptable. These men cared little for the rights of the players, Mills insisted; they only wanted to induce them to sign with the new league.

Mills pointed out that Warren White initially said his league didn't want any men who didn't want to play with them, but once players hinted at returning to their original teams, Lucas said he would engage a team of lawyers to fight them. "[H]e must be a child indeed," Mills noted sarcastically, "in law as well as in base ball, who believes that a ball player can be compelled to play a game of ball by legal process ... resorting to legal processes to compel him to pitch an in-shoot or make a home run."

The best the UA could do, Mills said, was to get an injunction to prevent the men from playing with another club. "A Union club with nine injunctions instead of nine ball players," he scoffed, "would probably not contribute materially to the exhibition of the National Game."

His long letter, Mills told Hadley, merely represented his own opinion, although he believed most of the League owners stood behind him. "Personally," he concluded, "I have no unkindly feeling toward gentlemen identified with the Union Association, but I sincerely believe that they are injuring the best interests of baseball without any reasonable prospect of deriving advantage for themselves."

Two of the biggest names to sign with the UA were second baseman Fred Dunlap of Cleveland and pitcher Larry Corcoran of Chicago. Dunlap, who signed with Lucas' St. Louis club, was one of the best players in baseball. He was a four-year NL veteran, a .300 hitter, and a great second baseman. Although many players wore gloves by 1884, Dunlap never did, relying on his small, supple hands. He was equally adept with either hand, although he didn't throw left-handed.

Dunlap also had star quality; he was a handsome man who was fastidious about his appearance. Mike Kelly, who knew about such things, called Dunlap the sharpest dresser in the game.[23] Although illiterate, he was clever and frugal, and was reported to be well off.

Corcoran, who'd won 134 games for the White Stockings the past four years, signed with Henderson's Chicago UA club for a reported $3,400 per year, with $1,000 in advance.[24] Henderson expected to have a strong rotation, for he had also signed pitcher Hugh "One Arm" Daily, who won 23 games for Cleveland in 1883.

Daily, who would have more accurately been nicknamed "One Hand," lost his left hand in a theater accident as a teen-ager. He was an irascible sort who generally made enemies wherever he went (he never spent more than one season with a club), railing at hitters, teammates, management, and reporters.[25] A man with a physical handicap is a naturally sympathetic figure, but Daily usually managed to make people dislike him. When he pitched for Buffalo in 1882, one paper claimed that his teammates were intentionally playing poorly behind him in the hopes that he would be released. When he was with the Metropolitans, he got angry with catcher Pat Deasley over the signs one day, called Deasley to the box, and punched him with his left stump.[26] The one place Daily seemed welcome was his home town of Baltimore, where he usually received a warm welcome as a visiting player. Of course, they didn't see him that often.

President Mills wrote a supportive letter to Cleveland president George Howe after hearing the news that Dunlap had signed with Lucas. "Dunlap is still one of your reserved players," Mills wrote, "whether he remains absent in the St. Louis club two months, or ten years. Nothing can terminate such reservation, except his release by your club." He urged Howe to stand strong for, "[I]f all our clubs toe the mark, and observe the rules this year, I have no doubt whatever that we will kill off the St. Louis Wrecker, and all other clubs which float the black flag."[27] He predicted that Dunlap would return to Cleveland and Corcoran would end up back with the White Stockings and reiterated that any player who was blacklisted for signing with the UA would never play for an NL or AA team again.

The NL waged a spirited battle to entice Dunlap, who would be the UA's best player, to return to the fold. NL and AA teams, particularly the Mets, tried to convince Cleveland to release him so they could sign him and keep him away from the UA. Dunlap, who came from Philadelphia, supposedly wanted to play for an eastern team, but Cleveland wouldn't budge and Dunlap stayed with Lucas.

For men who preached the sanctity of the contract, NL and AA owners tried very hard to get their former players to break their new agreements. "They have renounced players who have jumped the reserve rule to the extent of their vocabulary of invectives," said one paper, "and would have the public believe that these players are dishonest beyond reformation. At the same time they are laboring actively and incessantly to see them break faith with the Union Association and sign where they have been reserved."[28]

AA president McKnight was an eager collaborator when it came to poaching UA signees. "What has become of Denny McKnight?" the pro–UA *Cincinnati Enquirer* wrote in March. "He has not induced anyone to break a contract in five weeks."[29]

McKnight sent one UA signee a letter "to the effect that the latter should have joined such a weak cause as the Unions, and advising him to get out of it before he was lost."[30] McKnight didn't think much of the upstart league's long-term prospects. "They may pull through," he said, "but that is about all. The only manager who is putting up the money is Lucas, of St. Louis."[31] He thought that some of the men Lucas signed would desert him and some of his backers would pull out, and predicted that the St. Louis and Chicago franchises would do well but the others would struggle.

A.H. Henderson listed his signees and warned, "If any of the above players are tampered with, or if any of the said players attempt to break their contracts with us, both the player and the club engaging him will be dealt with to the full extent of the law, and, in every instance, an injunction will be laid against both the player and the club, preventing the said player from taking part in any game."[32]

Warren White announced that the UA intended to take legal action to prevent defectors from playing with another team and would put them on the UA blacklist. When they banned some contract jumpers in mid-season, the *Detroit Free Press* wrote, "The directors of the wrecking clubs met in Baltimore on Tuesday and voted to expel certain players, who, after they found what manner of company they were in, deserted the gang. This action can only find a parallel in a lot of tramps getting together and excommunicating one of their number who quits tramping and goes to work."[33]

Mills issued a fiery rebuttal to White. "There is not a single paragraph in Mr. White's letter," he wrote, "which does not contain a gross perversion of facts." Mills said that the Agreement was the idea of the Northwestern League; the NL and AA had simply gone along with it. He claimed that the UA was merely a scheme for making money while the other leagues had more lofty aims, although he was not specific. "A cause that needs bolstering up by lying, treachery, and thievery," he concluded, "must be on a good foundation, surely."[34]

During the months of December and January, Mills became deeply involved in trying to help his friend Al Spalding rescue Corcoran from the clutches of the UA, giving him legal advice on the best way to get Corcoran to sign a contract that would supersede that of the UA.[35]

Mills and Cap Anson met personally with Corcoran, a meeting the former described at length in a letter to Spalding. Mills appealed to Corcoran's loyalty and, in the event that was insufficient, threatened him with a life sentence on the blacklist.[36] Corcoran was sufficiently cowed and signed a new contract with the White Stockings. Or maybe he wasn't cowed. After all, Spalding himself said that Corcoran "has not been bulldozed, bribed, or coaxed or frightened."[37] Had anyone suggested he had been? Spalding added that Corcoran was not being compelled to sign due to the reserve clause, but because he had orally agreed to contract terms prior to signing the UA agreement.

The oral agreement was a complicating factor in many disputes and there were endless debates as to whether an agreement to sign a contract constituted a contract. When catcher Charlie Bennett went to court against the Alleghenies in 1882, the judge ruled that an agreement to contract was not a contract, but the issue remained the source of many squabbles.

Throughout the winter, the 1884 UA took shape. "You may say to the public," Lucas told a St. Louis paper, "that the arbitrary rules and dishonorable conduct of the League and American Association will not deter those who have invested their money in the Union Club here from carrying out their purpose. We will play ball this year, and not only this year, but the next, and will remain in the field after many of the League and American Association clubs have become things of the past."[38]

There would be Lucas' team in St. Louis, Henderson's teams in Chicago and Baltimore, Tom Pratt's Philadelphia nine, and the Washington club operated by Mike Scanlon, owner of a local billiard parlor and a long-time fixture in Washington baseball.

That made five teams, which were too few. A six-team league (the AA started with six in 1882) was probably viable, but Lucas wanted eight. There were rumors of a team in Boston (which materialized) and one in Hartford (which did not). In mid–December,

Lucas and Henderson made a trip to Cincinnati to try to boost efforts there and there was talk of teams in Detroit and Pittsburgh. Applications from Evansville, Kansas City, Rock Island, and Wheeling were rejected.

In February, Boston was still on the fence, thinking about the UA or maybe the Eastern League. The discussion was hypothetical, since Boston had neither a team nor a place to play. George Wright, brother of Philadelphia manager Harry Wright and once considered the best baseball player in America, was interested in backing the team and Pratt visited him to try to move things along.[39]

Wright decided to move forward, but by early March, just six weeks before the UA season was scheduled to open, Boston was still short of the capital needed to fund the operation, despite a $1,500 infusion from Lucas. The latter came to Boston and gave Wright until March 15 to raise the money and commit to the UA.

Boston raised a total of $25,000 by Lucas' deadline and engaged Harry McGlennen, treasurer of the Boston Theatre, as business manager. But by not starting until mid-March, they would be hard-pressed to sign enough talent to allow them to be competitive. The market for players was more spirited than ever, and with the season scheduled to begin in just four weeks, Wright and his cohorts had a formidable task ahead of them. A slew of players appeared for tryouts, and after sorting through them, Wright had a team, but it was a patchwork combination. "A nine never started out," said the local *Globe*, "under more discouraging circumstances, the men never having actually played together yet."[40]

Since their grounds had just been leased and needed a great deal of work, Boston arranged to play its early games on the road, with the hope that the park would be ready when they returned. Construction continued around the clock, with electric lights illuminating the field at night.

Cincinnati was expected to have a strong nine. Although the team did not officially join the UA until later, they were represented at the initial convention and Justus Thorner was elected a director. He would handle the baseball and his partner John McLean, owner of the local *Enquirer*, would provide publicity, which he did with enthusiasm, excoriating the local AA club and O.P. Caylor all summer.

The addition of Boston and Cincinnati gave the UA seven teams, one short of Lucas' goal. The final entry came as a surprise, for Altoona, Pennsylvania, was a lot different than UA cities like St. Louis and Cincinnati, which had large populations, mature infrastructure, and were connected by rail to other large cities. Altoona had not been established until 1849, and by the 1880 census had only about 20,000 residents. Although it was a railroad hub, Altoona was not near any large population centers, and not many spectators arrived at games on long distance train rides.

Small towns could produce talented baseball teams, and in 1883 Altoona won the championship of the Western Interstate League[41] while averaging about 1,600 fans per game, pretty good for a minor league team. They defeated the Alleghenies and Philadelphia in exhibitions and a game against the New York National League club drew between four and five thousand spectators.

The future of the Western Interstate League was uncertain, and Altoona planned to play in the Interstate Association in 1884. When that league failed to make it to the starting gate, the city was ready to listen when Henry Lucas came calling in February. Lucas had struck out in Pittsburgh, Detroit, and Hartford, Boston was on the fence, the beginning of the season was not far away, and Altoona, which had not interested him earlier, appealed to him now.

After Lucas' visit, the Altoona stockholders, who included executives of the Pennsylvania Railroad, called a special meeting at which they resolved to apply for admission to the UA. On February 20, they received notification that their application was approved. All they needed was players and the money to pay them and, like Boston, they didn't have much time to acquire either.

Lucas contributed $2,500 to the effort and a similar amount was raised from local businesses, including the Pennsylvania Railroad, which stood to gain additional revenue transporting players and fans. Most of the players were holdovers from the 1883 club, which did not bode well for Altoona's success in a circuit that claimed to be a major league. The UA might not be of the same quality as the NL and AA, but it was light years ahead of the Western Interstate League. "With a couple of exceptions," wrote James Forr, "these were decent, mid-level minor league players masquerading as big leaguers, like little boys parading around in their fathers' shirts."[42]

While last-minute entries Boston and Altoona scrambled to fill their lineups, it was evident that the best talent in the UA was on the roster of Henry Lucas' St. Louis club. It appeared that the UA, even more than the AA, might be an unbalanced league, with great disparities between the good teams and the not so good ones, which would make for very dull baseball. Early on, there had been rumors that all the UA players would be pooled and dispersed among the teams to create a more competitive situation,[43] but Lucas had not formed a league to have his team finish in the middle of the pack.

One of the players signed by Lucas was pitcher Tony Mullane, the first reserved NL or AA player to jump. At the end of 1883, word got around that Mullane would sign with the UA if he could get his release from St. Louis. He didn't but signed anyway, for a $2,500 contract with $500 paid in advance. Some thought Mullane only signed to get more money from the Browns and that his maneuvering wasn't over.

It wasn't long before Mullane started having doubts about the UA and approached the Washington AA team about signing with them. When they declined, he was reportedly ready to rejoin the Browns for $2,200, but then a better offer came along. In late January, Mullane went to Toledo and, after spending a few days with manager Charlie Morton, who'd managed him at Akron in 1881, agreed to sign for roughly the same terms he'd accepted from Lucas. The contract was contingent upon obtaining a release from the St. Louis AA club, and Browns president Chris Von der Ahe agreed to grant it, saying he didn't want Mullane back.

Meanwhile, Lucas said he would take legal action to prevent Mullane from playing with Toledo, although he wasn't sure he wanted to enforce his contract. If Mullane were compelled to play for St. Louis under protest, Lucas reasoned, he wasn't likely to give his best effort. But when Mullane offered to return the $500 advance he'd received from Lucas, the latter refused to accept it.

Lucas was so disgusted that he said if he could use the courts to get Mullane back on his team, he wouldn't be pitching, he would man the gate and take tickets. "If he has any tickets to take, or gates to guard," teased the *Detroit Free Press*.[44] The same paper, noting that Dunlap had a two-year contract, said, "What possible use Mr. Lucas will have for a base ball player in 1885 is a mystery."[45]

Even with a release from the Browns, Mullane couldn't sign with Toledo until ten days had passed. Lucas dispatched manager Ted Sullivan to Toledo to talk to Mullane, but Sullivan couldn't find him. When he arrived, Sullivan was taken in hand by an old friend, who also happened to be a friend of the Toledo club and made sure that

Sullivan wasn't successful. When Ted didn't find Mullane in Toledo, he followed his trail to Erie, Buffalo, and Cleveland, but didn't find him in any of those cities. When he returned to Toledo, he was told his quarry was in Akron, and off he went. But by that time, Mullane and Morton were on their way to Wheeling, and all the while the ten-day clock was ticking.[46]

There was a rumor afloat that the AA had pooled its funds to provide money to entice men to jump their UA contracts, and that Toledo had tapped it to sign Mullane. Cincinnati's Jacob Stern and St. Louis' Jimmy Williams hotly denied the existence of a fund and Williams wrote a long letter to *Sporting Life* denying that anyone in the AA had encouraged Mullane to break his UA contract.[47]

In early April, Lucas said Mullane had contacted him and said he would accept a contract for $3,000 per year for two years. When Lucas said he would accept, Mullane demanded the full $3,000 in advance, which Lucas refused. Mullane claimed it was Lucas who approached him, with the offer of a large advance, which he declined. After all the unsavory maneuvering and rampant rumors, Mullane opened the season with Toledo.

When the wandering hurler pitched for Toledo in St. Louis on May 4, the fans jeered his every move. Lucas, as promised, went to court and obtained an injunction prohibiting Mullane from appearing in the State of Missouri with any club other than his UA team and contemplated filing suit against Toledo for inducing Mullane to break his UA contract.[48] If the injunction held, Mullane would be unable to pitch against the Browns in St. Louis. In mid–May, however, the court vacated the temporary injunction,

Tony Mullane was one of the most talented and least principled players of his time. Before and after the 1884 season, Mullane was engaged in highly questionable contractual dealings. He wound up being suspended for the 1885 season for violating an agreement to sign a contract with St. Louis of the American Association (National Baseball Hall of Fame Library, Cooperstown, N.Y.).

on the grounds that the legal system shouldn't waste its time on frivolous activities like baseball.

The Mullane incident was the Fort Sumpter of the UA conflict. "The result of all this business," one paper wrote, "will be that there will be a deliberate and open beginning of operations on a war basis very soon and the Union clubs will get players anywhere and any way and, of course, there will be a series of retaliatory actions on the part of the League and American Associations. For a time it will be war to the knife and the mere existence of a contract will cut no figure in the matter."[49]

Mullane and Corcoran were not the only players to desert the UA. The pressure applied by the National League and American Association was effective, and in late February, *Sporting Life* reported that 16 men had deserted the Union ranks.[50]

Pitcher George Bradley, a 31-year-old veteran of nine big league seasons who'd signed with the Cincinnati UA club, was one of the AA's prime targets. Bradley, who pitched the first NL no-hitter and set a record with 16 shutouts in 1876, a mark that has never been bettered, appeared to be on the downhill side of his career. But he was a big name and enticing him away from the UA would be a coup.

In early April 1884, Horace Phillips, O.P. Caylor, and Chick Fulmer went to Cincinnati to try to convince Bradley to return to the Athletics. Situations like this were often facilitated by getting the target drunk, but unfortunately for the Philadelphians, Bradley didn't drink.[51] Nevertheless, the mission had all the cloak and dagger aspects of a spy thriller. Fulmer and Phillips, who was allegedly paid to turn Bradley around, coaxed him away from the Crawford House, where UA officials were keeping an eye on him. They put him in a hack, drove him around the city, told him the UA would never get off the ground and he would be blacklisted. They offered him money to go back on his contract. Fulmer gave Bradley $20 for train fare to Philadelphia and brought him to the station.

Two Cincinnati players heard of Bradley's attempted abduction and alerted manager Dan O'Leary, who was eating supper at the Gibson House. O'Leary dashed to the station and "In language more forceful than elegant he expressed his contempt for Fulmer and Phillips, who cringed before him like the lying whelps that they are."[52] O'Leary took Bradley in tow and brought him to meet with one of the Cincinnati directors, who apparently calmed whatever fears Bradley may have had about the UA. Shortly afterward, he sent a telegram to fellow UA signees Fred Dunlap and George Shaffer indicating that he planned to remain loyal to the UA.

Caylor, who was involved in several attempts to damage the UA, denied doing anything untoward. He said he simply told Bradley that if he didn't think the Union Association would last, he should return to Philadelphia. The pitcher had a wife and five children to support and would, Caylor warned him, end up like Jim Devlin, who'd been reduced to a beggar after he was expelled from the NL for throwing games.

The battle continued all summer. In June, 21-year-old first baseman Joe Quinn of the St. Louis Maroons was approached with an offer to join Washington of the AA. Leaving a team funded by the well-heeled Lucas for the shaky Washington franchise was a hard sell, and purportedly Ted Sullivan was involved in the attempt. Quinn was Sullivan's protégé from his Dubuque days, and when Ted resigned as the Maroons' manager, Quinn was concerned that he had no future in St. Louis.

Sullivan denied any involvement and Lucas said the approach was made in such an indirect manner that he wasn't sure who was behind it. Washington manager Hollingshead blamed the entire incident on the media. Quinn stayed put but the controversy, which came at about the same time Hugh Daily said he received a lucrative offer to desert the UA, played a role in Lucas' decision to declare war on NL and AA contracts beginning July 1.

That was in the future, and in mid–March, with a full complement of eight teams, the Union Association gathered for a final time to prepare for the season. "[T]he delegates," reported *Sporting Life*, "then found time to congratulate each other on the present brilliant outlook for a successful season. They do not expect to clear a barrel of money on the season, but will be satisfied with a fair return and will not grumble even at a loss on their investments the first season."[53]

Henry Lucas had formed an outlaw league, but he had little choice. Had he become a party to the National Agreement, he would have had to abide by the territorial restrictions that would keep his league out of virtually every major city. It was impossible for any league that aspired to major league status to consist of clubs from virgin territory. The open towns and cities were simply too small.

The second dilemma for a fledgling organization was finding players. Were the UA to acknowledge the reserve rule, it would be very difficult for them to sign any quality players, since the reserve had been expanded to include nearly everyone on a major league roster. A league with small town teams and second tier players could not, in the wildest throes of its imagination, claim to be a major league.

The Union Association was prepared for battle, but it was a fight against long odds, against the combined resources of the National League and American Association, plus minor leagues tied to them by the National Agreement. The primary weapon at the UA's disposal was the wealth of Henry Lucas, who not only financed his own club but helped capitalize some of his opponents. Historian David Voigt called the National Association "Harry Wright's League," but never before or since has a league been more clearly the creation of one person than the UA of Henry Lucas. "I am the Union Association," he once said. "Whatever I do is right."[54] Lucas against the rest of the baseball world was an uneven battle, but the young St. Louisan possessed the unbounded confidence that comes with inherited wealth and he was ready for the fight.

"All we have to do," he said, "is hold out this year, and next we can get all the players we want—the pick of the country, in fact. The players are praying for our success, because they know it will be the death of the reserve rule, and we propose to see that their prayers are answered."[55]

A National League man thought differently. "Yes," he said, "I think the Union Association will survive the season, but that is all. They will be unable to arrange games outside their own Association. Their clubs are unevenly matched and after the novelty of their first games the public will naturally drift over to the League and the American Association."[56] It was a prescient prediction.

# 12

## "He said he'd pitch his arm off to win the flag"

*National League Season*

The New York Gothams left the gate like John Day thought they would, winning their first 12 games, the best start of any NL team since the League was formed in 1876. Mickey Welch won seven games, John Ward three, and Ed Begley the other two. That was a good sign, for having three solid starting pitchers was a unique advantage.

The streak came to an end against Buffalo on May 17, and by June 4, New York, plagued by a rash of injuries, had slipped to 18–10, having lost 10 of 16 games. Apparently, there was already some dissatisfaction with the ability of manager James Price to control the nine, and on May 3, New York signed veteran infielder and manager Bob Ferguson. Ferguson was well-known in New York, having been the captain of the famous old Atlantic Club in the pre–NA era. He was one of the best umpires in baseball, known for his scrupulous honesty and knowledge of the rules. He was also one of the most despised managers in baseball, a domineering martinet hated by most men who played under him.

By 1884, Ferguson had been run out of Brooklyn, Hartford, Chicago, and Troy, dogged by tales of dissension and bullying. When he was brought to New York with the intention of placing him in charge of the Gothams, several of the players who'd been under his despotic thumb in Troy put up such a clamor that Ferguson was dismissed before he ever managed a game. He was a tough negotiator and the team supposedly had to pay him $1,000 to void his contract.

After a New York loss to Providence on May 26, the *Clipper* noted, "The New-Yorkers find the Providence team to be the only team they do not play with confidence against this season."[1] That would prove problematic, for the Grays had also gotten off to a flying start, boasting a 17–2 mark after their victory over New York. "The Providence men have started off with the lead," said the *New York Times*, "but the general impression is that they will not win the championship laurels, they being regarded as 'quitters.'"[2]

Perhaps the biggest surprise was the fact that Cap Anson's White Stockings were near the bottom of the pack. Chicago was the class of the league, winning the championship each year from 1880 to 1882 and finishing second in 1883. "The reasons why the public enjoy seeing the Chicagos play," said a Buffalo paper, "is because they are so admirably trained and their work from beginning to end is characterized by confidence, determination, courage and energy. There is more dash and brilliancy about their game than that of any other club and, although they are not always successful in winning, that is why they are so popular."[3]

### Standings on May 26

|            | W  | L  | Pct. | GB   |
|------------|----|----|------|------|
| Providence | 17 | 2  | .895 | —    |
| Boston     | 17 | 4  | .810 | 1    |
| New York   | 15 | 5  | .750 | 2½   |
| Buffalo    | 9  | 11 | .450 | 8½   |
| Philadelphia | 7 | 13 | .350 | 10½  |
| Cleveland  | 6  | 12 | .333 | 10½  |
| Chicago    | 5  | 14 | .263 | 12   |
| Detroit    | 2  | 17 | .105 | 15   |

The White Stockings' play in early 1884 was anything but dashing and brilliant. Spalding had decided not to send his team to a warmer climate for early practice and the cold of Chicago made it difficult to get the players in shape. While other clubs were barnstorming and playing top competition, Chicago battled rain and biting wind and only played against their reserve team.

When the season began, the White Stockings were hampered by injuries. Star outfielder George Gore was suffering from a bad ankle and infielder Tommy Burns from a sore arm, but the Chicago press wasn't interested in excuses. The *Tribune* complained, "It is a club capable of the best and worst playing of any in the league, and it has been with extraordinary persistency done its worst this year."[4] Anson's disciplinary plans were not working. "Chicago is wretchedly, hopelessly behind," added the *St. Louis Post-Dispatch*, "and they say that John Barleycorn has been aiding the opposing clubs in putting them there."[5] The *Tribune* suggested that some of the worst-behaved White Stockings be placed on the blacklist.

The Chicago press gave up early. "There is no evidence whatever," said the *Tribune* less than three weeks into the season, "that the pennant will return to Chicago" noting "the manner in which many of the games have been lost—by going to pieces when the game was well in hand."[6]

A superficial glance at statistics would seem to indicate that Chicago had a very powerful offense, but appearances were deceiving. The White Stockings hit 142 home runs (Buffalo had the second-best total with 39),[7] but that was because the outfield fences at Lake Front Park were ridiculously close to home plate. The left field fence was just 180 feet away and the right field barrier, although protected by a 17-and-a-half-foot tarpaulin above a 20-foot wooden fence, was an inviting 196 feet. The barrier angled back to 280 in left center, but only to 252 feet in right center. The center field fence was only 300 feet away.

Grounds rules were really grounds rules in the 19th century, and they varied from park to park and sometimes from game to game. A ball hit over the fence or into an overflow crowd on the fly or on the bounce wasn't necessarily a home run or a double. In 1883, a ball hit over the short fences at Lake Front Park on the fly was a double, but in 1884 the rule was changed and anything over the fence was a home run. The change had an immediate impact, as Abner Dalrymple, the first man to bat in the opening game, homered. In the bottom of the first inning, Detroit's George Wood led off with a home run. The White Stockings hit a total of five homers in the game.

The following day, Chicago's Ned Williamson became the first major leaguer to hit three home runs in a game (he added two doubles). On July 9, Anson hit two home runs and Williamson and Pfeffer one each. In the 855 games that were not played in Chicago in 1884, there were a total of 124 home runs. In 57 games at Lake Front Park, there were 197.

After Anson hit five homers in two games, the *Clipper* commented, "A correspondent states that Anson's three home-runs in the Chicago-Cleveland game, August 6, gives that player's record a big sound, but that on any other League grounds than those of Chicago the record would be about three singles. The writer further states that the over-the-fence-home-run rule is a sham and a burlesque."[8]

During one series between Buffalo and Chicago, the top two power hitting teams in the league, there were a total of 37 round-trippers. Late in the season, one paper commented, "Anson has passed O'Rourke in the batting list, and a certain ballist remarked that if the right field fence is moved up to first base, the Chicago team as a whole may lead the League."[9] The White Stockings wound up with the top four home run hitters in the NL. Williamson hit 27, Fred Pfeffer 25, Abner Dalrymple 22, and Anson 21, with big Dan Brouthers of Buffalo next at a legitimate 14.

Williamson's 27 homers (25 in Chicago) set a one-season record that would last until Babe Ruth hit 29 in 1919. He held the National League record until Rogers Hornsby hit 42 in 1922. Williamson was a fluky home run champion who hit a total of just 64 in his career, but he was a very good player. "Ed was, in my opinion," wrote Anson, "the greatest all-around ballplayer the country ever saw."[10] Playing in the Chicago bandbox, Williamson learned to clear the short fences and the previous season, when such hits counted as doubles, he had 49 of them.[11] At the end of the season, the National League passed a rule that any ball hit over a fence less than 210 feet from home plate would be a double.

Anson's biggest problem was the behavior of his team, which was just as bad as it had been for the past several years. The press urged expelling the worst offenders. Spalding suggested that Anson hire detectives to keep an eye

Ned Williamson hit an astonishing 27 home runs in 1884, nearly twice the previous record. The reason was that the fences in his home park were astonishingly close to home plate. Williamson may not have been a legitimate home run champion, but he was an excellent ballplayer who could play several positions skillfully (National Baseball Hall of Fame Library, Cooperstown, N.Y.).

on the players while the team was on the road and blamed his team's drinking on Henry Lucas. "This year," Spalding said, "it has been impossible to discipline and control the men in their habits on account of the bad influence exerted by the Union Association. If we rebuked or attempted to punish a player for dissipation we were met with the reply, 'Well, if you don't like it, I'll go elsewhere.'"[12]

One night in Boston, Anson decided to conduct a bed check. When he knocked on one door, he was refused entry by a player whose roommate was out on the town. Anson stood on a chair in the hallway, looked over the transom and lit a match to see what was going on inside. The player threw a pillow at Anson, which extinguished the match and dislodged Anson's head from above the transom, nearly knocking him to the floor. The player was fined $100.[13]

In Buffalo, Anson fined catcher Frank Flint a total of $170, which elicited an angry tirade from Flint. Anson and Williamson got into an argument over a poker game, during which Williamson threatened Anson with a water pitcher. By the end of the season, the two men weren't speaking. "The managers of the Chicago B.B.C. are disgusted with the club," said *Sporting Life*, "but not as much so as the public."[14] "The Chicagos are dissipating again," reported a Buffalo paper, "and two of them, names not given, have been fined $50."[15]

Previous Chicago teams had won in spite of their drinking, but they'd had strong pitching. In 1884, half of Anson's vaunted two-man rotation broke down. "Goldsmith," reported *Sporting Life*, "either cannot or will not do his share of the work properly."[16] For much of the previous winter, Goldsmith had been troubled by a bad ankle and when the season began it was apparent that he could no longer throw hard. Goldsmith always had a lackadaisical, somewhat odd manner, and Anson was often displeased with his work ethic but, like everyone's drinking, all was well when the White Stockings were winning. When Goldsmith pitched poorly, his quirky habits got on Anson's nerves. He hinted that Goldsmith was intentionally pitching poorly in order to get his release and sign a better contract elsewhere.

In a mid–June game against Buffalo, Goldsmith was unavailable and Anson had to start the sore-armed Corcoran, who was hit hard. By the end of the game Anson had employed four pitchers, a remarkable total for 1884, especially since Chicago had only two regular pitchers. The game was a farcical encounter won by Buffalo 20–9 and by the end of the afternoon Anson lost his temper, taking out his frustration on poor umpire Eugene Van Court. He and his players argued every close call, as if more favorable umpiring could make up an eleven-run deficit.

Finally, at the end of August, with a 9–11 record and a 4.26 ERA, Goldsmith was released. He signed with Baltimore, where he proved he was not faking by pitching in just four games before going down with a shoulder injury that ended his once-brilliant career. Goldsmith's departure left Anson with a one-man rotation, and although he experimented with a number of pitchers, he didn't find a capable one until late in the season. Meanwhile, the overworked Corcoran struggled. After pitching five games in a row in early August, his arm was so sore he was pounded for nine runs in the first inning of his next start.

From the time Chicago assembled its first professional team in 1870, the local press had blown hot and cold. When the team won, the papers were insufferably boastful, and when they lost, they lit into the club with venom. As the White Stockings fell off the pace in 1884, the press piled on Anson and his players. "We observe," noted the *Chicago News* wryly, "by the telegraphic dispatches that nine young persons, professing to be a Chicago base ball club, are wandering about the country for the evident purpose of bringing the athletes of this metropolis into disrepute. We refuse to recognize as genuine any alleged Chicago organization that suffers itself to become a door mat or lap-robe for other similar organizations."[17] The *Tribune* added, "The Chicago ball team is made up largely of cripples, bums, and bigheads. There are perhaps four players who do not belong in either of those classifications, and there are some who belong in all three."[18] "If another arctic expedition is organized, we want in time to speak for a berth for our base ball nine."[19]

It was a long season in Chicago. The team that had won three consecutive titles retained their swagger in the saloon but lost it on the ballfield. "[T]he day has gone by," said one journal, "when their 'dreaded name' beat the boys; they have to play ball now in order to do it."[20] Another added, "The once almost invincible Chicagos ... [are] no longer looked upon with awe and fear by the other contestants in the race, as they seem to have lost their vitality and are nothing more than an average League team."[21]

As the disappointing season went on, Anson got cranky. The Chicago captain was a "kicker" from way back, even during his early days in Marshalltown when it was considered rude. In the old NA, his Athletics were one of the more ill-behaved teams and Anson was right in the middle of it. "[W]hile his claims may be legitimate so far as the rule is concerned," wrote John Montgomery Ward, "they are not always in accord with a sense of fair play [and] he will occasionally stoop to certain questionable tricks upon the field and encourage these in his men."[22] In 1884, with things going badly, Anson was more belligerent than ever[23] and became one of the most heavily-booed visiting players in NL cities.

Philadelphia finished a dreadful last in 1883, and the high point of their 1884 season occurred when they won the 11th and deciding game and beat the 1883 AA champion Athletics in their intracity exhibition series. Attendance for the final game was more than 5,000, much larger than most of the crowds that attended regular season NL games, and it was estimated that the series drew 55,000 and grossed roughly $10,000.

Harry Wright's club was not quite as successful against NL competition. Wright was a managerial legend, but by 1884 the game had changed. "Harry Wright doesn't know as much as he used to,"[24] said one paper. In Cincinnati and Boston, he'd gotten by with one pitcher, but in 1884 Harry spent almost the entire season looking for replacements for his used-up battery men.

In late May, when the Eastern League Monumentals disbanded, Wright learned one evening that their pitcher, Jim McElroy, and catcher Joe Kappel were somewhere in Philadelphia. At nine o'clock, he and a friend climbed into a carriage and set out to find them. At the corner of Cedar and Dickinson, they encountered Joseph Fralinger, the manager of the August Flower club, who had seen Kappel at the corner of Fourth and Norris. Wright found Kappel at Fourth and Germantown and signed him to a contract. Kappel didn't know where McElroy was, but Wright found him and signed him as well. At 11, he departed for home with a new battery in hand.

Harry didn't get much for his efforts. McElroy was a drinker who was just 1–12 for Philadelphia (the only game he won was a contest that Providence finished with just eight men) and threw an astonishing 46 wild pitches in 111 innings. Philadelphia had catching problems all season, and never could find a receiver agile enough to handle McElroy. After he left Philadelphia, McElroy played one game for Wilmington before vanishing on a bender. Kappel played just four games for the Phillies.

Charley Ferguson was Philadelphia's best pitcher, and Wright eventually found a reliable second hurler in William Vinton, a tall (6'1"), cultured Yale graduate. Vinton didn't make his NL debut until July 30, when he was bombed by Boston in a 14–6 loss. He got better and in early September pitched a one-hitter against Detroit. For the season he was 10–10 for a team that finished well below .500 and posted an excellent 2.23 ERA.

Vinton wasn't the only Philadelphia pitcher who couldn't beat Boston. The club lost all 14 of their games to the Beaneaters in 1883 and in 1884 they extended the streak to 22 before finally winning a game in June. But the Phillies were playing better against the rest of the league and surpassed their 1883 win total on July 8.

Philadelphia's biggest problem was injuries, especially to their batteries. In September, the *Chicago Tribune* noted, "The Philadelphias, as is their custom, had a catcher knocked out."[25] In one game, Frank Ringo caught with hands that were so raw that he winced on every pitch. He said he needed a month off. "The Philadelphia Club ought to take an ambulance along," said the *Philadelphia Times*. "Pretty nearly all the players are disabled and it is only a question of time when they will all be in the hospital."[26]

By the end of the season, Philadelphia had used 11 different pitchers and 13 catchers. Of the latter, 11 played less than 10 games. The *Police Gazette* joked, "Harry Wright was seen down at the Battery the other day among a shipload of emigrants, looking for new pitchers and catchers. He has already tried all in this country and is now on a quest of foreign talent."[27]

Detroit appeared poised to assume Philadelphia's place at the bottom of the standings. They started the season on the road and lost 20 of their first 24 games. After a loss to Providence, the *Buffalo Times* described the Wolverines as "extremely weak at the bat and miserable in the field."[28] That would make for a rough season. A week later, when Buffalo returned from a poor road trip, a local paper said, "[A]dmirers of the club have only to look at the lot of the Detroits ... in order to obtain the comfort that is found in the thought of how much worse it might have been."[29]

Detroit's best asset was pitcher Fred (Dupee) Shaw, a left hander with a puzzling curve ball. After the Wolverines began the season with 11 straight losses, Shaw beat defending champion Boston for Detroit's first win. In his first five starts, Shaw struck out 48, including 12 in a loss to Boston on May 10.

After a couple of weeks of pre-season practice, manager Chapman concluded that his players were good fielders but weak hitters. Two weeks into the season, the team average was a miserable .159 and they finished the year with a .208 average. They were shut out 17 times. Twenty men played more than two games for the Wolverines, and 13 of them batted under .200, including eight under .150.

"Wanted," proclaimed the *Detroit Free Press*, "A dozen good batters. Apply to J.C. Chapman, Earle's Hotel, NYC. PS—Send along two dozen. Buffalo wants some."[30] "Hip! Hip! Hooray!," it declared later in the season. "Six base hits and one earned run! Tiger-r-r! The Detroits made 'em yesterday before dinner."[31]

Like every team, Detroit lost players to injury, and their replacements were woeful. Prior to the season, Chapman and captain Ned Hanlon spoke encouragingly of the team's depth, but in fact it had none. At one point, all three pitchers were suffering from sore arms and unable to pitch.

As always when a team is losing, the manager shouldered a good part of the blame. "One reason given for the unsatisfactory showing made by the Detroit Club," the *Free*

*Press* stated, "is that the team is being 'rattled' by Manager Chapman. He has been growling at the boys ever since the season commenced."[32]

A week later, ten Detroit players sent a letter to *Sporting Life* defending Chapman and denying that any of them had initiated the previous complaint. They said they were very happy with their manager and that their poor play was due to injuries.[33]

During a game against Boston, the precious left arm of Dupee Shaw gave out. But after backup Stump Weidman was injured, Chapman insisted that Shaw pitch with his damaged arm. He started nearly every game, and the more he pitched, the sorer his arm became. He said his arm hurt, but when he managed to pitch effectively with the pain, his detractors claimed he was faking.

During a game against Philadelphia, Shaw made a wild pickoff throw that allowed two men to score and was fined $30. Chapman said he knew the misplay was unintentional, but the directors insisted on levying a fine. After pitching with a very painful arm, being fined for making an error was the last straw. Shaw angrily left the team and went home in Charlestown, Massachusetts. He said that although Detroit promised to return the fine if he came back, he was so disgusted by their treatment that he had no intention of playing there again. He signed with the Boston Union Association club and Detroit placed him on the blacklist. Apparently, the brief rest did wonders for Shaw's arm, for he struck out 35 batters in his first two games with Boston.[34]

Detroit was in last place with Shaw and without him, they weren't going any higher, especially since Weidman, their other pitcher, had a sore arm and couldn't pitch for two months. When the team went on a brief spurt after Shaw left, his detractors insisted that the team was better off without him, but the Wolverines soon returned to their losing ways.

Chapman identified the problem. "The trouble is," he said, "that we can't get the players."[35] Suggestions rolled in. The *Detroit Journal* said, "the Detroit Club ... [should] imitate Congress—adjourn and go home."[36] "If the salaries of the Detroit Base Ball Club were as low as the low standard of their playing," said *Sporting Life*, "the club would make piles of money."[37] When there were rumors that the Saginaw team of the NWL was about to disband, the *Free Press* suggested that the Wolverines hire the entire nine.

As the Northwestern League began to unravel, Chapman saw an opportunity to get better players. When he received a telephone call telling him that the Grand Rapids team was about to disband, Chapman immediately telegraphed the team's president, who agreed to travel to Detroit and meet him at the Russell House. Chapman signed six Grand Rapids players, the most talented of whom was pitcher Charles Getzien. Although Getzien lost his first eight starts, he won five of his last nine decisions and finished the season with a 1.95 ERA. Three years later, he helped lead Detroit to the NL title.

As with most bad teams, things completely unraveled as the season wound down. Providence beat the Wolverines 15 straight times. "Lack of harmony in the ranks," summarized *Sporting Life*, "the desertion of Shaw and internal troubles handicapped the club until the season was nearly gone."[38] Also, as Chapman pointed out, the team didn't have very good players.

In late September, the *Clipper* reported, "President Thompson of the Detroit is so disgusted by the failure of his club that he says he will retire from the arena at the end of the season and never witness another professional game of ball,"[39] which would have brought great pleasure to most Wolverine players and several of Thompson's fellow owners.

As the season ended, the *Detroit Free Press* delivered the epitaph. "The Philadelphia agony is over [Detroit had played poorly in a series at Philadelphia], and when the Detroits have delivered five games to the New Yorks, the players will have completed their season's work in a very incomplete manner and been paid a much larger sum than they have earned ... they should hail with joy the opportunity to disappear from public gaze and practice throwing into a barn door for six months or more."⁴⁰

Hoss Radbourn of the Providence Grays wouldn't be throwing into a barn door in frustration when the season ended. First, his arm was too sore and, second, Radbourn had no reason to be frustrated after having perhaps the greatest season of any pitcher in the history of major league baseball. He was certainly the most durable. They called him Old Hoss, but any horse driven as hard as Radbourn was in 1884 wouldn't have lived to old age.

Providence manager Frank Bancroft hadn't intended it to be that way; he was a good baseball man who knew he needed more than one pitcher to get through a 114-game season. Young Charlie Sweeney had shown promise in 1883, and Bancroft thought he had a solid two-man staff, which was all a manager needed. But while his two pitchers had strong arms, each had a problematic personality and both had a penchant for alcohol.

The 21-year-old Sweeney was tall for the time at 5'10½" and handsome, with a thick mustache. He was born in San Francisco, where his father was a rather disreputable policeman. "Even by the standards of nineteenth century policing," wrote Edward Achorn, "which permitted a generous degree of brutality and corruption, the pitcher's dad proved to be a bad fit for the job."⁴¹

By the age of 17, Charlie was working as a butcher, and a year later he was pitching for the Athletic Club of San Francisco. He followed other Californians, like

In a season filled with remarkable events and achievements, the pitching of Charles (Hoss) Radbourn was perhaps the most impressive—59 wins, 679 innings pitched, and a 1.38 ERA, plus three straight wins in the World Series. Radbourn was a one-man staff in an era of pitching rotations, but he carried the Providence club on his back to the first World Series title (National Baseball Hall of Fame Library, Cooperstown, N.Y.).

Sandy Nava and Jerry Denny, to Providence and played one game in right field for the Grays in 1882. The following season, after his California team expelled him for dishonorable conduct, he went back to Providence, started 18 games, won seven and lost seven, and posted a 3.13 ERA.

Harry Wright managed the Grays in 1883, and Sweeney, who was egotistical and not particularly popular with his teammates, wasn't his type of player. In 1884, when Bancroft replaced Wright, he decided, after seeing Sweeney's blazing fastball, that he could tolerate his wildness, the strain he put on catchers, and his arrogant personality.

Sweeney justified Bancroft's confidence by winning 17 of his first 25 decisions, posting a 1.55 ERA and striking out 145 in 221 innings. His success only fueled his arrogance. In a game against New York at the Polo Grounds on May 29, he was hit hard and became disgusted. In the sixth inning, he pitched carelessly and let in four runs on wild pitches and a wild throw.

On June 27, while pitching against Chicago, Sweeney felt something pop in his arm. He kept pitching but couldn't get much on the ball. It didn't matter, since the White Stockings' Larry Corcoran pitched a no-hitter and Chicago won 6–0.

Sweeney had to lay off for a while, and Radbourn started six of the Grays' next seven games. He wasn't happy about the extra work load, for his arm wasn't feeling all that good either and said that if he was going to do all the pitching, he wanted more money. Supposedly, Sweeney had been paid extra when he took Radbourn's turn and Radbourn wanted the same treatment.

It wasn't long before pitching every game caused Radbourn's arm to give out, and Sweeney was asked to pitch on July 8, although *his* arm was still hurting badly. After pitching nine innings, he left with the game tied 5–5 and Radbourn came in to relieve him. The two pitchers had been jealous of each other from the start and the situation had become worse than ever. The feud divided the team into two contentious factions.[42]

"Radbourne and Sweeney," said Frank Wright of Cincinnati's UA team, "were jealous of each other, and when Radbourne was laid off and Miller was hired to pitch (see below) during Rad's illness, Sweeney held the same feeling toward him, and wanted to do all the twirling, although his arm was lame. He and Bancroft had words, as did the latter with Rad."[43]

Desperate for pitching, Bancroft pursued former Boston star Tommy Bond, who was bickering with his Union Association team over unpaid salary. When Bond was suspended, Bancroft attempted to sign him but Bond, realizing Providence was in dire straits, asked for more than Bancroft was willing to pay. Further, he had agreed to sign with Indianapolis, which put Bancroft on notice that it would protest if he attempted to use Bond.

That forced Bancroft to look elsewhere. He signed local gymnast John Cattanach, a remarkably skilled athlete who was a rower, wrestler, track star, and later a renowned professional boxer. Cattanach was not, however, a capable major league pitcher, and after one unsuccessful start, the Grays signed left-hander Joseph (Cyclone) Miller of the Union Association's Chicago club. Miller's contractual status was cloudy; he had been expelled by Worcester of the Massachusetts State League for jumping to Chicago. With a chance to strike a blow at the hated Union Association, Worcester agreed to release Miller.

Radbourn continued to carry the load, however, and on July 16, Bancroft sent him out to pitch his 12th game in 19 days. "[R]adbourn seemed to be on the edge of a nervous breakdown," Ed Achorn wrote. "Bancroft was willfully ignoring the loud warning signals that the veteran had endured more than enough and was headed for a collapse, or maybe something worse...."[44]

Radbourn was irritable under the best of conditions, and the grueling workload led to a meltdown that day. Angered by the umpiring of Stewart Decker, he began throwing wildly and erratically, exasperating catcher Barney Gilligan. By the end of the game, Gilligan's hands were a painful mass of reddened flesh.

After watching his churlish behavior, the board of directors suspended Radbourn without pay pending an investigation. "Radbourn's popularity with the Providence people is ruined," said the *Boston Globe*. Spotting Harry Wright sitting in the stands with Bancroft, the reporter wondered if the old veteran was giving Bancroft advice on how to handle his cranky pitcher.[45]

There was another story lurking in the background, for it was well-known that several Union Association teams were trying to sign the Grays' discontented pitchers. One story said that Radbourn would jump to Lucas' St. Louis club for a $5,000 contract.

Miller, who also had a sore arm, started the next day, but Sweeney came in from right field to save the game in the ninth inning. Bancroft, running out of options, signed former Holy Cross and Woonsocket pitcher Ed Conley, who had struck out 21 one day for the latter club. "Conley," said one unimpressed reporter, "is an undersized youth, a little lame, and looks more as if he was studying for holy orders than like a professional athlete."[46] But Conley provided a ray of hope by defeating Philadelphia 6–1 with a two-hitter in his debut.

With Radbourn suspended, Bancroft needed Sweeney, whose arm still hurt and whose behavior was becoming even more erratic. During an exhibition game in Woonsocket, he kept sneaking off to the dressing room for shots of whiskey, and afterwards refused to return to Providence with the team. He'd brought a woman to the game and insisted on staying with her and taking a later train.

Sweeney was still inebriated the following day when he reported for the game against Philadelphia. Even though he told his manager he was drunk, Bancroft put him in the box anyway, stationing Miller in right field in case Sweeney faltered. Amazingly, considering his condition, Sweeney was leading 6–2 after five innings when Bancroft decided he had pushed his luck far enough. He signaled for captain Joe Start to go to the mound and bring Miller in to pitch.

When Start told Sweeney that Bancroft wanted him to go to right field, he refused, and Start trotted back to his position. Sweeney continued to pitch but, two innings later, Bancroft called Start over to the scorer's stand and told him to bring Miller in. Sweeney again refused and he and Bancroft had a bitter argument. Bancroft said he would fine Sweeney if he didn't go to right field and Sweeney told him to go ahead. Then he stormed off the field.

Bancroft went to the dressing room and another violent argument ensued. Director Ned Allen joined the discussion and threatened to suspend Sweeney without pay. Sweeney said he didn't care, because he could make more money elsewhere.

When Sweeney left, Providence was forced to play with eight men. They lost in the ninth when the Phillies exploited the holes in the two-man outfield and scored eight runs. After the game, Sweeney left in the company of two women. The directors voted to expel him and within a week, after being seen frequently wandering drunk around Providence, Sweeney signed with St. Louis of the UA. "Lucas has secured a poor bargain in Sweeney," Bancroft said. "His arm has given out and he can only throw underhand. He was no good to the Providence Club the last two weeks we had him."[47]

Providence had lost their only reliable pitchers, one suspended and the other gone for good, and although they were just two and a half games behind Boston, they were in dire straits, both competitively and financially. Even with their two star pitchers, attendance had been disappointing and without them, it was hard to believe the club could draw well enough to cover expenses. The directors called a meeting to consider the possibility of disbanding the team.

After a lengthy discussion, the directors decided to soldier on. "The home management," reported the *New York Times*, "believe that they can weather the trouble which culminated yesterday in Sweeney's open revolt, and will go on and finish the season no matter how the club stands in the fight for the pennant."[48] The Grays were going to finish the season, the *Boston Globe* said, "if they have to put in cigar store Indians to represent the club."[49]

The departure of Sweeney left Radbourn in a very strong negotiating position. The directors told him he could return to the team and at the end of the season, he would be a free agent if he chose.[50] Perhaps the most positive impact of Radbourn's suspension was that it gave his ailing arm a week of rest. That didn't mean it was healed. "Morning after morning when Radbourne arose," wrote Jacob Morse, "he could not lift his arm as high as his waist. He had to brush his hair with his left hand.... He would slip out to the park about two hours before the rest of the team put in an appearance and would begin the excruciating process of loosening up. He could pitch the ball only a few feet when he would first go out; but he would keep on trying, time after time, rubbing his arm with his left hand. Sometimes his face would be drawn up into contortions, but never a word of complaint left his lips."[51]

Even though the Grays had nearly disbanded, they were right in the thick of the pennant race. New York dropped off the pace, and the contest developed into a two-team affair between Boston and Providence. In early July, Boston held the lead and one paper predicted, "[U]nless some accident happens, [Boston] will take the pennant again this year, as easily as they did last summer."[52]

| | W | L | Pct. | GB |
|---|---|---|---|---|
| Boston | 40 | 12 | .769 | — |
| Providence | 38 | 14 | .731 | 2 |
| New York | 33 | 21 | .611 | 8 |
| Buffalo | 25 | 25 | .500 | 14 |
| Chicago | 25 | 27 | .481 | 15 |
| Cleveland | 20 | 31 | .392 | 19½ |
| Philadelphia | 18 | 38 | .321 | 24 |
| Detroit | 11 | 42 | .208 | 29½ |

It was exciting to see Boston battling Providence for the title, because there had been an intense rivalry between the two cities ever since Providence entered the League. Boston was the defending champion from the older, more established city; Providence was the upstart underdog.

Brothers George and Harry Wright were at the center of the Boston-Providence rivalry. They were stalwarts of the Boston club that dominated the NA from 1872 to 1875, and in 1879, George took over as playing manager of Providence and won an NL title, while Harry's Boston club finished second. In 1882, after 11 years in Boston, Harry took over as Providence manager while George played shortstop. The Grays finished second, just three games behind the champion Chicago White Stockings, while Boston, without either Wright brother, was ten games back in third place. By 1884, Harry was in Philadelphia and George was back in Boston with the UA club, but the competition between the two cities was as hot as ever.

With a distance of only about 50 miles separating the two cities, fans could take the train to watch their team on the road and be home by bedtime. The 1884 games between the two clubs drew nearly 40,000 in Boston alone. Attendance wasn't as good in Providence, which had never been a great baseball city, even with a championship team. Providence was less populous than Boston and Messer Park was a 20-minute trolley ride from the center of the city. While Boston raked in profits, the Grays scrambled to stay solvent. Players knew that, and the Grays had trouble signing big names. They had already lost John Ward to New York, where he nearly doubled his salary.

The National League pennant race did not go down to the final day, or even the final week, but the two teams ran neck and neck for most of the summer and the head-to-head competition between the two teams generated as much excitement as a battle to the wire. The games were close, the crowds were large and enthusiastic, and the quality of play was everything one would expect of two contending teams. There were three series: a seven-game set in June, a five-game series in July, and four games in August. Since it was a short hop from one city to the other, the teams moved back and forth during each series rather than playing all games in one city.

When the first series began on June 6, Boston held a one-game lead. The margin was unchanged a day later, for in a game that set the tone for the rivalry, the two teams played 16 innings to a 1–1 tie when the proceedings were halted by darkness. Although Jim Whitney pitched the entire 16 innings for Boston, he came back strong the following day and lost only because Charlie Sweeney pitched even better, striking out a record 19 Beaneaters in a 2–1 win. The Grays returned home to a grand reception; they were met at the train depot, placed in carriages, and escorted by a band and a huge crowd to City Hall. Sweeney, the hero of the day, was lifted onto the shoulders of the fans and carried aloft.

Since National League teams didn't play on Sundays, Sweeney had a day to rest before he faced Boston at Providence on Monday. This time he squared off against Charley Buffinton, who beat him 2–0 in another tight pitchers' duel. Buffinton yielded just three hits and Sweeney but four. With Radbourn ailing, Sweeney pitched again the next day, losing 3–1 to Whitney. He struck out only five, an indication that his arm was getting a little tired.

Radbourn pitched the next day and lost 4–1 at Messer Park. The crowd of 1,838 was somewhat of a disappointment, given the stakes and the excitement of the previous games. The three Boston contests drew more than 15,000,[53] but while Grays fans might turn out at the train station, not many made it to Messer Park.

After a rainout, Boston won for the fourth straight time before Providence closed out the series with a dramatic 4–3 win in 15 innings. Radbourn beat Whitney when the Grays pushed across the winning run on doubles by Paul Radford and Cliff Carroll. The game was played in Boston on a Saturday afternoon and 5,424 saw a splendid display of championship baseball—good pitching, tight fielding, and a close extra inning affair.

The initial skirmish between the two contenders resulted in four wins for Boston, two for Providence and one tie. When the series ended, Boston had a three-game lead.

The next direct confrontation was a six-game series that took place July 11–17 and began with Boston holding a two-game lead. After losing the first game in Providence, Boston returned home for a Saturday game that attracted 6,137 fans (compared to 2,301 in Providence the previous day). A number of Providence fans made the trip to Boston, but they had little to cheer as the Beaneaters gained a 7–1 win in the most one-sided game the teams had played thus far.

The next game was equally inartistic, a 9–6 Providence win in which the *Boston Globe* reported 27 total errors. Since most papers called walks, wild pitches, and passed balls errors, the number is overstated, but it was a sloppy game. Whitney, who'd been ill for some time, pitched for Boston and was terrible. He looked thin and weak and didn't appear to be throwing very hard.

Boston won two of the remaining three games, the Providence win and one of the Boston victories the result of three-run ninth-inning rallies. When Round Two was over, each team had played 60 games and Boston had the same two-game lead they had when the series began.

The third leg of the series, consisting of four games alternating between the two cities, took place August 9–14 and essentially decided the pennant race, although there were two months left in the season. Like the series as a whole, the four-game series was baseball at its best, a great advertisement for the national game. After the final game, the *Boston Globe* said, "[A] better played string of games has never been witnessed in the history of the National League.... Probably never again will the pitcher's skill be shown to such advantage and with such wonderful results as in this series."[54]

For several weeks, the two teams had been jockeying for first, and when the series began, Providence led by a single game. By this point Radbourn was pitching virtually every game, and worked all four contests against Boston while allowing a total of just one run. The Grays won the opening game 1–0 in 11 innings on a home run by Art Irwin over the right field fence at the South End Grounds. They also won the next three, giving them a five-game lead, and the narrow margin that had separated the two teams all season was no longer narrow.

Buffalo, which finished third, was never a serious contender, mainly due to a slow start. The Bisons began their season on the road and lost ten of their first twelve games. The team was badly crippled by injuries in the early going, and in mid–May, Dan Brouthers, Jim Galvin, Hardy Richardson, and James White were all hurt. Top slugger Brouthers was home in Wappingers Falls with a fever (he missed 22 games) and top pitcher Galvin was suffering from a leg injury, a bad back incurred while lifting a suitcase at his hotel, and a sore arm. Richardson was playing, but he had lost weight and complained of chest pains, which were diagnosed as an inflammation of the lungs.

While Buffalo was in Baltimore preparing for the season, White was at his farm in Corning, New York. He said one of his farmhands left and he needed to stay and do chores, but at the age of 36, he might have been better off in Baltimore getting in shape. White didn't show up until April 17, and soon after he was injured.

The Buffalo press was disappointed by the slow start and didn't want to hear about injuries. "The Buffalo base ball association must be delighted," wrote *The Buffalo Commercial*, "with the hippodroming performance of the dozen or more so-called players who are drawing enormous salaries and living like princes. It is no longer sport for fame, but sport for money ... the directors will discuss the advisability of selling their $18,000 white elephant to Forepaugh or Barnum."[55]

When the team returned home to christen beautiful new Olympic Park and the injured stars began to heal, the Bisons began to play much better. Brouthers hit like the slugger he was and Galvin pitched like the ace *he* was. The Bisons kept getting better and by August 2, when they were 40–27, *Sporting Life* thought they might have a shot at the championship. "The Buffalos have shown splendid form of late," it said, "and as they are at present in better condition than any of the leaders it is just possible that they may repeat Boston's splendid steady up-hill fight to the top [in 1883]."[56]

Buffalo had a potent offense, led by Brouthers, who with 14 home runs was the leader among those who didn't play in Chicago. Future Hall of Famer White played third base and captain and future Hall of Famer Jim O'Rourke played mostly in the outfield. Despite having three future Hall of Famers in the lineup and a fourth in the pitchers' box, any title hopes Buffalo may have cherished were extinguished by the slow start and the injuries.

Despite a good season on the diamond, Buffalo was only able to break even financially. They got a very bad break when a home doubleheader scheduled for the Fourth of July, which probably would have drawn the largest crowd of the year, was rained out.

After the season, O'Rourke wrote a letter to Buffalo's directors stating that he was leaving the team to accept an offer from New York's NL club. It was the era of the reserve rule but O'Rourke, who was an attorney, insisted on a contract exempting him from the reserve. He burned no bridges and his resignation letter, which was widely praised in the Buffalo press, expressed a "deep sense of gratitude for the courteous and generous treatment that has uniformly been accorded me." O'Rourke said he left only because of a desire to return to the East, where he had been born and raised and played prior to signing with Buffalo in 1881. In closing, he said, "The memory of the seasons spent in Buffalo will always be regarded as among the most congenial of my experiences on the diamond."[57]

Cleveland was in trouble from the start, for before the season had even begun, they'd lost three of their best players, Fred Dunlap, George Shaffer, and Hugh Daily, to the UA. At first, the Blues managed to hold their own, hovering slightly below the .500 mark until a 4–18 July dropped them to 23–44.

The poor record led to dwindling attendance and consequent financial problems. For some time, there had been rumors that the team would disband or move, and they became more pervasive at the end of July. With the situation becoming tenuous, star pitcher Jim McCormick and shortstop Jack Glasscock were rumored to be negotiating with Henry Lucas. McCormick was pitching poorly, criticizing his teammates, and creating discord. The club had split into cliques and McCormick was the leader of one of them.

With the club suffering financially, management approached Captain Glasscock and asked him to convince his teammates to play on a cooperative basis, under which they would share the gate receipts rather than receive salaries. Glasscock had no intention of doing that, for he was making plans of his own.

For two weeks, Frank Wright, secretary of Cincinnati's UA team, had been following the Cleveland nine. He was eventually joined by president Thorner, who offered to pay Cleveland to release McCormick and Glasscock. Even though they desperately needed the money, Cleveland declined.

## 12. "He said he'd pitch his arm off to win the flag"

On the 8th of August, while Cleveland was playing an exhibition game in Grand Rapids, Michigan, Glasscock, McCormick, and catcher Fatty Briody told manager Charlie Hackett they had signed with Cincinnati and were leaving immediately. Each was reported to have received $1,000 in advance, with McCormick to get $2,300 and the others $1,500 each to finish the season.

Since there was a decent crowd on hand, Hackett asked the three men to play so that the gate money wouldn't have to be refunded. They said they would, but only if they were paid an additional $25 each. Hackett offered $10 and the deserters agreed. When the game was over, they left for Cincinnati.

Cleveland fans were upset and the move was denounced in most NL cities. Jumping a reserve was one thing, but walking out on an existing contract was worse. "They will be properly blacklisted," said *The Buffalo Times*, "and in a year's time when the Union Association is no more they will earn their livings by carrying hods or wheeling coal."[58]

Cleveland referred the matter to Attorney John M. White, with instructions to advise them as to the possibility of obtaining an injunction to prevent the three from playing in Ohio. It was convenient that the players had defected to a club in the same state, for an Ohio injunction would prevent them from playing any home games for Cincinnati. Cleveland's action was unsuccessful, however, and Glasscock, McCormick, and Briody were legally free to play in the Union Association.

Twenty games under .500, with dwindling attendance, and having lost three of their best players, the Cleveland directors decided to disband the team. Denny McKnight of the AA Alleghenies arrived in town trying to arrange a deal under which he would acquire the best of the remaining talent by paying a substantial bonus to the directors.

NL president Mills, attempting to salvage the franchise, sent a telegram to the directors offering a better split of receipts from Cleveland's road games. That was sufficient to change the board's collective mind and they decided to finish

Star shortstop Jack Glasscock, along with two teammates, jumped from the National League Cleveland nine to Cincinnati of the Union Association. The move stunned the NL but it was the last hurrah for the struggling UA (National Baseball Hall of Fame Library, Cooperstown, N.Y.).

the season.[59] It was suggested that NL teams with a surplus of players send one or two to Cleveland. Fortunately, the Northwestern League was disintegrating, and Cleveland picked up new men from Grand Rapids, Peoria, and Terre Haute.

Cleveland didn't fall apart immediately. It took about a week, during which there was brave talk that the desertions had actually made the club stronger by ridding it of three disruptive influences. McCormick's ego had damaged the team's chemistry, and now that he was gone, things would be better. "He was arrogant, conceited, and very largely overestimated," said the *Detroit Free Press*.[60] After defeating Detroit 1–0 on August 13, Cleveland had four victories in its first five games without the missing trio.

The bottom fell out after the win over Detroit and Cleveland lost 30 of its last 36 games. On August 21, their new pitcher, John Henry, gave up 26 total bases on hits and issued nine walks while losing 20–1. Perhaps McCormick was missed after all. As with so many teams, injuries played a major role in Cleveland's steep decline. Captain Jake Evans, who'd been hurting nearly all season, went home to rest his sore arm. After Briody left, catcher Jerry Moore was injured, leaving Doc Bushong to carry the load, and one healthy catcher wasn't enough. Replacements from the Northwestern League and Oil and Iron League were nowhere near the caliber of the players they replaced. Turnover was rapid and by the end of the schedule, only three players remained from the club that started the season.

After the loss of so many players and such a dreadful finish, there were rumors that Cleveland would leave the National League. On October 4, however, the team held a meeting, resolved to field a team in 1885, and sent a list of reserved players to the National League office.

After its hot start, New York faded quickly, plagued by injuries and lackluster management. After the 12-game winning streak at the start of the season, they played at exactly a .500 pace for the rest of the year. One of the Gothams' biggest problems was that they never found a strong pitcher to complement workhorse Mickey Welch. Welch started 65 games and posted a record of 39–21, and in a game against Cleveland in late August, he set a record by fanning the first nine batters. But when Welch wasn't involved in the decision, New York was 23–29. Welch's ERA was 2.50 while that of the other pitchers was 3.86. Johnny Ward, who'd been one of the top pitchers in the NL, was plagued by a bad arm that limited him to 61 innings. He spent most of his time at second base and the outfield, with limited success, batting just .253 and committing a total of 58 errors.

As with the White Stockings, many blamed off-field issues for New York's lack of success. "The New York team has been the same failure this year that it was in 1883," said the *Cleveland Herald*. "Its men play poker better than ball. That's the trouble."[61] "[Manager James] Price did not have the slightest control over the team," claimed the *Buffalo Commercial*. "They ran themselves and did just as they pleased, laying off when they felt like it, and staying up until all hours of the night, while in the city as well as abroad."[62]

In fairness, the club was also hampered by injuries to several key players; there were times when half the team was disabled. At the end of the disappointing season, Price was either discharged or resigned, depending on the source, with rumors of a defalcation hanging over his head. It had been another disappointing season for John Day's club.

The White Stockings, who played so miserably early in the season, caught fire after it was too late. One paper attributed the White Stockings' strong stretch run to more sobriety, caused by "lack of funds and the withdrawal of saloon credit."[63] A more likely reason was the addition of John Clarkson to support Larry Corcoran in the box. Like every team save Providence, the White Stockings had learned that one pitcher wasn't enough.

The search for a second pitcher was a long one. Candidates included a deaf-mute named Tom Lynch and Corcoran's brother Mike, who pitched one game and was bombed. Anson tried University of Michigan left-hander John Hibbard, a young man said to be in line to inherit half a million dollars from his father, a Chicago bankruptcy registrar. Hibbard got off to a good start, hurling a shutout in his debut and pitching well in his second start. Then he pitched no more, returning to Michigan, where, under the loose rules of the day, he pitched for three more seasons.[64]

The arrival of Clarkson gave Chicago a sound rotation for the first time all season. The handsome 23-year-old was a native of Cambridge, Massachusetts, who'd begun his career with the amateur Beacon Club of that city in 1880.[65] Clarkson was not the hardscrabble sort that often gravitated to professional baseball; his father was a prosperous jeweler. While his Chicago teammates were hard-drinking and boisterous, he was intelligent, quiet, and highly sensitive to criticism. Anson quickly learned not to use his bullying ways on the new pitcher; it caused him to shut down.

Clarkson's first major league experience was three games with Worcester in 1882. The following year, Bostonian Arthur Whitney, a former National League player, was named manager of Saginaw of the Northwestern League and convinced Clarkson to join the team. He was Saginaw's best pitcher, and the next year he dominated NWL batters, posting a 34–9 record with an astounding 0.64 ERA. He had 388 strikeouts for the season and struck out 73 in one five-game stretch, 19 in a single game. Clarkson did not possess an overpowering fastball; he had an assortment of effective pitches, good control, and a good head on his shoulders.

After the Saginaw club folded, Clarkson turned down an offer from Frank Bancroft, who was desperate for someone to support Radbourn, and signed with Chicago. National League teams were more interested in Clarkson than those in the AA, since his overhand delivery was illegal in the latter circuit.

Clarkson made his Chicago debut August 22 and wound up with a 10–3 record and a 2.14 ERA. With two talented pitchers, Chicago won its last nine games and 21 of its last 25, but it was too late. The surge lifted them to a final record of 62–50, which left them 22 games out of first place. They were 39–17 in the cozy confines of Lake Front Park, but only 23–33 on the road.

While the play of the 1884 White Stockings was very uneven, there was no variation in their behavior, which was consistently bad. After Chicago lost all four games of a series in Providence, a local paper said "[T]he condition of most of the Chicago players during their games in Providence [in September] was such that they did not know whether they were muffing, catching or hitting the ball. Some of them were fined for their conduct and one of them told Anson to go to—a certain hot place."[66] After the season, Spalding said he would have his club on the abstinence plan in 1885, and everyone wished him luck.

After Providence swept Boston in August, some thought the latter team was dead, but they bounced back to win 15 of their next 18 games—and fell farther behind, for Providence was in the midst of a 20-game winning streak, which featured several dramatic victories pulled out during the team's final at bat. After the streak was broken by Buffalo on September 9, the Grays won eight more in a row.

The man who fueled the Grays' remarkable run was Hoss Radbourn. When the irascible pitcher returned to the team in July, he appeared to be re-energized and threw harder and concentrated more than he had during his previous funk. The Grays played 18 games in August and Radbourn started 15 of them. In September he started 17 of 19 games, and when Conley took the box on September 25, it broke Radbourn's streak of 22 consecutive starts, each one of them a complete game. At one point, he won 18 games in a row.

When Providence lost Sweeney to desertion and Boston lost Whitney to illness, the race became a two-man contest. "For weeks past," said one paper, "it has been a question of endurance between [Buffinton] and Radbourn, and Radbourn has won the fight."[67]

Radbourn's ability to pitch day after day with his aching arm was partly due to the fact that speed was not his primary weapon. He was a strategist with a compact motion who relied on guile, changing speeds, and a variety of curveballs. Home runs were rare in 1884 (other than in Chicago), and a pitcher working with a lead and a tired arm could let up a bit without fear of yielding a three-run homer. Radbourn could get a strikeout when he needed one, but with no one on base and a light hitter up, he let his fielders do the work. Late in the season, when his arm was dragging, he threw hard only when the situation required it.

"He said he'd pitch his arm off to win the flag,"[68] Bancroft recalled, and he nearly did. Paced by their iron man pitcher, Providence had a league-leading 1.61 ERA, besting second place Boston's 2.47 by nearly a full run per game. Their 16 shutouts were also the best in the National League.

The champion Grays clinched the pennant with a win against Chicago September 26 and were welcomed home by a 21-gun salute and festive parade. Each member of the team was presented with a gold watch and a new set of clothes. Six thousand people (far more than attended games at Messer Park) turned out as the team rode in carriages to the Narragansett Hotel and was treated to a sumptuous meal at the Hotel Dorraine. The final standings showed the Grays' healthy margin.

|  | W | L | Pct. | GB |
|---|---|---|---|---|
| Providence | 84 | 28 | .750 | — |
| Boston | 73 | 38 | .658 | 10½ |
| Buffalo | 64 | 47 | .577 | 19½ |
| Chicago | 62 | 50 | .554 | 22 |
| New York | 62 | 50 | .554 | 22 |
| Philadelphia | 39 | 73 | .348 | 45 |
| Cleveland | 35 | 77 | .313 | 49 |
| Detroit | 28 | 84 | .250 | 56 |

On October 15, in Providence's final game of the season, Radbourn captured win #59, finishing with a 59–12 record and a 1.38 ERA. He pitched in 75 games and completed all 73 of his starts. In 679 innings, he'd given up only 528 hits and struck out 441 while walking just 98. "Radbourn has made a record," said the admiring *Boston Globe*, "which will probably never be equaled in the history of base ball. No man in the profession ever deserved what is due him."[69]

At the time, Radbourn was given credit for 60 wins, but later research by historian Frederick Ivor-Campbell determined that one of those wins had been awarded on June

28, when he relieved Cyclone Miller and pitched the last four innings. Miller started, pitched five innings, and left with a lead that was never lost, and under modern rules would have been credited with the win. Nineteenth-century scorers had more latitude, and that day's scorer awarded the victory to Radbourn. Most modern sources give him 59 wins.

Only one man, Cincinnati's Will White in 1879, has ever pitched more innings in a major league season, and he beat Radbourn by just one inning. But pitching rules had changed since 1879, with the front line of the pitcher's box being moved back from 45 to 50 feet, and the overhand pitching that was allowed in the NL put more strain on the pitcher's arm. In any event, it can safely be said that White's record and Radbourn's 59 wins will never be surpassed. It's hard to win 59 games throwing 90 pitches every fifth day.

While most observers marveled at Radbourn's iron man performance, the *St. Louis Post-Dispatch* thought his record showed not that he was extraordinarily durable but that other pitchers were shirkers. "[T]his wonderful success has been achieved at the cost of the complete overthrow of the claim of pitchers being unable to stand the 'great fatigue' incident to continuous work in their positions. What Radbourn can stand, hardier pitchers than he can stand more readily, and he has proved pretty conclusively the absurdity of the claim that consecutive work in the box is too trying an ordeal for pitchers to stand without their breaking down under the pressure. What is the work of a first-class League pitcher during a season's campaign? Why nothing more than pitching nine innings of pitching once a day—occupying less than two hours of labor out of the twenty-four—during an average of four days a week. Why it is simply nonsense to assert that this is an arduous task for any man of the healthy class of athletics who compose the leading pitchers of the day. What Radbourn has done they all can do."[70]

Thanks to their short fences, Chicago had most of the league batting leaders. Mike Kelly had the highest average (.354)[71] and the White Stockings had the top four home run hitters, led by Williamson with 27, plus the top four in RBI, paced by Anson with 102. The increasing dominance of pitching was shown by the fact that Sam Wise of Boston became the first major league batter to strike out more than 100 times. His 104 whiffs far exceeded the previous high of 79.[72] Another clue to the game of 1884 was the fact that John Morrill of Boston led the league in saves with two. Bringing in a reliever was a matter of desperation rather than strategy.

The NL established its superiority by winning 58 exhibition games and losing just 26 versus AA teams; two games ended as ties. The champion Providence nine won 13 times in 14 games against AA teams, while the Mets, their AA counterparts, were 7–15 against NL nines.[73]

In previous years, the season would be over, save for exhibitions, once the championship schedule was completed, but things would be different in 1884. Providence had an October date with the AA champion Metropolitans to determine whether the champion of the old NL was better than the best team in the upstart AA.

# 13

## "The Metropolitan Club is a strong one"
### *American Association Season*

After a month of play, it appeared that the battle for the top spot in the American Association would be a lively one. It was equally evident that there were a number of teams near the bottom of the list that would be hard pressed to finish the season. At the end of May, the standings showed a rather unbalanced league:

|                | W  | L  | Pct. | GB    |
|----------------|----|----|------|-------|
| Louisville     | 18 | 5  | .783 | —     |
| Metropolitans  | 17 | 6  | .739 | 1     |
| Athletics      | 15 | 8  | .652 | 3     |
| Columbus       | 14 | 9  | .609 | 4     |
| Cincinnati     | 12 | 8  | .600 | 4½    |
| St. Louis      | 13 | 9  | .591 | 4½    |
| Baltimore      | 12 | 10 | .545 | 5½    |
| Brooklyn       | 10 | 11 | .476 | 7     |
| Allegheny      | 8  | 15 | .348 | 10    |
| Toledo         | 6  | 17 | .261 | 12    |
| Washington     | 4  | 17 | .190 | 13    |
| Indianapolis   | 3  | 17 | .150 | 13½   |

Louisville benefited from an easy early schedule; of their 23 games, 14 had been against Toledo, Washington, and Indianapolis. In fact, the schedule favored all the top teams, pitting them against inferior competition in the early going. The second place Metropolitans had 15 games against Washington, Indianapolis, and the Alleghenies, plus six against Baltimore, which finished last in 1883. When they began playing against the rest of the league, Louisville and the Mets would find out how good they really were. The expansion teams already knew how good they weren't, for as *Sporting Life* noted, "Allegheny, Washington, and Indianapolis are still at the foot of the list with no prospect of immediate improvement."[1]

Indianapolis, which spent the first part of the season as cannon fodder for the contenders, had fired undisciplined manager Dan O'Leary, but his successor, Jim Gifford, was unable to control his undisciplined team. "Last Thursday," *Sporting Life* reported, "the Indianapolis Base Ball Directory read the riot act in unmistakable language to the players of the Hoosier nine. Dorgan was fined $100 for dissipating. Keenan, who wanted to resign the captaincy, was continued in office and the remaining members given to understand that his orders must be obeyed."[2]

Eighteen-year-old pitcher Larry McKeon was fined and suspended for drunkenness and insubordination, but since Indianapolis had no other reliable pitcher, he was reinstated two days later after promising to behave. In mid–July, a gentleman named James Hammill confronted McKeon and accused him of throwing games. The youngster angrily denied the charge, and Hammill followed him out to the sidewalk and threw a punch. McKeon retaliated and apparently got the better of the encounter.

McKeon, a holdover from the 1883 club, did lose a lot of games, 41 against 18 wins for the season, but in fairness to him, he had a lot of help. In fairness to Hammill, McKeon was typical of an 18-year-old with a little money in his pocket, and was an integral part of the Indianapolis drinking contingent. He had been fined the previous season for a drunken fight with a bootblack.

Since McKeon was Indianapolis' best pitcher, Gifford kept bringing him back on his promise of better behavior. But his behavior didn't improve. In July, he was sued for an unpaid board bill. One Sunday when he was supposed to pitch against Columbus, Gifford couldn't find him. The team left without him and he was eventually located in the Occidental Hotel saloon.

When McKeon went missing a second time, a young boy told Gifford he'd seen him board a train with his girlfriend headed for a picnic. That was on a Sunday; perhaps McKeon had moral objections to playing on the Sabbath. More likely it was additional evidence of his immaturity. He went on another spree in August and after he left Indianapolis, McKeon's life was a series of benders, arrests, and endless trouble.[3] Perhaps Hamill was not far from the mark.

In late July, with a 15–41 record, Indianapolis did what all failing entities do. They reorganized, releasing seven players and signing a number of new men from the defunct Bay City club of the Northwestern League. Since McKeon's arm was giving out, they engaged former NL star pitcher Tommy Bond, who lost all four of his starts. Then they signed former Washington pitcher Bob Barr, who lost 11 of 14 decisions but gave McKeon a rest—until *his* arm gave out.

Second baseman Ed Merrill disappeared in July, surfacing a few days later with a very unconvincing explanation for his absence. Since there was no one better available, he was taken back. For the season, Indianapolis employed 35 players, a remarkably high total, but the new men weren't any better or more reliable than the ones they replaced.

The Indianapolis major league team of 1884 paid higher salaries than the independent team of 1883, and the result was a late-season deficit of about $2,500, with another $500 shortfall projected through the end of the season. The directors made a call on the stockholders to raise $10,000 and there were brave noises about assembling a stronger team in 1885, plus rumors that either O'Leary or injured third baseman Bill Watkins would replace Gifford as manager.

The smaller shareholders balked at the prospect of coming up with more money and were forced out, leaving the directors in control of the team. One of their first moves was to fire Gifford and replace him with Watkins, who'd joined the club from the defunct Bay City nine. Since Watkins was an active player, that would save one salary.

Gifford, like so many managers of that era, was a smooth-talking promoter who acquired the nickname "Gift Show." He was well-respected in the baseball world, however, and his dismissal was widely criticized. "The directory complement [*sic*] Mr. Gifford," reported *Sporting Life*, "as an honest, straightforward gentleman, but say of him that he is too slow and about five years behind the times."[4] He may have been behind the times, but the players preferred him to Watkins, who was known as a strict disciplinarian. Gifford sued to get the remainder of his salary and the team threatened not to play unless he was reinstated.

When the former manager returned to Indianapolis after his dismissal, it was rumored that he was attempting to sow discord between Watkins and the players. The directors supported Watkins and fined captain Keenan for insubordination and drunkenness. He sobered up and was reinstated, then promptly got drunk again. He pleaded with the directors to forgive him, and his penitence earned him a third chance. Watkins then fined first baseman Bill Phillips for taking the field in a drunken condition. Finding nine sober players was becoming the manager's biggest challenge. The Hoosiers stumbled to the finish line, losing 18 of 22 games under Watkins.[5]

Indianapolis had a tradition of inebriated ballplayers. The previous season, four players were reprimanded for drinking and manager O'Leary was fined $75 for failing to enforce the rules. The *Indianapolis Times* suggested that the club get a letter from Mayor D.W. Grubbs, who was a baseball supporter, reading:

Office of the Mayor

Indianapolis, _____, 1883

Turnkey Clarke, Central Station House:

You are authorized to release _____ of the Indianapolis Ball Club, on condition that his friends deposit the required bond and take charge of him.

D.W. Grubbs

The writer suggested that the letter would save Grubbs the inconvenience of being woken in the middle of the night, as he had been frequently that summer.[6]

At least Indianapolis finished the season, which was more than could be said for Washington. Even before opening day, there had been questions about Lloyd Moxley's finances, and most experts thought the team would either finish last or not finish at all. On May 30, "Alhambra," *Sporting Life's* Washington correspondent, reported, "Until to-day both our clubs had been losing so many games the base ball patrons were becoming thoroughly disenchanted with the work of both nines."[7] After splitting a Decoration Day doubleheader with Columbus and Cincinnati, the Statesmen were 4–16.[8]

Washington achieved the remarkable feat of never winning more than one game in a row, partly because they won very few games in total. After noting the tight AA race, one paper said, "the only certainty for a bet would be that the Washingtons would cling tenaciously to the bottom."[9] The most excitement the team generated came from its location in the nation's capital. Moxley gave President Arthur a pass to the games, although it is not certain if he ever appeared. Other politicians did come to the games, and several of the players took a great interest in politics, frequently debating the issues of the day, including the Grover Cleveland–James Blaine presidential campaign.

As with most losing teams, there was a lot of turnover. The biggest problem was offense; the club had a team batting average of just .200 for the year, worst in the league. Their slugging percentage was a woeful .259, as they had just 91 extra base hits and only six home runs. Noting that eight of the lowest 20 averages in the Association belonged to Washington players, *Sporting Life* stated, "This fatal weakness in batting explains the club's ill success."[10] The team had a decent pitcher in Bob Barr, but he couldn't overcome the lack of offense and an .858 fielding average that was also the worst in the AA. There may have been room for two teams in Washington, but not if one of them was as bad as Moxley's crew.

By June, Barr, the most valuable player on the team, was feuding with manager Hollingshead and demanded his release. Hollingshead refused and accused Barr of intentionally pitching poorly to force a release. By the end of July, the entire team was in revolt. They returned from a month-long road trip, during which they lost 18 of 21 games, without being paid (they were owed a total of about $1,500) and told Moxley that if he didn't pay them by the next morning, they would stop playing. Moxley, who was in the country either ill or hiding, didn't deny owing money, but didn't promise to come up with it. There were rumors that Harry Clay Ford would replace Moxley and provide the money or that Mike Scanlon would shift from the UA to the AA and run the team.

When their heroes returned home after the long road trip, Washington fans were so excited to see them that less than 200 turned out. The gate didn't even give Moxley enough money to pay the visiting team's guaranty, let alone back salaries, but the team played anyway. The vultures began gathering, hoping to sign a player or two if the team disbanded. O.P. Caylor sat in the stands, fueling rumors that shortstop Frank Fennelly was headed to Cincinnati.

After the game, Fennelly stopped by Mike Scanlon's office. Catcher Pop Snyder of the Cincinnati club happened to be there and suggested Fennelly take a walk with him. When they were outside, a carriage pulled up and took them to a nearby office where Caylor awaited them. The three men repaired to a hotel and struck a deal in anticipation of Washington's demise.

They didn't have to wait long. Hollingshead was relieved of his duties and a day later, on August 3, the club officially disbanded, finishing the season with a record of 12–51. It was estimated that the unpaid debts were about $2,000, including the $1,500 due to the players. "Mr. Moxley stated," said *Sporting Life*, "that he was prepared to lose some money the first year, but it is probable that the amount already sunk, with the season only half over, exceeded the wildest calculations or expectations of the leaders of the club and he lost heart. Besides, he was in bad health, not able to keep on his feet, and under the discouraging circumstances, he concluded to give up the job."[11] Washington sold Fennelly's contract to Cincinnati for $1,000 and Moxley agreed to split the proceeds with the players in settlement of their unpaid salaries.

The AA approached the Wilmington Club of the Eastern League and asked them to replace Washington, but they declined. The second choice was Virginia, another EL club, whose application had been rejected by the AA before the season.[12] Virginia was an odd fit for the AA, since they didn't play on Sunday and didn't sell liquor at their park. In May, *Sporting Life* noted, "When the Virginia Club looks at its present standing in the Eastern League race and the position of the new teams in the American Association it must congratulate itself that it was not admitted to the latter organization. It would have made even a poorer showing than Indianapolis and Toledo."[13]

But the Eastern League was tottering, and when Billy Barnie of Baltimore approached Virginia about joining the AA, they accepted, resigning from the EL on August 4. Telegraphic approval was obtained from a majority of the AA clubs and Virginia was told to proceed to Philadelphia to play the Athletics. To strengthen the team, they signed three players from Trenton and to improve the financial situation the stockholders agreed to increase the capital from $5,000 to $10,000. The Virginia games would count for their opponents but, as a late entry, they were not eligible for the championship.

Virginia hadn't been a dominant team in the Eastern League and they were initially overmatched when they stepped up to the AA. They made an ignominious debut, losing 14–0 to the Athletics, and lost 10 of their first 12 games. "The visitors," said a Baltimore paper, "are not strong enough to play against AA teams, and the sooner the directors find this out and strengthen the club the better it will be for them and managers of opposing teams."[14] The *Richmond Dispatch* commented, "The weakness of the Virginia team lies in their batting," a comment made after a game in which the nine committed 14 errors, indicating that batting was not the only problem.

In Virginia, the Civil War was a fresh memory, and a couple of benefit games were played to raise funds for disabled Confederate veterans. That was a benevolent cause but when Toledo came to Richmond in early September, the darker side of the Confederacy showed its face and Toledo's manager received a letter informing him that there would be violence if he played Fleet Walker (see Chapter 3).

The Virginians added a few players and won a few games as the season wound down. "They do not present an especially fine appearance upon the field," said a Toledo paper after the southern nine left town, "but if they do look like hay-makers, their play is such as to put them in the first rank of base-ballists. Everybody was agreeably surprised."[15]

By the end of season, the Virginians had proven to be a little better than the Washington club they replaced, finishing with a record of 12–30. They looked forward to 1885, but the American Association had other ideas.

Toledo and Brooklyn, former champions of the Northwestern League and the Interstate Association, were the other new teams in the league, and both finished the season, achieving relatively comparable records (46–58 for Toledo and 40–64 for Brooklyn). Brooklyn had an estimated attendance of 65,000 for the year, while Toledo drew 55,000, which wasn't bad.

Toledo started slowly, losing its first eight games, and at the end of June had a 12–30 record, putting them in ninth place, ahead of only the woeful Indianapolis, Washington, and Allegheny clubs. Then they suddenly turned things around, posting a 34–28 mark after July 1. Tony Mullane was worth the trouble of getting him, with a 36–26 record and a 2.52 ERA that was well below the league average of 3.24. One good pitcher could make a difference in 1884, as proven by Providence, and Mullane lifted Toledo from a bad to a mediocre team. When Hank O'Day (9–28) pitched, Toledo was bad.

Fleet Walker was known as a good defensive catcher, but he led the league with 72 passed balls, perhaps in part because Mullane wouldn't tell him what was coming. Walker batted .263, pretty good for a catcher, but had only five extra base hits. He also missed several games with a badly injured shoulder, which led to his eventual release.

In August, there were strong rumors that Toledo was about to disband. They'd lost their biggest financial backer before the season began, the club was $6,000 in debt, and another $4,000 was needed to finish the season. Fortunately, the stockholders were able to raise the money and the season went on.

Brooklyn's opening exhibition game against the Cleveland NL team drew an impressive crowd. "If the highly-respectable assemblage of spectators who crowded the Washington Park Ballgrounds on April 12 to the number of over four thousand," said the *Clipper*, "is at all indicative of the general patronage which is likely to be given the Brooklyn Club this season then it is evident that that club has struck a bonanza for 1884."[16] Brooklyn didn't draw 4,000 every day, and their total attendance was eighth among AA clubs, but it was the best of the four new entries, better than half the National League teams, and only 3,000 less than the Metropolitans attracted while winning the AA pennant.

The official opening day, against the weak Washington Club, was a gala event, with entertainment provided by the Ninth Regiment Band and a good crowd of 3,000 paying customers plus a numerous gathering of ladies, who were admitted free. "Large audiences are the rule at the games in Brooklyn," *Sporting Life* reported in June. "Defeat does not diminish the enthusiasm."[17] Frequently noted were the respectable behavior of the crowd (a trait not generally attributed to 20th-century Brooklyn fans) and the significant number of ladies.[18]

Brooklyn often disappointed those enthusiastic, well-behaved fans, finishing below .500 at home. Overall, they had a so-so season, and as so often happens when a team does not meet expectations, even if those expectations were unrealistic, the press blamed it on a lack of character. "The play of the Brooklyns," wrote the local *Eagle*, "in these games has shown pretty conclusively that it is not from lack of good material that they have not succeeded. The players are there, but not the team work to make their play effective."[19] "They can play," the journal added eleven days later, "and they should be made to play."[20]

Manager George Taylor was unable to make the nine play better, but they completed the season without any rumors of financial difficulty. They didn't win the pennant and didn't even get close to .500, but it was the beginning of major league baseball in Brooklyn, which would have a team for the next 74 years until Walter O'Malley pulled up stakes after the 1957 season.

The primary pre-season goals of the Alleghenies were to put a sober team in the field and accumulate sufficient capital to get through the season. Both proved to be a struggle. Early in the year, there were rumors that lushing was taking place, but it may have been an attempt, as in Brooklyn, to blame losing on something other than a lack of talent.

After Denny McKnight managed the team to a 4–8 record, he stepped back to his executive role and engaged despotic Bob Ferguson, who'd been hustled out of New York, as manager. Perhaps McKnight thought more discipline was needed. "When Ferguson took charge of the team," reported *Sporting Life*, "he called the members into a room in the hotel and delivered a lecture, which continued for three hours. He informed the men as to what he expected of them and laid down rules which he said would be strictly enforced."[21]

Ferguson wasn't the answer. He lasted 42 games, of which the Alleghenies won just 11. "The Allegheny Club is not a whit more successful under Ferguson" it was noted, "than it was under Denny McKnight, which shows the lack of success is not due to mismanagement but to the inherent weakness of the team."[22]

On July 10, the club held a stockholders' meeting to address the sorry 14–37 record, nagging financial problems, and rumors that the club would disband. The directors said the team's performance was unacceptable and changes would be made. They released pitcher Frank Beck and outfielder George (Live Oak) Taylor and made it clear that Ferguson would have to go. The abrasive manager, as he'd done at every stop during his long career, had alienated the players, which was tolerable if the team was winning but problematic with a record like the Alleghenies.' "Since Bob Ferguson joined the Alleghenys," said the *Buffalo Times*, "they have gone all to pieces."[23] In addition to being a losing manager and a pain in the neck, he'd been of little help on the field, batting just .146 in ten games. They were the last ten games of his active playing career. On September 9, Ferguson became an NL umpire, which is what he did best.

Ferguson criticized the press for their negative reporting, but in their defense, his team really *was* bad, and it would have taken some very imaginative writing to paint a pretty picture. Not that anyone tried very hard. The season had barely begun when the *Post-Gazette* declared, "The public are not prepared to stand as much nonsense this year as last from the reconstructed team."[24] When the team got off to a bad start, the *Post-Gazette* showed *they* weren't going to stand for it. "The Alleghenys played a splendid game yesterday," they said sarcastically, "getting one score to the Metropolitans 8."[25] The sarcasm continued through the summer and even a win couldn't curb it. "Here at Last," read the headline after a victory over Brooklyn "A Club Happens Along That We Can Whip"[26] and "The Alleghenys did win a game yesterday; it's an actual fact, the score shows it."[27]

Mostly there were losses, marked by comments like, "Comedy of Errors,"[28] "Whipped, Of Course,"[29] "Simply Disgusting—The Worst Game Ever Played in Pittsburgh,"[30] and "The Alleghenys played a splendid game, making no runs and nine errors."[31]

It took three more managers to finish the Allegheny season, making five in total. Veteran infielder Joe Battin was in charge for 13 games (6–7) and second baseman George Creamer managed for eight losses. In mid–August, the Alleghenies hired peripatetic Horace Phillips to manage the final 35 games.

Phillips was popular in Pittsburgh. The local press, which didn't like much that season, had been excited when he brought his Grand Rapids team to the city for some pre-season exhibitions and when he was hired, they claimed that Hustling Horace was just the man to light a fire under the struggling team.

Part of their optimism was based on the belief that Phillips would be able to keep his charges away from the bottle. "Mr. Phillips says it is too near the close of the season to do much but keep sober and play ball."[32] He promised heavy fines for inebriation and brought a few of the best Grand Rapids players with him to upgrade the talent. By mid–September, only three players remained from the nine that started the season. Getting better players and winning a few games would be nice, but what Phillips was really good at was promotion, and the directors were eager to see him put some money in the nearly-barren till.

The Alleghenies won Phillips' first game as manager. They didn't win many more, and lost their last eight decisions of the year to finish with a 30–78 record, even worse than the 31-67 mark posted the previous year by the drinking nine. "As the ball season closes," said the *Post-Gazette*, "the play of the Alleghenys gets worse and the number of spectators smaller."[33]

The *Cincinnati Enquirer*, a UA organ, described the Allegheny team that came to the city at the end of the season as "the worst coached crew that has been in the city yet. In fact, it would be hard to point out any redeeming feature in their work.... Horace, you must do more hustling. Your present crew is naught but a mob. Take a net and go out among the vineyards and the bottoms. If you are zealous you can gather a real nine."[34] Only 100 attended the final home game and there was talk of changing the team's name to Pittsburgh (or Pittsburg, as it was known then) in order to forget the sorry history of the Alleghenies.

On April 5, before an exhibition game with Yale, the defending champion Athletics planned to raise the 1883 championship banner for the first time. The players marched proudly out to the flagstaff, grabbed the ropes, and hoisted the flag upward. When it was about five feet from the top, there was a loud crack. The pole splintered and the players ran for cover as pole and flag crashed to earth. It was a bad omen.[35]

In May, there were more troubles when Thomas Smith, an officer of the old Athletic Base Ball Club that played in the National Association, filed a suit to prevent the AA club from using the Athletic name. Smith claimed that although his team had not played in several years, the corporation owned the exclusive right to the name. The suit was dismissed, but it was another bad portent.

The surprise of the Athletics' early season was a no-hitter by Al Atkinson, a 23-year-old rookie making just the eighth start of his major league career. The previous season, Atkinson had petitioned Dan O'Leary for a job with Indianapolis. O'Leary had the youngster pitch in an exhibition against his club and he beat them, striking out either 16 or 18 (depending on the source). When O'Leary offered Atkinson a job, he declined, either peeved that it had taken so long to receive the offer or believing that his strong performance would get him a better deal elsewhere. It did, and he signed with the Athletics.

Other than his no-hitter, in which he allowed a run on a hit batsman, a wild pitch, and a passed ball, Atkinson had a mediocre run for the Athletics, posting an 11–11 record. In July, he went home, supposedly suffering from an inflammation of the bowels, but before he left, he told some of his teammates he was so disgusted with baseball he was going to quit. Very shortly thereafter, Atkinson surfaced in Chicago playing for the Union Association, earning himself a place on the blacklist.[36]

One of the reasons Atkinson was dissatisfied in Philadelphia is that the Athletics had snatched pitcher Billy Taylor from St. Louis of the UA after he posted a 25–4 record. Taylor, who wasn't needed in St. Louis after Lucas signed Charlie Sweeney, was a big man, nearly six feet tall and over 200 pounds, and a problematic sort. He was a gregarious, likeable man when sober, but his proclivity for drink caused him to bounce around a lot. In 1881 he played for four different clubs. He pitched for the Alleghenies in 1882 and 1883 and whenever they spoke of getting rid of the troublesome elements in the nine, Taylor's name was at the top of the list.

At the end of the 1883 season, Taylor was arrested for stealing a $1,000 pin from Charles Brown, a wealthy Pittsburgh coal merchant. Brown had been an admirer of the Allegheny pitcher and had either loaned or given him the pin. Apparently, Taylor thought it was a gift, and when Brown declared it a loan and demanded it back, Taylor refused and Brown had him arrested. The most likely explanation was that Brown had been drinking when he gave Taylor the pin, and demanded it back once he realized what he'd done.

Just a couple of weeks after the diamond pin incident, Taylor umpired a game between two teams of blondes and brunettes (see Chapter 17) and shortly afterwards, under the influence of alcohol, wound up married to one of the brunettes. "Now that he is married," said *Sporting Life* hopefully, "it is to be hoped that Taylor will cancel his saloon dates and lay away some of his advance money to fight old Crimp until the opening of next season."[37] Of course, Taylor had not married the girl next door; ballplaying blondes and brunettes were not considered the highest strata of womanhood. By the end of the year, as one journal said, "Love's young dream is over."[38] Taylor and his bride were separated and she was performing in Jaima at the Academy of Music.

In early July 1884, Taylor received a $500 advance from Lew Simmons of the Athletics to jump from the UA to the AA, but changed his mind and asked Henry Lucas to give him money to repay his advance. Lucas believed that Taylor had received only $300 and was trying to keep $200 for himself, and refused to give him the money. Taylor then decided to go through with his deal with the Athletics,[39] supposedly using the advance to obtain a divorce from his estranged wife. He pitched well for the Athletics, his 18–12 record supplementing the 30–18 mark posted by Bobby Mathews.

Despite having two strong pitchers, the Athletics were unable to defend their championship; they had too many injuries. They suffered through one particularly rough and unsuccessful road trip, as several players were debilitated by the midwestern heat and others drank bad water that affected their digestive systems. Like their cross-town rivals from the National League, the Athletics suffered a series of injuries to their catchers. No team could succeed without a reliable backstop, and the Athletics wound up in seventh place, 14 games out of first, a precipitous drop from the first-place finish of 1883.

Baltimore had been the worst team in the AA in 1883, and manager Billy Barnie was determined to do better in 1884. "The most radical changes in composition and greatest improvement," reported *Sporting Life*, "have been made in the Baltimore Club, whose manager, Mr. Barnie, has spared no pains or expense to give the Monumental City a club worthy of such a balltown."[40]

Barnie was as good as his word. "The Baltimores of 1883," the same journal said in July, "were a large, juicy pudding which hung at the tail end of the Association.… The Baltimores of 1884 are an entirely different organization. They are ballplayers, and a football for nobody."[41] At that point, Barnie's club had a 26–23 record, compared to a 13–36 mark after the same number of games in 1883.

Baltimore didn't have any stars, but they had a good 1–2 pitching combination; Bob Emslie finished with a 32–17 record and Hardie Henderson was 27–23. Henderson led the league in walks by a wide margin, but was second to Guy Hecker in strikeouts with 346, despite pitching far fewer innings. He averaged 7.1 strikeouts per nine innings while Hecker managed just 5.2. There were several reasons Henderson pitched fewer innings than Hecker, including a sore arm, a suspension for a drunken escapade (see Chapter 8), and a weight problem that required the use of a courtesy runner for most of the season.

While Baltimore did not have a strong offense to support their good pitching, Barnie had them playing good, hustling baseball, and their baserunning, particularly after Oyster Burns and Dennis Casey joined the club from Wilmington, was very good. The drinking that plagued the club in 1883 was reduced (other than Henderson and Gid Gardner) and unlike the Alleghenies, better behavior translated into more wins. Baltimore finished the season 63–43, a remarkable improvement from the 28–68 mark of a year earlier, and established a reputation for gentlemanly behavior and respect for umpires (although their fans were notoriously hard on umpires).

The Baltimore season would have been even sweeter had it not been for the disastrous western trip on which Henderson and a couple of pals got into a fracas at a bordello over a couple of gals. The team left in fourth place, but lost 11 of 17 games and returned in seventh and out of contention. When Baltimore limped home, a local fan sent the following poem to the *Baltimore Sun*:

> The Baltimore Club has come back from the West
> Its catchers are sick and the pitchers need rest.
> The field has been playing a very poor game;

> The short stop's all right but the batsmen are lame.
> The change catcher's hands are a terrible sight
> But barring these trifles the club is all right.

Still, it had been a good season and at its conclusion, the players presented Barnie with a $300 ring and a letter extolling his virtues.

Chris Von der Ahe expected the 1884 Browns to give him the pennant he'd barely missed in 1883. He kicked off the season in his usual style, entertaining the opening day crowd with a cornetist backed by a full band. The Browns got off to a good start, winning 10 of their first 11 games, before losing eight of their next 11 and dropping to sixth place at the end of May. The streaky team then went 15–4 in June, bringing them to within nine percentage points of the league-leading Louisville Eclipse. They played well in July but lost the pennant in August, when a 9–11 mark dropped them eight games off the pace.

Problems off the field played a major role in the Browns' failure to win the pennant. "It is strongly hinted," one paper confided, "that a storm is brewing in the St. Louis club. Several of the men are at 'outs' and it is thought a serious split will occur."[42]

The season wasn't three weeks old before the St. Louis players were misbehaving, with embarrassing incidents in Indianapolis and Toledo. Outfielder Fred Lewis and catcher Pat Deasley were two of the most egregious offenders, and although they sometimes got into trouble together, they were cut from different cloth. Deasley was a generally sympathetic character who just couldn't control his drinking. He was always remorseful afterwards and when sober, wasn't a bad fellow. Lewis, on the other hand, was an incorrigible boozer and a thoroughly unlikeable person, not much better sober than drunk.

When troubles arose, Von der Ahe, as he had the previous season, decided to get personally involved and look over the shoulder of manager Jimmy Williams. Williams, 37, was a well-respected baseball man, a long-time government employee who served as secretary of the AA but had never managed a major league team. Von der Ahe thought he was too easy-going and that the players were taking advantage of him.

Williams was well aware of the troubles of 1883, and prior to the season insisted he would enforce discipline, but he had been unable to do so. When Von der Ahe started watching the team more closely they won eight of 11 games and, despite all the problems, were tied for first on July 1. As late as August 15, they were just four games behind, but they would get no closer.

In early September, Von der Ahe replaced Williams with Comiskey. This time the appointment was permanent, and the young first baseman would lead the Browns to four pennants from 1885 through 1888.

During the second half of the season, when Tip O'Neil's arm injury prevented him from pitching and Jumbo McGinnis missed time with a bad arm, the Browns picked up two pitchers from the staggering Northwestern League who would become stalwarts of the championship teams of the next four years.

Dave Foutz, who'd had an 18–4 record for the Bay City Club when it folded in July, made his debut with the Browns on July 29. Bob Caruthers, who'd been pitching for Minneapolis, made *his* first appearance September 7. For the remainder of the season, Foutz was 15–6 and Caruthers 7–2. During the next three years, each pitcher won the identical total of 99 games, and the Browns won the pennant each year.

The 27-year-old Foutz was 6'2" and a wispy 161 pounds. A native of Maryland, he went west to prospect for silver with his brother but wound up playing baseball instead.

He threw hard and by 1882 had developed an effective sidearm curve and sinker that made him the star pitcher for a Leadville, Colorado, team that was one of the best in the western territories. Foutz always exaggerated his accomplishments with Leadville, but even unadorned they were quite good. He joined Bay City in 1883 and attracted the notice of the Browns by pitching well against them in an exhibition game the following April. Foutz also played the outfield and was a good hitter with quite a bit of power, hitting 31 career home runs.

Foutz did not come cheaply; Von der Ahe paid Bay City $2,000 for his release and gave Foutz a salary of $1,600 for the remainder of the season.[43] When he first appeared with St. Louis, Cincinnati protested on the grounds that ten days had not passed since he obtained his release from Bay City. The protest was disallowed, but O.P. Caylor continued to press the issue, producing a letter from A.G. Mills regarding a somewhat similar situation in which it was determined that the ten days didn't begin to run until notice had been given to the other teams.

Von der Ahe dismissed Caylor's claim, saying, "Even in Cincinnati no one pays any attention to it ... it was a silly, childish appeal and not worth the attention which has been given it."[44] For once the Browns' owner was right; the protest *was* silly. First, the ten-day rule was intended to keep players from jumping teams, whereas Foutz's team had gone out of business. Second, the reason the pitcher's eligibility was in question was that AA secretary Morton was traveling and had waited four days before forwarding notice of Foutz's release to the other AA teams.

President McKnight ruled that Foutz was eligible and Caylor absorbed a full ration of abuse. The St. Louis press called the protest "disgraceful" and "infantile."[45] A rival Cincinnati paper said, "The mendacious cadaver of the Cincinnati American Club, who is so handy with the word asinine when speaking of people who happen to have a different opinion from his own, must by this time realize that his repeated brays about the St. Louis protested games have caused unprejudiced individuals to think that there is an animal that would answer to the description of a jackass filling the position of Secretary of the Cincinnati Club."[46]

Nineteenth-century sports writing was brutal and some of it was downright mean, like the words of a Minnesota paper describing the visiting Fort Wayne team as "the worst looking lot of cornfield sailors that ever stole fodder from a blind hog. They had countenances like imitation monkeys and brains like a crippled canary."[47]

Writers frequently ground their axes without bylines or under pseudonyms. Caylor, who studied as a lawyer but opted for journalism instead, was second to none when it came to dishing out vitriol. Physically, he was a small, frail man, described as "a pimple on the end of a stick" and "a mongrel skeleton" by his enemies but, as David Nemec wrote, "with a pen in his hand, Caylor was lethal, the most superlatively caustic baseball writer in an era when journalism was a full-contact sport."[48]

Caylor used his acerbic pen to unleash virulent attacks on the NL, UA, and rival AA clubs.[49] When the Cincinnati club was dismissed from the NL in 1880 after differences with Hulbert, he suggested an investigation of the large number of prostitutes who allegedly attended games in Chicago. He carried on a running battle with Al Spink of St. Louis for many years. Caylor was a lightning rod for criticism and journalists from rival cities delighted in roasting him when he was proven wrong.

Caylor had been active in the management of Cincinnati major league clubs since the city joined the National League in 1876; in 1880, he and Justus Thorner ran the

Reds.[50] He was one of the organizers of the AA, and since he was intimately involved with the Cincinnati club's operations, Caylor made a better target than most writers. Further, his physical appearance lent itself to caricature.

By 1884, Harry Weldon, scorer of Cincinnati's UA club, was in charge of the baseball department at the *Cincinnati Enquirer*, Caylor's old paper, and savaged him almost daily. He referred to Caylor on various occasions as "The bilious cadaver on the American organ,"[51] "the ghoulish secretary of the Cincinnati American Club,"[52] "The poor dyspeptic idiot of the Cincinnati American Club,"[53] "the skeleton-headed crank of the Cincinnati American Club,"[54] and "the poor old half-demented Secretary of the Americans."[55] But it was all in good fun.

The *Enquirer* gleefully reported every small AA crowd, while light UA attendance was excused by bad weather, competing attractions, or lack of promotion. The AA club was accused of falsifying attendance figures and *Enquirer* reporters were dispatched to manually count the house.

The rivalry between Louisville and Cincinnati was particularly heated, and the *Louisville Courier* entertained itself throughout the summer at Caylor's expense. In late July, when Louisville visited Cincinnati, the Louisville officers and members of the press delegation learned they were required to buy tickets rather than being given the customary passes. They even claimed that a player, who did not arrive in uniform, was forced to pay to get in. "Mr. Caylor," said the *Courier*, "should be given a front seat and a tab when he comes here with the club next week."[56] Then the paper carped about the unruly nature of the Cincinnati fans and the inability of the club to maintain order.

Things were calm when the Reds played in Louisville a week later, and the *Courier* made sure no one missed it. "It was certainly surprising to the ghoulish Secretary of the Cincinnati Club to see the reception the Cincinnati nine met with yesterday. He has been trying to work up a sentiment of sympathy in favor of them by saying there was a danger of a mob, etc., and the thing was even carried so far that policemen were asked to ride home with the players in the carriages.... It must have made the individual who has been whining so piteously about being 'mobbed' blush to find that he was in the presence of a crowd of gentlemen who knew the principles of common decency."[57]

Apparently Caylor didn't see things in the same light, for he accused the Louisville fans of throwing stones at the Cincinnati players. That earned him another barrage of invective from Louisville, which said he had "the instincts of a blackguard and the intellect of a street-scraper ... the members of the Cincinnati club have no enemies in this city, and the only thing that can be said against them is that such a man as this Caylor is connected with the club."[58] "Caylor left for home last night," they informed their readers, "so as to be there in ample time to work up his customary mob when the Louisvilles arrive in Cincinnati."[59]

Sure enough, when Louisville went to Cincinnati, the *Courier* reported that the Louisville players were attacked while riding to the park in a hack. Ren Deagle and Joe Gerhardt were hit with stones, the former suffering a gash behind his ear. They jumped out and tried to run to safety, with a pack of rowdy Cincinnatians at their heels, intent on mayhem.

Louisville's biggest complaint about their games in Cincinnati was not the behavior of the crowd but the biased umpiring of Robert Ross. A Louisville paper said that, in contrast to the established custom of using nine players, Cincinnati had ten. "The extra stood just behind the batter and was ironically called the umpire."[60]

Ross' major league umpiring career consisted of four games, which was four too many to suit Louisville. "Ross having resigned," said the same journal, "it is now seen that a game may be won by visiting clubs in Cincinnati."[61] They sarcastically predicted that former president Rutherford B. Hayes of Ohio would umpire the next game in Cincinnati. Even the Cincinnati press was embarrassed. The *Enquirer* said, "nothing like the umpiring of Mr. Ross has ever been seen on the [St. Louis] grounds."[62]

Louisville wasn't finished with Ross, printing a poem the following day.

> What shall we do with Umpire Ross
> Who threw from us the game
> How would it do at once to toss
> Into some sewer his frame
>
> Oh, just to me this dandy yield
> This cunning base ball boss
> I'll take him to some center field
> And nail him to the cross[63]

In our discussion of Caylor and Ross, we digress from David Foutz, who was declared eligible and proved a godsend to the pitching-starved Browns. He won his first game, striking out 13. Foutz started ten games during his first 20 days in St. Louis, but then contracted malaria, which put him on the sidelines for several weeks.

That left 20-year-old Caruthers, who came from a wealthy family and supposedly inherited enough money to be financially independent. Despite being laid low by dysentery in late July, Carruthers had a 0.83 ERA with Minneapolis and struck out 17 in one game.[64] He was a "strategic" pitcher who had a variety of deliveries in addition to his fastball. Like Foutz, he was also an excellent hitter who played the outfield as often as he pitched, accumulating a lifetime major league average of .282 and, despite his 140-pound frame, hit 29 home runs.[65]

By the time Caruthers joined the Browns, it was too late—they'd fallen out of contention. After his debut, St. Louis won 16 of 22 games to finish the year with a 67–40 mark, good for fourth place. The Browns had a pretty good offense, with the fourth highest run total in the league and the fifth best batting average. Their best hitter was the troublesome Fred Lewis, who batted .323, followed by equally but differently troublesome Arlie Latham at .274. Charley Comiskey, whose strength was defense, batted just .237. O'Neil, moved to the outfield when his arm gave out, became one of the best hitters in baseball. Although he batted just .276 in 1884, O'Neil hit over .300 every year from 1885 through 1891. In 1887, when walks counted as hits, he led the AA with a remarkable .492 average. The rule was repealed the next season but O'Neil led the league again with a .335 mark.

The 1884 team had little power, hitting just 11 home runs, but if their offense had been backed by Foutz and Caruthers for the entire season, they might well have captured the pennant. They also might have won if their players had remained sober a bit more often. "St. Louis," said the *Boston Globe*, "can ascribe its position to the discreditable composition of the nine, which had too many unsteady players."[66]

Although the Browns lost the pennant, they won the battle for local patronage against Henry Lucas' Maroons. On Sunday, May 11, both teams played at home and the Browns outdrew the Maroons 12,000 to 1,500. The Maroons led the UA in attendance, but the Browns had the best attendance in baseball.

Cincinnati's season got off to a rough start when the stands collapsed on opening day, throwing a number of spectators to the ground with serious injuries.[67] That wasn't an omen of things to come, for Cincinnati played about as well in 1884 as they had the previous season, their .624 winning percentage almost identical to 1883's .622. Will White was again the team's leading pitcher, but he wasn't quite as good as he had been in previous seasons. In 1883, White led the AA with 43 wins and a 2.09 ERA, but in 1884 he dropped to 34 wins and his ERA rose to 3.32, which was slightly higher than the league average. While 34 wins was nothing to sneeze at, White was on the downside of a great career. Early in the 1884 season the *Enquirer* said, "Will White's pitching days are past."[68] "All the clubs," said another paper, "seem to have got the range of Will White's pitching this year."[69] "Trouncing of a Tea Merchant,"[70] read one headline.

Late in the season, White, who'd been an old underhanded thrower, tried raising his arm angle, but that didn't help. The new AA rule on hit batsmen hurt him badly, for hitting batters was one of the mild-mannered White's favorite tactics. In 1884, for the first time, AA batters who were hit by pitches were awarded first base. White led the AA by plunking 35—35 batters who would not have reached base a year earlier.

White began the season as the Reds manager, but when he struggled in the box, he decided that the responsibility was too much and resigned the position in favor of Pop Snyder. But increased concentration couldn't revive a dead arm, and although he was only 29, White won just 19 games over the next two seasons, the last of his major league career.

It was unfortunate that White suffered a decline in 1884, for the Cincinnati offense led the league in runs scored. While St. Louis might have won the pennant if they had Foutz and Caruthers all season, Cincinnati might have won if they had the Will White of previous years.

Charley Jones batted .314 with 17 triples, seven home runs, 114 runs scored, and 71 RBI. He led the AA with an on base average of .376. The batting star of the Reds, however, was first baseman Long John Reilly, who led the league with 11 home runs and a .551 slugging percentage and was second in batting average (.339), hits (152), triples (19), and RBI (91). He, like Jones, scored 114 runs. Future Hall of Fame second baseman Bid McPhee scored 107 runs.

The Reds played steadily all season, but were never able to ignite the spark that would vault them into the lead.[71] They had a major problem at shortstop, where they tried a number of players before acquiring Frank Fennelly when the Washington Club folded.

Louisville edged out Cincinnati and St. Louis to finish third, largely on the strong right arm of Guy Hecker. At the end of June, Louisville was in first place by a few percentage points, but they soon fell behind when the Metropolitans went on a long winning streak. The Eclipse hung on, however, and on September 22 were just two games out of first.

"The boys held up remarkably well," said the *Louisville Courier-Journal*, "until the last eastern trip, when all their misfortunes crowed upon them in a heap...."[72] Crippled by injuries to their key players, including Hecker, who just wore out, the Eclipse lost eight of nine games to end their chances of winning the pennant. But the close race captured the fancy of their fans. "Louisville is base-ball crazy," said a St. Louis paper. "They talk base-ball at breakfast, dinner, supper and all the rest of the time.... Even the deacons on Sunday, while they don't quite attend to the games, go and watch the returns scored on the pool-boards.... The whole town is base-ball crazy and when the club is home business is entirely suspended."[73] The enthusiasm translated to financial success, and the club that was barely hanging on when the season began found itself with money in the treasury at the end.

Hecker was the fans' favorite, toasted and feted almost everywhere the club traveled. Cigars, canes, and hats were named after him and a druggist sold a Hecker brand of salts. It was said that Hecker had been promised a plot of land and a house if Louisville won the pennant.

The leading Eclipse hitters were Hecker, Pete Browning, who batted .336 (3rd in the AA) and outfielder Chicken Wolf, who hit .300 and led the team by driving in 73 runs. The pitching, other than Hecker, was spotty (a combined 16–20 record) but since Hecker pitched nearly every day, that wasn't a huge problem. "With Hecker in the box," said *Sporting Life*, "the Louisvilles are well-nigh invincible; without him they are weak, because they then lack confidence."[74]

On July 4, Hecker pitched and won both ends of a doubleheader against Brooklyn. From August 15 through September 11, he started 14 of 16 games, including a stretch of seven in a row. On two other occasions, he started five or more consecutive games. Five times he started three in a row, and back-to-back starts were a regular occurrence.

For most of the season, the workload didn't affect Hecker's performance. During the stretch in which he started 14 of 16 games, he pitched a one-hitter on August 21 and took a no-hitter into the eighth inning four days later. Overall, he won 10 of the 14, with one tie. Although Hecker seemed to wear down late in the season, 19th-century pitchers didn't stop pitching just because the season was over. When Louisville's schedule ended, he barnstormed through Texas and pitched into the winter months.

Perhaps the most surprising club of 1884 was Columbus which, under the management of former newspaperman Gus Schmelz, went from a 32–65 mark in 1883 to second place and a 69–39 record in 1884.[75] Before the season, the club rid itself of some of the bad influences from the previous year (including manager Horace Phillips), but the turnaround was mostly due to the left-right pitching combination of Ed Morris and Frank Mountain. Morris was 34–13 and Mountain 23–17; the strong two-man rotation enabled Columbus to stay in the race all season. The .240 team average was in the middle of the AA pack but their 40 home runs led the league. Centerfielder Fred Mann, a holdover from 1883, led the club with seven home runs and 18 triples. Third baseman Bill Kuehne was right behind him with 16 triples and five homers.[76]

By July, Columbus had bested their 1883 win total. They were superb on their home grounds, winning 38 of 54 games, including 17 of 20 at one point. Unfortunately, the people of Columbus, unlike those in Louisville, did not catch the fever, and attendance was disappointing. Operating with limited financial resources, Columbus was unable to sign good players that became available when teams failed.

Like so many teams during the course of the long season, Columbus fell prey to injuries and was referred to as "The Cripples."[77] A number of regulars were hurt and Morris and Mountain both suffered from sore arms. That forced Columbus to use their third pitcher Ed (Dummy) Dundon, the first deaf-mute to play major league baseball. Dundon, who lost his hearing at the age of five from typhoid fever, learned to pitch while attending the Ohio Institute for the Education of the Deaf and Dumb, which had a prominent baseball program.[78] He joined the Columbus club in 1882 and stayed with them when they became a member of the AA the following year. Dundon was popular with fans and was welcomed by the deaf community wherever the Columbus team traveled. He even found a way to join in the abuse of umpires. When he was displeased with a call, Dundon raised his hands up in the air and made a face.

Despite their sore arms, Mountain and Morris pitched when they could, and Columbus hung in until the end, finishing six and a half games behind the Metropolitans and a game ahead of third place Louisville. It was a terrific performance and great credit was given to Schmelz, an unknown when the season began. "The second position...," said a local paper, "is a remarkable showing for what was regarding in the beginning of the season as one of the weaker clubs."

The only team to finish ahead of Columbus was the Metropolitans, the poor stepchildren of the Metropolitan Exhibition Company. In the city series that preceded the championship season, the Mets surprised everyone by winning four of seven games from the supposedly superior Gothams. When both teams started well, *Sporting Life* said, "New York has a much better lead for the League championship than the Mets have for that of the American Association, yet we would stake more on the latter's ultimate chances."[79] The *New York Times* stated, "The Metropolitan Club is a strong one and it is thought that their chances of coming out ahead this season are bright."[80]

At the end of June, the race was tight as could be, with six teams within two and a half games of first place.

|  | W | L | Pct. | GB |
|---|---|---|---|---|
| Louisville | 27 | 12 | .692 | ½ |
| Metropolitans | 29 | 13 | .690 | — |
| St. Louis | 28 | 13 | .683 | ½ |
| Cincinnati | 26 | 14 | .650 | 2 |
| Baltimore | 25 | 14 | .641 | 2½ |
| Columbus | 27 | 16 | .628 | 2½ |

"Not since the organization of the first professional organization," said the *Philadelphia Times*, "has there ever been such a close and exciting race for supremacy as that now going on for the American Association championship."[81] Despite the fact that the Mets were right in the thick of the pennant race, they were dogged by rumors that they were about to disband and send their best players to the Gothams. The problem was financial; playing most of their schedule in a downtrodden facility, the Mets were losing money.

One rumor said the Mets would generate as much money as they could playing home games and disband before their last western trip, as the old Mutuals had done in 1876. Another was that the Mets had been offered $30,000 to move to Pittsburgh and a third that they would consolidate with the Athletics.[82] Jim Mutrie was supposedly helping the Gothams sign players, which led *Sporting Life* to wonder, "[H]ow is it that Mutrie is so busy with the affairs of the New York Club, when all his attention is required to run the Metropolitan Club properly?"[83]

While rumors and speculation swirled about, the Mets took care of business on the field. They had an excellent pitching rotation of Tim Keefe and Jack Lynch, who started all but one of the Mets games. Each won 37 games, tied for second in the AA behind Hecker. Keefe posted a record of 37–15 and Lynch was 37–17, winning 14 in a row at one point. Keefe struck out 334 and Lynch 292. The two pitchers generally alternated starts and thus avoided the continuous strain that Louisville and Providence put on Hecker and Radbourn.

For offense, the Mets had big Dave Orr, who led the AA in average with a .354 mark,[84] in hits with 162, and in RBI with 112. His nine home runs placed him third behind Long John Reilly's 11 and Harry Stovey's 10.

The Mets did not always exhibit championship harmony. On June 28 in Cincinnati, Lynch engaged in a public brawl with teammate James (Chief) Roseman. What began as good-natured horseplay escalated when Lynch realized he was taking the worst of it and went after Roseman. Roseman threw Lynch to the ground and the two men began exchanging blows, while their teammates surrounded them and egged them on. Finally, the owner of a nearby bar separated the two men, both of whom were bleeding profusely. "The fight was disgraceful," a journal said, "and carried on in a manner common to bar-room loafers."[85]

In mid–July, after the Mets played the first half of the season at their sorry facility at Metropolitan Park, the Metropolitan Exhibition Company announced that they would play in the Polo Grounds whenever the Gothams weren't using it. That was a good idea, for by that time, the Mets were in first place and in a position to draw well in a decent park.

|  | W | L | Pct. | GB |
|---|---|---|---|---|
| Metropolitans | 47 | 18 | .723 | — |
| Columbus | 43 | 19 | .694 | 2½ |
| Louisville | 42 | 20 | .677 | 3½ |
| St. Louis | 41 | 21 | .661 | 4½ |
| Cincinnati | 41 | 22 | .651 | 5 |

The Mets got red-hot, winning 16 of 17. On August 26, they commenced an 18-game road trip that would send them to Baltimore, Brooklyn, Cincinnati, Louisville, St. Louis, Indianapolis, Toledo, and Columbus over a four-week period. If the Mets could survive that grueling stretch of road games, they would be in good shape, for their final 14 games of the year would be played at home.

When the Mets left on their trip, they held a two-and-a-half game lead over Columbus, and after returning on September 22 with a 9–8–1 mark, they were two games in front of Louisville and three and a half over Columbus. The Mets had 16 games remaining, Louisville had 14, including two against the Mets, and Columbus had 12, only one with the Mets.

Baltimore helped the Mets by beating Columbus three straight times in mid–September and besting Louisville on September 25 and 26. When the Mets commenced their two-game series against Louisville on September 27, they had a three-and-a-half-game lead; even if they lost both games, they would still be in first place. Each team had their best pitcher in the box for the first game, Keefe for the Metropolitans and Hecker for Louisville. Hecker had pitched seven of Louisville's last nine games while Keefe was well-rested (at least by 1884 standards).

Hecker hit a home run, but gave up nine runs and ten hits, as the Mets won 9–4, breaking a 4–4 tie with five runs in the last two innings. Bill Holbert caught Keefe skillfully, while the Louisville catchers had six passed balls, which led to several unearned runs.

Louisville manager Mike Walsh apparently thought Hecker needed a rest, so Phil Reccius pitched for the Eclipse against Lynch on the 29th. The Metropolitans ripped into

Reccius for seven runs on ten hits, while his teammates managed to score just a single run. The Mets had a sweep and the two games at the Polo Grounds drew a total of more than 6,500 fans.

The Mets beat Columbus two days later, giving them a five-and-a-half-game lead. A five-and-a-half-game lead with 10 games to play is not a sure thing, but it would require a total collapse on the part of the Metropolitans to lose. They didn't collapse, and Baltimore again provided help by beating Louisville three straight times and defeating Columbus the following day.

The final standings reflected a six-and-a-half-game margin.

|  | W | L | Pct. | GB |
|---|---|---|---|---|
| Metropolitans | 75 | 32 | .701 | — |
| Columbus | 69 | 39 | .639 | 6½ |
| Louisville | 68 | 40 | .630 | 7½ |
| St. Louis | 67 | 40 | .626 | 8 |
| Cincinnati | 68 | 41 | .624 | 8 |
| Baltimore | 63 | 43 | .594 | 11½ |
| Athletics | 61 | 46 | .570 | 14 |
| Toledo | 46 | 58 | .442 | 27½ |
| Brooklyn | 40 | 64 | .385 | 33½ |
| Richmond | 12 | 30 | .286 | 30½ |
| Allegheny | 30 | 78 | .278 | 45½ |
| Indianapolis | 29 | 78 | .271 | 46 |
| Washington | 12 | 51 | .190 | 41 |

Before the season began, many thought the AA had expanded unwisely, and the final standings supported that conclusion. The Association was a two-tiered league, with a large gap between the seventh place Athletics and eighth place Toledo. Still, nearly all AA clubs reported profits. A St. Louis paper[86] estimated them as follows:

| St. Louis | $40,000 |
|---|---|
| Athletics | 35,000 |
| Cincinnati | 20,000 |
| Baltimore | 15,000 |
| Brooklyn | 10,000 |
| Columbus | 5,000 |
| Metropolitans | 3,000 |
| Pittsburgh | 3,000 |
| Virginia | 1,000 |
| Indianapolis | (5,000) |
| Toledo | (5,000) |

The Metropolitans had big plans to celebrate the first major league baseball championship by a New York team, but celebrations were very problematic in 1884. The pennant raisings of the Athletics and Bostons resulted in a snapped pole and a pennant hoisted upside down, and the Metropolitans grand parade planned for October 22 was washed out.

The parade was finally held on the 27th and it was a grand affair. At 8:00 p.m., members of approximately 50 baseball clubs gathered at Central Park Plaza at 59th Street and 8th Avenue, the current site of Columbus Circle. Former catcher John Clapp, the Grand Marshal, led the procession on a dark brown charger. The Seventh Regiment Band played martial tunes, fireworks were shot into the sky, and 1,500 marchers paraded in front of about ten thousand spectators. The players and officers rode in coaches all the way to Union Square at 14th Street.

The postponement made the Mets' pennant celebration somewhat anti-climactic, for in the interim they had played the National League champion Providence Grays in what would later be recognized as the first World Series and they had not played like champions.

# 14

## "To keep a correct record of the Union Association is worse than solving a Chinese puzzle"

*Union Association Season*

The 1884 Union Association season was not very exciting unless you were a St. Louis fan, or if you enjoyed the drama of franchises folding, moving, or teetering on the brink of insolvency. Even for Henry Lucas, the biggest St. Louis fan of all, it was stressful summer, as he spent most of the season trying to keep his shaky league in one piece.

St. Louis fans were eager to see the fabulous park Lucas built for his team and when the Maroons made their first appearance for an April exhibition contest, nearly all 8,000 grandstand seats were filled. In order to get the jump on the established leagues, the Association began its season in mid–April, with St. Louis scheduled to play its first championship game on the 19th. Rain caused a postponement until the 20th, when the Maroons defeated Chicago 7–3 on a cold, rainy day before a huge crowd estimated variously between 6–10,000. Only 400 attended a Browns exhibition game played the same day.

The cold and rain that put a damper on the Maroons' opening day were the consequence of starting play in April, and several early season UA games were plagued by bad weather. On a deathly cold day in Cincinnati, the *Enquirer* said, "If there had been bonfires built at each of the bases and stoves distributed all through the stands, the crowd at the Union Athletic Park might have enjoyed the second championship game better than they did. It was cold enough for everything but icicles."[1] Despite the elements, the play in early UA games was decent and gave rise to cautious optimism.

The St. Louis victory over Chicago was the start of a 20-game winning streak during which the Maroons outscored their opponents by a 234–67 margin. On twelve occasions they scored more than ten runs, and twice more than 20. Billy Taylor pitched ten of the wins and Charlie Hodnett eight. Taylor had been 4–7 with Pittsburgh in 1883, while Hodnett pitched just four games for St. Louis. The fact that they were dominating the UA was testimony to the potent St. Louis offense and the feeble batting of their opponents. It also helped that the owner was president of the league; the club played 21 of its first 26 games at home.

The presence of a new team enhanced the baseball fever that already existed in St. Louis. "If Mr. Lucas," said the local *Post-Dispatch*, "after all of his lavish and tremendous expenditures, does not make a success of his Union venture, he will have at least the mild satisfaction of knowing that his rivalry has provoked at least the most wide-spread interest ever manifested in the national game in this city.... [T]he man, woman or child who cannot discuss the merits of every player in the field and of every fine point in a game finds himself or herself cut off from conversation."²

Lucas ran a classy operation. When the Maroons were on the road, carriages conveyed his team from the hotel to the park and a black valet was on hand to wait on the players. During the early part of the season, the Maroons drew well, often more than the Browns, but as the summer went on attendance declined; the UA pennant race simply wasn't interesting.

St. Louis didn't expect to go through the season undefeated, and on May 24, Boston ended their long winning streak. After the loss, the standings were as follows:

|  | W | L | Pct. | GB |
|---|---|---|---|---|
| St. Louis | 20 | 1 | .952 | — |
| Boston | 14 | 7 | .667 | 6 |
| Cincinnati | 15 | 8 | .652 | 6 |
| Chicago | 11 | 9 | .550 | 8½ |
| Baltimore | 11 | 11 | .500 | 9½ |
| Philadelphia | 6 | 17 | .261 | 15 |
| Washington | 5 | 17 | .227 | 15½ |
| Altoona | 4 | 16 | .200 | 15½ |

While life was rosy at the top, there was trouble at the bottom, where uncompetitive teams in a new league during an over-crowded season were having a difficult time drawing enough fans to survive. In a small town like Altoona, the task was nearly impossible. The little Pennsylvania town had been added to the league almost as an afterthought, and perhaps it had been a mistake.

Altoona played its first seven games on the road, the final four against St. Louis, and lost all seven.³ Their opening effort was unencouraging, a sloppy, error-filled 9–2 loss at Cincinnati on a chilly afternoon before just 350 spectators. Although they dropped four games to the Maroons, the St. Louis press attributed the losses to bad luck. "That there is good material in the Altoona club can no longer be doubted, for their work yesterday would have done credit to any nine in the country."⁴ The *Cleveland Herald* was less enthusiastic. Altoona, it said "seems to be a sort of harbor of refuge for all the cripples and poor relatives of the players in the Lucas crowd."⁵

When they finally returned home, Altoona's first four games were against the Maroons, making eight in a row against the league's powerhouse team. Altoona lost all four by a combined score of 57–12, dropping them to 0–11. Despite the losses, they received more praise from the St. Louis press. "The Altoona Club played magnificently in the field ... arousing, at times, the audience to a high pitch of excitement over wonderful stops." While the Altoonas were celebrated in St. Louis, the home folk weren't quite as optimistic and desperation was beginning to set in; the team had already released five players from the roster that began the season.

Once Altoona began playing the other bad teams in the league, it managed to garner a few wins, but the franchise was clearly untenable; most home "crowds" were less than a thousand. Lucas, facing a problem he should have anticipated, paid a visit to the Pennsylvania city on May 29. He and about 200 other people saw a 13–0 loss to Baltimore and a team in the latter stages of disintegration. There was no money in the treasury and the payroll was in arrears.

Angry that they hadn't been paid, three Altoona players went on strike, making it difficult in those days of limited rosters to field a team. Somehow, manager Ed Curtis managed to scrape a lineup together that played competitively in a 5–3 loss to Baltimore. That gave Altoona a 6–19 record on the field and a loss of about $12,000 on the books. They'd drawn an average of just over 600 per game, not enough to cover expenses. There was no one in Altoona willing to sink more money into the team, and after a few days in the city Lucas concluded that it would be unwise to use his own funds to keep the franchise alive. He decided to let the club die, the first major league casualty of 1884, but not the last.

To replace the Mountain Citys, the UA placed a team in Kansas City, which had expressed an interest in joining the new league in March. Four of the Altoona players joined the new franchise and the rest scrambled to get engagements. In 1884, with teams everywhere, there were a lot of jobs available, although many involved the risk of missing a few paychecks. The Altoona player with the most staying power was shortstop George (Germany) Smith, who was snapped up by Cleveland and wound up playing 15 major league seasons.[6]

Prior to Kansas City's entry into the UA, a local paper had written, "One thing to the credit of Kansas City is that she is the only city in the country of 100,000 population that has no professional base ball club. The grown people of this metropolis are too busy to sit in the sun and listen to 18 men quarreling with an umpire."[7]

When Altoona failed, the people of Kansas City apparently found time for a baseball club, and joined the UA with the understanding that they would not be eligible for the championship, although their games would count in the records of their opponents. As it turned out, that was irrelevant, as Kansas City had a lower winning percentage than even Altoona. Backed by a substantial local businessman named A.V. McKim, they did, however, have staying power, which was most important to Lucas.[8]

The formation of the Kansas City team was an *ad hoc* affair. McKim had money, but his team had no players, no manager, and no place to play. The latter shortcoming was remedied with the addition of 2,000 seats to Athletic Park, bringing the total capacity to 4,000. Today, such a project would take months, but in 1884 it took just a couple of days to get the park ready for opening day. The speed with which 19th-century workmen were able to accomplish such feats was a tribute to the work ethic and can-do spirit of the times, but on the other hand, the stands weren't much to look at and they sometimes collapsed.

McKim had four days to assemble a team before the opening game with Chicago, and with most players already engaged, there was not a lot to choose from. Lucas arrived with eight players in tow, and when the Chicago nine arrived, Captain Harry Wheeler had nine men to oppose them. Even though it was the first time they had played together, and some were in unfamiliar positions, the new club, with Lucas watching from the stands, took Chicago to 12 innings before losing 6–5 on a bad error by one of the new players. Kansas City lost all four games of the series but played well enough to give their fans hope that with a little practice they could be respectable. They were just 3–17, however, when Ted Sullivan arrived to take over the team.

Sullivan had resigned as manager of the St. Louis club despite its 35–4 record. In 1883 he had problems with his owner, and in 1884 he couldn't get along with the players.

There was a faction, consisting of captain Fred Dunlap, George Shaffer, and Dave Rowe, who didn't like Sullivan and tried to turn the other players against him.[9] The ringleaders were the three stars of the team, acquired at great expense, and if there was a choice between them and Sullivan, the latter would have to go. "Three of the leading spirits tried to run the club," Sullivan said, "and opposed all others in it. I would not tolerate this, and as I was not backed up in my actions by President Lucas I tendered my resignation." Dunlap took over as manager.

Sullivan became manager and reportedly 50 percent owner of the floundering Kansas City club and spent the rest of the summer scouring the country for new talent. When he took over, he admitted that the team was not competitive, said he would spare no effort to improve it, and asked the fans to be patient. Then Sullivan went to work with his typical energy. When the Northwestern League began to disintegrate in mid-summer, Kansas City signed six players from the Quincy and Bay City clubs. When the UA decided to raid other leagues, Sullivan took the lead, although one paper commented, "while they were about it, it seems as though they could get far better prizes than Blaisdell and Oxley of the Lynn."[10]

The roster evolved throughout the season, and the team wound up using the remarkable total of 51 players. The Providence Grays, on the other hand, used just 17. Sullivan even put himself at shortstop for a few games. When the club appeared in Washington at the end of August, it had just one player who'd been with them on the last visit to the city.

Sullivan recruited some impressive looking specimens. When the Cowboys appeared in Boston, the *Clipper* correspondent noted, "The Kansas Citys have been here and gone. They are a large, long-limbed aggregation, and attracted fair crowds, who were much in admiration of their stature, but were not overly enthusiastic about their ball playing."[11]

The Kansas City press maintained its enthusiasm for most of the season, asking the fans to be patient, but they slipped into sarcasm when the club continued to lose. "It was a glowing tribute to the invincible club of Kansas City," said the *Times*, "that the Wilmington nine disbanded as soon as they heard of its approach. It seems that the Wilmington club was formed with the resolution of never winning a game, and it knew that it could not meet the Kansas City nine and sustain that resolution; therefore it disbanded...."[12] The *Star* added, "The Kansas City Unions have not been heard from for a day or two, but they are believed to be wandering in some of the eastern states in search of another defeat."[13]

The club's biggest problem was the lack of a quality pitcher; they used 20 different starters. But Sullivan kept adding players right up to the final game of the season, and after posting a 7–55 record through mid–September, Kansas City won nine of its last 17 games, including four in a row over Boston, and finished the season with a 12–1 win. The final record of 16–63 wasn't impressive, but finishing the schedule was somewhat of a triumph, and Sullivan claimed he cleared a $7,000 profit, an even more amazing accomplishment.

"Tremendous crowds are attending the games in Kansas City," reported the *Boston Globe*, "where the national sport is somewhat of a novelty.... Judging from the enormous crowds which attend the games ... the people of that place would go base ball crazy should their nine win a few games."[14]

The Boston club, which had been assembled at the last minute, proved to be one of the stronger UA entries. Boston had wisely signed some recognizable names, including pitcher Tommy Bond, who was the best pitcher in baseball in the late '70s, winning more than 40 games three seasons in a row and leading Boston to two pennants. Bond, who served as captain, had gotten badly out of shape, but worked out during the winter and reduced his weight from 200 to 168 pounds.

Catching Bond was Lew (Blower) Brown, another veteran of the old Boston pennant winners. Brown was tough and could catch the ball, but he had a drinking problem (he'd been released by Detroit in 1881 for that reason) and a bad arm; base runners took great advantage of him. Manager and first baseman Tim Murnane was yet another member of the old NL champions, but he was 33 and hadn't played in the majors since 1878.

Amidst the veterans were a couple of young outfielders, 17-year-old Mike Slattery and 20-year-old Tommy McCarthy. There have been other 17-year-olds, such as Bob Feller, who played in the majors, but none who, like Slattery, played in nearly every one of their team's games (106 of 111). The diminutive (5'7") McCarthy played in just 53 games and his .215 batting average didn't impress anyone. But McCarthy had a future, eventually joining Boston's National League team, where he and Hugh Duffy became known as the "Heavenly Twins." In 1946, McCarthy became one of the least deserving members of the Hall of Fame.[15]

There were a lot more people in Boston than in Altoona, and the opening game, to which the team graciously invited the Boston NL players, drew a crowd of about 2,500, even though the grandstand was not yet complete. But for the next three games, the Beaneaters were playing on the South End Grounds instead of sitting in the UA club's grandstand and attendance at the UA games dropped precipitously.

Whenever the UA club went head-to-head with the Beaneaters, they came out second best. One Saturday in June, a Boston-Providence game drew 5,000 while the UA contest attracted less than a hundred.[16] A couple of weeks later, the *Clipper* stated, "The attendance at the Union games in the city this week has improved visibly, and on Saturday one thousand people were present. This seems insignificant, of course, when compared with League audiences; the newness of the Union movement must be considered, as well as the short existence of the team."[17] The local *Globe* was supportive, consistently producing positive articles and encouraging locals to check out the UA games, but not many did. During a home stand in late August, attendance did not exceed 250 at any game. Overall, average attendance was about 500, and it was almost impossible to turn a profit at that level.

There was dissension on the Boston team and it centered on the battery. On July 8, the club fined Bond and Brown $100 each and expelled them, despite the fact that Bond had a 13–9 record and Brown had played reasonably well behind the bat. Brown was charged with excessive drinking, including playing one game when he was visibly drunk, and Bond was accused of trying to rally the players against management.

Both men had reason to be unhappy, for the team owed Bond $208 and Brown $180 in unpaid salaries. Bond said it wasn't the first time his pay was late, he was tired of hearing excuses, and he wasn't playing until he got his money. Murnane told him he'd have it (less his fine) within a week but Bond said that was too late. He signed with Indianapolis of the AA. Brown was forgiven and reinstated. He didn't deny drinking to excess but said he'd never been drunk during a game.[18]

Despite its tribulations, the club made it through the season, finishing with a respectable 58–51 record. They were much better after signing former Detroit pitcher Fred Shaw, who struck out 14, 16, and 18 in his first three games. In late September, Shaw beat the champion St. Louis team three games in a row and in about half a season accounted for six of St. Louis' 19 defeats.[19] But after finishing the season and paying the final salary installment, Boston's management estimated its losses at $10,000 and announced that, whether the UA survived or not, it had no intention of fielding a team in 1885.

In Baltimore, the rivalry between the UA and AA was spirited but friendly, as AA manager Bill Barnie and Al Henderson of the UA got on reasonably well. The UA club got off to a promising start, as an opening day crowd of 4,500 witnessed a close 8–7 loss to Washington. Henderson had acquired an attractive, easily accessible site in the central part of the city, and his club played good ball. Unlike many major league teams, they won plaudits for their conduct. "Not only is the cool and brilliant style of their teamwork much admired," wrote *Sporting Life*, "but they are highly commended for their uniformly gentlemanly deportment upon the ball field. They are not only good ballplayers, but an exceptionally good class of men."[20]

Baltimore heated up during the humid southern summer, winning 12 of 13 games from June 6 through July 2 and ripping off a 16-game winning streak from July 14 through August 8, which gave them a 46–20 mark and put them in second place. Then they went cold, suffering through an 11-game losing streak in August and September and finishing the season by losing six of their last seven games. They wound up fourth, 32½ games behind St. Louis. One of the club's problems was an over-reliance on pitcher Bill Sweeney, who started 60 games; no other Baltimore pitcher started more than 14.

Throughout the summer, the most pressing question was not who would win the UA pennant; St. Louis had that well in hand after the first month. It was which teams would finish the season. Not only were the NL and AA doing everything they could to sink the new league; teams from the Northwestern League were trying to steal their players as well.

In late June, a UA insider from St. Louis said the local franchise was doing fine. "We take in enough money at our bar to pay the nine," he said.[21] The weak spots, he confided, were Philadelphia and Washington and he indicated that Lucas was pumping money into some clubs. If $100,000 was needed, he added, the money was available.

A couple of weeks later, the Association issued a report on the financial condition of its franchises:

> St. Louis—"Large surplus in treasury and prospects favorable for heavy excess of receipts over expenditures…."
> Cincinnati—"A trifle behind, but with games yet to be played, confident of coming out on the right side of the ledger."
> Chicago—"Expenditures a trifle in excess of receipts, but confidence expressed of a successful season."
> Baltimore—"Crowds attending all games, and the club daily growing in popular estimation. July 1 the receipts and expenditures just balanced."
> Washington—"The National Club of Washington, which has been classed by several papers as weekly on the point of disbanding—all obligations paid in full to July 1, and a handsome surplus in the treasury, the club being almost level with St. Louis from a financial standpoint."

Keystone—"Greatly encouraged by the prospects ahead, having twenty-four games to play, and a growing increase in popular favor manifested toward the new organization."

Boston—"Boston has not made any money thus far, but the indications showed that there was no lack of interest in the club, and its patronage was steadily improving."

Kansas City—"Kansas City was ahead financially, and assured of popular support at home."[22]

While hopeful, the reports were in most cases somewhat vague and, as it would turn out, not especially accurate. Frank Wright of the Cincinnati UA club, when asked about the league's prospects, said, "They could not be better. All the clubs are paying expenses and St. Louis, Washington, Baltimore, and Boston are making money. The association is bound to go through. Having lasted thus far against almost overwhelming opposition the backers are determined to see it out. Never has a base-ball organization experienced the obstacles the union has. All the best players were kept out of the reach of its clubs and in every way the supporters of the National agreement have tried to kill it, but still it flourishes."[23] The NL and AA insisted that the UA was in bigger trouble than it admitted and that turnstile counts had been inflated.

Around the first of July, stung by the attacks of the NL and AA and their raids upon his players, Lucas said he would no longer respect contracts, and that any player was fair game. There was a rumor that Lucas offered Louisville's iron man pitcher Guy Hecker the phenomenal sum of $4,000 for the rest of the season if he would break his contract.

With Lucas on the prowl, the NL became defensive. "Ballplayers never think for themselves," said Philadelphia manager Harry Wright, "they jump first and think afterward. How is it possible for a club drawing 500 and 600 people to a game to offer $3,000 and $4,000 salaries is a mystery ... and players never stop to think."[24]

"What chance has a player," added Providence manager Frank Bancroft, "who jumps from a National Agreement Club to a Union Club to live? He may make a good salary for one year, by the next season he will be at the mercy of the Union managers. He is ostracized by all National Agreement Clubs, and if he does not accept any offer the Unions may make him he can not play ball."[25] When it was learned that UA clubs had agreed not to poach players from each other, they were accused of hypocrisy. Wasn't that the equivalent of the reserve rule?

Kansas City got the ball rolling by raiding the NWL. Baltimore made offers to four players on the EL-leading Wilmington team, including pitcher Edward (The Only) Nolan. The *St. Louis Post-Dispatch* cautioned, "[A]t no time since it sprung into popularity and became the national game has its existence been so alarmingly threatened ... unless a cessation of hostilities is brought about, and that soon, a cut-throat policy is to prevail which will send to the wall a number of the clubs that are now in existence."[26]

The *Post-Dispatch* had a number of suggestions for righting the situation, including recognizing the UA, reinstating any player blacklisted for violating the reserve rule, appointing a National Board of Arbitration, with representation from each of the three leagues, and a modification of the reserve rule. None of those things were going to happen, for the NL and AA believed the UA was drowning, and planned to watch Lucas' league collapse one team at a time.

The Keystones were the next to fall. As the third team in a three-team city, they faced nearly impossible odds. Most of their players were not well-known, and in an attempt to show Philadelphia fans some familiar names and faces, the Keystones signed two members of the 1871 NA champion Athletics team, 34-year-old Levi Meyerle, major league baseball's first batting champion, and 39-year-old Ferguson Malone, who also served as business manager. Neither lasted long, playing a combined total of just four games.

Attendance was poor from the start. In April, while the Athletics played Philadelphia before 8,000 people, the Keystones played an exhibition against the Foley Club in front of 300. The home opener drew just 500, and the Keystone's 14–2 loss did little to convince anyone to return. For most games, attendance did not exceed 500. On the first home game after a long Western trip, on a day when the National League club also played at home, attendance was a paltry 100. The Keystones drew 1,500 on June 27 when the first place Maroons came to town with native Philadelphians Dunlap and Shaffer, and on the Fourth of July they attracted 4,000 for each game of a doubleheader. But most days only a few hundred came to watch. In desperation, the Keystones reduced the admission fee to fifteen cents.

In addition to stiff competition for Philadelphia fans, the Keystones played under the handicap of a poor record. When they beat Chicago in early July, the *Inquirer* exclaimed, "The Keystones actually won a game."[27] The victory kicked off an eight-game winning streak that boosted the club's record to 18–34, but the hot streak was followed by nine straight losses.

When Fred Dunlap visited his Philadelphia home in May, Tom Pratt told him that despite rumors to the contrary, his Keystone Club was making money and would weather the season. The rumors to the contrary were true, however, and on August 7, the Keystones disbanded. Losses had been about $12,000, the club was about two weeks in arrears on salaries, and the players were getting restless.[28] A long road trip was coming up, with the prospect of realizing only the $75 per game guarantee, which was insufficient to cover salaries and traveling expenses.

Pratt flirted with the idea of joining the Eastern League, where salaries would be lower and traveling expenses lighter, but Lew Simmons of the Athletics vetoed the Keystones under the territorial rule. Some of the players organized a new version of the team, which played a few exhibitions, and that was the end of the Keystones.

The Wilmington Quicksteps, who lost $4,000 while dominating the Eastern League with a 50–12 record, were selected to replace the Keystones. The club had spurned an earlier offer, but they weren't making money in the Eastern League and needed to do something to survive.

The Quicksteps played their first UA game on August 18 and found the competition much tougher than it was in the Eastern League. They lost 16 of 18 UA games and the team that batted .291 against EL opponents managed to hit just .175 in the UA.[29]

As soon as Wilmington joined the UA, Baltimore poached two of its best players. Others began jumping and the situation became chaotic. Historian Jon Springer summarized a three-game series against Cincinnati in early September, during which umpire Pat Dutton was seriously injured. "[O]ne win, two losses, one player down an elevator well, one umpire nearly dead on the field, two players defected, one player released and 17 errors including seven by outfielders."[30]

Whistling in the dark was standard operating procedure for the UA, and as the troubles mounted, Quickstep manager Joe Simmons[31] insisted his club would finish the season and talked about assembling a strong nine for 1885. He said Wilmington had been induced to join the UA by the promise that Lucas would cover the club's expenses (including salaries) on its western trip.[32] But a league meeting to authorize the expense kept getting postponed, the reason for which, Wilmington claimed, was to force them out of the league and replace them with a franchise in Milwaukee.

When the Kansas City club arrived in Wilmington for a game on September 15, and owner John West and Simmons saw less than 200 people in the stands, they called it quits. Attendance had been just three to four hundred a game, West lost between $3,000 and $4,000, and he didn't intend to lose any more. He asked the players to take a discount on the amount owed them, but when they refused, paid them in full. Three of the Wilmington players signed with Kansas City.

Cincinnati had a strong team; of the 23 players who appeared for the club during the season, 13 had prior NL experience. After a quick start, however, they fell into a slump and decided to get rid of some of the troublesome members in the nine, including shortstop Frank McLaughlin. The Unions claimed they did not know of McLaughlin's reputation when they signed him, but since he came from the 1883 Alleghenies, nearly every one of which was a lusher, they probably should have. McLaughlin behaved himself until a trip to Chicago, where he started drinking and didn't stop. He was released after twice showing up too drunk to play. Once the disharmonizing elements were dispatched, the Unions played better, and were a respectable 34–29 in early August.

On August 8, Cincinnati scored a coup that sent shock waves throughout the baseball world, enticing Jack Glasscock, one of the National League's best shortstops, Jim McCormick, one of the League's best pitchers, and Fatty Briody, one the League's chubbiest players, to break their Cleveland contracts and sign with the UA. Either the three hadn't been reading the newspapers or they were blinded by the size of their contracts and advances, for their action earned them immediate blacklisting. If there was no Union Association in 1885, they would be ineligible to play major league baseball. "I presume we will be blacklisted," Briody said, "but we have been playing ball for glory long enough. It is now a matter of dollars and cents."[33] With the defection of McCormick, the UA now boasted four of the NL's top pitchers from 1883 in McCormick, Daily, Sweeney, and Shaw.

Although Glasscock was an outstanding shortstop, he was not the most popular player in the major leagues. He was a combative, irascible man who battled with umpires and teammates and eventually incurred the enmity of many players by going back on the Brotherhood in 1890 in return for a rich contract. "[John] Ward was always a gentleman," said one writer, "on and off the field; Glasscock was just the opposite. I have heard him use language during the progress of the game that would put the meanest tough in the country to shame." He noted that a group of ladies formed for the purpose of attending baseball games refused to go to any match in which Glasscock played and recommended that men like him be banned from the game.[34]

Glasscock didn't care what people thought of him, for he knew what he wanted out of baseball, and it wasn't admiration. In 1887, when there was speculation over where he would play that season, Glasscock told a reporter, "The reports in my wanting to go to this club and that club are all bosh. I want to go where I can get the most money."[35] In 1884, the place he could get the most money was the Union Association, and that was where he went.

The acquisition of the three players made Cincinnati the equal of the first place

Maroons; after the signing they won 30 of 34 overall and beat St. Louis four times in five games. Glasscock batted .419 in 38 games, Briody hit .337 in 22 games, and McCormick was 21–3 with a 1.54 ERA.

There were also financial benefits. The first time the trio appeared in Cincinnati uniforms, attendance was more than 4,000, and when the season ended, Cincinnati was one of the few UA clubs that could boast of at least modest financial success. They reportedly paid all their players in full and after the final game, Justus Thorner took them on a festive outing in the country to celebrate the team's second place finish.

The Cincinnati signing was a great victory for Lucas. "I feel better over Thorner's success in getting McCormick, Glasscock and Briody," he said, "than if someone had given me $10,000. I don't take any pride in contract-breaking as a regular business, but it is a good thing to succeed when self-preservation forces you to engage in it. There is also great pleasure in going into the enemy's camp, capturing their guns, and using them on your own side."[36]

Lucas said things were never better in the UA. "Why, there is no battle," he said, "the strife ended some weeks since. We won the fight against great odds and are now on top."[37] He said the 1885 UA would operate with eight clubs, with franchises in Philadelphia and Cleveland replacing Kansas City and Wilmington. He would force the other leagues to recognize UA contracts and the reserve rule would be abolished. The breakup of the Northwestern League would depress salaries due to greater competition for jobs. Lucas predicted that four AA clubs would be dropped and that the continuing existence of NL franchises in Cleveland, Detroit, and Buffalo depended on additional investment. He considered few AA players worthy of chasing, but was confident that a number of NL players would be playing in the UA in 1885.

Lucas' joy over cuckolding the National League was short-lived, for there was trouble elsewhere. Chicago had been unable to compete with the strong National League franchise, and the local *Tribune* reported its results under the heading "Minor Games" along with those of the NWL and semi-pro contests. By August, rent was several months in arrears and the earlier reported "trifle" by which expenditures exceeded revenue was apparently between $30,000 and $35,000. By the time the season was over, Henderson lost a total of $42,000 operating the Chicago and Baltimore franchises.

In January, there had been talk of a UA franchise in Pittsburgh, but nothing had come of it. In mid–August, Henderson went to Pittsburgh with Warren White to negotiate for the use of Exposition Park. Soon afterward, on a day the UA organ in Cincinnati proclaimed the Chicago club "one of the strongest in the country,"[38] it was announced that the team would move to Pittsburgh, to operate under the auspices of the Exposition Park Association, "which will divide the profits, should there be any to handle, with President Henderson."[39]

The *Pittsburgh Post-Gazette,* which had eviscerated the Alleghenies all season, was enthusiastic about the arrival of a new club. It spoke highly of the new park and noted that with the Alleghenies about to embark on a long road trip, the UA club would have an opportunity to win over Pittsburgh fans, who were eager to see some good ball. Although the team was just 34–39 when they arrived, that was a lot better than the Alleghenies' record. The UA opened on August 25, before a brass band and a reported crowd of 3,000, which saw a win over Lucas' first place team. "The Alleghenys couldn't hunt the ball for these fellows,"[40] one fan was quoted as saying.

The Pittsburgh Club had been operating less than three weeks when the *Clipper* reported rumors that it would disband and its best players would be sent to Henderson's Baltimore Club.⁴¹ The *Clipper* was usually on the mark and, sure enough, the club packed its tent on September 19, having posted a 7–11 mark in Pittsburgh. Six players went to Baltimore. Henderson insisted that the Pittsburgh club had not lost money and was disbanded only to strengthen the Baltimore nine.

Better players were not necessarily the answer; what Henderson really needed was more fans. In early September, when the Maroons were scheduled to play at Baltimore, the two teams arrived at the field and found only a handful of spectators. A couple of the players were sick, so the managers decided to refund the fans' money and cancel the game.

There was better news in Washington. Many had doubted that the city could support two teams, and they were correct, but the UA team was the one that survived. Mike Scanlon was an experienced baseball man with a loyal following who'd kept salaries down and done a good job of shepherding his team through a difficult season. He'd acquired well-located grounds at the intersection of C Street and New Jersey Avenue, in the center of the city near the Capitol, and managed to draw well enough to survive, which was no mean accomplishment in 1884.

When the local AA team failed, Scanlon had Washington to himself. He graciously put on a benefit game for the disenfranchised players that netted them $35–40 each, enough to pay their way back home. Unlike Moxley, who'd spent too much, Scanlon managed prudently and added players judiciously. After starting the season by losing 31 of their first 43 games, the Nationals went 35–34 to finish with a nearly respectable 47–65 mark. "It is a matter of regret," said the *National Republican*, "that we did not have the same nine at the beginning of the season."⁴² If so, the paper surmised, the club would be battling for first place.

With the walls crumbling around them, the UA held a meeting on September 20 at the National Hotel in Washington. St. Louis, Washington, and Kansas City reported profits, while the other clubs admitted they were losing money. The disbandment of the Wilmington and Pittsburgh clubs was formalized and Milwaukee was admitted. Someone (reportedly Lucas) said the Mets and Athletics had made overtures about joining the league, a story that was quickly denied by the latter two organizations.

Lucas admitted there were problems but said "all would be plain sailing in the future."⁴³ The solvent owners agreed to help struggling franchises, if the latter furnished sound collateral, and all expressed a desire to work with the NL and AA to reduce salaries and stop stealing each other's players. Having brought the UA to its knees, the other leagues had no desire to work with them on anything.

Milwaukee, which played its first UA game September 27, was fighting on several fronts almost immediately. They were trying to survive, they were trying to keep other teams from stealing their players, and they were trying to come up with some semblance of a schedule. In order to eliminate the expense of traveling, the club was allowed to play all of its 12 games at home.

The same day Milwaukee made its debut, a new franchise in St. Paul played its first game. St. Paul had been a member of the NWL and continued to play exhibitions after the league disbanded. Since the team was already on the road, they played all of their UA games away from home, losing six of eight.

By the end of the season, the UA looked nothing like it had when it took its hopeful first steps in April. Of the eight teams that started the season, only St. Louis, Cincinnati,

Baltimore, Boston, and Washington made it to the finish line. Chicago, Philadelphia, and Altoona perished along the way, as did Wilmington, which lasted just a month. Lucas was said to have pumped a total of $40,000 into some of the weaker franchises to keep them afloat.

The pennant race had long been decided and the only excitement was in seeing which teams would survive. The final standings reflected the league's imbalance and its turnover.

|  | W | L | Pct. | GB |
|---|---|---|---|---|
| St. Louis | 94 | 19 | .832 | — |
| Milwaukee | 8 | 4 | .667 | 35½ |
| Cincinnati | 69 | 36 | .657 | 21 |
| Baltimore | 58 | 47 | .552 | 32 |
| Chicago-Pittsburgh | 41 | 50 | .451 | 42 |
| Washington | 47 | 65 | .420 | 46½ |
| Philadelphia | 21 | 46 | .313 | 50 |
| St. Paul | 2 | 6 | .250 | 39½ |
| Altoona | 6 | 19 | .240 | 44 |
| Kansas City | 16 | 63 | .203 | 61 |
| Wilmington | 2 | 16 | .111 | 44½ |

NOTE: The standings are based on winning percentage, regardless of the number of games played. "To keep a correct record of the Union Association," said the *Boston Globe*, "is worse than solving a Chinese puzzle."[44] The standings were so muddled that many papers ceased publishing them. The rules of the UA called for a replacement for a disbanded team to assume the schedule of the old team, with the games to count on the record of the original team. Most gave up trying to determine the status of teams that played a partial season.

Lucas had his championship by a wide margin and Kansas City managed to finish 61 lengths behind while playing just 79 games; by comparison, the 1962 Mets, often used as a standard of ineptitude, finished 60 games behind over 160 games.

The best individual performer was St. Louis second baseman Fred Dunlap. Playing 101 games, Dunlap won the UA batting title by hitting .412, besting second place George Shaffer by 52 points. He scored 160 runs, had 185 hits and hit 39 doubles, which would equate to 227 runs, 263 hits and 55 doubles had St. Louis played a 162-game schedule. Dunlap also led the league with 13 home runs. Teammate Shaffer, a 32-year-old veteran of the National Association and National League, was second in batting average (.360), runs (130), and hits (168), and surpassed Dunlap by hitting 40 doubles. Bill Sweeney of Baltimore threw 538 innings and was league's top winner with 40 victories and 21 defeats. While Dunlap and Shaffer played in the National League in subsequent seasons, Sweeney never pitched another major league game.

The weakness of applying modern day statistical analysis to 19th-century performances is neatly demonstrated by the fact that Retrosheet's Batter-Fielder Wins (BFW) category shows the Maroons with an aggregate of *negative* 2.2! The team record was 94–19, so someone must have been doing *something* to win those games, but modern analysis doesn't recognize it.

There were hopes that the UA would play post-season exhibitions against NL and AA clubs, especially in St. Louis. "What stupendous humbug the national agreement is anyhow," said a local paper. "Here is St. Louis with two rival clubs, and the entire local base ball patronage anxious to see them play a series of games, but because one organization is a subscriber to the national agreement they can not meet."[45]

In mid–October, on hearing that Browns manager Charlie Comiskey said his team would play the Maroons if each player put up $100 as a purse, Fred Dunlap accepted and said he would personally put up the money for any teammate who was hesitant. Von der Ahe even promised to donate the proceeds to charity, but the AA was unwilling to give the UA an opportunity to challenge them on the playing field. They were winning off the field.

The Cincinnati UA team challenged any nine in Ohio to play a series for the championship of the state and a cash prize. The team they wanted to play, of course, was Caylor's AA team, which wouldn't take the bait. The *Enquirer* published the challenge for several days at the head of its sports section, and each notice announced how many days the challenge had been running without being accepted. It never was.

Kansas City and Louisville scheduled a series, but when the

Fred Dunlap, considered by many the finest second baseman of his era, was easily the best player in the 1884 Union Association. He led the upstart league with a .412 average, 160 runs scored and 185 hits in just 101 games. When the Union Association collapsed after the season, he stayed with owner Henry Lucas' Maroons when they entered the National League (National Baseball Hall of Fame Library, Cooperstown, N.Y.).

latter went to Kansas City, they were stymied by bad weather and misunderstandings, and left without playing a single game. Mills told Louisville they could not play without risking expulsion, even if the season was over. The players were under reserve, Mills reminded Louisville, and while it was not strictly illegal, "such an act would be injurious to us and a direct benefit to the common enemy, and I trust that means will be found to prevent it."[46] The UA, he said, "has managed to exist to the present time with the corpses of but four of its clubs buried by the wayside this season. What promises of permanence, much less of reputation and prosperity, can be found in its career I leave for others to estimate. But I invite clubs of the national agreement to consider what chance of success *they* would have should they recognize or in any way affiliate with the clubs of the Union Association, and thereby not only aid in perpetuating that association but also condone acts which they have pledged themselves to resist and which, if sanctioned and persisted in, cannot fail to wreck professional ball playing."[47]

Apparently, someone was listening to Mills, for when Von der Ahe learned that Louisville planned to play UA teams, he cancelled an exhibition series with them. Louisville did play against the Cincinnati and St. Louis UA clubs, splitting two games with Cincinnati and losing 15–1 to St. Louis. Guy Hecker, who had to be exhausted after carrying the pitching load all season, was hit hard by UA batters.

Despite the fact that the UA was crumbling, it was bravely making plans for 1885, featuring an eight-team league, a guarantee fund to prop up shaky franchises, and a split of gate proceeds for road teams rather than a flat $75 payment. But it seemed unlikely that there would be a Union Association in 1885. What Henry Lucas really wanted was a major league franchise. He'd had to form his own league to get one in 1884, and for 1885, he was looking for a less painful way to become part of the big leagues.

# 15

# The Pitchers

In 1884, pitching was more dominant than in any previous season. From the 1840s to the 1880s, the roles of the pitcher and catcher gradually evolved from ones of relative inconsequence to the two most important positions on the field. While the job of early pitchers had been merely to put the ball in play, the 1884 pitcher was a formidable defensive weapon, primarily due to changes to the rules regulating his delivery. In baseball's early days, the pitcher was restricted to underhand pitching with a stiff wrist, but over the decades the rules were relaxed to allow the pitcher more freedom of movement, which enabled them to generate more speed and make their deliveries much harder to hit.

As the role of the pitcher evolved, so did that of the catcher, whose initial function was to stand well behind the bat and return the ball to the pitcher. By the 1880s the catcher had become perhaps even more important than the pitcher; a good pitcher without a capable catcher was useless. And the better the pitcher and the harder he threw, the more he needed a tough, agile, athletic man behind the plate.

Catchers were chewed up rapidly and no backstop, no matter how tough he was, could play every game. His hands couldn't take it. The primary task of the catcher was defense; the hitting of 19th-century catchers was similar to that of pitchers in the 20th century, and there were many pitchers who were better hitters than their catchers. Pitchers knew how important their catcher was to their success and many refused to join a new team unless they were assured of good support behind the bat. When pitcher Ed Morris signed with Columbus in 1884, he did so on the condition that his catcher, Fred Carroll, would be signed as well.

Pitching dominance was a relatively recent phenomenon. In the National League's first season (1876) failure to put a ball in play was relatively rare. Pitchers issued 336 bases on balls and racked up 589 strikeouts in 520 games, less than one walk and slightly more than one strikeout per game. In 1883, NL clubs played 790 games and there were 1,121 walks and 2,877 strikeouts, more than four and a half strikeouts per game. That's not a lot by current standards, but it was a dramatic change over just seven years.[1] In 1871, the first season of major league baseball, Al Pratt led the league with 34 strikeouts. Al Spalding, the best pitcher of the National Association era, fanned 23 in 257 innings. In 1883, Boston's Jim Whitney led the National League with 345 strikeouts in 514 innings, while the Mets' Tim Keefe led the AA with 359. Many baseball people, most prominently Henry Chadwick, thought the game was becoming too focused on a pair of men playing pitch and catch while the other seven stood idly by.

Baseball's rules were amended frequently during its early years, often to maintain a balance between offense and defense. As pitchers began throwing harder and trying to prevent the hitter from making solid contact, the front line of the pitchers' box was moved back from 45 to 50 feet and the calling of balls and strikes was initiated. The rules governing balls and strikes changed nearly every year. By 1884, it took six called balls for a walk in the NL, while the AA required seven. Then, as now, three strikes sent a batter back to the bench. In a new and controversial change, AA batters who were hit by a pitch were awarded first base. Those in the NL just rubbed a little, glared at the pitcher, and stepped back up to the plate.

By 1884, National League pitchers were totally unrestricted in their delivery while American Association and Union Association hurlers had to deliver the ball from below the shoulder.[2] Rule changes invariably came after the fact, after pitchers ignored the previous rule and umpires didn't enforce it. In 1883, while NL pitchers were ostensibly required to keep their arm below the shoulder, many didn't, and at the end of the year, the rules committee dropped the requirement to conform to actual practice.

With the elimination of all restrictions, many feared that pitchers would dominate the game. "It has not been decided," quipped the *Buffalo Times*, "whether to use a cannon or continue the present system of delivering the ball."[3] Tim Keefe, star pitcher of the Metropolitans, said that even though NL pitchers could throw from above the shoulder, most wouldn't because of the strain it would place on their arm. "Whitney, Radbourn and Galvin," Keefe said, "kept their arms up as high as they cared to last season ... they won't throw any higher this season. They would not be able to ever stand the strain if they ever tried it."[4] Keefe and Radbourn continued to use their sidearm styles even after the AA rules changed. Will White, who'd pitched since the mid–1870s, was one of the last underhand throwers.

"Nineteenth century pitching was somewhat of a variety show," wrote Bryan Di Salvatore,[5] for other than arm angle, there were few restrictions on a pitcher's delivery. With no pitching rubber, some pitchers, such as Jim Whitney and Mickey Welch, raced forward and leapt toward the front line of the pitching box. Whitney was nicknamed "Grasshopper" because of the way he approached the line at a gallop and jumped at the batter.

When the NL banned preliminary contortions after the 1884 season, the *Buffalo Commercial* noted with relief, "Under the new rule the pitcher cannot take the ball in his two-thousand-apiece-dollar hands and fumble it, and then moisten his finger and thumb with saliva and wipe them on the side of his trousers, cross his right foot around in front of his left, just touching the toes of the former to the ground, stand in this picturesque attitude several seconds, while the feelings of the spectators are wrought up to fever heat, and then suddenly untie his legs and go down into his pocket for a chew of tobacco, and wink at the pretty girl who is watching his contortion through an opera glass."[6]

Many pitchers, including Charlie Buffinton and Guy Hecker, had a delivery that routinely brought them over the front line of the pitchers' box before they delivered the ball. If a team thought the visiting pitcher had a habit of stepping over the line, they put stones on the boundary. "When Indianapolis strikes Cincinnati," said one paper, "McKeon may find the box fenced in by tombstones."[7] Jumbo McGinnis of St. Louis injured his feet on the stones, damning evidence of his transgression. Hecker, expecting his opponent to use the stone strategy, wore a pair of tennis shoes to thwart them.

Even with the liberalized rules, the limit on a pitcher's speed was his catcher. By

1884, most backstops were using some form of bodily protection. It was nothing like today's equipment, but a giant leap from baseball's early days, when the catcher's only protection was his agility and courage. Catchers now had gloves, a mask, and a chest protector. The *New Haven News* noted "With his frontal liver-pad, his hands cased in thick gloves, the familiar wire helmet on his head, the average baseball catcher looks for all the world like an animated combination of a modern bed-bolster and a medieval knight."[8]

Teams needed multiple catchers, for they invariably wore out during the season. There were rare exceptions, such as Emil Gross, who achieved the remarkable feat of catching every one of Providence's 87 games in 1880. But for the rest, it was only a matter of time before fingers were broken, hands swollen, teeth loosened, or worse. The *Cincinnati Enquirer* reported that a catcher from the local Clipper team lost two fingernails, had two teeth knocked out, with hit on the head with a foul tip, and fell off a cliff chasing a foul pop, which cost him most of his pants. It was all in a day's work.

Injuries were also a way of life for 1884 pitchers. Each team had just one or two good ones and they were worked until their arms wore out. Then, after a day or two of rest, they were back in the box again. Every regular pitcher had a sore arm by the end of the season, and it was an endurance contest to make it to the end.

The life span of pitchers was brief, and Bobby Mathews was the only 1871 major league hurler still active in 1884. The concept of preserving a pitcher's arm was a foreign one and the only reason for not pitching was ineffectiveness. If a manager found a reliable pitcher, he kept running him out to the box until he became ineffective, which he inevitably did when his arm finally gave out.

Often the man chosen to pitch was the one whose arm hurt the least that day. There was a spirited debate as to whether managers should rotate their pitchers to conserve their strength or go with the hot hand until it wore out. They were usually criticized when a second-line pitcher lost while the star rested.

Most National Association teams had one regular pitcher who started every game and nearly always finished what he started. As the schedule expanded and a longer pitching distance put more strain on pitchers' arms, managers realized they would wear out one pitcher. The first true pitching rotation was that of Fred Goldsmith and Larry Corcoran in Chicago. At first, pitchers resented a second man sharing their position, but when the White Stockings began winning pennants, it wasn't long before other teams followed suit.

Even with a two-man rotation, 1884 pitchers threw a staggering number of innings. Ten logged more than 500 and three exceeded 600. A relief pitcher was rarely used, even when a game went deep into extra innings. In early July 1884, Bob Emslie of Baltimore and Guy Hecker of Louisville each went the 15-inning distance against each other, and no one was surprised.

One of the principal jobs of a manager was to fill the schedule with revenue-producing exhibition games, which gave small town fans a chance to see big-time players. They especially wanted to see a team's star pitcher and thus, during the course of a summer, pitchers threw far more innings than were counted in the official statistics.

Old Hoss Radbourn was the pitcher whose 1884 season would be remembered through the ages, but there were a number of other iron men. Boston, like Providence, found itself down to just one pitcher after Jim Whitney became ill. While Charley Buffinton wasn't Radbourn, he started 67 games, despite being hampered by a sore arm for six weeks. The fact that his arm was sore, of course, did not mean he wasn't pitching; he merely wasn't pitching comfortably or well. During one stretch Buffinton pitched nine games in a row and 11 of 12 and during another started seven games in a row and nine of 10. After he lost to Philadelphia on August 2, the *Clipper* noted, "Buffinton showed signs of the strain of continuous work in the pitcher's position."⁹

When he was healthy, Whitney also logged a lot of innings. In early June, he pitched 25 innings in two days against Providence. Twenty-five innings in two days was a heavy load for any pitcher, but it was even tougher for Whitney, with his hard fastball and all the gyrations in his delivery.¹⁰

By the end of the season, both Whitney and Buffinton were worn out and with his team out of the race, manager John Morrill decided not to break them. Whitney did not start a game after September 17 and Buffinton started just four of the last ten games. Without their two best pitchers, Boston stumbled to the finish, winning just eight of their last 22 games.

Buffinton racked up 417 strikeouts in 584 innings, second in the NL to Radbourn. On September 2, he struck out 17 Cleveland Blues. While Whitney relied almost exclusively on his speed, Buffinton had an excellent curve ball and what observers referred to as a "slow drop," which sank quickly due to a peculiar twist he put on the ball.

Unlike Providence and Boston, Buffalo started the season knowing they had a one-man rotation in an era that demanded two. Jim Galvin, a stocky 5'8" hurler who eventually ballooned to 250 pounds, made his major league debut in 1875 with St. Louis of the old NA, then pitched for professional teams that were not members of the National League. In 1878, when Buffalo played in the International Association, Galvin was an iron man. Statistics are incomplete, but his biographer Brian (Chip) Martin stated that Galvin pitched in 101

**In the late summer of 1884, Pud Galvin had a remarkable streak of pitching in which he threw a no-hitter, a one-hitter, and a three hitter within six days. For the season, he was 46–22 and allowed less than two earned runs per game. Galvin was baseball's first 300-game winner and was elected to the Hall of Fame in 1965 (National Baseball Hall of Fame Library, Cooperstown, N.Y.).**

of his team's 117 games, starting 95 of them. In an estimated 895 innings, he won 72, lost 25, and tied three. He pitched 17 shutouts and got 10 wins against NL clubs. In 1879 he started 66 of his team's 79 games and completed 65 of them, throwing 593 innings. Galvin's primary weapon was a good fastball; he never mastered the curve due to his relatively small hands.

In 1884, Galvin started 72 of Buffalo's 114 games and posted a 46–22 record. When Galvin didn't pitch, Buffalo was 17–25. "Buffalo made the fight with Galvin alone,"[11] said the *New York Sun*. Galvin was injured and ill early in the year, and by August, his arm was shot from overwork. When the Bisons went to Utica for an exhibition game, Captain Jim O'Rourke planned to give his star pitcher a much-needed rest. But the Utica fans had turned out to see Galvin, and wouldn't be happy until they saw him. Galvin pitched the ninth inning, sore arm and all.

Just prior to the Utica game, Galvin had one of the most remarkable pitching streaks in the long history of baseball. On the 2nd of August, he pitched a one-hitter against Detroit. Two days later, he pitched a no-hitter against the Wolverines. He had a perfect game until the ninth inning when, with one out, Dan Brouthers dropped Deacon White's throw to first base. Galvin struck out the next two batters to complete the no-hitter, but missed hurling baseball's third perfect game. He'd been down that road before. In 1880 he pitched a no-hitter that would have been a perfect game had his teammates not committed six errors behind him. Three days after his 1884 no-hitter, in Buffalo's next game, Galvin shut out Detroit once more, this time allowing just three hits.

Over the space of six days, Galvin had thrown a one-hitter, a no-hitter, and a three hitter—just four hits and no runs in 27 innings. He'd faced just 87 batters, only six over the minimum, and at one point retired 54 of 56. In his next game, Galvin lost 1–0 in 12 innings.

In a year of remarkable pitching performances, Guy Hecker of Louisville took a back seat to no one. He had one of the most amazing seasons in the history of major league baseball, ranking in the top ten all-time single-season marks for the following categories:

| Wins | 52 | 3rd |
| Starts | 73 | tied for 4th |
| Complete Games | 72 | tied for 3rd |
| Innings Pitched | 671 | 3rd |
| Strikeouts | 385 | 7th |

Hecker led the AA in games pitched, games started, complete games, wins, innings pitched, and strikeouts, including 17 in one game. Radbourn's statistics were just a little better than Hecker's, but what set the Louisville pitcher apart was that he was also one of the best hitters on his team. In 316 at bats, he hit .297 with four home runs and 42 RBI. He tied for the team lead in homers and was third in RBI, despite playing in just 78 of Louisville's 110 games. "His combined skill as a pitcher, a batsman, fielder and a base runner," said the *Clipper*, "render him the most effective all-round player in the professional fraternity."[12] When Hecker began playing more frequently at first base and the outfield, he accumulated even more impressive statistics, leading the AA with a .341 average in 1886 and batting .319 the following season.

The term "no-hitter" was not yet in use nor was the accomplishment feted as it would be in the 20th century. It was mentioned in game accounts, but almost as a quirky oddity rather than a great achievement. Thirty years after he pitched major league baseball's first perfect game, John Lee Richmond told a reporter, "I do not recall that any particular fuss was made about it by any newspaper or any set of 'fans'...."[13]

When Al Atkinson of the Athletics tossed his no-hitter, the *Philadelphia Times* said, "[A]s the contest was so one-sided there was no interest manifested, save towards the close of the game, when the majority of the spectators stayed to see if the Alleghenies would succeed in making a base hit."[14]

The longest no-hitter of 1884 (and the longest to date by a pitcher not involved in a decision) was thrown by Sam Kimber of the Brooklyn AA club, who had several low-hit games during the season. Kimber pitched a rain-shortened one-hitter against the Athletics, a two-hitter against Baltimore, and on October 4 against Toledo, he pitched a ten-inning no-hitter in a game that ended in a scoreless tie. The *Clipper* was thoroughly unimpressed. After briefly noting that it was the first time in history a pitcher had ever held a team hitless for ten innings, the *Clipper* declared, "It was a battle between the pitchers throughout and a fine sample of what the game will ultimately become unless the batsmen are given equal chances with the pitchers."[15]

The *Clipper*'s concern was based upon the fact that there were eight major league no-hitters in 1884, the most ever in a major league season until 13 were thrown in 2021. There had been only two no-hitters in 1883 and a total of just ten since major league baseball began in 1871.

The first 1884 no-hitter was by Atkinson on May 24, and over a six-day period in late May and early June, Ed Morris and Frank Mountain of Columbus each threw one. Morris got the usual blasé response. "Not a single safe hit was made off Morris, while Neagle was hit pretty hard."[16] Mountain added to the luster of his no-hitter by adding a home run.

In 1884, Guy Hecker of Louisville had one of the best seasons in the history of major league pitching. Unfortunately, he chose the year that Hoss Radbourn had perhaps *the* best year a pitcher ever had, which cast Hecker into the shadow. The latter was also an excellent hitter, and batted a healthy .341 while pitching and playing first base and the outfield in 1886 (National Baseball Hall of Fame Library, Cooperstown, N.Y.).

On June 27, Larry Corcoran of the White Stockings achieved the remarkable feat of no-hitting the powerful Providence Grays in Chicago's tiny park with its ridiculously short fences. In the other three games of the series the Grays scored 25 runs, which was more typical in Chicago. It was the third no-hitter of Corcoran's career[17]; no pitcher threw four until Sandy Koufax pitched his perfect game against the Cubs in 1965. The game report said only, "they did not secure anything approaching a base hit from Corcoran's delivery."[18]

There were two no-hitters in the Union Association, by Dick Burns of Cincinnati against Kansas City and Ed Cushman of Milwaukee against Washington. There were a few tainted no-hitters as well, including a six-inning, 10-strikeout darkness-shortened gem by Charles Getzien of Detroit, in which Philadelphia hit just one ball out of the infield. Charlie Geggus (whose name was spelled in a variety of ways in press reports), pitched just 21 games in his major league career, but in one of them he didn't allow a hit in eight innings. The game was then called by mutual consent.

Larry McKeon pitched six hitless innings for Indianapolis before the game was called due to rain. The *Cincinnati Enquirer* was so unimpressed that its headline was "A Tiresome Affair." Near the end of the season, Charlie Sweeney (two innings) and Henry Boyle (three innings) of the St. Louis Maroons combined for five hitless innings in a rain-shortened game, in which Sweeney garnered the only hit by either team.

It may not have been the liberalized pitching rules that led to the flurry of no-hitters, as only two occurred in the NL, the only league that allowed complete freedom of delivery. The common denominator among no-hit victims was that they were weak-hitting teams. The Alleghenies, with a team average of .211, were the victims on two occasions, while Kansas City (.199), Washington (AA) (.200), Washington (UA) (.237), and Detroit (.208) were held hitless once. The only strong club to have a no-hitter pitched against them was Providence, and their main strength was Hoss Radbourn rather than their offense, which ranked fifth in the NL with a .241 average.

In addition to the no-hitters, there were other noteworthy pitching feats, including Galvin's remarkable run and Sweeney's 19-strikeout game. On July 7, Hugh (One Arm) Daily of the UA's Chicago club pitched a one-hitter against Boston and tied Sweeney's major league mark by fanning 19. Under current rules, he would have had 20 strikeouts; he was not credited with one when his catcher dropped a third strike and threw wildly to first.

The great pitching feats of 1884 were alarming to some. "It seems to be now generally recognized in base ball circles here," said the *Pittsburgh Post-Gazette* at the end of the season, "that the rules of the game must be amended as to give the batsman a better chance to make runs, such general complaint of the shortness of the games, and of their monotony by reason of the constant putting out of men without their reaching even first base ... the fear is entertained by base ball managers that general interest in the game will die out."[19]

Baseball's rule makers had been equal to the task in previous years, and before long, the pitcher was moved back a few feet and offensive baseball made a comeback. For more than a hundred years, there would be periods in which pitchers dominated the action and others when home runs flew over outfield fences in record numbers. But the likes of Hoss Radbourn, Guy Hecker, and Pud Galvin, workhorses who toiled more than 500 innings and carried a team on their backs, would not be seen again.

# 16

## "Shadows of their former selves"

If the major leagues were unstable in 1884, they were a pillar of strength compared to the minor leagues, where one needed to be a forensic wizard just to determine a league's standings. Eighteen eighty-four was perhaps the most challenging year in the history of minor league baseball, even rougher than the two 20th-century war eras. During the world wars, minor leagues had their rosters decimated by government conscription. In 1884, they were victims of the expanded major leagues.

In 1881, the eight-team National League was the only major league, but in 1884 there were three leagues and 34 teams, each of which needed players and a home city. Major league teams took the best cities and players, leaving the minors scrambling for talent and unclaimed territory. They wound up saddled with secondary cities and marginal, unreliable players, to whom they had to pay inflated salaries. The difference between minor and major league players was not as pronounced as it is today, and many minor league teams paid salaries nearly equivalent to those paid major leaguers. In an increasingly competitive field in which revenue generation was a challenge, high salaries made a difficult situation almost impossible. Before the season, the *Cleveland Leader* offered some cautionary advice to members of the Ohio League. "The clubs who enter it," the *Leader* said, "should do so with one determination paramount to all the rest. That is to stay out the season, come what may."[1]

But minor league operators were entrepreneurial and optimistic and not inclined to hunker down and control expenses. They seemed determined to put themselves in jeopardy by expanding too rapidly, becoming too widely dispersed, and in their quest to bring glory to their home towns, spending too much money on salaries.

The results were predictable. The Northwestern League, the most prominent minor circuit, folded, as did several other leagues. The Eastern League, which began the season with high hopes, staggered to the finish line with just five teams remaining. "The trouble in the Northwestern and Eastern Leagues," said one journalist, "has been too big salaries, too large circuits for too small towns, and too many games per week."[2] That's a lot of trouble.

The Eastern League was a new venture that essentially took the place of the Interstate Association. The IA began the 1883 season with seven teams in New York, Pennsylvania, and New Jersey and finished with five. During the winter, there was an attempt to organize for 1884, but two of the league's strongest prospective franchises, Altoona and Brooklyn, joined the UA and AA, respectively. It would be difficult to survive without those teams and the Interstate decided not to try, one of the few sensible decisions in the baseball world of 1884.

When it became apparent that the Interstate Association wasn't going to answer the bell, the Union League, covering a similar geographical area, was established in its stead. The organizers understood the value of a compact footprint and decreed that all clubs should be located within an imaginary line running through New York, Richmond, and Harrisburg. "I know very little about the Eastern League," one National League man said before the season, "except that it has the shortest circuit of any association and one that there is scarcely a chance of losing money on."[3]

The *Clipper* suggested that the Union League join forces with the Union Association, but when the NL and AA learned of the possible alliance, AA president Denny McKnight approached the UL with the promise of concessions if they steered clear of the UA. The UL, leery of being banned from exhibition games with NL and AA teams, signed on to the National Agreement February 19 and became an official member of organized baseball. To eliminate the confusion between the two organizations, they changed their name to the Eastern League.

The Eastern League began the season with eight teams located in New Jersey, Pennsylvania, Delaware, Maryland, and Virginia. Four of them, Harrisburg, Trenton, the Active of Reading, and the Quicksteps of Wilmington (Quickstep was a Civil War term for a brisk march) were former members of the Interstate Association. The Virginia franchise, formed in the summer of 1883, was the first team from a former Confederate state to participate in a professional league. In their first year, using mostly local players, they finished with a 33–14 record, doing very well against inferior competition but generally coming out second best against AA, NL, and Interstate Association teams.

The only EL club sharing a city with a major league team was the Monumental of Baltimore. Both the AA and UA were in Baltimore, and three teams was probably two too many but the AA and NL felt that a having a third team might help drive the UA out of business. Billy Barnie, manager of the city's AA team, didn't think there were enough fans in Baltimore to support three teams and waged a spirited battle to keep the Monumentals out of the Eastern League.

Although Barnie was unsuccessful, it wasn't long before natural causes accomplished what Barnie could not. On May 20, after losing 10 of their 13 games, the short life of the Monumentals came to an inglorious end, the first of many fatalities that would mar the 1884 season. "The Monumentals are gone," said *Sporting Life*, "to that bourne from whence no base ball club returns."[4]

The team had an almost impossible financial burden, having spent a reported $10,000 to improve their grounds[5, 6] and having a lease payment that was more than that paid by some major league clubs. When attendance averaged only about one hundred per game, it didn't take long for the team to run out of money. The hotel where the players lived moved to evict them.

With their pay a month in arrears for a season that was only a month old, the players showed up for a scheduled game with Harrisburg and refused to dress unless they were paid. There were about 75 spectators on hand, not nearly enough to pay expenses. The Harrisburg players took the field and when no Monumental appeared at the plate, umpire Wes Curry told the pitcher to deliver. When he threw nine pitches over the plate, Curry awarded the game to Harrisburg. The Monumentals' career had come to an end, and according to *Sporting Life*, it was a miracle they had lasted that long. "It is wonderful to contemplate," said the paper, "what was done by Manager Spence with the little he had at command."[7]

Despite the sorry state of affairs, Monumental president George Massamore insisted he could have gone on had the players not balked. He claimed he was but $200 behind and that there were investors ready to put in more money. "It was a foolish act on the part of the men to stop when they did," he claimed. "They ought to have gone ahead and played the game with the Harrisburg Club."[8]

Without consulting his colleagues, EL secretary Henry Diddlebock assigned the Ironsides of Lancaster to assume the Monumentals' schedule. NL president Mills declared that the Ironsides were ineligible to enter the Eastern League, but could play as long as their games didn't count. After some hemming and hawing, it was announced that the games already played by the Monumentals would count in the standings, and the Ironsides would play as outsiders. It was a muddled affair, but in fairness to Diddlebock, he was dealing with a fairly novel situation. By the end of the year, baseball executives would become much more experienced in handling franchise failures.

By mid-summer, several Eastern League teams were suffering from a lack of patronage, particularly those in Harrisburg, Reading, and Wilmington, even though the latter had by far the strongest team in the league. They were too good, and their dominance robbed their games of interest and depressed attendance. It was uncertain whether they would last long enough to capture the pennant so readily within their grasp.

It wasn't long before Harrisburg disbanded and was replaced by the Atlantics of Brooklyn, which played just two games before being expelled for failing to pay a guarantee to the Virginia Club. At a July 16 league meeting, the Lancaster (PA) Club and the York (PA) Club applied for admission and the Ironsides asked to move from their hybrid status to full membership. The league urged the two clubs from Lancaster to consolidate and apply as one team, but they had a history of squabbling and couldn't get together. To complicate matters further, the Monumentals applied for re-admission.[9] The league admitted the Ironside and York nines, which would play the schedules of the Monumental and Harrisburg Clubs, respectively.

Amidst all the turmoil, the action on the field became almost incidental, and with the confusion over the status of the Ironsides and whether or not to count the games of disbanded teams, the standings were a hopeless mess. To complicate things even further, the league ruled that the Ironsides could count the games played prior to their full admission. Regardless of how the standings were calculated, it was clear that on July 21, Wilmington, thanks to a 19-game winning streak, had a substantial lead.

|  | W | L | Pct. | GB |
|---|---|---|---|---|
| Wilmington | 40 | 7 | .851 | — |
| Active | 24 | 20 | .545 | 14½ |
| Virginia | 25 | 21 | .543 | 14½ |
| Trenton | 27 | 24 | .529 | 15 |
| Domestic | 23 | 24 | .489 | 17 |
| Ironsides | 17 | 20 | .459 | 18 |
| Allentown | 20 | 26 | .435 | 19½ |
| York | 0 | 3 | .000 | 17 |

On July 25, Allentown disbanded and dropped out. Jersey City applied to fill the vacancy, as did the Atlantics, who claimed their failure to pay the guarantee money to Virginia was the fault of their manager, Charles Endler. Once the other officers found out the money hadn't been paid, they discharged Endler and now wanted a second chance.

The league was reaching the desperate stage, losing teams and having to choose replacements from prospects that, like the Ironsides and Atlantics, were flawed. But 19th-century magnates, even the small-time magnates who ran the Eastern League, were made of stern stuff. *Sporting Life* said, "The Eastern League, which started out with such a rosy prospect, has had considerable hard luck, but the officers are not discouraged and will keep the League afloat to finish the season, and also be in the field next year, when, however, a much better circuit will be established."[10]

Those were brave words, for there were still two months left in the 1884 season, and if many more clubs dropped out, the officers wouldn't have to worry about 1885. Sure enough, it wasn't long before more bad news was afloat. Shortly after Allentown disbanded, the league received the ominous news that their best team, Wilmington, was being seduced by the Union Association to replace the defunct Philadelphia Keystones. If Wilmington left the Eastern League, there would be a big hole to fill and not much to fill it with.

Wilmington's rotund young president, John West, who ran a gambling den known as the "Sweat Box," was sorely tempted. But he decided against moving, at least until he could negotiate a better deal. In the meantime, the Eastern League got some rare good news. Allentown was back; their disbandment had lasted just a few days. "Drunkenness and dissensions among the players," reported *Sporting Life*, "were the cause of the trouble. The players promised to do better and the club directors decided to give them another chance."[11]

Allentown was back but it wasn't long before the Actives of Reading were gone. The Actives had encountered trouble as early as May, in the form of heavy drinking by the players and a revolt against manager Frank Heifert. The team was divided into two cliques, one of Eastern players and the other of Californians. With dissension and slim attendance, the club was in dire circumstances.

At the end of July, the directors held a closed-door meeting and decided to keep going and try to boost attendance by scheduling exhibitions with National League and American Association clubs. That was a sound plan but difficult to execute, for major league teams were not eager to play in a city that couldn't draw. Not surprisingly, the plan was unsuccessful, and the Actives were eventually expelled from the Eastern League for nonpayment of dues. On August 30, the team's fixtures were sold at auction.

On August 5, Diddlebock announced that he had expelled the Virginia Club because they owed the league $44.50, consisting of $24.50 that president W.C. Seddon charged the league for travel to the meeting and $20 in fines against their players. Given the difficulty the league was having keeping their teams alive, it seemed odd that they would expel a team for owing less than $50 and there was, in fact, more to the story. Virginia had accepted an offer to join the American Association as Washington's replacement.

When Virginia left, the league lost its president, for Seddon went with them. S. Reineman of Trenton was elected in his place, a new board of directors was appointed, and the league trundled on with six teams.

This was the summer of deals, and Seddon approached Wilmington's West to propose combining the two teams and joining the AA as one. West, however, was moving in another direction. He'd received a visit from UA secretary Warren White to see if the Quicksteps might now be interesting in switching. West again declined, citing the increased travel costs associated with the UA. If he was going to leave the protection of the National Agreement, he wanted a better deal. Eventually, the UA made West the proverbial offer he couldn't refuse. They reportedly offered to pay the salaries of Wilmington's players and traveling expenses for the next road trip, and give the team 50 percent of gate receipts. It was a great deal for the struggling Quicksteps, but perhaps the death knell for the Eastern League. "The secession of the Wilmington Club," said the *Clipper*, "will prove damaging to this association, and it is likely that its days are numbered."[12]

The Eastern League was resilient, however, and the Virginia and Wilmington defections were just two more in a long string of tribulations. But they were running out of solutions, and a meeting convened to deal with the situation produced none, only plans for another meeting. Supposedly, there were a number of applicants looking to fill the open positions, and more time was needed to make a decision.

The subsequent meeting took place at the Trenton House in Trenton, New Jersey, on August 26. There were applicants who were ready and willing, but apparently they were not able, for none were admitted. Jersey City, which had played against several Eastern League clubs, was denied admission because their grounds were not in suitable condition. Despite the dire situation and the fact that nothing productive had been done, the talk turned hopefully to 1885 and the promise of a reorganized league and more teams.

On August 30, the standings were published as follows:

|  | W | L | Pct. | GB |
|---|---|---|---|---|
| Wilmington | 50 | 12 | .806 | — |
| Trenton | 41 | 29 | .586 | 13 |
| Ironsides | 26 | 25 | .510 | 18½ |
| Active | 27 | 27 | .500 | 19 |
| Virginia | 28 | 30 | .483 | 20 |
| Allentown | 25 | 30 | .455 | 21½ |
| Domestic | 31 | 38 | .449 | 22½ |
| Harrisburg | 15 | 24 | .385 | 23½ |
| Monumental | 3 | 10 | .231 | 22½ |
| York | 5 | 17 | .227 | 25 |

Of the teams listed in the standings, Wilmington, the Actives, Virginia, Harrisburg, and the Monumentals were no longer in existence, leaving just five teams in the field. Of the survivors, the Domestics were the only ones up to date on salaries and expenses. "The Northwestern and Eastern Leagues," reported the *Clipper*, "are now but the 'shadows of their former selves' having been dwindled down gradually by disbandment and otherwise."[13]

In mid–September, *Sporting Life* reported, "It is stated that an effort may be made in a day or two to close the Eastern League season without further delay as the clubs do not draw. This would relieve the clubs from paying the $65 guarantee several times every week and would enable them to arrange exhibition games with clubs of the older organizations."[14]

Of course, it would also relieve the visiting teams from collecting the $65 guarantee, which was their main source of revenue. In the event, the Eastern League elected to soldier on to the finish, which came at the end of September. The schedule was a shambles by that time, but Diddlebock said the season was over, so it was over. Trenton, with the best record among the survivors, was awarded the pennant. "There have been so many disbandments and changes," said the *Clipper*, "that the secretary alone probably knows the standings of the different clubs. According to our record, the Trenton team have the lead for the pennant."[15]

|  | W | L | Pct. | GB |
|---|---|---|---|---|
| Trenton | 46 | 38 | .548 | — |
| Ironsides | 30 | 31 | .492 | 4½ |
| Domestic | 32 | 40 | .444 | 8 |
| Allentown | 30 | 41 | .423 | 9½ |
| York | 11 | 20 | .355 | 8½ |

When the Eastern League crossed its self-declared finish line, Trenton, Allentown, the Ironsides, and York were in arrears to the league and the salaries of the umpires remained unpaid. The Trenton club had finished the season on the cooperative plan, with the players sharing in gate receipts rather than receiving salaries. Undeterred, the Eastern League met on October 23 to make plans for 1885.

Crippled though it was, the Eastern League managed to complete the season, which was more than the Northwestern League was able to accomplish. The saga of the Northwestern League epitomized the turmoil of 1884. The league had a spotty history; the first NWL, formed by Ted Sullivan in 1879, didn't survive the season. On October 27, 1882, a second, eight-team version of the NWL was formed under the leadership of Elias Matter of Grand Rapids, co-owner of Nelson, Matter and Company, a furniture manufacturing, wholesale, and retail company. Matter contacted Abraham Mills and told him of his league's desire to become a party to the National Agreement, and Mills was enthusiastic. "Assuming that your clubs have in view rather a pure exhibition of manly sport," he said, "than the aim of money making, I cannot believe that your enterprise will fail."[16] That was prescient advice, but without money-making, an enterprise will eventually fail.

The new league completed a relatively successful 1883 season, leaving only a smattering of unpaid bills in its wake.[17] During the winter, the pennant-winning Toledo club, one of the NWL's strongest members, left to join the expanded AA. Matter, the guiding force behind the NWL who was well-respected by his counterparts in the NL and AA, also departed and was succeeded by 28-year-old John Rust of Saginaw, president of the Detroit Stamping Company. Rust was a large man, weighing 230 pounds, and was, according to the *Chicago Herald*, "a much handsomer man than Mr. A.G. Mills, H.D. McKnight, or even Max Nirdlinger [president of the Fort Wayne club]."[18] But good looks didn't go far in the challenging world of minor league baseball.

The going would be tougher in 1884 than it had been in the NWL's first season, and the NWL unwisely compounded its problems by expanding to 12 teams. The marginal 1883 financial results had not discouraged potential applicants, and there were more than could be accommodated.

The time seemed unripe for expansion. "Indeed," said *Sporting Life* in December 1883, "the prospects look very discouraging for the North-western League itself. Two or three ... teams are in straitened circumstances, and since the Toledo Club, the strongest in the organization, may be admitted to the American Association, rumors are afloat that the association itself will pass out of existence."[19]

"Exactly what use Muskegon has for a salaried base ball club had been a fifteen puzzle all along," said the *Detroit Free Press*. "And yet it would probably be a difficult matter to convince any one of these fond nurses that her particular nurseling [sic] will not come toddling home in the fall proudly flaunting the Northwestern pennant."[20]

The *Milwaukee Sentinel* also sounded a warning. "When baseball players ask salaries equal to ministers," it said, "towns like Muskegon, Fort Wayne, and Stillwater ought not to meddle with them." But meddle with high-priced players is exactly what the NWL did. Milwaukee signed pitcher Ed Cushman for a reported $3,000 and the team's expenses, including the cost of its grounds, were estimated at $53,000.[21]

Apparently, the NWL harbored its own doubts, for it made an informal arrangement with Evansville to wait in the wings as a potential replacement in the event that one of the league teams folded.

The twelve NWL franchises, including six holdovers and six new teams, were:

| Bay City | Fort Wayne | Grand Rapids | Milwaukee |
| Muskegon | Peoria | Quincy | Saginaw |
| Stillwater | Terre Haute | St. Paul | Minneapolis |

In addition to paying salaries that were too high, the league was too widely dispersed. The Eastern League made a conscious effort to contain its franchises within a relatively tight footprint, but the NWL had teams spread all across the upper Midwest, which would require some long road trips:

- Bay City to St. Paul—720
- Bay City to Stillwater—708
- Stillwater to Saginaw—595
- Grand Rapids to Minneapolis—590
- Grand Rapids to Stillwater—571
- Fort Wayne to Minneapolis—498
- Grand Rapids to Quincy—460

Bay City had a couple of jaunts of more than 700 miles, and to transport ten players 700 miles and receive a $75 guarantee is a losing proposition. There were National League teams that took long trips, like the 1,177-mile journey from Boston to St. Louis (the longest major league haul), but major league teams drew major league crowds, which NWL teams did not.

Another problem was that several NWL cities had relatively small populations. Only 15,000 people lived in Stillwater, much too small a base for a league just a notch below the majors. Only Milwaukee, Minneapolis, St. Paul, and Grand Rapids had populations in excess of 30,000. The Eastern League, which was comparable in terms of status and aspirations, had nine teams in cities with more than 30,000, and those cities were closer together. The NWL hoped to offset some of its weaknesses by permitting Sunday baseball and the sale of liquor on its clubs' grounds.

By the end of June, Grand Rapids, which had been the pre-season favorite, was comfortably in first place. Manager Horace Phillips, never shy about spending money, had assembled a talented team with a payroll of $12,650. He had an excellent chance of bringing his team in first if he could just bring in his team.[22]

Sure enough, it wasn't long before financial troubles were threatening the league's existence, with almost every franchise seemingly on the brink of failure. The *Clipper* stated, "The disbandment of some of the NWL clubs is looked for. It is hard for 'The Ghost' to walk."[23]

In a cost-cutting measure, Terre Haute released manager Al Buckenberger on July 2 and appointed one of the team's directors to manage the team.[24] The Quincy players had to move from their hotel into private boarding homes when the hotel bills went unpaid. Muskegon defaulted on its players' board bill. In Peoria they were wondering what happened to the reported $1,200 earned during a trip to Quincy and Milwaukee, since it hadn't been accounted for and the players hadn't been paid.

At the end of July, the *Cleveland Leader* painted a bleak picture. It said that Bay City was $7,500 behind, Peoria $3,000, Quincy $4,500, Saginaw $8,000, Fort Wayne and Terre Haute $2,000, and Muskegon $6,000. Milwaukee and St. Paul were reportedly breaking even.[25]

Bay City, which had a 37–14 record, was the first team to fail, ceasing operations after their July 22 game against Peoria. When news of the impending failure became known, managers from across the country converged on Bay City. Ted Sullivan of Kansas City made off with several players, supposedly fifteen minutes after his arrival.

Evansville, which had been waiting patiently in the wings for a team to fail, was brought in as a replacement. They assumed the Bay City schedule, but their games were not supposed to count in the standings; they were added in order to give the remaining teams someone to play and generate gate money. There were rumors that several other clubs were in trouble, but at a July 25 meeting the league announced its determination to finish the season. With Evansville in the league, there was no more dry powder to cover for another failure.

League-leading Grand Rapids averaged 911 fans per game in May, which enabled them to make money. When a succession of weak teams visited the city in June, attendance dropped to 368 per game, and the team lost an estimated $800. When Grand Rapids complained that Milwaukee fans were rowdy, Milwaukee retorted that Grand Rapids didn't have enough fans to create a disturbance. At 25 cents per head, a club had to draw 300 just to pay the visiting team guaranty of $75, which meant that at 368, they had about $17 left to cover salaries and overhead. By the end of June, Grand Rapids was $2,500 in the hole and ten local citizens raised about $2,700 to keep the team afloat.

About a week and a half after Bay City folded, Fort Wayne and Stillwater dropped out. Fort Wayne wasn't in deep trouble (owing less than $1,000 in unpaid salaries), but saw the handwriting on the wall and decided to get out before they got in any deeper. They reportedly paid their players in full.

Stillwater's season was as chaotic as might have been expected, given the fact that they lost their first 16 games and were located in the league's smallest city. "This club should never have been admitted to the League," said *Sporting Life*, "as the city had not the population to support a professional club. The one-horse character of the village can best be gleaned from the fact that it was not able to sustain a newspaper."[26] When Bud Fowler, the NWL's only black player, began to pitch more often, Stillwater rallied, but the overall results were disappointing. The team went through four managers and at the time it was dissolved, its record was 22–41 and financial losses were estimated at $3,500 to $4,000, although the players were supposedly paid in full. Fowler finished the season with a .302 batting average and a pitching record of 7–8 for a team that was 19 games under .500. The Stillwater fans were so impressed they presented him with ten dollars and a suit of clothes in appreciation of his efforts.

Terre Haute, like Stillwater, seemed doomed from the start, drawing just 109 fans to its opening game. Although they began the season with 28 straight home games, crowds were disappointing. Perhaps there were too many games. On July 30, the Terre Haute stockholders announced that the club was $2,200 in debt and needed to raise $4,200 in order to finish the season. Five days later, the goal was reduced to $1,000, but only $300 was contributed. It wasn't nearly enough, and on August 5, the club disbanded.[27]

The *Detroit Free Press* said, "[B]ye and bye when the big salaries become due, and it is found that people had about as soon go fishing, or to a picnic, as to attend ball games, and another 'assessment' is levied, stockholders begin to grow weary, don't care much about the pennant anyway, especially when pennants come so high, and disband their club."[28]

Peoria was wracked by dissension and bickering among the players, a little too much carousing, and the desertion of a couple of key performers. There was a lot of dissension in the 1884 Northwestern League, as players who aren't paid have a tendency to get irritable. In May, manager James Whitfield got into a dispute with the directors and was fired and replaced by Charles Flynn. Noting the controversy over Sunday baseball, a local paper said, "We are glad to note that no such charge can be brought against the Peoria Reds. They have not been playing base ball on the Sabbath. And the same may be said of the other days of the week."[29]

Peoria held a meeting on July 7 at which they raised what they believed would be enough money to carry them through the season. "[T]here is no likelihood of the club disbanding before the season is over,"[30] the Peoria *Transcript* said confidently. They were wrong. A couple of weeks later, after failing to pay guarantee money to Terre Haute, they made a second attempt to raise money, but this time they were unsuccessful. The team was disbanded and the players were forced to accept 30 cents on the dollar in order to obtain releases.

Muskegon was also in dire straits, with $3,900 in debt and $34 in the treasury. Like almost every other NWL team, they tried to raise additional funds—$7,000 in this case. Although the *Clipper* opined that there were "good prospects of success"[31] that was wildly optimistic. Anyone who could read a newspaper realized that the league's status was tenuous, and apparently the residents of Muskegon had enough sense to keep their money in their wallets. A week later, the *Clipper* changed its tune. "The report that Muskegon has raised $7,000 to tide over the storm," it reported, "is not generally believed, to put it mildly."[32]

Amidst the chaos, the NWL met in Chicago on August 9 to try to salvage the season. With virtually all the remaining clubs on the brink of insolvency, the league required $500 bonds from each team to assure they would finish the season. When president T.M. Weston of Grand Rapids received a telegram informing him of the new requirement, he replied that he would submit the proposition to the directors. Before he could do so, manager Phillips received a notice indicating that the reply was unsatisfactory and the team was being dropped from the league. Muskegon was eliminated for the same reason.[33] Both teams protested that the league had no right to require a bond at this point, since it had never been a condition of membership. The protest was ignored, but it was largely irrelevant, since neither team had the resources to last much longer, bond or no bond.

As the NWL began to unravel, players saw the handwriting on the wall and were receptive when the UA came calling. Kansas City corralled Quincy's battery of Black and Baldwin, cutting out the heart of the latter team. Once the league's best players began to leave, the end of the NWL became almost a foregone conclusion.

Several Grand Rapids players went to Detroit, for which the club was apparently compensated, allowing them to pay most of their outstanding bills. Manager Phillips and another group went to the Alleghenies. Movement was fast and furious. "Hardly a day passes," reported the *Boston Globe*, "that there is not an addition to the list of disbanded clubs."[34]

"The past week has been a disastrous one for this association," said the *Clipper*, "no fewer than four of its clubs disbanding, while two more clubs went to pieces on account of being dropped."[35] There were five clubs left in a 2,000-mile circuit, an impossible situation, but the survivors gamely attempted to finish the season, even though by that time most teams weren't taking in enough at the gate to pay the visiting team their guaranty.

Losses of the NWL were estimated as follows:

| Bay City | $7,500 |
| Peoria | 3,000 |
| Quincy | 4,500 |
| Saginaw | 8,000 |
| Fort Wayne | 2,000 |
| Terre Haute | 2,000 |
| Stillwater | 10,000 |
| Grand Rapids | 10,000 |
| Muskegon | 6,000[36] |

Milwaukee and St. Paul were supposedly breaking even.

President Rust resigned and was replaced by W.D. Whitmore of Quincy, who didn't last long. Quincy, which had raised $2,000 to stave off bankruptcy, got hot, winning 10 of 12 games. They believed the only way their team could survive was to join the Union Association and managed to get an audition in the form of an exhibition game against the St. Louis Maroons. They lost 5–1 and apparently, Henry Lucas wasn't impressed, because he didn't invite Quincy to join his league. They therefore disbanded, taking the league president with them.

Saginaw sent an appeal to 400 citizens asking for funds. Just 40 responded, with pledges of $2–25 each. It wasn't nearly enough, and on August 16, Saginaw was expelled for failing to pay a guaranty to a visiting team. Evansville was dropped, and the salaried umpiring staff was released; each home team was required to supply its own umpire.

On the plus side, Winona enthusiastically boarded the sinking vessel, signing six former Muskegon players, who were forced to sign documents releasing the shareholders from liability before they were given their releases. Winona's entry, in addition to providing a much-needed franchise, contracted the league's geography.

At this point, with the wholesale addition and subtraction of teams, no one had any idea what the standings might be, and the schedule was a complete shambles. It was suggested that the season be ended and Milwaukee declared the champion, on the basis that they had won the most games against teams that were still extant. They declined, preferring to soldier on.

The Minneapolis stockholders met with president Merrill of St. Paul, and the two teams, along with Milwaukee and Winona, decided to take a mulligan and start over again, with a new schedule and new standings. With Whitmore gone, the league got its third president, Welcome Kirby of Milwaukee. It had taken all season, but finally the Northwestern League was comprised of cities that were large enough to support a team and close enough together to keep travel expenses to a minimum. When Omaha applied for admission, they were denied, most likely because the remaining teams finally realized that the travel expenses to the Nebraska city would bankrupt them.

It was just as well for Omaha, for by that time, the Northwestern League was a lost cause. On August 26, the Minneapolis directors met to discuss the perilous financial situation of their franchise. All they came up with was the hope that somehow the club would come up with money from somewhere. They didn't, and disbanded eight days later. Salaries had not been paid in full since July 15, and the total unpaid debts were more than $2,500.[37]

With Minneapolis gone, the jig was up, and on September 7 the remaining teams threw in the towel. "The Northwestern League has at last reached that stage of dissolution," the *St. Paul Globe* eulogized, "at which it is proper to pronounce its funeral oration."[38] The league that survived the 1883 season could not survive 1884.

Some teams, like the armless, legless knight of Monty Python's *Holy Grail*, weren't ready to give up. Omaha, persistent if not wise, applied to replace Minneapolis, but there was no longer any league to join. St. Paul claimed it was the champion of the league since it was the best of the two remaining clubs, but it was a hollow honor.

The end of the league did not mean the end of the teams. Milwaukee and St. Paul had drawn reasonably well and were still solvent. The former club was supposedly waiting for Wilmington to collapse so it could join the UA. St. Paul embarked on a tour with the intention of scheduling games as they went.

Eventually, both St. Paul and Milwaukee joined the Union Association, which was experiencing franchise problems of its own. Winona disbanded and several of the players went back to Muskegon looking for their unpaid salary. During the second season, 28 games had been played and Milwaukee was in the lead with a 12–3 record. Winona won just one game. The final standings, including both segments of the season and all teams that had been members, were as follows:

|  | W | L | Pct. | GB |
|---|---|---|---|---|
| Evansville | 4 | 1 | .800 | 16 |
| Grand Rapids | 48 | 13 | .787 | — |
| Bay City | 37 | 14 | .725 | 6 |
| Saginaw | 45 | 20 | .692 | 5 |
| Quincy | 40 | 23 | .635 | 9 |
| Peoria | 38 | 24 | .613 | 10½ |
| Minneapolis | 35 | 46 | .432 | 18 |
| St. Paul | 29 | 54 | .349 | 30 |
| Muskegon | 19 | 37 | .339 | 26½ |
| Fort Wayne | 19 | 38 | .333 | 27 |
| Stillwater | 20 | 42 | .323 | 28½ |
| Terre Haute | 13 | 48 | .213 | 35 |
| Winona | 1 | 10 | .091 | 22 |

The teams are ranked by winning percentage, but Evansville, the team with the highest percentage, played just five games and can hardly be declared the league champion. That honor should probably go to the Grand Rapids nine of Horace Phillips. They didn't complete the season, but then neither did the league.

Although the 1884 NWL season was a collective fiasco, it wasn't due to a lack of talent. Pitcher John Clarkson of Saginaw was 34–9 with a 0.64 ERA before joining the Chicago White Stockings late in the season; he struck out 19 Grand Rapids batters in one game. Bob Caruthers of Minneapolis and Dave Foutz of Bay City went to St. Louis after their teams folded and pitched the Browns to a World Championship later in the decade. Bud Fowler, Stillwater's black pitcher-infielder, rather than going to the majors like so many white NWL stars, stayed in Stillwater to pursue his barbering profession.[39]

Other leagues found the going equally difficult. The Western Interstate Association, comprised of teams in Pennsylvania and Ohio, never left the starting gate. In February 1884, some of the teams that had planned to play in the WIA formed a circuit called the Iron and Oil League Base Ball Association, consisting of the following towns and cities:

| East Liberty, Ohio | Franklin, Pennsylvania |
| Youngstown, Ohio | New Brighton, Pennsylvania |
| New Castle, Pennsylvania | Oil City, Pennsylvania |

Attendance was a challenge for the Iron and Oil League, as it was for all minor leagues in 1884, and by mid–July Youngstown was on the verge of collapse. The original club disbanded, but a new organization, which retained the same players, took its place, supported in part by the local streetcar company, which hoped to continue hauling fans to the grounds.

Shortly thereafter, New Brighton disbanded and was replaced by a team from Johnstown, Pennsylvania. Just days after that, however, the Oil City team folded and in early August the Iron and Oil League ceased operations, leaving unemployed players and distressed creditors in its wake. Several of the players went to the Ohio State League and the creditors went to court. Franklin, which had the most wins at the time the league shut down, was declared the champion.

The Ohio League, which operated under the protection of the National Agreement and had teams in Springfield, Dayton, Ironton, Hamilton, Portsmouth, and Chillicothe, was plagued with problems from the start.[40] There were contract problems, such as that of Red Mack, who signed a Dayton contract on June 16 and signed a second contract with Springfield four days later after being supposedly plied with drink. His status became a major bone of contention. Portsmouth employed the ubiquitous boozer Frank McLaughlin, who was under contract to Baltimore and therefore ineligible. The Dayton owners were accused of gambling away the club's funds. When Dayton visited Springfield, Cox, their catcher, got drunk and attacked another player. He and two others were arrested and jailed.

With all the confusion, it wasn't surprising that there was a dispute as to which team finished in first place. Springfield said they had a record of 58–22 to Dayton's 55–21 and should be declared champions. They claimed three forfeits from Portsmouth while Dayton claimed two from Chillicothe. Springfield also claimed three forfeits from Portsmouth for the use of McLaughlin, while Dayton claimed one. Dayton wanted four wins from Springfield due to the use of Mack. It was a mess, and the season ended without a resolution but, unlike that of many minor leagues, the season ended when it was supposed to end.

Pennsylvania's Keystone Association began to fall apart in mid–June when Chester and Chambersburg dropped out, leaving just York, Littlestown, and Lancaster. When Littlestown dropped out, Lancaster and York, which were feuding, refused to play each other. Since there was no one else left to play, the season came to an ignominious conclusion.

The six-team Connecticut League managed to finish the season, losing just one team in the process. Waterbury, with a 34–13 record, won the championship by a wide margin. Connecticut is not very big, which minimized travel expenses, and the teams, which were clustered around the center of the state, played just two days a week. The catcher for the Meriden team, in his first professional season, was a 21-year-old youngster who played under the name Connie Mack.

Massachusetts is about twice the size of Connecticut and apparently that was too much ground for a minor league to cover, for after Springfield disbanded on August 23, the Massachusetts Association was down to only two of the eight teams that began the season. Springfield was preceded in death by Waltham, Lynn, Salem, Worcester, and Holyoke. Even with just two teams left, there was a dispute over the championship. The Boston Reserves had the best record, but the pennant was awarded to Lawrence on the premise that the Reserves had not reported its players and roster changes properly.

There was limited activity in the south, where the most prominent circuit was the Georgia State League, which had teams in Columbus (which won the championship), Savannah, Macon, and Augusta. The Texas League, with teams in Waco, Fort Worth, Galveston, and Houston, was late to the party, which was probably a good idea, since it had less time to fail. Play didn't begin until July 13 and continued through the end of October. The schedule was flexible and somewhat irregular, but the league made it to the finish line.

There were other leagues that did not operate under the National Agreement, such as the Western League, a loose combination of amateur and semi-pro clubs. California, which had a history of professional baseball dating back several years, had a number of teams, which played in both winter and summer.

All in all, it was a disastrous season for the minor leagues, doomed from the start by too many teams, too much competition, a lackluster economy, and expenses that greatly exceeded potential revenue. Making the situation worse was the fact that few of the leagues had competitive pennant races, and many couldn't begin to unravel their standings. After analyzing the National League and American Association races in August, the *Brooklyn Eagle* stated, "The records of all the other association races have been too one sided and mixed up to be worth printing any longer."[41]

There were many lessons to be learned from the tribulations of the 1884 season, but most could have been learned from 1883 and earlier. The experiences of 1884 were so painful, however, that many cities would think long and hard before organizing teams for 1885.

# 17

# The Others

Press coverage of baseball in the 1880s focused predominately on white male professionals. There were other people playing baseball, but one would scarcely know it by reading the sporting press. Collegians received a little attention, but the play of women, blacks, and others was largely ignored or satirized.

Baseball had been played informally at colleges for decades and inter-collegiate games had been popular since the middle of the 1860s. College teams of the 19th century were typically social clubs whose expenses were paid by their members rather than the college.[1] The best teams played exhibitions against professionals, as well as competing among themselves for various regional championships. Several college players, including John Lee Richmond of Brown and Jumping Jack Jones of Yale, went on to play in the major leagues. Yale's Bill Hutchison, a star pitcher for the Chicago teams of the 1890s, made his debut with Kansas City in 1884. A number of professional pitchers, including Tim Keefe, John Montgomery Ward, Bobby Mathews, and Larry Corcoran, coached college teams before the major league season began. In addition to working with the pitchers, they threw batting practice to give the collegians experience hitting against top-flight talent.

The most publicized collegiate action was among the teams that now comprise the Ivy League, and the battles between Yale and Harvard had the same intensity as the current day football rivalry between the two schools. Walter Camp, father of college football, was also one of Yale's best baseball players. Prior to the start of the 1884 season, John Day tried to get him to manage the New York club, but Camp, despite the attractive financial tender, was attached to Yale and declined. He would have been a much better manager than the eventual choice, James Price, for Camp had a sterling reputation and understood physical conditioning, human nature, and the game of baseball.

Collegiate eligibility rules were very loose, and it was not unusual for men to continue to play for their alma mater after they'd graduated. Some Harvard players stayed with the team while they pursued post-graduate courses. Others didn't attend graduate school but played anyway. A few college associations allowed a limited number of professional players, which instigated some very spirited debates.

What was a professional? Was it someone who was paid for playing a sport? For teaching it? Someone who had been paid in the past but no longer was? The issue bedeviled amateur athletics and the Olympic Games well into the 20th century and was no less murky in the 19th. Jumping Jack Jones, who helped pitch the Athletics to the AA pennant in 1883, said that if he were barred from playing for Yale the following season because of his professionalism, the Elis would make certain that at least two or three players from other schools were disqualified for the same reason.

Colleges that abided by the letter of the law risked falling behind, and there was an intense debate about the issue at Harvard, where the fortunes of its baseball team had declined in recent years. "Base ball," said one paper, "formerly the leading college sport, has almost fallen into desuetude [a suitable word to describe a Harvard sport] and the nine, formerly the glory of the college, is now regarded with little less than pity and contempt."[2]

The paper blamed the faculty. Harvard, concerned about the direction in which college sports was heading, had formed a committee of three faculty members to govern the school's sporting activity. In December 1883, the committee declared that no professionals would be allowed to coach the school baseball team nor would the Harvard nine be permitted to play exhibitions against professional clubs or college teams that employed professional coaches. The decision was uniformly unpopular and the *Harvard Herald Crimson* protested, "As long as we have professional trainers in sparring, fencing and general athletics, we cannot see why we should not have professional trainers in base ball playing."[3]

During the winter before the 1884 season, eastern colleges had some spirited discussions concerning the suitability of sport for students. The subject was a series of resolutions advocating a ban on the use of professional coaches, appointing a faculty committee to oversee athletics, limiting participation to four years per athlete, and restricting competition to schools that adhered to those standards.

Yale was generally supportive of athletics while Harvard wanted to de-emphasize sports, which the faculty and administration thought were taking too much time away from studies and had acquired an unwarranted importance in college life. Princeton and Amherst lined up behind Harvard while Brown supported Yale.[4]

Sports had been controversial at Harvard ever since they began, and the concept of professionalism was perhaps the most contentious topic. As historian Richard Hershberger explained, "[Harvard president Charles] Eliot's vision of the role of college athletics was informed by the assumptions of Victorian English society."[5] In Victorian England, there were gentlemen and there were others. Gentlemen did not play sports for money; they were financially secure and played sports solely for physical and moral benefit. They considered those who competed for money to be their inferiors. By the 1870s, the most popular professional team sport was baseball, which Eliot thought unfit for college undergraduates. "I think it is a wretched game," he said, "I call it one of the worst games, although I know it is called the American national game."[6] That boded ill for baseball at Harvard.

Football was in even greater danger than baseball, with good reason. The football played in 1884 was brutal, even deadly, and there was widespread pressure to end the carnage that invariably ensued when 22 strapping young men met on the gridiron without protective equipment or many rules. "Football games had degenerated into slugging matches," wrote the *Boston Globe*.[7]

Under pressure, the Harvard faculty relented and allowed the school to hire Keefe as a coach. They still insisted, however, that the Crimson not compete with non-college teams. "The action of Harvard's faculty," said *Sporting Life*, "is regarded as narrow and bigoted and as a death-blow to the National game in that institution."[8]

A month later, *Sporting Life* took another shot. Eliot was perhaps the most transformative president in the long history of Harvard, but he couldn't please the editors of *Sporting Life*. "It is easy to see why President Eliot speaks slightingly of the base ball game," they wrote. "Professional jealousy is at the bottom of it. It costs more to hire nine base ball professors for six months than nine first-rate college professors for a year. President Eliot has mistaken his vocation and he is mad about it."[9]

The *Clipper* was also upset. "So obnoxious are the resolutions at Harvard that there is a strong sentiment of abandoning the gymnasiums and dissolving all the athletic organizations."[10] The paper's Boston correspondent declared, "In other words, [Eliot] wants to control college athletics." The *Clipper* applauded Yale for standing up to Harvard and declared that it wouldn't matter if Harvard refused to play them, for public opinion would be overwhelmingly on Yale's side. Returning to Eliot, they concluded, "President Eliot of Harvard knows about as much concerning sports as the average woman," as damning a criticism as could be delivered to any man in 1884.[11]

Baseball had been played at Harvard since 1858, and the school had a long history of competing against professional teams. In the mid–1860s they fielded one of the best nines, college or amateur, in New England, and played competitively with some of the top teams in the New York area. One of the highlights of the Harvard spring season was the annual exhibition against the Boston National League club. If the 1884 ban held, the game would have to be cancelled.[12]

The 1884 college season was plagued by endless wrangles over player eligibility, including one involving William H. Coolidge, who'd already played five seasons for Harvard. In 1884, he was a student at Harvard Law School, which would have made him eligible for a sixth season, but when he played for the amateur Beacon Club in an exhibition against Boston's National League team, Harvard banned him from its team.

Other schools were not as scrupulous and in mid–May, Cornell complained that nearly all the other teams in the New York State Intercollegiate Base Ball Association employed professional players. They said that Hamilton College and Union College actually advertised for players in the New York papers. Between them, Cornell claimed, the two schools had seven paid players who were not students. They provided a sworn affidavit that all Cornell players were legitimate students. Emory College, which lost the collegiate championship of Georgia to the University of Georgia, protested on the basis that five players on the Georgia team had no connection with the college. At the end of the season, the New York association decided not to award the championship to any team, claiming that every single one of them, apparently even Cornell, had broken the rules by using outside players.

It was apparent that the honorable conduct attributed to college athletics and presumed to have existed in the "good old days" was nowhere to be found in 1884. The Princeton faculty prohibited any college baseball games from taking place on their campus and Yale and Princeton hired New York lawyers to file suit over a cancelled game. "The most grasping of professional clubs," said *Sporting Life*, "would scarcely have attempted such a thing."[13]

The Eastern title came down to the wire between Yale and Harvard. The former had been undefeated in 1883 but Harvard gave them a run for their money in 1884. The Crimson beat Yale on June 21 before a Cambridge crowd of 6,000 (apparently the school had regained its enthusiasm for sports), giving each team eight wins and forcing a play-off, which took place on neutral ground at Brooklyn's Washington Park on June 27. Three thousand fans turned out and the cheering was loud and enthusiastic. Yale fans had more to cheer about, as the Bulldogs won 4–2 to claim their fourth consecutive title with a 9–2 record. Harvard was 8–3.[14]

Women weren't playing a lot of baseball in 1884, having been warned by physicians that excessive physical activity was harmful and might affect their ability to bear children. Those who chose to ignore the warnings and engage in sports were hindered by the cumbersome clothing they wore to protect their modesty. Bloomers, which would have given them more freedom of movement, were rejected as too unfeminine.

Some enlightened women believed that exercise was good for them, one of them being Dr. Helen Webster of Vassar College, which fielded several baseball teams in the 1860s and 1870s. There was a well-publicized team at Peterboro, New York, and two teams at Bridgton Academy in Maine, where of course, "the question of uniforms is the all-absorbing topic."[15]

By 1884, there were several women's teams in the field, including the occasional professional nine; the first was organized in Springfield, Illinois, in 1875. The most publicized form of women's baseball, however, was the vaudeville-like attractions put on by shifty promoters, games that were one part baseball and nine parts prurient interest and comedy. Most women's troupes divided into teams based upon hair color, with blondes versus brunettes being the standard matchup.

The most infamous promoter was a man operating under the alias of Harry Freeman, who in late 1883 took a group of ladies from Philadelphia on tour. Freeman apparently anticipated the groundbreaking work of historian David Block, stating that women had played baseball in England during the 14th century and it was therefore natural that modern women should take up the game. He claimed his girls were all between the ages of 15 and 22. "Maybe he means twenty-two and fifty-eight," suggested *Sporting Life*. Freeman said that only three of the young ladies "had been on the stage," which was not a reputable place to be.[16] The women wore red caps, "very short" white skirts trimmed with red braid, black stockings, and baseball shoes.

The women appeared to have been chosen for their looks rather than their ability to hit, throw, or catch a baseball. Reporters noted that they threw in an awkward feminine manner and did not seem especially skilled at the game. "The ball was pitched in," said one description, "not according to any rule, high, low, in the air or on the ground indiscriminately. Then the girl at the bat would poke at it ... with the exception of a catcher in red or a short-stop in blue, the girls seemed afraid of the ball ... the girls paid more attention to the boys on the stand."[17]

Freeman's troupe played to poor reviews on opening day in Columbus. "The effect was, if anything, depressing, that women should allow themselves to so far depart from every instinct of womanly modesty as to make a field exhibition of themselves."[18] The second game in Columbus was cancelled and the show moved on to Cincinnati, where the same critic noted, "The club managers should be ashamed of itself [sic] for renting its ground for a purpose degrading the national game."[19]

From Cincinnati, Freeman took the ladies to St. Louis, where his show came to an end. He could not get any grounds and was forced to play in a rented hall. After the first performance drew poorly, Freeman skipped town, leaving the women to find their own way home. They could only raise enough money to get to Chicago, where they were stranded again. When their remaining funds ran out, they were forced to abandon their hotel and stay at the train depot. "Several of the better looking ones were furnished railway passes,"[20] while the less pulchritudinous remained at the depot.

At about the same time, another group of female players from Philadelphia was stranded in St. Louis, where the local Union Association club raised money to send them

A number of female "ballplayers" traveled the country playing exhibitions in various cities. Many were led by the odious Sylvester Wilson, who spent time in prison for defrauding and exploiting the women (courtesy John Thorn).

home. The girls hadn't been paid in three weeks and their baggage was held hostage by the Indianapolis and St. Louis railroad for unpaid fees. The sponsor of this troupe was known as Sylvester F. Wilson, who had organized an ill-fated tour of the New York Female Base Ball club several years earlier. "[Wilson] will give up his female base-ball project," sighed the *St. Louis Post-Dispatch,* "when there are no more girls."[21]

Meanwhile, Freeman and his partner, William Phillips, were in Buffalo planning another excursion, this time taking along a canvas fence that created a 300 by 400-foot enclosure within which to play. "The female baseball tramps are at it again," said *Sporting Life.* "The one-legged and one-armed teams have not yet been heard from."[22]

Like the previous season's adventure, the 1884 journey came to a sorry end, this time in Newark, New Jersey, where, after generating just $92 in revenue from the game, the treasurer had no money to pay the ladies, who were once again left on their own. *Sporting Life* delivered the eulogy for the tour and for female baseball in general. "Females cannot play base ball even a little bit, and all attempts to organize and run such clubs must end in disaster and disgrace. Let us hear no more of female base ball clubs. The public want none of it."[23]

The public was going to get it whether they wanted it or not. In July, after attracting 32 spectators in Baltimore, the girls were abandoned again when an unscrupulous local promoter took off with the meager receipts. They were evicted from their hotel for non-payment and temporarily housed in the Monumental Theater, where the kindly proprietor gave them breakfast. "All the girls," said the *Philadelphia Times,* "were respectable working girls and were inveigled away from home by the promise that they were to be gone only two days."[24]

Later that summer of 1884 yet another group of young ladies was stranded in Philadelphia. In September, Freeman was trying to raise $500 to take a team to New Orleans, promising the players profits of $50–100 per day. In the meantime, he was hauling the girls around Pennsylvania, where he reportedly took in five dollars in Easton and ten in Allentown, after which he had to pawn his watch in order to get out of town.

Somehow, Freeman managed to get the girls to Washington and Richmond, and in the latter city a few major leaguers, including Charley Ferguson and Billy Nash, took part in an exhibition game with them. By this time, Freeman had taken enough vitriol from the press, and dashed off an angry letter to *Sporting Life*. After branding Freeman's charges as vicious lies, editor Francis Richter added, "We, however, warn H.H. Freeman, better known to infamy as Sylvester Wilson, the ticket scalper, that if he ever shows his face in Philadelphia again he will find himself on a charge of criminal libel, in his old quarters in Moyamensing Prison."[25]

Freeman, however, was headed in the opposite direction, and while he was in Albany, Georgia, Richter took another whack at him, in an article titled, "The Female Tramps, Disgraceful Conduct of the Girl Players in Georgia." "The girls are from 15 to 19 years of age," Richter wrote, "jaunty in style, brazen in manner, and peculiar in dress. When they reached this place, their agent obtained rooms for them at the Artesia Hotel. It was not long before the proprietor discovered that the character of his house was suffering. All the swells of the city were around the place like a swarm of bees. The proprietor promptly ejected the ball players, and they had to amuse themselves for several hours at the depot until the train arrived which was to take them away. They were accompanied by some of the local swells. Their conduct was of such a character that respectable ladies got off the cars and waited for the next train."[26] "The female has no place in baseball," Richter concluded, "except to the degradation of the game."

"Freeman" was indeed Sylvester Wilson, who had a long and disreputable history in women's baseball.[27] His first group of English Blondes and American Brunettes set sail in March 1879, but the tour ended abruptly when Wilson and his partner, William Powell, were arrested for "engaging girls under 16 for immoral purposes" and having sexual relations with the girls.

Historian Debra Shattuck described Wilson as a "narcissist, career criminal and pedophile,"[28] whose career lasted until 1903 despite several arrests and incarcerations. He operated under numerous aliases, including Freeman, and always seemed able to find girls willing to follow him. He even ventured into women's basketball after that sport was invented. Wilson died in prison in 1921.

The fact that Wilson's career lasted as long as it did despite his reputation and prison sentences was a tribute to his marketing ability. In 1883, attendance at Wilson's games averaged more than 1,600 (which was better than some major league teams) and in 1890, long after he acquired his sordid reputation, one of his games in New Jersey drew a crowd estimated at 7–10,000. "Had Wilson not been the crook he was," Shattuck wrote, "he might have made a positive contribution to the history of professional women's baseball."[29]

Not all female players were as untalented and exploited as Wilson's blonds and brunettes. In Philadelphia, the Dolly Varden and Jinks clubs, composed of black women, took their baseball seriously, as did the Colored Female Base Ball Club in Montgomery, Alabama. In 1887, there was a New York nine known as the Sadie Thompsons and captained by first baseperson Annie Jones.

Reporters were surprised at the skill of the Dolly Vardens. "They ran like deer," said one paper, "threw the ball like a boy, with the right arm, and batted with lusty grace and freedom from restraint that was, to say the least, novel."[30]

Some female teams suffered from the same problems as major league clubs. In 1885, Amelia Bradley, captain of the black Rough and Ready club, was reported to be drunk and disorderly after a big win, for which she was sentenced to a $10 fine or 30 days in jail.[31]

The Dolly Vardens and their like were few and far between and women baseball players would not be much heard from for the remainder of the 19th century. When they played, they often played privately, on college campuses, in attire that was so cumbersome that it was difficult to move, let alone play ball. Title IX was nearly a century in the future and fortunately, by that time, Francis Richter was long in his grave.

Black players were only slightly more welcome than females, and their play was for the most part treated as an amusing novelty rather than serious baseball. Black baseball teams were formed as early as the 1850s, although data on those first teams is scarce. Two of the most enduring organizations were the Fearless Club of Utica, New York, which lasted from 1866 to 1908, and The Uniques of Chicago, who played from 1871 to 1893. Many clubs were formed around professions, with barbers and hotel workers, two of the more lucrative jobs available to blacks, the most common. Many of the leading players were light-skinned mulattoes and some passed for white.[32] In order to attract fans and minimize hard feelings if they happened to beat a white nine, black clubs frequently played to white stereotypes by sporting dandified uniforms or engaging in minstrel-like clowning on the field, in the fashion of the Harlem Globetrotters.

The 1884 season was the 19th-century high water mark for blacks in the major leagues, with the Walker brothers (see Chapter 3) playing for Toledo and Bud Fowler a step behind in the Northwestern League. The demand for players created by the rapid expansion of teams was undoubtedly a motivating factor. The unanswered question is why more teams, particularly those on the brink of failure, didn't sign blacks. There were talented men available who probably could have been obtained at cheaper prices than white players, yet only the Walkers broke through. Perhaps inbred prejudice overcame financial incentives, or maybe managers felt as some owners did in the 20th century—black players would drive away their fans.

Whatever the reason, virtually all blacks were relegated to their own teams in 1884. Two of the best were Henry Bridgewater's Black Stockings of St. Louis and the Gordons of Chicago. The Black Stockings, who played into the 20th century, dominated black baseball in St. Louis for many years and once took an 80-game tour through the United States and Canada. Their shortstop in 1884 was 26-year-old Frank Hart, who earned a fair degree of celebrity as a long-distance walking champion. In the pedestrian world, his race didn't prevent him from competing with whites, but when Hart (whose real name was Fred Hichborn) decided he wanted to play baseball, he had to play for a "colored team."[33]

The Gordons, professionals[34] who were paid an estimated $35–50 per week,[35] claimed the title of colored champions of the United States. Many of the Gordons were prominent in the Chicago community and the club was financed in part by gamblers Henry Jones, who served as president, and Fenton Harsh. Their headquarters was a gathering place for the black clubs of the city.

Nearly all black teams were independent, playing for informal championships of geographic regions, for there were virtually no black leagues. The Alerts of Washington, D.C., applied to the white D.C. Baseball Association and the Pythians of Philadelphia to the Pennsylvania Baseball Association in 1867, but both applications were rejected.

The Union Colored Base Ball League was formed in New Orleans in the early 1880s and in 1884 there was a league that included teams in Maryland and Pennsylvania. Prior to the 1884 season, there was talk of forming a Colored League of Base Ball Clubs, including teams in Baltimore, Harrisburg, Pottsville, Reading, and Washington, but it does not appear to have come to fruition. Talk of a league in Ohio and Indiana likewise came to nothing.

Black clubs played mostly against each other, but occasionally they played against whites, especially in the north. In May 1884, Milwaukee's Northwestern League team drew 4,000 for a game against an African American team. In August, the black Orions of Philadelphia played the Millville Club, and since no mention was made of Millville's race, they were likely white. Some umpires were black, and there were a number who became proficient (as proficient as a 19th-century umpire could become) but quite often the umpire in a game between two black teams was white. If there was one black player on an otherwise all-white team, it was usually the pitcher or catcher, the two most important positions on the field.

It was rare for the results of games between black teams to be reported in the press; their activity was more likely to be noted if it reflected poorly on them. A newspaper reported a game between teams from Newark and Paterson, New Jersey, that ended in a dispute over prize money. A similar incident was reported in August 1884, when the Mutuals of Philadelphia failed to get their share of the gate proceeds from the Athletics of Baltimore. The Mutuals, with no money to cover their fare home, went to City Hall to ask for transport. "There being no fund for that purpose," the *Clipper* reported, "the probabilities are that some of the colored brethren are footing it back to the Quaker City. Anyhow, walking is pleasant at this time of the year."[36]

One of the few serious reports of black baseball activity in a major sporting paper was an account of the Alpines defeating the Remsens 6–3 for the "colored championship" at Brooklyn's Washington Park on September 30, 1884. It was not clear what championship was involved, but it is interesting to note that the game was played at the home field of Brooklyn's AA team.[37]

Most articles about games involving black players employed heavy use of dialect, such as "Dat's a dandy! Jee Christmast! Go 'way dar chile!"[38] Even compliments were backhanded. "It must be said of the Giants," said one paper, "that although they are colored, they are among the most gentlemanly lot of men that have ever played ball in Lancaster."[39]

Other ethnic groups were likewise viewed as curiosities when they played ball. "Philadelphia," said the *Clipper*, "…had a mania for novelties in baseball, games having been announced there between Chinese nines, between colored male and female teams, between nines composed of cripples, the qualification for membership being a lost arm or leg, and between sides made up of sixteen young girls."[40] Promotor John F. Lang catered to the curious with teams composed of blacks, women, and Chinese players. The latter wore exotic uniforms and their names alone sent reporters into paroxysms of laughter. The baseball was incidental.

Tom Oran, an outfielder for the NA St. Louis Red Stockings in 1875, was the first Native American to play major league baseball. The *Cincinnati Enquirer* wasn't expecting many more, noting, "An Indian base ball club has just been formed out West. As the umpire is likely to be killed at the conclusion of every game, the introduction of base ball among them probably marks the disappearance of the noble red man."[41]

Baseball was still primarily an American game, although a number of Canadians played in the U.S. major leagues, the most prominent of whom were pitcher Bob Emslie and outfielder Tip O'Neill. Others, such as George Latham and pitcher Fred Goldsmith, were born in the United States but made their reputation in Canada.

The story of the origin of baseball in Canada had an eerie similarity to its American counterpart. The account of the celebrated first game that allegedly took place in Beachville in 1838 has as many holes as the Doubleday myth. But somehow or another baseball did take hold north of the border and during the late 1860s and early 1870s, top American teams toured Canada, played exhibitions against local teams, and usually beat them soundly. The beatings were the highlights of the season, for without television, it was the only chance Canadians had to see the best players in the world.

The Canadian Association of Base Ball Players, consisting of teams from Toronto, Guelph, London, Hamilton, and Dunnville, was formed in 1876 at the instigation of brewer George Sleeman, a leading figure in Canadian baseball for many years. Many Canadian teams used American imports[42] and, bolstered by their Yankees, the Tecumsehs[43] of London, Ontario won the International Association title in 1877. The Maple Leafs of Guelph also provided strong competition for touring American teams and engaged in a bitter feud with the Tecumsehs that lasted several seasons.

Prior to the 1878 season, Tecumseh was invited to the annual NL meeting and briefly considered joining the league, which would have made them Canada's first major league team. They decided their population base was too small and the travel expenses too great and did not take the leap. It would be nearly one hundred years before another Canadian team was invited to join the major leagues.

The 1877 championship was the highlight of the Tecumsehs' career. By the following season, with financial difficulties and rumors of suspicious play haunting them, they disbanded at the end of August. By 1884, there was not much top-flight baseball north of the border.[44]

It would have been unusual for any aspect of 1884 baseball to be absent of controversy and Canada was no exception. On October 4, when the Clippers of Hamilton showed up in Toronto to play for the Canadian championship, they brought Dan Brouthers, Billy Serad, and George Myers of the Buffalo Club with them. Communication was limited in 1884, and the Clippers were hoping no one recognized the Americans, although the fame, size, and bushy mustache of Brouthers made him quite conspicuous. Toronto spotted the three ringers immediately and raised a howl of protest, but the Clippers countered that Toronto had engaged Boston's battery of pitcher Charlie Buffinton and catcher Mert Hackett at a cost of $25 each. After a lengthy squabble, the teams left the major leaguers on the sidelines and played their regular lineups. The game wound up in a tie when darkness forced its termination.

Baseball was becoming popular on the island of Cuba. The sport was introduced to the natives by the U.S. military in the 1860s, but the Spaniards were leery of an American sport and discouraged it. Esteban Bellan, a Cuban who attended St. John's College in New York and played major league baseball from 1871 to 1873, returned to the island in 1874 and played a leading role in the development of Cuban baseball.

With their temperate climate, the Cubans played primarily in the winter months, which gave American teams the opportunity to visit during their off-season. During the winter of 1879, Frank Bancroft took a team there to play exhibitions and a New Orleans team followed in 1884.

The quality of baseball in Cuba wasn't bad. About the time of Bancroft's visit, an American expatriate sent an encouraging letter home describing a game between two Cuban teams that "would have done no discredit to two League clubs in the States." To his delight, the umpire made his calls in English, but to his disappointment, the game took place on the Sabbath. His sorrow was somewhat assuaged by the presence of "hundreds of the dark-haired senoritas." When the game became exciting near the end, "The Spanish blood was excited, men shouted, gesticulated and threw their hats in the air, while the Cuban maidens waved their handkerchiefs in wild delight at the success of their favorites."[45]

*Sporting Life* published an article on Cuban baseball titled, "Base Ball as a Civilizing Agent," which noted approvingly that baseball was replacing the primitive sport of bull-fighting and that games were attended by "dark-eyed senoritas and fashionable gentlemen."[46] By 1884, Cuban baseball had gotten quite serious, and those hot-blooded Spanish men started looking for some blue-eyed Americans to strengthen their teams for the winter months.

One can't learn much about women's baseball, baseball among African Americans, or baseball in Cuba by reading the major sporting journals. But we *can* learn quite a bit about how the mainstream media viewed these groups. Women had no place in baseball, and those who played publicly were harlots. Blacks bickered over trivialities but were always good for a laugh. Hot-blooded Cubans were cheered on by dark-eyed senoritas. That was the baseball world of 1884 and would be the baseball world for many years to come.

# 18

# "Champions of the world"

Football's Super Bowl is the biggest sporting event in the United States. And while the World Cup and Olympics may generate more interest internationally, the Super Bowl is the most popular one-day sporting event in the world. American cities vie for the honor of hosting it, and it is probably only a matter of time before some foreign city overwhelms the NFL with an offer it won't refuse. Today the game is awarded several years in advance to give the host city plenty of time to prepare, but preparations for the first Super Bowl, then known as the NFL-AFL Championship Game, were much less elaborate. In mid–December 1966, about a month before the game was played, NFL commissioner Pete Rozelle announced that it would probably take place in Los Angeles, most likely on January 15, 1967. That is where and when the game did take place, and the Los Angeles Coliseum was not even close to being sold out, despite an average ticket price of about $12.

Baseball's World Series began in equally modest fashion. Until 1882, there had been just one major league and the regular season champion was *the* champion. When the American Association was formed in 1882, fans wanted to see the two leagues play each other, but they were at war. A series between the AA pennant winners from Cincinnati and the National League champion Chicago nine ended after each team won one game. AA president Denny McKnight was angry over the way the NL had treated his new league and told Cincinnati to terminate the series or risk expulsion. In any event, it was never considered a contest for the championship of professional baseball, just an exhibition series played for gate receipts.

When the two leagues made peace in 1883, there were no post season championship contests, partly because the AA champion Athletics were so devastated by injuries, they were in no condition to play another series. Further, there was no tradition of post-season playoffs. There was, however, a long tradition of pre- and post-season exhibitions, and when the AA and NL established amicable relations, teams from the two leagues regularly played each other, with contests for city championships generating tremendous interest.[1]

Not everyone thought that a series for the championship of professional baseball was a good idea. Henry Chadwick worried that it would encourage more betting. A Louisville paper agreed. "[It] will speedily bring professional ball playing down to the level of prize ring encounters. Once allow this kind of business, and the door will be left open to the crookedness of a dozen years ago, and games and players will be bought and sold by the gamblers as was formerly done."[2]

In the late summer of 1884, with the Providence Grays leading the NL and the Metropolitans in the van in the AA, Grays manager Frank Bancroft sent a challenge to his counterpart Jim Mutrie of the Mets proposing a post-season series. Each team would put up $1,000 and the team that won a best-of-three series would take the entire purse and all gate receipts.

In its October 1 edition, *Sporting Life* reported, "If the Metropolitans win the American Association championship they will play a series of games with Providence, to be played in New York, if the weather be at all favorable."[3] There was no indication that the series would result in what we now know as a World Champion, or that it was more important than the Mets' competition with the New York National League club.[4]

A day later, it appeared that the series was off. An October 2 letter from Bancroft listed a number of scheduled exhibitions, but a series with the Mets was not among them. The Grays' last game would be in Cincinnati on October 20. "Then," Bancroft concluded, "we sing 'Auld Lang Syne' and depart for home to lay plans for '85." Mutrie added, "For good and sufficient reasons, the League champions will not play the Mets and that settles it."[5]

Bancroft blamed Mutrie for the cancellation. "[A]t our meeting in Detroit Sept. 19," he said, "he not only refused an offer for three games, half gross receipts each, and pitchers to pitch according to their respective rules, but had the gall to offer us half *gate* [emphasis in original] receipts and pitchers to pitch under American rules, which I, of course, declined, and having closed my dates now cannot make dates under any consideration, at least until the season ends. I presume the Providence players will accommodate him if he decides to accept the original challenge."[6]

There was no dispute over where the games would be played, for Providence, despite winning the pennant, had not drawn well at home. Mutrie initially offered to play a five-game series, two in each city and the deciding game at a neutral site, but Bancroft didn't trust his home town fans to turn out and didn't want to incur the cost of going back and forth. He wanted to play three games, all in New York.

Bancroft and Mutrie were well-schooled in the art of generating publicity, and a public feud was just the ticket for giving the impression that the series would be a hard-fought grudge match. A week after Bancroft accused Mutrie of quashing the deal, Mutrie said that if Providence did not accept his terms, he would claim the "championship of the world"[7] for the Metropolitans. He proposed that each club put up $1,000 and that the entire sum be donated to charity. That sounded like a publicity stunt, for the Mets had lost money during the season and could use the extra cash.

After skirmishing in the press for several days, Bancroft and Mutrie unknotted their shorts and made concrete plans to play in New York on October 23, 24, and 25. Gradually, the series became acknowledged as a contest to decide the baseball champion of the United States, although no one would call it a World Series. The next year, when the Browns met the White Stockings for the title, St. Louis sportswriter Al Spink called it the World's Series, and by the 20th century it was known by its current appellation.

Ever since baseball became popular in the 1850s, there had been an obsession with championships—of states, cities, towns, regions, professions, races, and virtually any kingdom that could be defined. Now, with two major leagues, baseball had an opportunity to play a series with, as the *Cincinnati Enquirer* said "the winning club to be entitled to the championship of America." It added, "These will probably be the greatest games ever played."[8] *Sporting Life* also anticipated "the greatest games ever played" and expected that, with good weather, there would be more fans at the Polo Grounds than ever attended a baseball game before.[9]

### 18. "Champions of the world"

Attendance proved more of a challenge than *Sporting Life* anticipated. In the 24 hours before the first game, the temperature in New York dropped about 25 degrees and a rainstorm left a stiff wind in its wake. On October 23, as the teams took the field, "Some 2,500 people huddle in the stands at the Polo Grounds, their eyes tearing up when gusts blast them in the face and make the ballpark's flags snap like gunfire."[10] The size of the crowd was disappointing, but the spectators compensated in quality for what they lacked in quantity. Henry Chadwick was there to report the action; Detroit manager Jack Chapman was also in attendance, as was old veteran Dicky Pearce and several major league players and executives.

Bancroft announced before the series began that Hoss Radbourn would pitch every game, which came as no great surprise since he'd pitched nearly every game the second half of the season. The teams agreed to use AA pitching rules, which limited throws to below the shoulder. While that might have been problematic for some National League pitchers, it didn't bother Radbourn. The use of AA rules also meant that hit batsmen were entitled to first base.

Tim Keefe, who won 37 games for the Mets during the regular season, seemed to have more trouble than Radbourn with the swirling wind, and his delivery was wilder than usual. He was also hampered by the absence of injured catcher Bill Holbert, and the Grays took advantage of Keefe's two wild pitches and Charley Reipslager's four passed balls.

Keefe hit the first two batters, Paul Hines and Cliff Carroll. Under AA rules, umpire John Kelly awarded them first base. Veteran first baseman Joe Start drove in Hines with the first run in World Series history and Carroll scored on a wild pitch, giving Providence a quick 2–0 lead. Keefe allowed just one hit during the first six innings, but in the eighth inning, the Grays unleashed a flurry of hits, including two doubles and a triple, scored three runs, and boosted their final margin to 6–0. Radbourn gave the Mets nothing, allowing just two hits before the game was called due to darkness during the eighth inning.

For Friday's second game, the weather was colder and the crowd even smaller than the previous day, numbering only about 1,000. The teams battled through four scoreless innings before Providence broke through with three runs in the top of the fifth. The features of the rally were a disputed safe call on an attempted steal of second by Jack Farrell and the first World Series home run, a blast over the center field fence by Jerry Denny, who led the Grays with six during the season. The Mets scored a run in the bottom of the fifth and the Grays plated two more in the top of the eighth, but just before 5:00, umpire Jack Remsen suspended play due to darkness and the score reverted to the end of the seventh. Although the Mets were one-sided losers once more, they did a little better against Radbourn the second time around, touching him for three hits.

Although Providence had already clinched the series with two victories, a third game was played on Saturday, October 25. The cold snap continued and, with the issue already decided, less than 500 fans showed up. By that point, even the Grays had had enough. It was uncomfortably cold, there wasn't much money to be realized from the meager crowd, and the Providence players just wanted to go home. They objected to each umpire proposed by the Mets, hoping to have the game cancelled. But the Mets wanted to play. They were already home and wanted to collect the gate receipts. Mutrie told Providence they could have any umpire they wanted, even Bancroft. Arthur Bell, treasurer of the Metropolitan Exhibition Company, finally convinced the Grays to play, with Keefe as umpire.

The Mets played like a beaten team, putting Buck Becannon, who'd pitched only one

The 1884 Providence Grays were the first major league team to win a championship in a post-season playoff. Standing (left to right): Paul Hines (CF), Jerry Denny (3B), Jack Farrell (2B), Joe Start (1B), Miah Murray (C), Frank Bancroft (Mgr.), Charles (Hoss) Radbourn (P), Charlie Sweeney (P), and John Cattanach (P). Seated (left to right): Art Irwin (SS), Cliff Carroll (LF), Sandy Nava (C), Barney Gilligan (C), and Paul Radford (RF). Insets: (left): Charley Bassett (SS/3B); (right) Ed Conley (P)(National Baseball Hall of Fame Library, Cooperstown, N.Y.).

game all season, in the pitcher's box. New York's other pitcher, Jack Lynch, who'd equaled Keefe with 37 wins, was sidelined with an injured wrist. Even though Providence had already won the series and Radbourn had pitched a staggering number of innings, Bancroft sent him out for the third day in a row. After all, he had all winter to rest.

The Grays rolled to an easy 11–2 victory, for what it was worth, making them the undisputed champions of the United States. "After beating up the Metropolitans," Bancroft wrote, "no fields remained to be conquered, and we patted each other on the back and called ourselves the best on earth."[11] Although UA adherents called for a round-robin series among the Grays, Mets, and St. Louis Maroons, *Sporting Life* called the Grays "Champions of the World."

When the American Association was folded into the National League in 1892, the 19th-century World Series came to an end. The National League tried a split season format, and then the Temple Cup, in which the first-place team played the runner up, but neither generated much enthusiasm. It was not until the 20th century, when the American League became a viable rival for the National, that a new World Series caught the fancy of baseball fans. Most current fans call the 1903 meeting between the Pittsburgh Pirates and Boston Pilgrims the first World Series, but they are wrong. A hastily arranged, poorly-attended three-game match in New York began the tradition, and the Providence Grays were the first team in the history of professional baseball to win a title in head-to-head competition.

# 19

# "On the Ragged Edge"

When the 1884 season ended, *Sporting Life* wrote, "The past year in base ball has been the most successful in the period of modern revival. The season opened earlier and lasted longer.... It has been a prosperous year for players. Base ball can now be ranked as an established occupation."[1]

It may have been a long season and a prosperous one for players, but many teams that started the season did not finish it, and many players who had been prosperous in 1884 would be unemployed in 1885. It was too much, too soon. "It is very clear," said the *Baltimore Sun*, "that the base-ball business has been overdone this season."[2]

What was good for the players was certainly not good for management, as the dilution of talent and the option of a third league gave many players a sense of entitlement, as least by the standards of the day. "In 1884," said the *Clipper*, "all of the League and American clubs found it difficult, if not impossible, to bring any strong coercive laws to bear on their players in the way of penalties for slighted field-services or for acts of insubordination; the stumbling-block in the way of the application of strict club rules in punishing violations thereof being the existence of the rival Union Association."[3] "The course of the Union Association," added the *Baltimore Sun*, "in antagonizing the national agreement … had a very injurious effect upon the discipline of clubs in all the associations."[4]

The birth of the Union Association and the expansion of the American Association also led to higher salaries. Yet, despite increased expenses, it was believed that all National League clubs except Detroit and Cleveland, which finished at the bottom of the standings, made money, and the losses of those two clubs were nominal. Al Spalding, however, hinted that Chicago, which had always been profitable, might incur a small loss. Boston supposedly had $50,000 in the treasury at the end of the season, while the Metropolitan Exhibition Company had mixed results. The NL club made $35,000 while the Mets, despite winning the AA title, lost $15,000. The Mets' attendance was hampered by the fact that there were 27 occasions on which both the Mets and Gothams played at home on the same day—and the Gothams had a much better park.

In the AA, only Toledo, Indianapolis, and the Alleghenies lost money. The new UA was much less successful—just St. Louis, Washington, and Kansas City were profitable—and the only minor league club believed to be in the black was the Domestic Club of Newark.[5]

Kansas City's profit came despite a late entry and a 16–63 record. Ted Sullivan was enthusiastic when the season ended, happy with the reception from local fans and encouraged by his late season success. During the winter, he tried to get the city to build a new stadium and announced that he had signed a number of stars, including Fred Shaw, Hugh Daily, and others.

Despite the fact that the majority of teams were profitable, the experience of 1884 convinced even the most hard-headed expansionist that there had been too many teams. The one thing that every major league executive agreed upon was that salaries needed to be curtailed. That would be much easier to accomplish if there were fewer teams and therefore a contraction appeared to be in order.

Almost as soon as the season was over, speculation began about the lineup for 1885, and the most pressing question was what would become of the UA. While the *Spalding Guide,* the official yearbook of the NL, wrote, "The record of the inaugural campaign of the financially disastrous Union Association is appended by way of record,"[6] at least they called it the "inaugural" campaign, hinting that there might be another season.

There were hopeful rumors about star players like Ned Williamson and George Gore of Chicago possibly signing with the UA. But after the instability of 1884, it would be difficult to entice players to risk blacklisting by joining a league that didn't appear to have much staying power. Paul Hines of Providence said he would not entertain any UA offers because he had no confidence that the circuit would last.

It appeared certain that the UA was going to lose its Baltimore and Boston franchises. Nashville, Columbus, and Rochester were mentioned as possible replacements, but the general consensus was that the association would be composed only of western teams. While Lucas denied it, Warren White admitted that the eastern part of the league was in a "chaotic state."[7] Of the eastern teams that set sail in 1884, Baltimore and Boston were out and Philadelphia was long gone. Washington wanted to get into the AA to replace Moxley's defunct team. *Sporting Life* revealed that NL president Mills had delegated Henry Diddlebock of the Eastern League, Billy Barnie of Baltimore, and Jim Mutrie of the Metropolitans to entice the Washington and Boston UA teams to join the Eastern League.[8]

In late November, *Sporting Life* predicted that the 1885 UA would consist of Columbus (or possibly Pittsburgh), Cincinnati, Indianapolis, St. Louis, Kansas City, Omaha, St. Paul, and Milwaukee.[9] If that supposition was correct, the UA would look more like a western minor league than a major league.

While the NL and AA were trying to steal Lucas' franchises, he was trying to do the same to theirs, telling people in Indianapolis they were going to be dropped from the AA and urging them to join his league. "He didn't wish to be understood," said *Sporting Life*, "as making any threats against Indianapolis, and didn't want any of its players himself, but he simply wanted to let them know that they would be subserving [sic] their own interests by joining the Unions."[10] He pointed out that Ted Sullivan, who accompanied him, had signed several Indianapolis players to conditional contracts and with a weaker team they would be doormats in the AA. He also pointed out that Sunday ball was nearly universal in the UA and that he was considering moving to a percentage gate distribution system in 1885. Lucas left town believing that Indianapolis would join the UA if it was dropped by the AA. He also targeted Detroit and Cleveland of the NL.

The Union Association held a meeting December 18 at the Laclede Hotel in St. Louis with Cincinnati, St. Louis, Milwaukee, St. Paul, and Kansas City represented in person, and one other city, whose identity was withheld, represented by proxy. Baltimore's resignation was accepted, and Boston and Washington, which did not sent delegates, were dropped. A number of cities were discussed as possibilities for 1885 franchises. Philadelphia, which Lucas had tried to revive three months earlier, did not come through. The prospective investors turned out to be better at pledging money than delivering it.

Lucas was re-elected president, each club was assessed $131.29 to make up the deficit from the previous season, and it was announced that four cities had officially applied for membership. Good faith deposits would be required in order to avoid the disasters of 1884. The plan was to admit three clubs to supplement the five in attendance, a decision expected to be made at the annual meeting scheduled for January 15 in Milwaukee. The *Enquirer* predicted that the January meeting would be a "whopper."[11]

No one expected there to be a meeting on January 15, for *Sporting Life* had just printed a bombshell titled "A Startling Story—Mr. Lucas to Desert the Union Association—Ready to Put a League Club in St. Louis."[12] The story was based on two pieces of evidence: a dispatch from New York and a letter from a friend of Lucas who signed his name A.L. Bird.

The dispatch stated that Lucas intended to join the National League as a replacement for Cleveland and Bird's letter confirmed it. "[H]e made the fight against [the reserve rule]," said Bird, "for the protection of the players, but since he has had experience with them, he has found them to be an ungrateful lot, and he has come to the conclusion that the reserve rule is a necessity."[13] The biggest question was whether Lucas would be allowed to retain his players that were on the NL and AA blacklist.

*Sporting Life* said that when Lucas was asked whether he was going to join the NL, he replied that "he had been admitted to that organization so far as its action could go under the National Agreement."[14] Under the Agreement, it was necessary to get the consent of the AA, and the most likely person to object was Chris Von der Ahe of the Browns. Von der Ahe assumed that Lucas would be prohibited from playing on Sundays and that he would have to charge the 50-cent admission required of all NL teams. When he found that the NL could unilaterally remove these constraints if they chose, the Browns owner decided to fight.

It wouldn't be an easy fight, because the NL wanted Lucas, for it would mean the end of the despised UA; there was no way it could survive without him. The *Clipper* supported Lucas, noting that baseball owners were practical businessmen, and the best way for them to realize a profit on their investments was to let Lucas into their league and rid themselves of the Union Association. "It is all a matter of business," Chadwick wrote. "Each club in both Associations works for its own special pecuniary interests, leaving sentiment in the matter good enough to wind up a constitutional paragraph on a club address."[15]

The UA annual meeting took place as planned, but without Lucas it was a waste of time. "The meeting of the Union Association set for January 15, at Milwaukee," said *Sporting Life*, "was a funeral."[16] Only Milwaukee and Kansas City were represented, the latter by Ted Sullivan. After waiting in vain for Lucas to appear, Sullivan dissolved the Union Association and formed the Western League, which is essentially what the UA would have been if it had survived.

With the UA gone, there would be eight less teams in major league baseball in 1885, and probably fewer, for the American Association, which had expanded quickly and unwisely the previous season, was due for a contraction. Shortly after the 1884 season ended, Toledo and Columbus withdrew, reducing the membership to ten. Toledo lost $10,000 and was unable or unwilling to commit additional capital for 1885. Columbus had been profitable, supposedly clearing $7,500, but the team had overachieved in 1884 and would be hard-pressed to pay the salaries their players expected after their good seasons. Further, they knew that the AA was planning to contract and thought they might be one of the victims.

Columbus saw opportunity. So did Allegheny manager Hustling Horace Phillips, who'd been deposed as Columbus manager a year earlier and had signed most of the players now on the roster. As soon as the season ended, he appeared in Columbus trying to filch some of the club's top players, but quickly learned that all the reserved players but one had signed.

Phillips sent a telegram to the Columbus stockholders offering to pay $3,000 if they would release the battery of Morris and Carroll or $5,000 for the entire team. If Columbus was dropped from the AA the players could be had for nothing, but Phillips wanted to secure them without bidding against other teams. One of the Columbus stockholders visited Pittsburgh and said the $5,000 offer was too low, but thought the players could be had for $6,000. He promised to return to Columbus and find out.

The Columbus stockholders considered their options. If they raised advance money to pay their signees and the AA dropped them, they would be left with nothing. Even if they remained in the league, the city might prohibit Sunday baseball, which was critical to their survival. They decided to sell out, received approval from the other AA teams, and the transaction was finalized for $6,900.

The transaction was novel and controversial. The *Cincinnati Enquirer,* always ready to take a shot at the AA, headlined its article "Selling Players Like Slaves."[17] "The recent action of the Columbus club," said the *Brooklyn Eagle,* "in transferring their players to Pittsburgh, just as they would dispose of any of their club house furniture, is in direct violation of the rules of the national agreement."[18]

Under the rules, Columbus could not actually sell its players. They could accept payment in return for a release, after which the players promised to sign a contract with the new team after the ten-day waiting period expired. Of course, if those promises were as binding as a contract, the ten-day rule was meaningless. When the Arbitration Committee met on November 7, it re-affirmed that a team could release its players but not directly transfer them to another team.

The AA was in the process of choosing a president. "The need of a general executive officer to govern the American Association is undeniable," said *Sporting Life*.[19] The leader, it added, should have no connection with any club and should have the power to run the Association, blacklist players, and enforce discipline without interference.

Incumbent Denny McKnight, who was recovering from a broken shoulder suffered in a fall, had reportedly severed his association with the Allegheny Club, and was the man *Sporting Life*'s Francis Richter wanted in the job. McKnight's primary competitor was Charles Byrne, president of the Brooklyn Club. In early October, Henry Chadwick predicted confidently that Byrne would be the next AA president.[20] Richter left no doubt where he stood. "Byrne," Richter said, "is a nervous little man, full of life and grit, a good talker, very earnest and aggressive, and has a very high opinion of the American Association, the Brooklyn Club and—himself. Byrne is also ambitious, and his candidacy was probably brought about by his own exertions."[21]

Byrne proved a most reluctant candidate, while McKnight made no attempt to disguise his eagerness to continue in the position. He was re-elected with a minimum of controversy, at a salary of $1,800 plus $500 for expenses. In an attempt to solve what had been a major problem in 1884, McKnight was given full authority over the Association's umpires.

The bigger issue for the Association was how many teams it would have in 1885 and, if it were to go back to eight, which teams would be dropped. At the annual convention, the Domestic Club of Newark (an 1884 member of the Eastern League) and the Nationals of Washington (a UA club in 1884) applied for membership. This precipitated a debate as to the number of teams and the issue was referred to a three-man committee.

The committee reported back with the recommendation that it would be difficult to make up a schedule for a ten-team circuit (which the American and National Leagues did from 1961 to 1968) and that the league should be limited to eight teams. The two clubs left outside looking in would be Indianapolis and Virginia.

The exclusion of Indianapolis was no surprise to most people, since the Hoosiers ended the season in disarray, with the players in revolt against manager Bill Watkins. The club's directors, however, were shocked, angry, and defiant. In November, when rumors began circulating that the team might be a victim of the AA contraction, Watkins said he would fight any effort to drive his team out; as long as a team paid its dues and its players, he said, they couldn't be ousted. Indianapolis president Schwabacher hinted that the club might go to court if the AA tried to remove them.

According to one of the Indianapolis officers, the club had contacted some AA directors and asked whether it was advisable to expend money for the next season. He said they were assured they wouldn't be expelled, and therefore improved their grounds and paid advance money under 1885 contracts.[22]

There was talk of joining the UA, combining with Cleveland as an NL team, or playing as an independent team. If they chose the latter route, they could meet NL and AA teams in exhibitions, but would have no protection for their player contracts. Eventually, Indianapolis decided to join the Western League.

Although the decision didn't seem particularly fair to Virginia, which had been enticed to join the league late in the 1884 season, they went quietly and joined the Eastern League, where they experienced great success on the field and dismal failure in the coffers, folding in mid-season 1885 with a 67–26 record.

Indianapolis and Virginia had not played well in 1884, and Indianapolis had a very rocky season off the field. If teams had to be jettisoned in the interest of efficiency, they were probably the best candidates. But throughout the winter there was rumor that the AA's best team might not be around to defend its title in 1885.

The Mets had a winter very different than that of most champions. There was no basking in the glory of the 1884 season; they spent most of their off-season denying rumors. One was that Lucas was going to buy the Mets as his entree into the major leagues; he said later that the team had been offered to him, but the price was too high. A second rumor claimed that the Mets would disband and the Metropolitan Exhibition Company would acquire the Brooklyn AA club and transfer the best Met players to Brooklyn. The Mets' place in the AA would be taken by Mike Scanlon's Washington nine. Another possibility was that, if it should acquire the Mets players, Brooklyn would apply for admission to the National League if Detroit pulled out. Yet another rumor said that Brooklyn would acquire the Providence players and enter the NL as the Atlantics.

The situation became even more puzzling when Brooklyn president Byrne announced that he had obtained a ten-year lease on a field at Coney Island, beyond the Brooklyn city limits, where he thought he would be permitted to play Sunday games. Since playing on Sunday was not allowed in the NL, it did not appear he was planning to move in that direction.[23] But it did appear that something was afoot in Brooklyn, because when December came to an end, the team had not signed any players.

Just after the beginning of the new year, rumors of the Mets' disbandment ebbed.

Byrne said that there had been discussions in November, but they terminated in early December. Reportedly, the Mets began the talks by offering to buy the stock of the Brooklyn club. When that offer was declined, Brooklyn proposed transferring the Met franchise to Brooklyn. The Mets asked for $75,000 to do that, and Brooklyn declined. A second sticking point was the reluctance of Bryne to reimburse the Mets for improvements they'd made to their grounds. A third was that Brooklyn wanted all the Mets' players, while the Metropolitan Exhibition Company wanted to transfer some of the best talent to their New York Club and send the rest to Brooklyn.

When it appeared that negotiations were over, the *Clipper* said of Brooklyn, "[C]lub officials are quietly attending to their own business in regard to getting a strong team together." It praised the club's adherence to honesty and square dealing and said, "This policy pays best in the end, and they have had the wisdom to follow it."[24]

On January 17, Jim Mutrie told *Sporting Life* that Brooklyn approached the Mets with the idea of consolidating, and there had been a number of meetings, but when the Mets refused to soften their terms, the deal collapsed. He said the Mets would have an AA team in 1885. That didn't stop the rumors, and at the end of January, there was speculation that the Mets would drop out of the AA and be replaced by Washington.

One of the issues the National League faced during the winter was the selection of a new president, for Abraham Mills, who had to be convinced to continue in the job in 1884, told the owners he intended to resign. It had been a difficult year, particularly with the battle against the UA, and Mills had numerous other business interests. He had taken a hard line with the UA, and was disappointed that Lucas, who he'd tried so hard to destroy, was going to be admitted to the NL. There was even talk that the blacklisted players might be allowed to return.

Mills' successor would be the fourth president in NL history, and the first not selected by William Hulbert. Morgan Bulkeley had been an honorary appointment, and Hulbert, the driving force behind the league even when Bulkeley was president, succeeded him after a single season. Mills had been Hulbert's somewhat reluctant hand-picked successor.

There had never been a spirited fight for the office and there would not be one in 1884. Josiah Jewett of Buffalo was a possibility and some favored Arthur Soden of Boston, who'd served as interim president after Hulbert's death. But it was good old Nick Young's turn. At the League's annual meeting on November 19, Mills resigned, as expected, and was replaced by Young in a process notably lacking in controversy.

Nick Young had been connected with baseball since the Civil War. He'd been the leader of the early Washington professional teams and it was his initiative that led to the organizational meeting of the National Association in 1871. Young was active in the management of the NA and shifted his loyalty to the NL when it was formed in 1876; since the league's inception he had served as secretary and treasurer. Loyalty and diligence were his finest traits, and because of his genial personality he had few enemies. In a small, contentious group such as the National League, a lack of enemies is a sure path to electoral victory.

One thing that prevented Young from being NL president earlier was the fact that he held a full-time job with the Treasury Department in Washington, which he was loath to give up. When Young agreed to serve the League on a full-time basis, the job of president was combined with those of secretary and treasurer, in order to provide a salary sufficient to induce him to leave government service.

Young served as president until 1902, but he was not a strong leader. During the critical discussions of January 1885 regarding the admission of Lucas to the NL, the *Brooklyn Eagle* noted, "It was made plainly manifest during the session that the 'power behind the throne' in the League gathering was in the hands of the Chicago, Boston and New York club delegates, the president of the League apparently being but a mere salaried official."[25]

Throughout the winter, there was intense speculation as to the status of Detroit and Cleveland. Detroit president Thompson had always been a loose cannon; on one occasion he stormed out of an NL meeting in protest of a proposal to pay president Mills a $4,000 annual salary. Prior to the 1883 season, he complained, "If there is a ball player in the country in whose promise you can place reliance, and not be disappointed, I have not met him." After the sorry 1884 campaign, he was even less enamored of his players. He had done everything he could to build a championship team, Thompson said, and had paid top salaries to get the best talent. Why hadn't it worked? Why had his team played so poorly?

The reason, Thompson said, was "the dishonesty and ungratefulness of players. They contract with us at a salary larger than the income of a large majority of professional men, to remain sober and play the best ball of which they are capable. We have kept our faith with them, but they have not with us. I do not believe there is a League team in the country that has not among its members two or three who will not throw a game at any time in the interest of the pool box.... Only two or three months ago, I said to one of them, who hadn't made a hit in six weeks. 'What's the matter with you? You are not batting as well as you ought' and he instantly responded, 'If you do not like the way I play ball, you can give me my release.'"

"I believe them to be the most ungrateful set of men I ever met," Thompson concluded, "and I am done with them." Just as well, said *Sporting Life*. "The man who would talk in the above strain of a game with which he has been associated so pleasantly as has Mr. Thompson is no loss. It is a good thing for the League that he does retire."[26]

A week after Thompson's outburst, a letter to *Sporting Life* signed "An Ex-Member" blamed Thompson for Detroit's problems, claiming he had cursed players, interfered with personnel decisions, and made a general nuisance of himself. He claimed that Thompson's reputation was so bad that good players wouldn't sign with Detroit no matter how much they were offered.[27]

The players were as unhappy with Thompson as he was with them. When the team's star pitcher, Dupee Shaw, left for the UA, he said the situation in Detroit was intolerable. At the end of the season, several players were due salary payments and threatened never to play for the team again. Stump Weidman and Charlie Bennett claimed they were owed $500 each.

The Detroit situation was cloudy, for while the club had reserved its top players, they had signed no one as of early December. The board of directors had resigned and Thompson was feuding with the other stockholders. He said if he couldn't force them out, he would dissolve the team and form a new one.

The Wolverines had no manager, for Jack Chapman would not return in 1885. There was talk that he would return to Brooklyn, where he began his career, to manage the AA club. Although his team had finished deep in the basement, Chapman had a remarkable talent for emerging unscathed from one disaster after another. He managed in the major leagues for 11 years despite a sorry 350–500 record. In seven of his 11 seasons, his team won less than 40 percent of its games. Chapman was invariably described as genial and a great story-teller, and had the middle-aged rotundity that traditionally accompanied a pleasant nature. That geniality and a reputation for baseball knowledge allowed him to have a long, though not terribly successful, managerial career.

Henry Chadwick, who had admired Chapman since the latter played for the old Atlantics, blamed Thompson's interference for the poor record of the Detroit club. Frank Bancroft and Chapman had failed to overcome Thompson's negative influence, Chadwick said, and "Harry Wright [whom Chadwick worshipped] would also fail under the same bossing."[28]

As 1884 turned into 1885, there were rumors that Milwaukee would replace Detroit, and the National League passed a special resolution intended to prevent Detroit from selling all of its players. On January 7, the team held a meeting and raised over $4,000. New management took over, led by Frederick Stearns, owner of a pharmaceutical company and a former player at the University of Michigan. At an NL meeting on January 10, the Wolverines convinced the league that they had the financial wherewithal to continue operations, and the application of Cincinnati's UA club to replace them was denied. The *Clipper* was unconvinced, however, and thought that Detroit's intention was to stay alive only long enough to sell its reserved players, as Toledo and Columbus had done, after which they would take the money and drop out of the League.[29]

Finally, at the end of January, the club held a meeting and elected a new slate of officers. Charley Morton, out of work after his Toledo club resigned from the AA, was signed as manager and a complement of players was engaged. There would be baseball in Detroit in 1885 after all. By 1887, after some wholesale acquisitions from Indianapolis and Buffalo, the Wolverines won the World Series.

That was not to be the case in Cleveland. Although the club finished 1884 with a 35–77 record, 49 games out of first, they reserved their players and raised money for 1885. There was no overt controversy, as there was in Detroit with Thompson, but there was an unsettling feeling that something was amiss, particularly when no players were signed. In late November, the club announced that it had reserved its grounds for 1885, but when third baseman Mike Muldoon, who'd played 110 games in 1884, was released rather than reserved, it fueled rumors that the club was going to disband. The *Clipper* declared in December that Cleveland was on the "ragged edge" and that if they folded, Brooklyn had the inside track on signing their players.

In early January, *Sporting Life* reported, "Nothing new has developed concerning Cleveland's future during the past week. The situation is still full of uncertainty and our belief is that Cleveland will not have a League club in 1885. Of this we are convinced."[30]

Apparently, the stockholders wanted out. They spent a good deal of money in 1884 only to see Fred Dunlap, George Shaffer, and Hugh Daily leave for the Union Association before the season started and three of their best players jump to Cincinnati in August. They'd had enough.

When it became known that Cleveland might be in play, rumors began circulating furiously. There were rumors (mostly initiated by Lucas) that the St. Louis owner was going to buy the Cleveland franchise and place Detroit and Cleveland in the UA, while St. Louis and Cincinnati took their places in the NL. Or maybe Cleveland would join the AA and Baltimore would switch to the NL. Or perhaps the Cleveland franchise was moving to Pittsburgh.

In the end, all that happened was that Cleveland disbanded and dropped out of the

NL. That left them, however, with a roster of reserved players, who became hot commodities. Apparently, Lucas was interested, and on December 22, he and his attorney, Newton Crane, met with Cleveland manager Charles Hackett. They offered Hackett[31] the St. Louis manager's job with the understanding that he would bring most of the Cleveland players with him. Hackett was coy.

The reason for Hackett's reticence was that he had already met with Charles Byrne and agreed to manage Brooklyn in 1885, with the same caveat. That not only explained Hackett's hesitation to deal with Lucas, but also the fact that Brooklyn had signed almost no players.

Hackett had attended the AA convention in mid–December and insisted that Cleveland would have a National League team in 1885. The reason he was at the meeting, however, was to talk to Byrne. After the two men reached an agreement, Hackett went on the road. First, he went to Ilion, New York, to meet with Pete Hotaling. Then, he went to Chicago and met with Bill Phillips. He found George Pinkney in Peoria, Illinois, and in Chillicothe, Illinois, he met with Bill Krieg, who'd played in the UA in 1884. He spoke with Doc Bushong and Germany Smith and believed both had agreed to play in Brooklyn, although Bushong was later released from his pledge and eventually signed with St. Louis. By the time Cleveland officially disbanded, Hackett had seven players in tow.

Other than an informal agreement with Hackett, however, there was nothing to bind the players to Brooklyn until they signed contracts, for the ruling after the Columbus-Allegheny deal confirmed the ten-day waiting period. Byrne was taking no chances. He reportedly sequestered the players in a remote location close to the Canadian border so that no other team could find and sign them. Another rumor had them in Oil City, Pennsylvania.

Cleveland gave notice of the players' releases to NL president Young on January 3. Young was out skating, and didn't get it until the 5th (apparently it was quite a long skate). He was supposed to send notice to all clubs promptly upon receipt, but did not do so until the 10th, under a letter dated the 6th. Supposedly, he delayed sending the letter in order to give Henry Lucas a chance to sign the players.[32]

Despite the rumors of sequestration in exotic locations, the released players were in a Cleveland hotel under the close watch of Byrne and Hackett. Their whereabouts was no secret, for other clubs began sending contract offers to the hotel. On the 13th, the players issued a statement saying they were not interested in receiving offers because they were planning to sign with Brooklyn.

At 12:10 a.m. on January 16, ten minutes after the expiration of the ten-day waiting period, Byrne signed contracts with Phillips, Hotaling, John Harkins, Pinkney, Smith, Krieg, and Bill McClellan, who'd played with Philadelphia of the AA in 1884. AA president Denny McKnight was there to witness the act. For its cooperation, Cleveland was reportedly paid $4,000 by Brooklyn, which also paid $5,000 in advances to the players.

The hometown *Brooklyn Eagle,* which had castigated the Columbus club for an identical act, somehow imputed honor to the wholesale raid. It was the admirable qualities of Byrne and the Brooklyn club, said Chadwick, that led Cleveland to deal with them rather than the less reputable Lucas. "Had the arrangement been one controlled by mere money consideration," he wrote, "then the St. Louis financier would probably have won the day."[33] "It is understood that every step taken by Mr. Byrne ... and by Mr. Hackett ... has been with the full knowledge, consent and cooperation of the Cleveland Club previous to the release of its players, and therefore in no way conflicting with the national agreement.... It has been charged that the Brooklyn club's negotiations with the Cleveland men was a violation of the national agreement. This is nonsense."[34] Chadwick, who nearly always took the side of the AA, attributed the indignation to sour grapes that Lucas was unable to get the Cleveland players.

At a subsequent NL meeting, a resolution was passed mandating the expulsion of any team negotiating contracts with players under reserve with another club but it was, of course, too late to affect the Cleveland-Brooklyn transaction.

The Metropolitan Exhibition Company employed similar guile in contract negotiations. They wanted to move Tim Keefe and Dude Esterbrook from the Mets to the Gothams, but if they released the two men other teams could sign them within the ten-day window. Therefore, when the Mets gave Keefe and Esterbrook their releases, they put them on a boat to Bermuda with Mutrie and John Day's brother-in-law. When the ten days were up, they signed contracts with the Gothams. The Mets were fined $500 but paid it willingly. Mutrie was rewarded with the NL team manager's job, vacant after the firing of James Price the previous October.

For the second straight winter, the contractual situation that created the most excitement was that of pitcher Tony Mullane. Prior to the 1884 season, Mullane had created a stir by jumping to Lucas' St. Louis team and then jumping back to the AA with Toledo. When Toledo dropped out of the AA, that left Mullane without a team.

Apparently, at some point during the 1884 season, when Toledo was having financial difficulties, they offered to sell some of their players, including Mullane, to Louisville. When Toledo was able to raise enough money to continue, Mullane stayed, but the *Commercial* indicated that Louisville agreed to contingent contracts that would be effective in the event that Toledo folded.[35] At the same time, Cincinnati expressed an interest in signing Mullane if Toledo bit the dust.

When Toledo did fold, Louisville contacted Mullane and the others about making their contingent agreements binding. In the meantime, however, Toledo had agreed, in return for $5,000, to release five players, including Mullane, in order to allow them to sign with St. Louis. St. Louis paid half of the amount for the releases in advance, with the rest due after the players had signed.

Mullane was in an interesting position. He pitched for St. Louis in 1883 before leaving for the Union Association, and Chris Von der Ahe hadn't seemed eager to have him back. Apparently, the Browns owner was willing to forgive and forget, and the two agreed on terms, but when the players gathered to sign contracts, Mullane excused himself, saying he wasn't feeling well. Sometime that evening, he regained his health and signed with Cincinnati for $5,000, with a $2,000 advance.[36] Cincinnati's Oliver Caylor claimed that since Mullane had only agreed to sign a contract with St. Louis, but never actually signed, the Cincinnati contract was valid. He did not use the explanation that since Mullane was ambidextrous, perhaps he'd simultaneously signed two contracts.

While it was clear that Mullane's conduct was not admirable, it was not clear that he had broken any rules. Cincinnati claimed he hadn't and that reneging on a promise to contract was different from reneging on a contract. Von der Ahe, now twice burned, said he didn't want Mullane back and wouldn't hold him to his oral agreement to sign a contract. That didn't mean that Mullane and Cincinnati were in the clear, however, because the AA had to approve the Cincinnati contract.

Prior to the AA's annual meeting, there was considerable sentiment that Mullane should be expelled. John Day said that if Mullane had given his word to play in St. Louis, "he should be forever prevented from playing baseball, at least with clubs of the national agreement, and I will be in favor of his expulsion."[37] St. Louis, Pittsburgh, Baltimore, and Louisville were also reported to be in favor of expulsion.

Mills said that the AA should determine which contract was legal, enforce it, and move on without expelling anyone. The other AA clubs, however, weren't just concerned with the legal aspects of the case. By expelling Mullane, they would greatly weaken a strong Cincinnati team. "When Caylor goes to blow down the barrel of the Mullane shot gun," said the *Philadelphia Times*, "he will discover that it is loaded."[38]

The AA Board of Directors met December 9, the night before the annual meeting. It was a stormy session during which Von der Ahe and his associate, Congressman John O'Neill, argued for Mullane's suspension or expulsion, Mullane defended himself, and Caylor supported him. At one point, Von der Ahe called Caylor a liar and O'Neil said he and Mullane were a disgrace to baseball.

Mullane was one of the few players at the meeting and his situation was the main topic of discussion. The delegates voted to suspend him for the 1885 season and ordered him to repay $1,000 of the $2,000 advance he received from Cincinnati. Despite Cincinnati's strenuous efforts to get Mullane reinstated, including a threat to jump to the NL, the AA wouldn't budge.[39]

The Cincinnati team said they would find Mullane a job and a place to practice, with the expectation that he would pitch for them in 1886. The AA called Caylor's bluff about jumping to the NL by offering his spot to the local UA team, at which point he quickly backtracked. The *Enquirer*, always ready to pounce on Caylor, was beside itself. "The professional reputation of the ghoulish Secretary of the Cincinnati Club has been staked so often and lost that it is thinner than church festival oyster soup."[40] It gleefully reproduced a letter from Billy Barnie offering the UA club a spot in the AA.

As he had the previous year, Mullane, who appeared outwardly unconcerned, took a beating in the press. "Mullane," wrote the *Brooklyn Eagle*, "very plainly exhibited his true character by the remarks he made in the lobby of the Fifth Avenue Hotel during the convention. The penalty, disgracing him, did not affect him in the least, but the fun did. It's money he is avowedly after. Character is nothing to him."[41]

Mullane, said the *Enquirer*, "is one of the most despicable and characterless men in the profession. He does not care a particle for his word or written contract and has broken promises time and again during his career."[42] "Treacherous Tony is wintering in Erie, Pennsylvania," the *Enquirer* added a couple of weeks later, "and the mayor has doubled the police force."[43]

Toledo, whose team didn't even exist anymore, jumped into the fray. They said St. Louis owed them for releasing Mullane, even though he hadn't signed, and said they planned to sue if they weren't paid.[44]

While the major leagues jettisoned teams, sold players, stole players, and bickered among themselves, minor league executives tried to determine whether there would be any minor leagues in 1885. The previous year had been a disaster. The Eastern League was the only prominent circuit to survive, and it barely did so. During the off season, when no money was being lost and no teams were folding, potential franchise holders were optimistic, crafting ambitious plans for the upcoming season. In November, the Eastern League expelled Allentown, York, and Trenton, and petitioned the Arbitration Committee to allow it to continue to operate under the National Agreement.

At the Arbitration Committee meeting of November 7, the following resolution was passed:

> *Resolved*, "That in view of the alleged disorganized state of the Eastern League ... it is hereby ordered that, unless the said league shall, by its secretary, exhibit to the spring meeting of this committee, to be held in April 1885, satisfactory documentary evidence showing an active membership of not less than six clubs, the said Eastern League shall forfeit its membership in this committee...."[45]

Virginia, which was about to be jettisoned by the AA, signed on and a number of other clubs expressed interest. All were in the same general geographic area, and apparently Henry Diddlebock had learned the lesson of the Northwestern League. His revamped league would be as compact as possible.

On December 12, the Eastern League held a meeting at the Bingham House in Philadelphia to organize for 1885 and try to meet the conditions of the Arbitration Committee. Diddlebock was elected to fill the combined offices of president, secretary, and treasurer, at a salary of $1,000. Virginia was re-admitted, as were the Nationals of Washington under Michael Scanlon, who had been unsuccessful in gaining admission to the AA.[46] As in 1884, two clubs from Lancaster vied for admission and the Lancaster Club was chosen. Other clubs would be located in Norfolk, Trenton, Newark and Jersey City. It was expected that one more club would be added, either Baltimore, Wilmington, or Bridgeport, Connecticut.

There couldn't be an Eastern League team in Baltimore unless Billy Barnie gave his permission, and Bob Ferguson was working to obtain it.[47] Diddlebock indicated that if Barnie was uncooperative, he would oppose the idea of a St. Louis club in the NL. But Barnie said no, Nick Young supported him, and no one cared what Diddlebock thought about the St. Louis situation. There would be no EL team in Baltimore.[48]

The *Clipper* had an interesting suggestion, which did not appear to be in jest. If Bridgeport was added to the Eastern League, they said, perhaps Bridgeport native P.T. Barnum could be persuaded to become president of the league. Who better to preside over the circus the Eastern League had been in 1884?[49]

Other leagues were organizing, including the New York State League, under the leadership of James Jackson, and the Southeastern League, which planned to have teams in Louisiana, Georgia, Tennessee, and Alabama. There was also a Southern League of eight franchises and there was talk of a Tri-State League in Ohio, Indiana, and Michigan.

The most important and controversial issue of the 1884–85 off-season involved Henry Lucas, who had been the primary cause of the chaos of the previous winter. This time, Lucas wasn't a threat; he was a supplicant. Throughout the early part of the winter, Lucas maintained the charade of keeping his league alive, but what he had always wanted was a major league franchise. To get one in 1884, he had had to support the entire league nearly single-handedly and he didn't intend to do it again.

A St. Louis man said that Al Spalding and Josiah Jewett of Buffalo approached Lucas in June about joining the NL. After the season, when asked if he wanted the enter the League, Lucas replied, "I think as a financial investment it would be a good thing, but I have not yet reached that point where I think it would be advisable to sell my honor for a little gold. You understand what I mean; I will not go back on Dunlap, Shaeffer [*sic*], Sweeney, Rowe, Dolan and other players I had with me last season. Unless the League will reinstate all the blacklisted players in my club as it now stands I could not for a minute think of dropping the Union Association."⁵⁰ In mid–December the UA organ *Cincinnati Enquirer* categorized the story of Lucas wanting to join the NL as an "absurd rumor"⁵¹ and Warren White insisted it was untrue. Nick Young said that all he knew of the situation was what he read in the newspapers.

The National League and American Association wanted to put a stake through the heart of the gasping UA, and the best way to accomplish that was to let Lucas into one of their leagues. Since Lucas' home base was St. Louis, and Chris Von der Ahe already had a franchise in the AA, the National League was the logical place for him to land.⁵²

The NL was willing to let Lucas in, and with Cleveland out, there was room for him. But there were a couple of potential problems. First was the issue of the blacklisted players on Lucas' roster and the second was that under the terms of the National Agreement, two-thirds of the AA clubs, or six of the remaining eight, would need to vote in favor of admitting St. Louis to the NL. In mid–December, Mike Scanlon of the Nationals told a reporter he thought a deal had been struck, for he saw Lucas, Newton Crane, and Von der Ahe shake hands after a meeting.

There had been no deal. Lucas was not willing to compensate Von der Ahe for sharing his territory and upset the Browns owner by not paying sufficient homage in order to gain his approval. If he were admitted to the NL, Lucas would be at a competitive disadvantage, since he would have to charge a higher admission fee than the Browns, could not play on Sunday, and could not sell beer. Of course, if Von der Ahe kept Lucas out of the League, he would be no competition at all.

When the National League met on January 10, Lucas acted as if he was an owner, participating in discussions and obtaining consent to form a club and sign players. Meanwhile, Von der Ahe went to Cleveland, where Charley Byrne was busy signing the former Cleveland players, and enlisted Byrne's aid in blocking Lucas. He also believed he had Cincinnati and Louisville in his camp, more than enough votes to carry the day.

It wasn't certain if Von der Ahe's goal was to keep Lucas out of the NL or to cause enough trouble to shake some money out of someone. But he clearly wanted something, and wasn't going to give in easily. "Von der Ahe remains as stubborn as he is capable of being," said the Boston correspondent to *Sporting Life*.⁵³ The journal's January 28 headline read, "On the Ragged Edge, The National Agreement in Danger, The League to Stand by Lucas."⁵⁴ Root of Providence, Soden of Boston, and Day of New York were selected by the NL to meet with the AA to try to find a solution.

The fight had gone beyond Lucas and Von der Ahe and become a conflict between the NL and AA, which the NL believed was attempting to use its veto power to extort money and concessions from an erstwhile NL owner. The League was prepared to support Lucas even, it appeared, at the risk of abrogating the National Agreement. The Philadelphia owners were the only ones not backing the St. Louis magnate.

Each side had its grievances. The AA was angry about the NL's attempt to ram Lucas down its collective throat after having spent 1884 calling him the devil incarnate. The NL was angry about Brooklyn signing the Cleveland players after the latter club had apparently made a deal with Lucas. Arthur Soden was upset that Brooklyn had signed Ed Swartwood, whom he wanted. Each side tried to cloak its cause with righteousness, but in the end, it was only a conflict of self-interest.

Francis Richter of *Sporting Life* thought the NL would benefit if the National Agreement was scrapped and the leagues went back to war. "The League in its present situation," he wrote, "has everything to gain by a war; it needs new blood, new clubs, new players. The American Association, on the contrary, has everything to lose; it is growing, it is compact, but it has not yet arrived at maturity."[55]

At first, Lucas chose not to negotiate directly with Von der Ahe, leaving the situation to the NL owners. He hinted that he would use his political connections to get the Missouri legislature to pass a bill prohibiting Sunday baseball if the League was unable to strike a satisfactory deal with the AA.

It was the political connections of his opponent, however, that brought the sides together. Congressman John O'Neill, an old friend of Von der Ahe's and a vice president of the Browns, arranged a meeting between the two St. Louis owners and in just 30 minutes, they reached an agreement. When the AA met on January 27, Von Ahe issued the following statement:

"The differences between Henry V. Lucas and myself have been amicably settled, and I hereby withdraw my objections to the admission of a League baseball club in the city of St. Louis."

Von der Ahe said he would have agreed earlier except for some misunderstandings. "I have all along thought that the two clubs," he said, "should play together, and carry on a friendly strife, as I think each can add to the financial strength of the other."[56]

What had caused the change of heart? The *Clipper* knew. It reported that Lucas' lawyer, Newton Crane, said, "We read with interest the *Clipper's* editorials, and I am confident they had much to do towards bringing this pleasant result about."[57]

Once the issue of Lucas' admission to the NL was resolved, and the Union Association was officially defunct, discussion turned to the former UA players who were on the blacklist. Initially, the AA and NL had taken a hard line. In early November, the Arbitration Committee considered the case of Clarence (Kid) Baldwin, who'd left Quincy of the Northwestern League to sign with Kansas City of the UA. "*Whereas*," the committee said, "This committee will never consent to the reinstatement of any player who has deserted, or may hereafter desert, any club identified with the National Agreement, therefore, *Resolved*, that the application of said Baldwin is denied."[58]

It was one thing to take a tough stand against a rookie like Kid Baldwin, but it might be different when the cases of established stars Fred Dunlap, Jack Glasscock, and Hugh Daily came up. The first case of a prominent player was considered at an NL meeting on November 22, when the applications for re-admission of Fred Shaw and several other players were denied with the same strong language used by the Arbitration Committee in the Baldwin case.

In January, Denny McKnight wrote a letter to *Sporting Life* arguing against re-admitting the jumpers. If they were taken back, McKnight said, and they were better than players who had remained loyal to their team, the latter would be released, a bitter reward for their allegiance. The jumpers would have jobs and the loyal players would be out in the cold, which McKnight said would be a grave injustice.[59] Mills was also strongly against letting the jumpers return.

John Montgomery Ward, who a year later would form the Brotherhood of Professional Base Ball Players, believed the contract breakers should not be subject to expulsion, which he said should only be used in cases of dishonest play. He also thought it was hypocritical for the AA and NL to ban those who jumped their reserve when they had encouraged players who contracted with the UA to break those contracts. Henry Chadwick agreed.

Some reserve jumpers had sympathetic stories. Dave Rowe said that in March of

1884 he asked Von der Ahe about a contract, but did not hear from him for six weeks. In the meantime, he signed with St. Louis of the UA. When Von der Ahe finally offered him a contract and Rowe told him he'd signed with the UA, he was placed on the blacklist. In March 1885, Rowe sued the Browns owner for $25,000.

By the time Rowe filed his suit, the hard line had been tempered by realism. Could the NL and AA ban some of the game's best players, depriving themselves of talent and revenue in the name of principle? If the owners had forgiven Lucas, the man who enticed the jumpers, and given him an NL franchise, how could they ban the players he'd signed? Two of Lucas' best players, Dunlap and George Shaffer, had committed the venial sin of reserve jumping rather than the mortal sin of contract breaking. The reserve rule was in its early stages, and many in baseball were uncomfortable with it. The NL was also hesitant about admitting Lucas but crippling his team from the start.

Billy Barnie proposed a compromise under which those who jumped contracts to join other AA or NL clubs would be banned, but those who went to the UA would not. Charley Byrne shot back, "Do you think we can respect such fellows as Dunlap, McCormick, Glasscock, Shaw, Mullane, Gleason, Bradley, and the rest of them? Have you any idea the amount of money, labor and trouble these fellows have cost the League and Association?"[60] On March 2 and 3, the AA held a meeting and resolved that no contract or reserve jumpers would be allowed in the Association. The only negative vote was cast by Cincinnati, which wanted Mullane to play for them in 1885.

Eventually, the NL and AA granted a near blanket amnesty to the blacklisted players, who had to pay $1,000 each to be reinstated. Most of the money was paid by their clubs. Although Dunlap, Sweeney, and Shaffer played with St. Louis in 1885, none was able to replicate his UA performances, an indication of the league's inferior standard of play. Sweeney's elbow gave out early in the season and he posted an 11–21 record. The Maroons, nicknamed the "Black Diamonds" for the number of formerly blacklisted players on the roster, finished in last place.[61]

Attendance was low, and in desperation, Lucas unsuccessfully petitioned the NL to allow him to play on Sundays. After losing money for two years, Lucas sold the team to John Brush, who moved it to Indianapolis. The man who had done so much to create the chaos of 1884 was gone by 1886. He said he had dropped $70,000 in three years and eventually lost all the money he inherited from his father. His wife divorced him and he ended his working career in a menial job for the City of St. Louis.

The biggest difference in major league baseball from 1884 to 1885 was that there were only 16 teams, rather than 28, and many men who played in the majors in 1884 were minor leaguers in 1885. The January 14 edition of *Sporting Life* contained 91 ads from players looking for jobs, including such well-known veterans as Dave Eggler, Herman Dehlman, and Denny Mack.[62] Those who remained in the majors had to accept lower salaries, usually without the generous advances of previous seasons. At the National League meeting of March 7, 1885, a committee reported that it had met with the AA and issued "a joint resolution announcing to the fraternity that hereafter no advance money would be paid to any club player or manager. This is but the beginning of an effort which will be made next Winter to reduce the high salaries which prevail at present."[63]

Some players didn't take the changed conditions quietly. Sid Farrar said he had other career options and wouldn't sign with Philadelphia unless he got what he thought he was worth. Mert Hackett was a Boston holdout, but the odds were against him. "He has been offered what everyone," said the *Clipper*, "save himself, concedes to be a fine salary. The Bostons will not bulldoze him into signing, but it might be well for him to learn that two catchers of reputation are anxious to come to the Hub."[64]

The *Clipper* tried to put a positive spin on a controversial winter, pointing out that all of the activity had gained national attention to baseball and enlivened the normally dull off-season. "Not since the National League was organized, in 1876" it said, "has the opening of a season in the professional arena looked more promising for the best interests of professional ball-playing than does the coming season of 1885."[65]

Many of the teams that participated in the 1884 season were not around in 1885, and by the following season, more fell by the wayside. Of the 34 teams that were considered major league franchises in 1884, only 14 were major league teams in 1886. The 1884 season was the high point for franchises and the low point for a lot of other things. There were many lessons that could have been learned; some were and some weren't. Six years later, baseball would foolishly plunge into another abyss, the Players League fiasco. Magnates are slow learners.

# Appendix A: Rules of the Brooklyn American Association Club

Rule I—Each player must make himself thoroughly familiar with the constitution and playing rules of the American Association of Base Ball Clubs.

Rule II—Each player must at all times keep his uniforms clean, neat and in fit condition for immediate use.

Rule III—When the club is traveling, players must retire at 11 p.m., if, in the judgment of the manager, that is practicable, and report to the manager next morning at such hour as he may name.

Rule IV—When the club is at home, players must report on the ground every morning at ten o'clock sharp, and practice for such time as the manager directs.

Rule V—Players must be on the ground, dressed for a game, forty-five (45) minutes before the time scheduled for it to begin.

Rule VI—Players must go out to and come in from their positions on the run.

Rule VII—All orders of the team captain must be promptly obeyed, and any player who violates this rule, or who questions in any way the decision of the umpire, will be rigorously dealt with.

Rule VIII—No matter what the provocation may be players must not reply to or take any notice of any remarks or criticisms of a spectator. If insulted or abused in any [way] they will at once request the captain to inform the manager, who will at once take such action as the case requires. All members of the club may rest assured that they will be protected from all annoyances of this kind.

Rule IX—Smoking while in uniform is strictly forbidden, and the use of liquors, at home or abroad, will subject a player to very summary punishment.

Rule X—A player who finds fault with or censures another, in public or private, for any errors he may make or lack of judgment displayed in playing, will incur a severe penalty or find his stay with this club very brief. The manager will do the necessary censuring.

Rule XI—All equipments furnished to members of the club are the property of this association, and are to be returned or accounted for.

SOURCE: *Brooklyn Eagle,* April 13, 1884.

NOTE: Other clubs had similar rules but, as can be seen throughout this text, they were uniformly ignored.

# Appendix B:
# The Lake Front Battleground

The Chicago White Stockings had occupied their Lake Front Grounds on Michigan Avenue since 1878 and intended to play there in 1884. On the 2nd day of January, however, Chicago mayor Carter Harrison, Sr., made their prospects very uncertain when he signed a contract with Michigan Central Railroad and Illinois Central Railroad to sell the parcel of land on which Lake Front Grounds were located. On January 7, Harrison sent the contract, which included a purchase price of $800,000, to the City Council for its approval.

The railroads intended to construct a depot on the property, which meant that the White Stockings would have to leave. They hung their hopes of remaining on the fact that there were several complications that might prevent the transaction from being consummated. The biggest impediment was that the City of Chicago didn't own the parcel it had agreed to sell. The land was part of the old Fort Dearborn, constructed on the shore of the Chicago River in 1803. After the original fort was destroyed by the British in the War of 1812, a second fort was constructed on the site. In 1839, the rebuilt fort was decommissioned and most of the property subdivided into a number of lots, which were sold individually. A portion of the site, three blocks between Randolph and Monroe Streets, was reserved for public use. Two blocks were owned by the federal government and one by the State of Illinois. The role of the City of Chicago was to maintain the public portion of the land and give the lot owners an open view to Lake Michigan and the "benefit of the fresh, pure, and invigorating breezes therefrom."[1]

Selling property one doesn't own is a tricky business. Chicago attempted to sell the Lake Front parcel in 1869 and convinced the state legislature to enact a law granting it the right to do so. Their efforts were frustrated, however, by the adjoining property owners, who claimed the sale would violate the open space requirement, and by the federal government, which obtained an injunction prohibiting the transaction. The 1869 act was repealed in 1873, in the wake of the devastating Chicago fire. A second attempt was made in 1881, but the U.S. Congress wouldn't consent to the sale of the federally-owned portion of the land.

In 1884, the city and the railroads determined to try again. To further cloud an already complicated scenario, the sales contract allowed the city to retain title to a one-inch strip along the shoreline in order to preserve riparian and other underground rights.

Captain John F. Stafford, Chairman of the Citizens Committee of Lake Front property owners, apparently played a role in arranging the sale and was the most vocal advocate for the eviction of the White Stockings. He sent a letter to the mayor in mid-February urging that the White Stockings be removed, and in April he appeared before the Judiciary Committee of the city council with a petition signed by a number of property owners urging the council to terminate the baseball club's occupancy. Stafford claimed he had an injunction that would oust the White Stockings, while the club denied that any injunction existed.

Stafford said that the baseball club and the local militia, which occupied a portion of the grounds, were using political influence to stymie his efforts to eject them. White Stocking president A.G. Spalding denied he had done anything untoward. "But," he added, "some zealous and overofficious member or friend of the club may have done a little buttonholing on his own hook and without my knowledge."[2] Apparently, someone *was* on their own hook, for the aldermen reported a vigorous lobbying effort.

Although Chicago has a long history of corruption, Mayor Harrison was relatively free of stain, other than a minor scandal involving fraudulent Civil War pensions. He had an aristocratic heritage (he was a distant cousin of the late president William Henry Harrison) but was considered a friend of labor and the working man rather than subservient to special interests.

Harrison was not the one who wielded the power in this case; the aldermen needed to approve the sale and then seek the approval of Congress. As opening day of the baseball season approached, the aldermen had done nothing. The *Tribune* urged them to get moving, since pocketing $800,000 for land the city didn't even own was a windfall. The railroads were probably the only buyer the federal government would approve, since rail travel was at least a quasi-public function. A sale to private parties wouldn't have a chance.

"The city is confined, therefore," the *Tribune* stated, "to the alternative of selling to the railroad at the price they are willing to pay, which is believed to be a fair one, or of retaining the property for the benefit of squatter, circuses, and base-ball players, who give little or no compensation for the use thereof ... it is a question between allowing the property to remain in its present unproductive and unsightly condition or accepting $800,000 in cash and adding largely to the taxable property of the city and at the same time beautifying and improving that particular locality."[3]

"The interest of the public undoubtedly favor the sale," the *Tribune* said later, "but the Aldermen are not accustomed to yielding to that consideration."[4] When the Aldermen continued to dawdle, Stafford claimed it was because Spalding had given them season tickets and all the free tickets they desired. Spalding said he did that every year and Stafford was upset that he hadn't gotten one.[5]

The *Tribune* thought the delay was due to the aldermen's hope that the railroads might realize that a bit of graft would speed the process along. In the meantime, the Illinois Central withdrew from the proposed purchase and the Michigan Central, controlled by the Vanderbilts, proceeded alone.

Stafford filed a suit asking that the White Stockings, who he repeatedly referred to as squatters, be evicted. The club was represented by W.I. Culver of McCagg and Culver, whose primary arguments were that the club had occupied the site since 1878 without harming anyone, had invested a substantial sum in property improvements, and that an eviction at this late date would cause undue hardship. "It is safe to say the club will play there this season at least," Culver said. "No one is objecting but Stafford."[6]

When Culver said the White Sox would be unable to find an alternative site if they were evicted, Stafford countered by saying that Spalding had known of the prospective sale since the beginning of the year and done nothing.[7] He produced a letter from Chicago's Union Association club offering to let the White Stockings use their field at Wabash and 39th.

Chicago was scheduled to spend the first month of the season on the road, and did not have a home game until May 29. On May 1, Controller Gurney, without any authority to do so, signed a lease with the White Stockings for the 1884 season. Mayor Harrison said he knew nothing of the matter.

Prior to the White Stockings' scheduled home opener, the U.S. District Attorney filed suit to evict them. Culver was out of town and asked that the hearing be postponed until June 4. The D.A. agreed, clearing the way for the White Stockings to hold their opening game. On May 29, Chicago and the Detroit Wolverines inaugurated the home season with a 15–5 Chicago win before a crowd of roughly 2,000.

On June 10, the case was delayed for another week. At that point, the White Stockings offered to leave after the season, which was somewhat disingenuous since their lease expired anyway. Judge Blodgett was looking for a way out, however, and that gave him the graceful exit he wanted.

"They have occupied [the grounds] six or seven seasons," Blodgett said, "and the city has been allowed without complaint from the United States, and without complaint from the abutting owners of the ground, to permit these parties to occupy the ground. It therefore seems to me it would be a great hardship at this time to impose unnecessarily on these parties a loss of their season's campaign because the United States and certain property-holders at this late day arouse themselves to the conviction that they must assert their rights.... No harm can come now to the United States, and no special harm to those abutting-property owners that I can see, to allow these parties to use the grounds for the present season; and therefore I shall have to deny an injunction as against the base-ball club for the use of the ground during the season."[8] "The base-ball people were pleased at the result,"[9] reported the *Tribune*.

Chicago was able to use the Lake Front grounds for the entire 1884 season, and fashioned an impressive 39–17 home record. The home field advantage, however, was never more evident than in the case of the Lake Front Grounds.

# Appendix C: Players Active in Multiple Leagues

*Men Who Played in the First Major League Season of 1871 and Were Active in 1884*

| Name | 1871 Team | 1876 Team | 1884 Team | Notable |
|---|---|---|---|---|
| Adrian Anson | Rockford | Chicago | Chicago (NL) | |
| Joe Battin | Cleveland | St. Louis | Pitts (AA)/Chi-Pitts (U) and Balt (U) | played only one game in 1871 |
| Ned Cuthbert | Athletics | St. Louis | Balt (U) | Played in four major leagues |
| Dave Eggler | Mutuals | Philadelphia | Buffalo (NL) | |
| Bob Ferguson | Mutuals | Hartford | Pittsburgh (AA) | |
| Davy Force | Olympics | Phi-NY | Buffalo | |
| Chick Fulmer | Rockford | Louisville | Cincinnati (AA) | |
| Ferguson Malone | Athletics | Philadelphia | Philadelphia (U) | didn't play MLB from 1877 to 1883 |
| Bobby Mathews | Fort Wayne | New York | Philadelphia (AA) | |
| Levi Meyerle | Athletics | Philadelphia | Philadelphia (U) | didn't play MLB from 1878 to 1883 |
| Joe Start | Mutuals | New York | Providence (NL) | |
| Ezra Sutton | Cleveland | Philadelphia | Boston (NL) | |
| Deacon White | Cleveland | Chicago | Buffalo (NL) | |
| Warren White | Olympics | none | Washington (U) | didn't play MLB from 1876 to 1883. Played just one game in 1871 and four in 1884 |
| Tom York | Troy | Hartford | Baltimore (AA) | |

NOTE: Charlie Sweasy, a member of the undefeated Red Stocking team of 1869 who played with the Olympics of Washington in 1871, played two games with the Domestics of the Eastern League in 1884.

*Men Who Played in the Union Association and Players League or American League*

| Name | UA Team | PL Team | AL Team | Notable |
|---|---|---|---|---|
| Jersey Bakley | Philadelphia | Cleveland | | |

# Appendix C: Players Active in Multiple Leagues

| Name | UA Team | PL Team | AL Team | Notable |
|---|---|---|---|---|
| Lady Baldwin | Milwaukee | Buffalo | | |
| Charlie Bastian | Kansas City | Chicago | | |
| Jack Brennan | St. Louis | Cleveland | | |
| Ed Crane | Boston | New York | | |
| Tom Daly | Philadelphia | | Chicago | Played in '02 and '03 |
| Fred Dunlap | St. Louis | New York | | Only one game in PL |
| John Ewing | Cincinnati | New York | | |
| Frank Foreman | Kansas City | Baltimore | | Played in '01 and '02 |
| John Irwin | Boston | Buffalo | | |
| Al Maul | Philadelphia | Pittsburgh | | |
| Joe Quinn | St. Louis | Boston | Washington | |
| Yank Robinson | Baltimore | Pittsburgh | | |
| Emmett Seery | Baltimore | Brooklyn | | |
| Mike Slattery | Boston | New York | | |

# Chapter Notes

## Introduction

1. During the 19th century, baseball was almost always written as two distinct words. Unless taken from quotations, I will follow the modern custom of using one word.
2. Spink, p. 11.
3. Melville, p. 97.
4. In 1881, on a rainy day in Troy, the game between Troy and Chicago drew just 12 fans.
5. Melville, pp. 83–4.
6. Attendance is taken from *Total Baseball, Sixth Edition*, Chapter 4, "Major League Attendance," by Robert L. Tiemann and Pete Palmer. Despite being outdrawn by the AA in 1882, the NL surpassed 1875 NA attendance for the first time.
7. *New York Clipper*, April 21, 1883.
8. Wright and Ditson, pp. 62–63.
9. *Chicago Tribune*, August 17, 1884.
10. *Detroit Free Press*, August 13, 1884.
11. *Saint Paul Globe*, September 15, 1884.

## Chapter 1

1. Much of the information on the economic conditions of the second half of the 19th century was taken from *Thirty Years of American Finance* by Alexander Dana Noyes.
2. http://socialdemocracy21stcentury.blogspot.com/2013/02/us-unemployment-graph-18691899.html.
3. http://www.pbs.org/wgbh/americanexperience/features/general-article/grant-panic/.
4. An income tax had been instituted during the Civil War, but it was eliminated after the war and not re-instituted until 1913.
5. *Sporting Life*, October 1, 1883.
6. *Ibid.*, October 8, 1883.
7. Achorn, *Summer of Beer and Whiskey*, pp. 240–41, said St. Louis made $50–70,000 and Philadelphia cleared $78,320.
8. The actual report of the Allegheny team showed total revenue of $29,000, player salaries of $14,000, and a deficit of $1,200 after expenses (*Sporting Life*, October 22, 1883). Some also said the Mets lost money.
9. In mid–October, Columbus reported revenue of just under $20,000 and about $1,000 in the treasury. Columbus was managed by Hustling Horace Phillips, and the finances of any team operated by Hustling Horace were bound to contain a few surprises. A week after their initial announcement, the Columbus directors said that the records were in such disarray they couldn't determine the club's financial condition. Phillips was asked to explain some of the more questionable expenditures but he never did and was not re-hired for 1884. It did not appear that Columbus realized a $5,000 profit.
10. *Sporting Life*, January 2, 1884. Another possible reason for the secrecy was that George Wright was talking about organizing a Union Association club in the city and the NL officers didn't want him to learn about the financial condition of his prospective competitors (*Sporting Life*, January 9, 1884).
11. *Ibid.*, October 22, 1883.
12. *Ibid.*, November 7, 1883.
13. Both are still in existence, as the Chicago Cubs and Atlanta Braves.

## Chapter 2

1. Two of the best sources on the evolution of baseball and rule changes are *Game of Inches* by Peter Morris and *Strike Four* by Richard Hershberger. Both gentlemen write about a potentially arcane subject with humor and insight, explaining how and why baseball evolved.
2. When examining fielding statistics, one must keep in mind that official scorers had widely varying opinions as to what constituted an error. According to historian David Nemec, AA and UA scorers were much harsher than those in the NL.
3. *1885 Spalding Guide*, p. 31.
4. *Buffalo Commercial*, March 8, 1884.
5. *St. Louis Post Dispatch*, May 2, 1884.
6. *Richmond Dispatch*, May 2, 1884.
7. *Buffalo Times*, May 2, 1884.
8. Hofmann, p. 26.
9. *Cincinnati Enquirer* quoted in *St. Louis Globe-Democrat*, March 17, 1884.
10. Ball clubs were often able to negotiate favorable rates from the railroads due to their frequent usage.
11. Di Salvatore. p. 187.

12. There have been many references to baseball players as undesirable hotel guests due to their behavior, but there were multiple ads in the UA Guide placed by hotels offering discounts to baseball teams.

13. Labor Day did not become a national holiday until 1894.

14. *Baltimore Sun*, July 5, 1884.

15. The prohibition extended to casual play and many ordinary citizens, mostly youngsters, were arrested for gathering to play informal games on Sunday. A group in Baltimore was fined $1.45 each.

16. *Sporting Life*, October 15, 1883.

17. Boston played a road game on Sunday in September, the first time any team from Puritan Boston had ever played on the Sabbath.

18. The habit persisted into the 20th century when player, manager, and renowned executive Branch Rickey took Sundays off in deference to his religious beliefs.

19. The term "shoulder-hitter" was 19th-century slang for a bully or ruffian.

20. *Louisville Courier-Journal*, May 16, 1884.

21. *Boston Globe*, May 14, 1884.

22. It was not until 1887 that the home team had the choice and 1950 when the current rule that the home team batted last became official.

## Chapter 3

1. https://www.ssa.gov/history/lifeexpect.html; https://usafacts.org/state-of-the-union/population/?utm_source=google&utm_medium=cpc&utm_campaign=ND-Competitors&gclid=EAIaIQobChMIpPXR7LiO8gIVbMqzCh2ahg6cEAMYASAAEgIvxvD_BwE.

2. http://baseballcrank.com/archives2/2007/05/baseball_enter_1.php.

3. *Detroit Free Press*, October 1, 1884.

4. The information on Olin was taken from his Bioproject article by Guy Waterman, https://sabr.org/bioproj/person/frank-olin/.

5. *Kansas City Times*, August 13, 1884.

6. Jerrold Casway, *Ed Delahanty and the Emerald Age of Baseball* (Notre Dame University Press, Notre Dame, 2005).

7. Many, including historian Peter Morris, credit William White, a Brown University student who played one game with Providence on June 21, 1879, with being the first African American major leaguer. White was 25 percent black, identified as white, and apparently was regarded as white by others. At the time he played for Providence, there was no mention that he was black.

8. Anson, p. 46. The pages of the edition of Anson's autobiography in my possession are not numbered. I have numbered them manually.

9. Fleitz, pp. 310–11.

10. Anson, p. 104. Anson once presented a gray Chicago jersey to Horace Haywood, a player known as the "Black Anson." Haywood cherished the jersey and supposedly wore it during games. Perhaps Anson had no problem with black players so long as they didn't want to play with whites.

11. Fleitz, p. 182.

12. *Toledo Blade*, August 11, 1883, quoted in Fleitz, p. 112.

13. *Sporting Life*, May 7, 1884.

14. Walker was elected to the Oberlin Hall of Fame in 1990.

15. Quoted in Zang, p. 41.

16. *Louisville Commercial*, May 2, 1884, quoted in Zang p. 26.

17. *Oberlin News-Tribune*, November 14, 1946, quoting the *Toledo Blade* of May 5, 1884.

18. On September 11, 1884, the umpire scheduled to work the Toledo-Athletic game failed to show, and O'Day took his place. He became a full-time umpire in 1887 and officiated National League games through the 1927 season, appearing in ten World Series, including the first modern classic in 1903.

19. *The Sporting News*, June 18, 1887.

20. *Sporting Life*, October 15, 1883.

21. *Washington Post*, June 7, 1884.

22. *Sporting Life*, September 24, 1884.

23. Zang, p. 57.

24. Young Clark Gable watched movies at Walker's theater.

25. Esteban Bellan of Cuba, who played with the Haymakers of Troy and Mutuals of New York from 1871 through 1873, was the first Hispanic major leaguer.

26. *New York Clipper*, August 5, 1882.

27. *Kansas City Times*, August 31, 1884.

28. *Cincinnati Enquirer*, October 21, 1884.

29. Information on Nava can be found in Nava's Bioproject essay by Brian McKenna, http://sabr.org/bioproj/person/1ac63c02.

30. Laing, p. 87.

31. *Binghamton Leader*, July 12, 1887, quoted in Laing, p. 92.

32. A story announcing Fowler's winning of the prize was headlined "Fowler Gets the Award: A Life Size Picture of the Leading Batter Won by the 'Coon'" (Laing, p. 90).

33. For an opinion of Fowler's change in attitude see Laing, p. 123.

## Chapter 4

1. Bauer, *The Finances of 1880s Baseball*, p. 7.

2. Although it was later referred to as the reserve clause, it was not included in player contracts until 1887. Prior to that it was merely the "reserve rule."

3. In 1887, the AA decided to blacklist reserved players who refused to sign.

4. Quoted in Bauer, *The Finances of 1880s Baseball*, p. 21.

5. *New York Clipper*, July 24, 1880.

6. *Ibid.*, September 11, 1880.

7. While Jones may have been a martyr to the cause of labor, he was no saint. He was known to have an active night life, and his wife once

damaged his eyes by throwing pepper in them when she suspected him of infidelity.
   8. *New York Clipper*, March 19, 1881.
   9. *Ibid.*, June 4, 1881.
   10. *Ibid.*, October 22, 1881.
   11. *Boston Globe*, May 7, 1884.
   12. *New York Clipper*, quoted in *St. Louis Globe-Democrat*, February 3, 1884.
   13. *St. Louis Globe-Democrat*, February 29, 1884.
   14. *St. Louis Post-Dispatch*, February 25, 1884.
   15. Overbeck played for Baltimore and Kansas City of the Union Association in 1884 and batted a combined .186 in 60 games. They were the last of his major league career.
   16. *St. Louis Post-Dispatch*, January 26, 1884.

## Chapter 5

   1. Levine, p. 50.
   2. Spalding urged the introduction of a rule requiring bats to be wound with tape which, of course, his company could supply.
   3. By 1884, the 40-year-old Day was part of the Day and Davis tobacco company.
   4. Achorn, *The Summer of Beer and Whiskey*, p. 1.
   5. Cash, p. 55.
   6. Al Spink claimed he also played a role in bringing Sullivan to St. Louis.
   7. Hetrick, pp. 72–73.
   8. In an appendix, Hetrick listed 50 lawsuits involving Von der Ahe (Hetrick, p. 307).
   9. The National League furnished bail on the condition that Von der Ahe sell the Browns and get out of baseball.
   10. *Buffalo Morning Express and Illustrated Buffalo Express*, October 19, 1884.
   11. The town of Jewett City, Connecticut is named after Josiah's ancestor Eliezer Jewett, who founded a settlement there in 1771.
   12. SABR Bioproject article by Brian McKenna, https://sabr.org/bioproj/person/arthur-soden/.
   13. Hofmann, p. 33.
   14. *Ibid.*, p. 28.
   15. *Ibid.*, p. 22.
   16. A good profile of Byrne is the SABR Bioproject article by Ronald G. Shafer, https://sabr.org/bioproj/person/charles-byrne/.
   17. *Sporting Life*, October 11, 1890, quoted in Shafer.

## Chapter 6

   1. *New York Clipper*, January 26, 1878.
   2. *Ibid.*
   3. *Ibid.*
   4. Author Paul Browne believes that O'Leary may actually have been born in 1853 rather than his claimed birth date of 1856.
   5. An excellent source on O'Leary is Browne's article in the SABR Bioproject collection, http://sabr.org/bioproj/person/22dc582f.
   6. O'Leary discovered 19th-century slugger Sam Thompson in Danville, Indiana, although he stretched the truth a bit to make for a good story.
   7. *Sporting Life*, January 2, 1884.
   8. *Cincinnati Enquirer*, June 15, 1884.
   9. *St. Louis Post-Dispatch*, January 9, 1884.
   10. *Detroit Free Press*, March 9, 1884.
   11. O'Leary said that $100 of the amount owed was a disputed fine that he refused to pay on principle.
   12. *Sporting Life*, March 19, 1884.
   13. *Ibid.*, December 10, 1884.
   14. *Cincinnati Enquirer*, November 30, 1884.
   15. The Scranton-Elmira story is told by Paul Browne in "The Elmira-Scranton Patent Double Back Action Combination Base Ball Team," *Nineteenth Century Notes*, Summer 2019.
   16. Kerr, p. 16.
   17. Quoted in *New York Clipper*, July 27, 1878.
   18. *Ibid.*, September 7, 1878.
   19. *Cincinnati Enquirer*, reprinted in *Grand Rapids Daily Democrat*, August 14, 1883 (quoted in Morris, *Game of Inches*, p. 207).
   20. *Sporting Life*, February 2, 1884. Two weeks later, the *Sporting Life* correspondent reported that the negotiations between Phillips and O'Leary had been very amicable. Phillips had written to O'Leary, asking if he could have games with Indianapolis on certain dates. "You bet your life you can," was Dan's reported reply. "We got the dates and better terms," Phillips said, "than with any other club, notwithstanding the 'picnic'" (*Sporting Life*, February 20, 1884).
   21. *New York Clipper*, August 14, 1880.
   22. Nemec, *The Beer and Whisky League*, pp. 19–20.
   23. *Columbus Dispatch*, October 21, 1882.
   24. *New York Times*, June 7, 1883.
   25. *Sporting Life*, December 19, 1883.
   26. *St. Louis Post-Dispatch*, January 14, 1884.
   27. Shortly thereafter, Phillips, who was a prolific correspondent, wrote to *Sporting Life* stating that he had been offered the Milwaukee manager's job, but was perfectly happy in Grand Rapids and had declined (*Sporting Life*, July 23, 1884). At about the same time, he signed to promote Harry Miner's Comedy Four Company beginning October 1 but, fickle as ever, Phillips wound up hawking for the Murphy and Mack Comedy Four Company.
   28. *Sporting Life*, August 20, 1884.
   29. Martin, *Pud Galvin*, p. 158.
   30. https://mightycaseybaseball.com/2017/05/15/happy-birthday-hustling-horace-phillips/.
   31. http://sabr.org/cmsFiles/Files/Civil%20War%20veterans.pdf.
   32. *St. Louis Post-Dispatch*, August 25, 1884.
   33. *New York Clipper*, January 3, 1880. Bancroft was so enthused by the trip to Cuba that he talked to Harry Wright about an expedition to Australia, a plan which never came to fruition (*New York Clipper*, February 7, 1880).
   34. *New York Clipper*, October 9, 1880, and January 15, 1881.

35. *Ibid.*, July 23, 1881.
36. *Sporting Life,* November 7, 1883.
37. *Ibid.*, October 29, 1883.
38. *Ibid.*, January 2, 1884.
39. *Buffalo Evening Telegraph*, April 22, 1884.
40. Much of the information on Mutrie was taken from the comprehensive SABR Bioproject article by Peter Mancuso, http://sabr.org/bioproj/person/430838fd.
41. The name was taken from a Bret Harte poem written during the 1870s and applied to Mutrie by Henry Chadwick.
42. *New York Clipper,* June 26, 1880.
43. Sullivan had three hits in nine times at bat, and retired with a lifetime .333 average.
44. Sullivan resigned after experiencing the abuse typical of umpiring in that era.
45. Spink, p. 286.
46. SABR Bioproject article on Hal O'Hagan by David Nemec, http://www.sabr.org/bioproj/person/332f0b3a.
47. Sullivan's birth year has been reported as 1851, 1854, 1855, and 1856. Retrosheet claimed it was 1851, and that seems the most likely date, based upon the start of his baseball career, subsequent references, and his *Sporting News* obituary.
48. Most of Sullivan's players worked on trains, selling food or newspapers, while not playing ball.
49. SABR Bioproject article on Hoss Radbourn by Brian McKenna, http://www.sabr.org/bioproj/person/83bf739e. Sullivan had a charming tale about how he signed Comiskey, which may or may not be true. It involved $50 given to him to repair a fence by Sir Thomas Shaughnessy of the Canadian Pacific Railway, who later became a noted executive and a British peer. The bit players in Sullivan's dramas were never run-of-the-mill extras.
50. Like George Steinbrenner, Von der Ahe liked to change managers. He had 18 of them over a seven-year period.
51. *The Sporting News*, October 4, 1886.
52. Despite their troubled relationship, Sullivan was a pallbearer at Von der Ahe's funeral.
53. *The Sporting News*, February 16, 1895.
54. *Ibid.*, December 12, 1918.

## Chapter 7

1. *St. Louis Post-Dispatch*, May 14, 1884.
2. *Sporting Life*, June 10, 1884.
3. *The Buffalo Commercial*, July 10, 1884.
4. *New York Clipper*, January 19, 1878.
5. *Ibid.*, June 7, 1879.
6. *Ibid.* In 1878, umpire George Campbell sued the *Buffalo Express* for claiming that he had been paid by gamblers to make biased decisions during a game between Rochester and Buffalo. The case was settled and the newspaper issued an apology.
7. *Sporting Life*, April 23, 1884.
8. *Brooklyn Eagle*, June 10, 1884.
9. *Ibid.*, August 17, 1884.
10. *New York Clipper*, February 7, 1880. In the earliest days of baseball, there were two umpires, one from each team, and a referee to decide all questions on which the two umpires were divided. Since each umpire tended to rule in favor of their own team and the referee had to decide all close calls, it was decided to go to a single umpire system. Of course, two impartial umpires would have been a significant improvement.
11. *Sporting Life*, May 21, 1884.
12. *Ibid.*, October 8, 1884.
13. *Ibid.*, July 23, 1884.
14. *The National Pastime*, Number 20, 2000, pp. 20–31.
15. *Columbus Times*, May 23, 1884.
16. Ironically, Honest John Kelly operated a saloon in partnership with Mike (King) Kelly and became a gambling impresario after leaving baseball, although he always prided himself on running honest games of chance.
17. *New York Clipper*, November 25, 1882.
18. *Boston Globe*, January 6, 1884.
19. Martin, *The Detroit Wolverines*, p. 81.
20. It was estimated that in 1883 the AA spent $4,000 on umpires (*Sporting Life*, December 26, 1883) and the NL spent $6,500 (*Sporting Life*, November 14, 1883).
21. The UA reported paying a total of $4,700 for the expenses of its umpires.
22. *Sporting Life*, May 28, 1884.
23. Gunkle abandoned umpiring and later in the season became manager of the Stillwater club.
24. *Sporting Life*, June 4, 1884.
25. One day while visiting Philadelphia owner John Rogers, Connell put his police skills to use. He discovered an intruder upstairs and arrested the man and brought him to the station house.
26. *Cincinnati Enquirer* quoted in *Sporting Life*, March 26, 1884.
27. The bullying of baseball umpires became so pervasive that when the *Brooklyn Eagle* reported on a cricket match, it noted, "Some of them on that occasion thought they were at a base ball match, and they kicked against the decision of the Staten Island umpire just as the roughs do on a base ball field" (*Brooklyn Eagle*, July 13, 1884).
28. *Sporting Life*, July 16, 1884.
29. *Ibid.*, March 19, 1884.
30. *Cincinnati Enquirer*, June 22, 1884.
31. *Boston Globe*, June 13, 1884.
32. *Sporting Life*, June 18, 1884.
33. *Ibid.*, July 2, 1884.
34. *Ibid.*, November 19, 1884.
35. *Cleveland Leader* quoted in *Louisville Courier-Journal*, July 20, 1884.
36. *Kansas City Times*, September 4, 1884.
37. *Columbus Dispatch*, August 31, 1884.
38. *Cincinnati Enquirer*, July 25, 1884.
39. *Buffalo Commercial*, July 19, 1884.
40. Hoover umpired in the Northwestern League later in the season, where his work was no more popular than it had been in the Eastern League. A St. Paul player named Brown became so enraged

by one call that he slapped Hoover in the face, for which he was released.

41. *Sporting Life*, July 23, 1884. The actual quotation is "d—n thief" but I have used literary license in my interpretation.

42. *Commercial* quoted in *Sporting Life*, July 16, 1884.

43. *Sporting Life*, July 23, 1884.

44. *Police Gazette*, quoted in Nemec, *Major League Baseball Profiles, 1871–1900*, pp. 201–02.

45. McLean gave Cap Anson boxing lessons when the latter was in Philadelphia.

46. *Buffalo Commercial*, July 3, 1884.

47. *Sporting Life*, August 6, 1884.

48. "The man who can umpire in Cleveland," said the *Police Gazette*, "without getting bailahoo from the press of that place, is a fit subject for the London Museum" (*Police Gazette* quoted in *Buffalo Evening Telegraph*, July 18, 1884).

49. After Anson umpired a game during the World Tour of 1888–89, he noted that he had taken a little abuse, which he understood, since "I have even been known to indulge in a little gentle remonstrance myself when I thought the circumstances were justifiable" (Anson p. 113). Anson wasn't much on humor, but a couple of the light-hearted remarks in his book concerned his propensity for umpire-baiting.

50. *Buffalo Commercial*, July 2, 1884.

51. *Chicago Tribune*, August 5, 1884.

52. Bauer, *Outside the Lines of Gilded Age Baseball: Alcohol, Fitness & Cheating in 1880s Baseball*, p. 141.

53. *Buffalo Times*, June 13, 1884.

54. *Buffalo Morning Express*, June 28, 1884.

55. *Chicago Tribune*, July 9, 1884.

56. *The Mirror of American Sports*, quoted in *Boston Globe*, September 15, 1884.

57. *Boston Globe*, September 15, 1884. Chicago, and Mike Kelly in particular, had such a reputation for cheating that when a player cut bases or tripped a runner it was referred to as a "Kellytrick."

58. *Boston Courier* quoted in *Sporting Life*, November 12, 1884.

59. *Boston Globe*, September 10, 1884.

60. *New York Times*, August 2, 1884.

61. *Baltimore Sun*, August 27, 1884.

62. *St. Louis Post-Dispatch*, August 5, 1884.

63. Reportedly, the AA had passed a rule stating that any game played without a regular umpire would be an exhibition, but it was inadvertently left out of the published rules.

64. Five years later, Gaffney umpired in the 1889 World Series and made several calls that were prejudicial to Ward's Giants. Perhaps he was getting his revenge.

65. *Brooklyn Eagle*, October 26, 1884.

66. *Sporting Life*, July 9, 1884.

67. Daniels umpired in Connecticut and also in the Western Association later in the season, but then became ill and had to stop officiating. Ironically, he had been offered a job in the National League prior to the season, but declined, choosing to remain in the AA, which fired him.

68. *Sporting Life*, July 30, 1884.

69. Many of the interpretations involved the hit-by-pitch rule and the rule that limited pitchers to delivering the ball below the shoulder. Several AA umpires were accused of allowing pitchers complete freedom of delivery.

70. *Sporting Life*, January 7, 1885.

71. *1885 Spalding Guide*, p. 83.

72. *St. Louis Post-Dispatch*, September 20, 1884.

## Chapter 8

1. *New York Clipper*, December 10, 1881.

2. *Ibid.*, May 14, 1881.

3. An excellent source on drinking and alcohol in 18th- and 19th-century America is *The Alcoholic Republic*, by W.J. Rorabaugh. The book contains statistics on alcohol consumption and a sociological analysis of the reasons Americans drank.

4. Rorabaugh, p. 97.

5. Many of Rush's purported cures have not stood up under modern science. Some of his medications contained massive amounts of mercury and his go-to treatment, bleeding, was more likely to kill patients than heal them. On their epic journey to the Pacific, Lewis and Clark took along a generous supply of Rush's laxatives, indelicately called "Thunderclappers," that contained about 50 percent mercury. One of his cures for mental illness was to stimulate the blood of the brain by placing the patient on a centrifugal spinning board. The primary benefit, like the old joke says, was that it felt so good when it stopped.

6. Information on the history of treatment for alcohol is taken from http://www.williamwhitepapers.com/pr/AddictionTreatment&RecoveryInAmerica.pdf.

7. http://eh.net/encyclopedia/fertility-and-mortality-in-the-united-states/.

8. The following winter, he was arrested for beating his girlfriend during a drunken rage.

9. *Sporting Life*, July 30, 1884.

10. Some of the 1886 Washington players were accused of smoking opium, but nothing was ever proven.

11. Bob Carruthers reportedly pitched in the 1886 World Series under the effects of morphine administered to treat an undisclosed illness. Pud Galvin's alleged use of a performance enhancing "elixir" is covered in great detail in Martin, *Pud Galvin*, pp. 4, 9, 15–16, 161–63.

12. Rorabaugh, p. 241.

13. *New York Clipper*, July 19, 1879.

14. *Cincinnati Enquirer*, July 13, 1884.

15. John Thorn, in the citation below, offers several alternative explanations as to how Nolan was given his nickname. The most plausible is that it was given to someone with a unique skill.

16. Thorn, in his "Our Game" blog, wrote a

feature article on Nolan, http://ourgame.mlblogs.com/2015/05/18/the-only-nolan/.

17. *New York Clipper*, September 8, 1877.
18. Nemec, *Major League Baseball Profiles, 1871–1900*, Vol. I, p. 143.
19. *Sporting Life*, June 25, 1884.
20. sabr.org/bioproj/person/b4fdac3f.
21. Bauer, *Alcohol, Fitness and Cheating, Volume 1 of Outside the Lines of Gilded Age Baseball*, p. 17.
22. Anson, p. 76.
23. Unidentified clipping in Flint's Hall of Fame file dated November 8, 1890. Mrs. Flint was experienced in divorce, having been previously married to minstrel performer Lew Benedict. Benedict was an irresponsible husband and when he ran out of money, Flint paid the couple's hotel bills. After her divorce, she married Flint in 1879.
24. Unidentified clipping in Flint's Hall of Fame file dated January 23, 1892.
25. Information on the case of Larkin is taken from the *New York Clipper*, May 5, 1883, and August 11, 1883, the *Brooklyn Eagle*, February 18, 1884, and Nemec, *Major League Baseball Profiles 1871–1900, Volume II*, pp. 396–98.
26. *New York Clipper*, January 11, 1879.
27. *Cincinnati Enquirer*, March 31, 1884.
28. *Sporting Life*, May 7, 1884.
29. *New York Clipper*, June 28, 1884.
30. *Richmond Dispatch*, October 17, 1884.
31. *Sporting Life*, January 23, 1884.
32. *Ibid.*, January 30, 1884.
33. *New York Times*, September 27, 1884.
34. *1885 Spalding Guide*, pp. 96–97.
35. Bauer, *Alcohol, Fitness and Cheating, Volume 1 of Outside the Lines of Gilded Age Baseball*, p. 7.
36. *Critic* quoted in *Sporting Life*, March 5, 1884.
37. *Cincinnati Enquirer*, March 2, 1884.
38. *Brooklyn Eagle*, April 13, 1884.
39. *Cincinnati Enquirer*, March 31, 1884.
40. *Brooklyn Eagle*, March 23, 1884.
41. *St. Louis Critic* quoted in *Cincinnati Enquirer*, January 13, 1884.
42. Bauer, *Alcohol, Fitness and Cheating, Volume 1 of Outside the Lines of Gilded Age Baseball*, p. 27.
43. *St. Louis Post-Dispatch*, May 31, 1884.
44. *Ibid.*, September 20, 1884.
45. *1885 Spalding Guide*, p. 96.
46. Bauer, *Alcohol, Fitness and Cheating, Volume 1 of Outside the Lines of Gilded Age Baseball*, p. 41.
47. *Sporting Life*, June 18, 1884.
48. *Cincinnati Enquirer*, September 21, 1884.
49. *Ibid.*, October 5, 1884.
50. *Sporting Life*, May 21, 1884.
51. Deasley's younger brother John was released by the UA Washington Club for dissipation.
52. Morris, *Catcher*, pp. 172–207.
53. *Louisville Courier*, December 15, 1884. Deasley may have had a contract that did not include a reserve clause, but apparently Von der Ahe demanded payment anyway. Supposedly, Deasley put up the $400 himself, encouraged by his wife, who was eager to see him out of St. Louis. He played three seasons with New York and another with Washington and it's likely that he straightened out at some point, for unlike so many alcohol-plagued players, he had a long life, dying at the ripe old age of 86 in 1943.
54. One morning, when Von der Ahe came to get Lewis out of jail, he supposedly commented that he'd told the players to get to bed by 11, but Lewis had ended up in the wrong room.
55. In 1883, Henderson got into a scrape over a woman after a masked ball at Kernan's Theater and ended up in jail.
56. *Baltimore Sun*, March 17, 1884.
57. *Ibid.*, April 28, 1884.
58. *Sporting Life*, July 9, 1884.
59. *Ibid.*, June 25, 1884.
60. *Cincinnati Enquirer*, September 28, 1884.
61. *Ibid.*, July 20, 1884.
62. *Ibid.*, September 7, 1884.
63. *Sporting Life*, July 16, 1884.
64. *Philadelphia Times*, June 1, 1884.
65. *Brooklyn Eagle*, October 12, 1884.
66. *Sporting Life*, November 19, 1884.
67. *Detroit Free Press*, December 15, 1884.

## Chapter 9

1. *Sporting Life*, March 12, 1884.
2. *Ibid.*, April 9, 1884.
3. When Al Spalding sent the team to Hot Springs, Arkansas, for spring training in 1886, he said, "I boil out all the alcoholic microbes, which may have impregnated the systems of the men, during the winter while they have been away from me," (Cash, p. 124).
4. Quoted in Appel, p. 79.
5. Appel, p. 61.
6. Goldsmith was one of several who claimed to have invented the curveball, demonstrating the pitch for journalist Henry Chadwick in 1870. David Arcidiacono wrote an article in the 2012 issue of *Base Ball* (published by McFarland) discussing the controversy and Goldsmith's claim to the distinction, which is also covered in Martin, *Tecumsehs*, pp. 224–33.
7. Martin, *Tecumsehs*, p. 192.
8. *Sporting Life*, October 8, 1883.
9. *Bill James Historical Baseball Abstract*, p. 15.
10. *Sporting Life*, January 9, 1884.
11. *Ibid.*, October 29, 1883.
12. *Ibid.*, April 30, 1884.
13. *Detroit Free Press*, May 18, 1884.
14. *Ibid.*, May 12, 1884.
15. John Ward and Larry Corcoran played for the 1877 Buffalo club. After signing Jim Galvin, Buffalo decided it didn't need the inexperienced Corcoran, who became a star in Chicago. One of the club's biggest problems in subsequent seasons was the lack of the second pitcher behind Galvin.
16. *Cincinnati Enquirer*, December 28, 1884.

17. In 1877, while playing for his hometown team in Wappinger's Falls, New York, Brouthers was involved in a collision at home plate that severely injured catcher John Quigley. Quigley died of his injuries a month later and Brouthers was so distraught that he played no more that season and considered giving up baseball.
18. Brouthers made a cameo two-game appearance in 1904.
19. The total of five strikeouts is from Retrosheet. Baseball Reference charged Brouthers with nine strikeouts.
20. *Detroit Free Press*, March 6, 1884.
21. *Cleveland Herald*, quoted in *Sporting Life*, November 7, 1883.
22. *Sporting Life*, January 9, 1884.
23. *Ibid.*, April 30, 1884.
24. *Ibid.*, March 19, 1884.
25. *Ibid.*, November 7, 1883.
26. *Boston Globe*, May 27, 1884.

## Chapter 10

1. *Sporting Life*, November 21, 1883.
2. *Ibid.*, December 19, 1883.
3. *Ibid.*, January 2, 1884.
4. *Brooklyn Eagle*, March 23, 1884.
5. *New York Clipper*, December 22, 1883.
6. A biographical sketch of Moxley is contained in *The Rank and File of Nineteenth Century Major League Baseball*, by David Nemec, pp. 290–91.
7. *St. Louis Post-Dispatch*, April 26, 1884. There were rumors, which Hollingshead denied, that the AA had helped Washington acquire players in order to bolster the team.
8. *Sporting Life*, November 14, 1883.
9. Nemec, *Major League Baseball Profiles, 1871–1900, Volume 2*, p. 99.
10. Jones next appeared in the sporting press when the glee club was involved in a train crash while on tour in the Midwest. Although he was not seriously injured, many others were. Jones never played in the major leagues again, although he did coach at Yale and pitch for some Connecticut minor league clubs. He came from a family of dentists (his mother was the first practicing female dentist in the United States), and after receiving a degree in dentistry and an M.D. degree, Jones practiced dentistry until the 1920s.
11. Stovey's given name was Stow. He used an alias to prevent his mother from knowing he was playing professional baseball.
12. Historian David Nemec pointed out that the AA made every effort to promote Stovey as its star and inflated his averages to give the impression that he was better than the NL's best players.
13. *Philadelphia Times*, February 10, 1884.
14. For an excellent reference on the history of 19th-century baseball in St. Louis, see *Before They Were Cardinals*, by Jon David Cash.
15. The 1878 season could have been worse, for St. Louis had signed Devlin and Hall, both implicated in the Louisville scandal, before they were expelled by the NL.
16. *Cincinnati Enquirer*, July 6, 1884. After divorcing Emma, Latham married Kate Conway, who played piano in a vaudeville show in which he appeared. That marriage also ended in divorce, with accusations of infidelity and cruelty.
17. Cash, p. 86.
18. In April, it was announced that the Mets were sold to Frank Rohner for $40,000, but that appeared to have been a feint to give the impression that the Mets were under independent management. The Metropolitan Exhibition Company continued to control the team.
19. Lowry, pp. 148–49.
20. As if the Mets' park didn't have enough flaws, it was severely damaged by a storm on March 30 and a large portion of the fence was blown into the water.
21. *Sporting Life*, May 28, 1884.
22. Spink, p. 178. Despite his lack of speed, Orr legged out 108 triples, with a high of 31 in 1886. In the spacious 19th-century playing fields, many of them would have been inside the park home runs for a faster man.
23. *Sporting Life*, April 9, 1884.
24. *Ibid.*, December 17, 1884.
25. The saloon was hit by a fire in February 1884, sustaining $1,700 in damage. Fortunately, most of the loss was covered by insurance and the establishment was repaired and reopened.
26. Pat Deasley, another excellent defensive catcher who played for the Browns in 1884, is fourth on the all-time list with 1,466 at bats without a homer.
27. A flood nearly destroyed the grandstand at the new UA park, necessitating about $5,000 in repairs. That probably brought a rare smile to Caylor's face.
28. *Sporting Life*, January 9, 1884.
29. Much of the information on Reilly is taken from the SABR Bioproject article by David Ball, http://sabr.org/bioproj/person/df50ad73.
30. *New York Clipper*, December 9, 1882.
31. For a good summary of Morris' career, see Nemec, *Major League Baseball Profiles*, pp. 136–37.
32. *New York Clipper*, November 23, 1878.
33. Wolf supposedly acquired the nickname "Chicken" from Pete Browning when both were teenagers playing with the Eclipse. After being advised to eat lightly before a game, Wolf gorged himself on stewed chicken and played poorly. This story and other information on Wolf was obtained from Bob Bailey's SABR bioproject entry, http://sabr.org/bioproj/person/3f8eac9e.
34. There are differing opinions as to Browning's ability as a fielder. The *Louisville Courier* said, "His chief virtue as a ball-player lies in his ability to bat" (*Louisville Courier*, August 3, 1884). Historian Bob Bailey called Browning's outfield play "dreadful" and one of the reasons Browning acquired the nickname "The Gladiator" was his battles with fly balls. Phillip von Borries, however,

believes Browning's defense may have been better than generally portrayed. He pointed to the crude equipment, the typical low fielding averages of the era, and the fact that Browning was generally employed in key defensive positions such as center field, short stop, and second base. David Nemec agrees with von Borries, pointing out that Browning was moved to the outfield primarily due to concern that his hearing difficulties would produce collisions in the infield.

35. Information on Browning can be obtained from Phillip von Borries' SABR bioproject article, http://sabr.org/bioproj/person/b4fdac3f.

36. *Cincinnati Enquirer*, August 10, 1884.

37. For information on Hecker, see Bob Bailey's bioproject entry, http://sabr.org/bioproj/person/4b471b76.

38. Maskery was involved in baseball for many years and one of his unique experiences was playing and coaching in England in 1890.

39. Perhaps the most valuable contributor to the sorry 1883 Baltimore club was an older black dog who sometimes wandered onto the field. No one seemed to know who he belonged to or where he came from. Yet it seemed that whenever the dog made an appearance, the Orioles won, coming from far behind on three occasions. "Whatever he was—dog or devil," wrote the Baltimore correspondent to *Sporting Life*, "we hope to welcome him for the season of '84" (*Sporting Life*, April 2, 1884).

40. Sommer and Macullar were both converted outfielders who had limited experience in the infield prior to the 1884 season.

41. *New York Clipper*, October 27, 1877.

42. *Ibid.*, May 27, 1882.

43. *Sporting Life*, February 27, 1884.

## Chapter 11

1. As in most stories of this sort, there were differing accounts as to exactly how much Lucas inherited from his father. The consensus seems to be that it was at least $1 million, the equivalent of more than $25 million in today's currency.

2. Quoted in *Sporting Life*, October 1, 1883.

3. Quoted in *Sporting Life*, October 1, 1883.

4. *New York Clipper*, December 15, 1883.

5. *Ibid.*, December 29, 1883.

6. *St. Louis Post-Dispatch*, March 11, 1884.

7. *Sporting Life*, December 12, 1883.

8. *Ibid.*, December 19, 1883.

9. *St. Louis Globe-Democrat*, April 1, 1884.

10. *Wright and Ditson's Union Association Guide*, p. 7.

11. *Sporting Life*, November 28, 1883.

12. Springer, p. 34.

13. H.B. Bennett was initially elected president of the UA, but was almost immediately replaced by Lucas.

14. *Sporting Life*, December 12, 1883.

15. *Ibid.*, November 28, 1883.

16. *New York Clipper*, December 15, 1883.

17. *Evening Star*, January 22, 1884.

18. *Cincinnati Enquirer*, March 23, 1884.

19. Abraham Mills to Denny McKnight, December 8, 1883.

20. Abraham Mills to Elias Matter, December 12, 1883.

21. Abraham Mills to Arthur Soden, December 17, 1883.

22. Abraham Mills to John Hadley Doyle, February 14, 1884.

23. Dunlap parlayed some large salaries into a small fortune for the time (reportedly $100,000) but the money mysteriously disappeared and he apparently died penniless.

24. *Sporting Life*, November 28, 1883. The advance was $200 per another account and $700 by a third.

25. Hitting with one hand was difficult for Daily, and he apparently used some form of "harness" to help him hold the bat (*Pittsburgh Post-Gazette*, August 28, 1884).

26. Author Roy Kerr pointed out that Daily was handicapped by the rule that prohibited substitutes. If he was relieved from his pitching duties, he had to take a position in the field, where he used a pad on his stump to trap the ball and did as well defensively as a one-handed man could be expected to do.

27. Abraham Mills to George Howe, December 1, 1883.

28. *St. Louis Globe-Democrat*, January 8, 1884.

29. *Cincinnati Enquirer*, March 9, 1884.

30. *St. Louis Globe-Democrat*, February 28, 1884.

31. *Philadelphia Times*, March 9, 1884.

32. *St. Louis Post-Dispatch*, January 29, 1884.

33. *Detroit Free Press*, July 3, 1884.

34. Quoted in *Louisville Courier-Journal*, March 10, 1884.

35. Abraham Mills to Albert Spalding, December 14, 1883.

36. Abraham Mills to Albert Spalding, December 14, 1883.

37. *The Buffalo Commercial*, January 8, 1884.

38. *St. Louis Globe-Democrat*, February 2, 1884.

39. Wright had supposedly been offered a substantial salary to run Cincinnati's UA team.

40. *Boston Globe*, April 17, 1884.

41. One of the reasons Altoona won the championship was its endurance. Four of the nine teams folded before the season ended.

42. SABR Bioproject article, Altoona Unions by James Forr, https://sabr.org/bioproj/team/213b8775.

43. *Sporting Life*, December 12, 1883.

44. *Detroit Free Press*, March 18, 1884.

45. *Ibid.*, March 13, 1884.

46. When he returned empty-handed, Sullivan denied he had set out to convince Mullane not to sign with Toledo. He said he just wanted to have a friendly talk with him, but it was quite a journey in quest of a friendly talk.

47. *Sporting Life*, February 27, 1884.

48. Justice was served in another fashion, as Vice President J.S. Rogers of the Toledo Club had his leg broken in two places as the result of a railroad accident while traveling to represent the club in the Mullane case.
49. *St. Louis Post-Dispatch*, February 2, 1884. The UA carefully set their schedule to avoid head-to-head competition in two-team cities. Philadelphia, the only city with three teams, posed more of a problem and there were a number of conflicts.
50. *Sporting Life*, February 24, 1884.
51. After the 1884 season, Boston outfielder Bill Crowley signed with Buffalo for the following year. He apologized to his Boston friends, saying that he was drunk when he signed.
52. *St. Louis Post-Dispatch*, April 8, 1884.
53. *Sporting Life*, March 26, 1884.
54. Martin, *The Detroit Wolverines*, p. 89.
55. *St. Louis Globe-Democrat*, March 16, 1884.
56. *Philadelphia Times*, February 10, 1884.

## Chapter 12

1. *New York Clipper*, May 31, 1884.
2. *New York Times*, May 26, 1884.
3. *Buffalo Commercial*, May 26, 1884.
4. *Chicago Tribune*, quoted in *St. Louis Post-Dispatch*, May 26, 1884.
5. *St. Louis Post-Dispatch*, June 7, 1884.
6. *Chicago Tribune*, May 18, 1884.
7. The 1877 White Stockings did not hit a single home run all season.
8. *New York Clipper*, August 16, 1884.
9. *Ibid.*, September 27, 1884.
10. Anson, p. 77.
11. Other teams could hit the ball over the fence as well, and Chicago pitcher Larry Corcoran surrendered 35 round-trippers.
12. Achorn, *Fifty-Nine in '84*, p. 239.
13. Policing his team's drinking was a career-long task for Anson. One night during the 1891 season, he stood outside his team's hotel to make sure none of his players left for a night on the town. Meanwhile, they were drinking upstairs, and after emptying a keg, heaved it out the window, nearly hitting Anson, who scurried for cover (Fleitz, p. 206).
14. *Sporting Life*, August 20, 1884.
15. *Buffalo Evening News*, May 23, 1884.
16. *Sporting Life*, July 23, 1884.
17. *Chicago News*, quoted in *St. Louis Post-Dispatch*, June 9, 1884.
18. *Chicago Tribune*, September 27, 1884.
19. *Chicago Inter Ocean*, September 7, 1884.
20. *Sporting Life*, May 21, 1884.
21. *Ibid.*, June 25, 1884.
22. Di Salvatore, p. 229.
23. Anson had such a reputation as a "kicker" that players who argued excessively with umpires were referred to as employing "Ansonian" tactics.
24. *Buffalo Times*, July 1, 1884.
25. *Chicago Tribune*, September 12, 1884.
26. *Philadelphia Times*, June 1, 1884.
27. Devine, p. 142.
28. *Buffalo Times*, May 14, 1884.
29. *Buffalo Morning Express and Illustrated Buffalo Express*, May 21, 1884.
30. *Detroit Free Press*, May 4, 1884.
31. *Ibid.*, August 9, 1884.
32. *Detroit Press*, quoted in *Sporting Life*, May 28, 1884.
33. *Sporting Life*, June 4, 1884.
34. Most NL pitchers who jumped to the UA had great success, in part because UA hitters were not as formidable as those in the NL.
35. *New York Clipper*, July 19, 1884.
36. *Ibid.*
37. *Sporting Life*, May 21, 1884.
38. *Ibid.*, October 22, 1884.
39. *New York Clipper*, September 27, 1884.
40. *Detroit Free Press*, October 5, 1884.
41. Achorn, *Fifty-Nine in '84*, p. 63. Achorn is an excellent source for the Grays 1884 season and the performances of Radbourn and Sweeney.
42. In addition to the Sweeney-Radbourn factions, the *New York Times* indicated that there was a rift between the Catholics and Protestants (*New York Times*, July 23, 1884).
43. *Buffalo Commercial*, July 29, 1884.
44. Achorn, *Fifty-Nine in '84*, p. 181.
45. *Boston Globe*, July 18, 1884.
46. *St. Louis Post-Dispatch*, August 7, 1884.
47. *Ibid.*, August 2, 1884.
48. *New York Times*, July 25, 1884.
49. *Boston Globe*, July 24, 1884.
50. Providence's offer for 1885 was sufficient and Radbourn signed rather than look for another team.
51. Jacob Morse, *Baseball Magazine*, January 1909, quoted in Spink, p. 150.
52. *Buffalo Times*, July 2, 1884.
53. The Boston-Providence rivalry was so lucrative that in August the two clubs took their show on the road, drawing 4,000 fans for an exhibition game in Portland, Maine.
54. *Boston Globe*, August 15, 1884.
55. *The Buffalo Commercial*, May 16, 1884.
56. *Sporting Life*, August 6, 1884.
57. *The Buffalo Commercial*, October 21, 1884.
58. *The Buffalo Times*, August 11, 1884.
59. Not everyone felt sorry for Cleveland. The Columbus *Journal* said, "Cleveland was not entitled to any sympathy for the desertion of McCormick, Briody and Glasscock, because the management was trying to sell them like cattle, and the players rightly came to the conclusion that if any money was to be made on their reputation they were the persons to profit by the transaction" (*Columbus Journal* quoted in *Louisville Courier*, August 14, 1884).
60. *Detroit Free Press*, August 16, 1884.
61. *Cleveland Herald*, quoted in *Buffalo Morning Express*, October 11, 1884.
62. *Buffalo Commercial*, October 21, 1884.
63. *Buffalo Morning Express*, July 13, 1884.

64. After his graduation, Hibbard began an engineering career and became president of the John Davis Company of Chicago, which was eventually acquired by United States Steel.

65. A prolife of Clarkson can be found in the SABR Bioproject article by Brian McKenna, http://sabr.org/bioproj/person/47feb015.

66. *Sporting Life*, September 10, 1884.

67. *Detroit Free Press*, August 15, 1884.

68. Achorn, *Fifty-Nine in '84*, p. 206.

69. *Boston Globe*, September 28, 1884.

70. *St. Louis Post-Dispatch*, September 23, 1884.

71. At the time, Jim O'Rourke of Buffalo was awarded the batting title with a .347 mark, but subsequent corrections gave the title to Kelly.

72. Neither Retrosheet nor Baseball Reference lists batter strikeouts for the 1884 AA and UA and did not report strikeout figures for the AA in prior seasons.

73. Results were similar to 1883, when NL teams were 66–23 versus the AA.

## Chapter 13

1. *Sporting Life*, May 28, 1884.
2. *Ibid.*
3. Information on McKeon's career can be found at http://sabr.org/bioproj/person/91d22fd2. According to Al Spink, McKeon and Keenan were known as the "Dago battery" due to their dark features. Since no photos of McKeon survive, we are reliant upon Spink's description (Spink, p. 103).
4. *Sporting Life*, September 17, 1884.
5. In December, Gifford applied for a job as an American Association umpire. Watkins continued managing and won the 1887 World Series with Detroit, but he was a harsh disciplinarian who was resented by his players at almost every stop.
6. *Indianapolis Times*, June 24, 1883.
7. *Sporting Life*, June 4, 1884.
8. During the 19th century, the holiday we now celebrate as Memorial Day was known as Decoration Day.
9. *Louisville Courier-Journal*, July 27, 1884.
10. *Sporting Life*, July 23, 1884.
11. *Ibid.*, August 13, 1884. After the season, outfielder Henry Mullin filed suit against Moxley for unpaid wages of $106.56. It was generally understood that if he was successful, other suits would follow, for the players believed Moxley had the resources to pay. Had second baseman Frank Olin been the owner and Moxley played second base, Washington might have had a better chance of surviving. If Olin employed the business savvy he used to found the Olin Corporation in 1889, the club might have made enough money to stay in business.
12. While Virginia was in the Eastern League, their shortstop, William Smiley, died on July 11 after a brief illness. Smiley, who played in the American Association in 1882, was a popular player and his death was greatly mourned. A large contingent of players attended his funeral and a game was played for the benefit of his mother.

13. *Sporting Life*, May 28, 1884.
14. *Baltimore American*, quoted in *The State* (Richmond), August 22, 1884.
15. Quoted in *Richmond Dispatch*, September 30, 1884.
16. *New York Clipper*, April 19, 1884.
17. *Sporting Life*, June 10, 1884.
18. Many baseball historians are skeptical of reports of significant numbers of ladies attending games, believing the numbers were exaggerated in the interest of emphasizing the game's respectability.
19. *Brooklyn Eagle*, August 3, 1884.
20. *Ibid.*, August 15, 1884.
21. *Sporting Life*, May 28, 1884.
22. *Ibid.*, July 2, 1884.
23. *Buffalo Times*, June 6, 1884.
24. *Pittsburgh Post-Gazette*, May 3, 1884.
25. *Ibid.*, May 9, 1884.
26. *Ibid.*, May 10, 1884.
27. *Ibid.*, August 16, 1884.
28. *Ibid.*, June 21, 1884.
29. *Ibid.*, August 5, 1884.
30. *Ibid.*, August 7, 1884.
31. *Ibid.*, August 14, 1884.
32. *Ibid.*, August 18, 1884.
33. *Ibid.*, October 15, 1884.
34. *Cincinnati Enquirer*, September 12, 1884.
35. When the National League champion Boston Club hoisted their championship banner on opening day, it was all the way to the top before they realized it was upside down.
36. Apparently, Atkinson did not burn his bridges in Philadelphia, for he pitched there in 1886 and 1887.
37. *Sporting Life*, November 21, 1883.
38. *Ibid.*, January 9, 1884.
39. Simmons insisted he paid a $500 advance and, had Lucas sent him the money, Taylor would have remained in St. Louis.
40. *Sporting Life*, April 30, 1884.
41. *Ibid.*, July 16, 1884.
42. *Louisville Courier-Journal*, June 24, 1884.
43. Cash, p. 91.
44. *St. Louis Post-Dispatch*, August 19, 1884.
45. *Ibid.*, July 30, 1884.
46. Quoted in *Louisville Courier*, August 11, 1884.
47. Bloomington, MN, *Eye* quoted in *St. Louis Globe-Democrat*, May 5, 1884.
48. SABR Bioproject article on Caylor by David Nemec, https://sabr.org/bioproj/person/o-p-caylor/.
49. Caylor's animus toward the NL dated to 1879 when Cincinnati manager Deacon White brought in his brother-in-law to take Caylor's place as official scorer.
50. Caylor managed Cincinnati in 1885 and 1886 and the Mets in 1887.
51. *Cincinnati Enquirer*, June 15, 1884.
52. *Ibid.*, August 24, 1884.
53. *Ibid.*, November 30, 1884.
54. *Ibid.*, August 26, 1884.

55. *Ibid.*, September 21, 1884.
56. *Louisville Courier-Journal*, July 30, 1884.
57. *Ibid.*, August 6, 1884.
58. *Ibid.*, August 9, 1884.
59. *Ibid.*, August 7, 1884.
60. *Ibid.*, July 27, 1884.
61. *Ibid.*, July 30, 1884.
62. *Cincinnati Enquirer*, July 24, 1884.
63. *Louisville Courier-Journal*, July 30, 1884.
64. In a post season exhibition against Columbus in October 1884, Carruthers struck out 18 in eight innings.
65. Caruthers later acquired the nickname Parisian Bob when he supposedly agreed to contract terms in Paris, where he was vacationing.
66. *Boston Globe*, October 19, 1884.
67. Several reports indicated that a spectator was killed in the collapse, but Philip Lowry, author of *Green Cathedrals*, an encyclopedic description of professional baseball parks, stated that there were no fatalities (Lowry, p. 63).
68. Quoted in *Sporting Life*, May 7, 1884.
69. *Sporting Life*, September 10, 1884.
70. *Cincinnati Enquirer*, August 7, 1884.
71. *Columbus Journal*, October 17, 1884.
72. *Louisville Courier-Journal*, October 17, 1884.
73. *St. Louis Post-Dispatch*, August 5, 1884.
74. *Sporting Life*, July 23, 1884.
75. Before the regular season began, Columbus posted two satisfying exhibition wins over Grand Rapids, managed by former Columbus skipper Horace Phillips.
76. In 1885 Kuehne set a record for hitting the most triples in a season (19) without hitting a home run, acquiring the nickname Dreisocker ("triple" in German) in the process.
77. *Cincinnati Enquirer*, September 8, 1884.
78. Future major league star William (Dummy) Hoy attended the same school.
79. *Sporting Life*, May 21, 1884.
80. *New York Times*, May 12, 1884.
81. *Philadelphia Times*, June 29, 1884.
82. One of the obstacles facing the Metropolitan Exhibition Company was the fact that the annual rent on the Polo Grounds, which both New York teams eventually shared, was $9,500, far more than most other clubs paid.
83. *Sporting Life*, July 2, 1884.
84. At the end of the 1884 season, Stovey was considered the AA batting champion, and later Esterbrook of the Metropolitans was awarded the title. It was not until years later than a more detailed analysis showed Orr to be the true champion.
85. *Sporting Life*, July 9, 1884. Although there were multiple witnesses, Lynch, Roseman, and Jim Mutrie denied that the fight took place.
86. *St. Louis Post-Dispatch*, October 11, 1884.

## Chapter 14

1. *Cincinnati Enquirer*, April 19, 1884.
2. *St. Louis Post-Dispatch*, May 10, 1884.
3. The story of the Altoona Unions can be found in James Forr's SABR Bioproject entry on the team. http://sabr.org/bioproj/team/213b8775.
4. *St. Louis Globe-Democrat*, April 28, 1884.
5. *Cleveland Herald* quoted in *Detroit Free Press*, May 18, 1884.
6. Two Altoona players, Jim Brown and Charley Manlove, became the subject of a bitter dispute between Indianapolis and New York when both clubs claimed them. They were awarded to New York.
7. *Kansas City Journal* quoted in *Boston Globe*, May 23, 1884.
8. In July, the UA decided to remove all of Altoona's games from the record, which was commonly done in that era. Most modern statisticians include them.
9. Apparently, the players also had problems getting along with each other. Al Spink related a story of Dunlap and a teammate engaging in an arranged boxing match, which Dunlap won (Spink, p. 198).
10. *St. Louis Post-Dispatch*, July 10, 1884.
11. *New York Clipper*, July 12, 1884. The players were large by 1884 standards, but not by those of the 21st century. "Jumbo" Davis was 5'11" and 195 pounds.
12. *Kansas City Times*, September 17, 1884.
13. *Kansas City Star*, September 17, 1884.
14. *Boston Globe*, August 16, 1884, and August 21, 1884.
15. McCarthy was inducted with an overweight class of ten. His main attributes were being associated with Duffy, having a handful of very good years for championship teams, being an innovative strategist, and staying in the game as a college coach after his playing career ended. In 13 seasons during an offensive era, McCarthy had 1,493 hits and a .292 career average. He had a reputation as a good defensive player, but despite a strong arm, he made a lot of errors and posted a lifetime fielding average of .897 as an outfielder, sub-par even for his era.
16. *New York Clipper*, June 21, 1884.
17. *Ibid.*, July 5, 1884.
18. At the end of the season, Brown was arrested for allegedly stealing a watch, but was exonerated.
19. One of the reasons Brown was reinstated was that Boston needed a good catcher to handle Shaw.
20. *Sporting Life*, May 28, 1884.
21. *Philadelphia Times*, June 27, 1884.
22. *Sporting Life*, July 9, 1884.
23. *The Buffalo Commercial*, July 29, 1884.
24. *St. Louis Post-Dispatch*, August 2, 1884.
25. *Ibid.*
26. *Ibid.*, July 17, 1884.
27. *Philadelphia Inquirer*, July 2, 1884.
28. In December, first baseman John McGuinness sued Pratt for $594 in unpaid salary.
29. Springer, p. 160.
30. *Ibid.*, pp. 159–60.
31. Simmons was an interesting footnote to

history. On the day that Fleet Walker fatally stabbed a man in Syracuse, he was on his way to visit Simmons when he came upon his victim.

32. There was some doubt that the promise had been made. Lucas denied it and said perhaps White had made the offer or that West simply was not telling the truth.
33. *Cincinnati Enquirer*, August 9, 1884.
34. Unidentified clipping in the Glasscock file at the Hall of Fame, dated April 2, 1890. Glasscock lived until 1947, and in his later years peppered *The Sporting News* with crotchety letters criticizing modern ballplayers and comparing them unfavorably with players from his era.
35. Unidentified clipping in Glasscock file at the Hall of Fame, dated February 23, 1887.
36. *St. Louis Globe-Democrat*, August 10, 1884.
37. *Ibid.*, August 27, 1884.
38. *Cincinnati Enquirer*, August 20, 1884.
39. *New York Clipper*, August 30, 1884.
40. *Pittsburgh Post-Gazette*, August 25, 1884.
41. *New York Clipper*, September 20, 1884.
42. *National Republican*, September 1, 1884.
43. *Cincinnati Enquirer*, September 20, 1884.
44. *Boston Globe*, September 28, 1884.
45. *St. Louis Globe-Democrat*, July 29, 1884.
46. *Ibid.*, October 6, 1884.
47. *Philadelphia Times*, September 29, 1884.

## Chapter 15

1. The number of strikeouts not only increased dramatically from previous years, but there were more than there would be in subsequent seasons. In 1933, NL teams averaged less than three strikeouts per game.
2. Jimmy Williams of St. Louis was the only AA manager who supported unrestricted pitching.
3. *Buffalo Times*, November 22, 1884.
4. *St. Louis Post-Dispatch*, April 3, 1884.
5. Di Salvatore, p. 127.
6. *Buffalo Commercial*, December 22, 1884.
7. *Columbus Times*, August 9, 1884.
8. *New Haven News*, quoted in *Buffalo Weekly Express*, May 29, 1884. Catchers' gloves could be obtained from A.G. Spalding and Brothers for $2.50–$3.50, a chest protector for $10.00, and a mask for $3.00.
9. *New York Clipper*, August 16, 1884.
10. Despite his awkward delivery, Whitney had excellent control. He walked just 27 in 336 innings in 1884, only 37 in 441 innings the following year, and was always among the league leaders in fewest walks per nine innings.
11. *New York Sun*, quoted in *Buffalo Times*, November 4, 1884.
12. *New York Clipper*, June 28, 1884.
13. Spink, p. 154.
14. *Philadelphia Times*, May 25, 1884.
15. *New York Clipper*, October 11, 1884.
16. *Columbus Dispatch*, May 30, 1884.
17. A few weeks later, Corcoran lost a one-hitter in which his team committed five errors.
18. *St. Louis Post-Dispatch*, July 9, 1884.
19. *Pittsburgh Post-Gazette*, November 12, 1884.

## Chapter 16

1. *Cleveland Leader* quoted in *Sporting Life*, January 30, 1884.
2. *Sporting Life*, August 13, 1884.
3. *Philadelphia Times*, February 10, 1884.
4. *Sporting Life*, May 28, 1884.
5. *The Baltimore Sun* said it was $4,000 (*Baltimore Sun*, May 21, 1884).
6. The Monumentals had done a fine job improving their park, and after they left the Eastern League, it continued to be used throughout the summer. The Union Association club, which had a well-located but small park, played its home games there later in the season.
7. *Sporting Life*, May 28, 1884. The club reorganized and played independently. It was still active in August, with plans to apply to the Eastern League for the 1885 season.
8. *Baltimore Sun*, May 22, 1884.
9. For all his tribulations in running the league, Diddlebock, a Philadelphia sports reporter who'd been involved with Philadelphia teams in the late 1870s, was voted a $100 raise.
10. *Sporting Life*, July 30, 1884.
11. *Ibid.*, August 6, 1884. Allentown's odds of success grew longer when the team reinstated pitcher Tom Healy. "Tom is a good pitcher," said *Sporting Life*, "but the love of firewater is his great weakness" (*Sporting Life*, July 23, 1884). In December, suits for unpaid salaries were brought to an Allentown alderman, who granted judgments in favor of several players for amounts up to $150.
12. *New York Clipper*, August 23, 1884.
13. *Ibid.*, September 6, 1884.
14. *Sporting Life*, September 17, 1884.
15. *New York Clipper*, September 27, 1884.
16. Abraham Mills to Elias Matter, December 16, 1882.
17. Including one to the Spalding company for $375 worth of baseballs.
18. *Chicago Herald*, quoted in *Sporting Life*, January 23, 1884.
19. *Sporting Life*, December 12, 1883.
20. *Detroit Free Press*, April 23, 1884.
21. *New York Times*, April 4, 1884.
22. At about that time, there were rumors that negotiations were underway that would transfer the Grand Rapids franchise to Milwaukee.
23. *New York Clipper*, July 19, 1884.
24. Buckenberger went on to manage for 21 seasons, including nine in the major leagues, and became an important figure in baseball administration.
25. *Cleveland Leader* quoted in *Sporting Life*, August 6, 1884. A month later, *Sporting Life* reported that all of the defunct teams had lost money and

Milwaukee, which was still active and had been reported earlier as breaking even, lost $1,800. St. Paul was said to have broken even and Fort Wayne supposedly did better than expected, posting a loss of just $500.
  26. *Sporting Life*, August 13, 1884.
  27. The story of the Terre Haute season is covered in a four-part series of articles in the *Tribune Star* of Terre Haute that ran on July 11, July 18, July 25, and August 1, 2009.
  28. *Detroit Free Press*, August 9, 1884.
  29. *Peoria Transcript* quoted in *St. Louis Post-Dispatch*, June 13, 1884.
  30. *Peoria Transcript* quoted in *St. Louis Globe-Democrat*, July 13, 1884.
  31. *New York Clipper*, August 9, 1884.
  32. *Ibid.*, August 16, 1884.
  33. In September, it was reported that the skeleton of a mastodon was found near Grand Rapids. *Sporting Life* quipped, "Wonder if it belongs to the defunct Northwestern League" (*Sporting Life*, September 17, 1884).
  34. *Boston Globe*, August 8, 1884.
  35. *New York Clipper*, August 16, 1884.
  36. *St. Louis Post-Dispatch*, August 2, 1884.
  37. The *Globe* of sister city St. Paul blamed Minneapolis' failure on having too many players and staying at expensive hotels, but since the entire league folded, it's doubtful that Minneapolis' extravagance was responsible for its fate.
  38. *St. Paul Globe*, September 8, 1884.
  39. In a fitting conclusion to the dismal Northwestern League season, all the records of the year's games were destroyed in a fire at the store of Spalding Sporting Goods.
  40. Two players were released after an incident with the female employees of a hotel where the team was staying.
  41. *Brooklyn Eagle*, August 17, 1884.

## Chapter 17

  1. Expenses were sometimes offset by admission fees, although charging to watch college sports was a controversial issue.
  2. *Boston Herald*, quoted in *St. Louis Globe-Democrat*, February 5, 1884.
  3. *Harvard Herald Crimson* quoted in *Sporting Life*, December 12, 1883.
  4. Amherst later passed a resolution that, beginning in 1885, games could take place only on Wednesdays, Saturdays, and holidays.
  5. Hershberger, p. 65. Hershberger asserts that the quote attributed to Eliot in Ken Burns' epic film *Baseball* claiming that pitchers who attempted to deceive batters by throwing curve balls were cheating should be attributed to his cousin, Harvard professor Charles Eliot Norton.
  6. *St. Louis Globe-Democrat*, April 12, 1884.
  7. *Boston Globe*, March 10, 1884.
  8. *Sporting Life*, March 5, 1884.
  9. *Ibid.*, May 21, 1884.
  10. *New York Clipper*, February 23, 1884.
  11. *Ibid.*, January 26, 1884.
  12. Before the season began, the Harvard faculty committee softened its position somewhat, conceding that Harvard could play against non-college teams if the games took place on Harvard's home field.
  13. *Sporting Life*, July 16, 1884.
  14. Harvard suffered a tragic loss in May with the death of shortstop Rueben Lovering.
  15. *Sporting Life*, October 29, 1884.
  16. *Ibid.*, November 7, 1883.
  17. *Baltimore Sun*, July 5, 1884.
  18. *Sporting Life*, November 14, 1883.
  19. *Ibid.*
  20. *Ibid.*, December 19, 1883.
  21. *St. Louis Post-Dispatch*, May 29, 1884.
  22. *Sporting Life*, April 23, 1884.
  23. *Ibid.*, May 28, 1884.
  24. *Philadelphia Times*, July 8, 1884.
  25. *Sporting Life*, November 26, 1884.
  26. *Ibid.*, December 24, 1884.
  27. A good source for Wilson's infamous career is Debra Shattuck, *Women's Baseball in Nineteenth Century New York and the Man Who Set Back Women's Professional Baseball for Decades,* The National Pastime, Baseball in the Big Apple (2017), published by Society for American Baseball Research, https://sabr.org/journal/article/womens-baseball-in-nineteenth-century-new-york-and-the-man-who-set-back-womens-professional-baseball-for-decades/.
  28. Shattuck.
  29. *Ibid.*
  30. Brunson, *Black Baseball*, p. 222.
  31. *Ibid.*, p. 195.
  32. Black ball even had its own One-Arm Daily, a pitcher named E. Daily who pitched for the Cuban Stars.
  33. Hart's nickname was "Black Dan," given him due to the resemblance of his style to champion walker Dan O'Leary (not Dan O'Leary the baseball manager).
  34. The information regarding the salaries of the Gordon Club is in *Sporting Life*, March 5, 1884.
  35. The Gordons were not the first black professionals; the concept was almost as old as white professionalism.
  36. *New York Clipper*, August 30, 1884.
  37. Later in the season, the Alpines played the Newark club at Washington Park, and it was reported that the Remsens had permission to use the field when Brooklyn was out of town. Since the team had the same name as Brooklyn outfielder Jack Remsen, it was possible that there was a loose affiliation with the Brooklyn team. *Sporting Life* noted, "Jack Remsen's cup of glory is full. A colored club in Brooklyn has been named after him" (*Sporting Life,* September 24, 1884).
  38. *Cincinnati Enquirer*, October 26, 1884.
  39. Brunson, *Black Baseball*, p. 219.
  40. *New York Clipper*, December 29, 1883. The Chinese game would have been of little interest to

Philadelphian Francis Richter, whose *Sporting Life* stated on another occasion, "Chinamen have not the pluck or nerve to play the game even as well as little boys" (*Sporting Life*, June 10, 1884).

41. *Cincinnati Enquirer*, July 8, 1884.

42. Had the Tecumsehs signed two more American players, the history of major league baseball might have been different. Prior to the 1877 season, Bill Craver and Jim Devlin wrote to owner George Sleeman requesting an engagement. When neither was signed, they played for Louisville and were involved in major league baseball's first big scandal. The situation is covered in Martin's book on the Tecumsehs (pp. 110–11).

43. The team was named for London's Tecumseh Hotel, which served as the unofficial headquarters of Canadian-based Confederates during the Civil War. The hotel was named for the Indian chief who fought with the British in the War of 1812 and was killed by the Americans.

44. For the history of the Tecumsehs, see Brian (Chip) Martin, *The Tecumsehs of the International Association*. In addition to telling the story of the club and its 1877 championship, Martin makes the case that the 1877 International Association was a major league and that the Tecumsehs, not the 1992 Toronto Blue Jays, were the first Canadian champions of major league baseball.

45. *Sporting Life*, April 9, 1884.

46. *Ibid.*, June 10, 1884.

## Chapter 18

1. The city series were so important that the 1885 World Series was interrupted while the St. Louis Browns played exhibitions against the NL Maroons for the championship of St. Louis.

2. *Louisville Courier-Journal*, August 4, 1884.

3. *Sporting Life*, October 1, 1884.

4. An excellent source on the 1884 World Series is the daily diary of the 1884 season compiled by Edward Achorn, author of *Fifty-Nine in '84*. The diary can be found on edwardachorn.com.

5. *Buffalo Commercial*, October 9, 1884.

6. *Sporting Life*, October 8, 1884.

7. The *Fall River News* scoffed at Mutrie's claim of a world championship and suggested he satisfy himself with the championship of the United States.

8. *Cincinnati Enquirer*, October 17, 1884.

9. *Sporting Life*, October 22, 1884. Although Providence and the Mets were in different leagues, they'd met once in a pre-season exhibition game at the Polo Grounds. Providence won 13–6, despite the fact that neither Radbourn nor Sweeney pitched.

10. *Achorn Diary*, October 23, 1884.

11. *Ibid.*, October 25, 1884.

## Chapter 19

1. *Sporting Life*, November 5, 1884.

2. *Baltimore Sun*, September 22, 1884.

3. *New York Clipper*, February 28, 1885.

4. *Baltimore Sun*, October 20, 1884.

5. *Sporting Life*, October 22, 1884.

6. *1885 Spalding Guide*, p. 68.

7. *Cincinnati Enquirer*, December 9, 1884.

8. *Sporting Life*, November 19, 1884.

9. *Ibid.*, November 26, 1884.

10. *Ibid.*, December 3, 1884.

11. *Cincinnati Enquirer*, December 21, 1884.

12. *Sporting Life*, December 17, 1884.

13. *Ibid.*

14. *Ibid.*, January 21, 1885.

15. *New York Clipper*, January 17, 1885.

16. *Sporting Life*, January 21, 1885.

17. *Cincinnati Enquirer*, October 31, 1884.

18. *Brooklyn Eagle*, November 9, 1884.

19. *Sporting Life*, November 12, 1884.

20. *Brooklyn Eagle*, October 5, 1884.

21. *Sporting Life*, November 19, 1884.

22. Apparently, at least two of the players signed conditional contracts, which would be void if Indianapolis did not field a team in 1885.

23. It was uncertain whether Brooklyn would be allowed to play on Sunday at Coney Island, for while their laws allowed amusements, it was not clear whether a professional endeavor was considered an "amusement."

24. *New York Clipper*, January 3, 1885. The *New York World* reported that the New York Club was willing to support Lucas' entry into the NL if he could obtain the rights to the former Cleveland players, which would therefore compel the Brooklyn Club to strike a deal with the Metropolitan Exhibition Company (*Brooklyn Eagle*, December 28, 1884). The New York club was also conflicted when several of the other NL owners wanted to abrogate the National Agreement, which would have a detrimental effect on their Metropolitans.

25. *Brooklyn Eagle*, January 22, 1885.

26. Interview with the *Free Press* and the *Sporting Life* rebuttal printed in *Sporting Life*, October 22, 1884.

27. *Sporting Life*, October 29, 1884.

28. *Brooklyn Eagle*, October 26, 1884.

29. *New York Clipper*, January 17, 1885.

30. *Sporting Life*, January 7, 1885.

31. According to historian David Nemec, Hackett was an excellent recruiter who was thoroughly disliked by most of his players. His reputation was sullied when he yielded to pressure from Cap Anson to refrain from using black pitcher George Stovey in an exhibition game (email from David Nemec, February 23, 2022).

32. It was later reported that Lucas had gained entry to the NL by buying out Cleveland, making a $500 down payment, with another $2,000 to be paid when his application was approved (*Sporting Life*, January 21, 1885).

33. *Brooklyn Eagle*, January 11, 1885.

34. *Ibid.*, January 18, 1885.

35. Quoted in *Sporting Life*, November 5, 1884.

36. When Toledo couldn't deliver Mullane, Von der Ahe refused to pay the remaining $1,250 of the

purchase price. Toledo sued and the judge split the difference.

37. *Buffalo Morning Express and Illustrated Buffalo Express*, December 8, 1884.

38. *Philadelphia Times*, December 7, 1884.

39. The *Louisville Courier*, which had a running feud with Caylor during the season, was delighted, noting, "Mr. Caylor was severely sat upon at the Association meeting" (*Louisville Courier*, December 14, 1884).

40. *Cincinnati Enquirer*, December 14, 1884.

41. *Brooklyn Eagle*, December 28, 1884.

42. *Cincinnati Enquirer*, November 9, 1884.

43. *Ibid.*, November 23, 1884.

44. After sitting out a year, Mullane held out for more money prior to the 1886 season. Despite all his machinations, he encountered financial problems and eventually went broke when his saloon business failed.

45. *New York Clipper*, November 15, 1884.

46. The shamelessly pro-UA *Cincinnati Enquirer* had lionized Scanlon when he ran one of the more successful UA franchises, but once he tried to join the AA and wound up in the EL, it abused him as much as it had other non-UA men. He'd become a bum.

47. When Barnie would not consent to an Eastern League team in Baltimore, Ferguson attempted to place a franchise in Brooklyn.

48. At its meeting on March 12, the Eastern League admitted the Monumental Club of Baltimore under the management of Dr. Massamore, the same club and management that failed the previous season, but the Arbitration Committee refused to allow it. The *Cincinnati Enquirer* didn't think any of it mattered. After noting the Mike Scanlon wanted to enter his Nationals in the EL, they stated, "By June Mike and Harry Diddlebock will be all that is left of it" (*Cincinnati Enquirer*, December 28, 1884).

49. *New York Clipper*, December 27, 1884.

50. *Boston Globe*, December 18, 1884.

51. *Cincinnati Enquirer*, December 14, 1884.

52. Assisting Lucas was his former manager Ted Sullivan, who was described that winter as Lucas' "right hand man."

53. *Sporting Life*, January 21, 1885.

54. *Ibid.*, January 28, 1885.

55. *Ibid.*

56. *New York Clipper*, January 31, 1885.

57. *Ibid.*, February 7, 1885. Albert Spalding put his own spin on the events. In 1911 in his epic *America's National Game*, he summarized the UA experience by writing, "The season was a humiliating failure ... Mr. Lucas then retired, with his fortune dissipated and his combativeness destroyed" (Spalding, p. 243). That was not exactly what happened, but one did not cross Albert G. Spalding and get the benefit of the doubt.

58. *Sporting Life*, November 12, 1884.

59. *Ibid.*, January 14, 1885.

60. Bauer, *The Finances of 1880s Baseball*, p. 60.

61. They actually wore a black diamond on their uniforms in 1886.

62. *Brooklyn Eagle*, January 18, 1885.

63. *New York Clipper*, March 14, 1885.

64. *Ibid.*

65. *Ibid.*, February 28, 1885.

## Appendix B

1. *Chicago Tribune*, May 27, 1884.

2. *Ibid.*, March 2, 1884.

3. *Chicago Tribune*, January 9, 1884. Joseph Medill, the publisher of the *Tribune*, was a former mayor of Chicago and a political opponent of Mayor Harrison.

4. *Chicago Tribune*, January 13, 1884.

5. Apparently, Spalding had given Stafford a free ticket in prior years but cut him off in 1884.

6. *Chicago Tribune*, March 31, 1884.

7. Today, three or four months' notice wouldn't give a club nearly enough time to find a new stadium, but in 1884 that was plenty of time. Several clubs whipped fields into shape in a month or less.

8. *Chicago Tribune*, June 25, 1884.

9. *Ibid.*

# Bibliography

## Newspapers

Baltimore American
Baltimore Sun
Binghamton Leader
Boston Courier
Boston Globe
Boston Herald
Brooklyn Eagle
Buffalo Commercial
Buffalo Evening News
Buffalo Evening Telegraph
Buffalo Morning Express and Illustrated Buffalo Express
Buffalo Times
Buffalo Weekly Express
Chicago Herald
Chicago Inter-Ocean
Chicago News
Chicago Tribune
Cincinnati Enquirer
Cleveland Herald
Cleveland Leader
Columbus Dispatch
Columbus Journal
Columbus Times
Detroit Free Press
Evening Star
The Eye (Bloomington, MN)
Fall River News
Grand Rapids Daily Democrat
Harvard Herald Crimson
Indianapolis Times
Kansas City Journal
Kansas City Star
Kansas City Times
Louisville Courier
Louisville Courier-Journal
The Mirror of American Sports
National Republican
New Haven News
New York Clipper
New York Sun
New York Times
New York World
Oberlin News-Tribune
Peoria Transcript
Philadelphia Inquirer
Pittsburgh Post-Gazette
Police Gazette
Richmond Dispatch
St. Louis Critic
St. Louis Globe-Democrat
St. Louis Post-Dispatch
St. Paul Globe
Sporting Life
The Sporting News
The State (Richmond, VA)
Toledo Blade
Tribune Star (Terre Haute, IN)
Washington Post

## Books

Achorn, Edward, *Fifty-Nine in '84: Ole Hoss Radbourn and the Greatest Season a Pitcher Ever Had,* Smithsonian Books, New York, 2010.
Achorn, Edward, *The Summer of Beer and Whiskey,* Public Affairs, New York, 2013.
Anson, Adrian C., *A Ball Player's Career.* The volume I used had no information on the publisher and no page numbering. The original citation is Era Publishing, Chicago, 1900.
Appel, Marty, *Slide, Kelly, Slide,* The Easton Press, Norwalk, 1996.
Bauer, Dr. Rob, *Alcohol, Fitness and Cheating,* Volume 1 *of Outside the Lines of Gilded Age Baseball,* self-published, 2018.
Bauer, Dr. Rob, *The Finances of 1880s Baseball,* Volume 4 of *Outside the Lines of Gilded Age Baseball,* self-published, 2020.
Bevis, Charlie, *Tim Keefe: A Biography of the Hall of Fame Pitcher and Player Rights Advocate,* McFarland, Jefferson, 2015.
Brunson, James E., III, *Black Baseball 1858–1900, Volumes I–III,* McFarland, Jefferson, 2019.
Brunson, James E., III, *The Early Image of Black Baseball,* McFarland, Jefferson, 2009.
Cash, Jon David, *Before They Were Cardinals,* University of Nebraska Press, Lincoln, 2002.
Casway, Jerrold, *Ed Delahanty and the Emerald Age of Baseball,* Notre Dame Press, Notre Dame, 2005.
Devine, Christopher, *Harry Wright: The Father of Professional Baseball,* McFarland, Jefferson, 2003.
DiSalvatore, Bryan, *A Clever Base-Ballist: The Life and Times of John Montgomery Ward,* Johns Hopkins University Press, Baltimore, 1999.
Fleitz, David L., *Cap Anson: The Grand Old Man of Baseball,* McFarland, Jefferson, 2005.
Hershberger, Richard, *Strike Four,* Rowman & Littlefield, Lanham, 2019.
Hetrick, J. Thomas, *Chris Von der Ahe and the St. Louis Browns,* Pocol Press, Clifton, 1999.
Hofmann, Paul, and Nowlin, Bill, editors, *The 1883 Philadelphia Athletics, American Association Champions,* Society for American Baseball Research, Phoenix, 2022.

James, Bill, *Bill James Historical Baseball Abstract*, Simon & Schuster, New York, 2010.
Kerr, Roy, *Big Dan Brouthers: Baseball's First Big Slugger*, McFarland, Jefferson, 2013.
Laing, Jeffrey Michael, *Bud Fowler: Baseball's First Black Professional*, McFarland, Jefferson, 2013.
Levine, Peter, *A.G. Spalding and the Rise of Baseball*, Oxford University Press, New York, 1985.
Lowry, Phillip J., *Green Cathedrals: The Ultimate Celebration of Major League and Negro League Ballparks*, Walker and Company, New York, 2006.
Martin, Brian, *The Detroit Wolverines: The Rise and Wreck of a National League Champion, 1881–1888*, McFarland, Jefferson, 2018.
Martin, Brian, *Pud Galvin: Baseball's First 300-Game Winner*, McFarland, Jefferson, 2016.
Martin, Brian, *The Tecumsehs of the International Association*, McFarland, Jefferson, 2015.
Melville, Thomas, *Early Baseball and the Rise of the National League*, McFarland, Jefferson, 2001.
Mogan, Jim, *19th Century Columbus Baseball*, self-published, 2020.
Morris, Peter, *Catcher: How the Man Behind the Plate Became an American Folk Hero*, Ivan R. Dee, Chicago, 2009.
Morris, Peter, *A Game of Inches: The Stories Behind the Innovations That Shaped Baseball*, Ivan R. Dee, Chicago, Revised Edition, 2010.
Nemec, David, *The Beer and Whisky League: The Illustrated History of the American Association—Baseball's Renegade Major League*, Lyons and Burford, New York, 1994.
Nemec, David, *Major League Baseball Profiles 1871–1900, Volume 1*, University of Nebraska Press, Lincoln, 2011.
Nemec, David, *Major League Baseball Profiles 1871–1900, Volume 2*, University of Nebraska Press, Lincoln, 2011.
Nemec, David, *The Rank and File of 19th Century Major League Baseball: Biographies of 1,084 Owners, Managers and Umpires*, McFarland, Jefferson, 2012.
Noyes, Alexander Dana, *Thirty Years of American Finance*, Greenwood, New York, 1969. Originally published by G.P. Putnam's Sons, 1900.
Rorabaugh, W.J., *The Alcoholic Republic*, Oxford University Press, New York, 1979.
Shiffert, John, *Baseball in Philadelphia: A History of the Early Game, 1831–1900*, McFarland, Jefferson, 2006.
Spalding, Albert G., *America's National Game*, University of Nebraska Press, Lincoln, 1992.
Spink, Alfred H., *The National Game*, Southern Illinois University Press, Carbondale, 2000.
Springer, Jon, *Once Upon a Team: The Epic Rise and Historic Fall of Baseball's Wilmington Quicksteps*, Sports Publishing, New York, 2018.
Terry, James L., *Long Before the Dodgers: Baseball in Brooklyn 1855–1884*, McFarland, Jefferson, 2002.
Theissen, Dennis, *Tip O'Neill and The St. Louis Browns of 1887*, McFarland, Jefferson, 2019.
Thorn, John, Palmer, Pete, Gershman, Michael, and Pietrusza, David, editors, *Total Baseball, Sixth Edition*, Total Sports, New York, 1999.
Zang, David W., *Fleet Walker's Divided Heart: The Life of Baseball's First Black Major Leaguer*, University of Nebraska Press, Lincoln, 1995.

## SABR Bioproject Articles

| Subject | Author |
|---|---|
| Altoona Unions | James Forr |
| Pete Browning | Phillip Von Borries |
| Charles Byrne | Ronald G. Shafer |
| Oliver P. Caylor | David Nemec |
| John Clarkson | Brian McKenna |
| Guy Hecker | Bob Bailey |
| Larry McKeon | David Nemec |
| Jim Mutrie | Peter Mancuso |
| Sandy Nava | Brian McKenna |
| Hal O'Hagen | David Nemec |
| Dan O'Leary | Paul Browne |
| Frank Olin | Guy Waterman |
| Hoss Radbourn | Brian McKenna |
| John Reilly | David Ball |
| Arthur Soden | Brian McKenna |
| Ted Sullivan | Frank Vaccaro |
| William "Chicken" Wolf | Bob Bailey |

## Player Files at Giamatti Research Center, National Baseball Hall of Fame

Frank Flint

Jack Glasscock

## Other

Edward Achorn Diary.
Browne, Paul, "The Elmira-Scranton Patent Double Back Action Combination Base Ball Team," *Nineteenth Century Notes*, Summer 2019.
*1884 Richmond AA* compiled by Peggy Simmer, Edward Simmer, and Walter Kephart.
*1883–1885 Indianapolis AA Newspaper Clippings and Notes* compiled by Bob Bailey and David Ball.

# Bibliography

*1882–1886 Baltimore AA Newspaper Clippings and Notes* compiled by Marty Payne.

Hershberger, Richard, "With a Deliberate Attempt to Deceive," *Baseball Research Journal*, Spring 2017, pp. 65–69.

Abraham Mills Correspondence.

Morse, Jacob, *Baseball Magazine*, 1900.

*The National Pastime*, Number 20, 2000.

Shattuck, Debra, "Women's Baseball in Nineteenth Century New York and the Man Who Set Back Women's Professional Baseball for Decades," *The National Pastime, Baseball in the Big Apple*, published by the Society for American Baseball Research, 2017.

*Spalding's Official 1885 Base Ball Guide.*

*Wright and Ditson's Baseball Guide, Union Association of Base Ball Clubs.*

## Websites

baseballreference.com

http://baseballcrank.com/archives2/2007/05/baseball_enter_1.php

http://eh.net/encyclopedia/fertility-and-mortality-in-the-united-states/

https://mightycaseybaseball.com/2017/05/15/happy-birthday-hustling-horace-phillips/

http://ourgame.mlblogs.com/2015/05/18/the-only-nolan/

http://sabr.org/cmsFiles/Files/Civil%20War%20veterans.pdf

http://socialdemocracy21stcentury.blogspot.com/2013/02/us-unemployment-graph-18691899.html

https://usafacts.org/state-of-the-union/population/?utm_source=google&utm_medium=cpc&utm_campaign=ND-Competitors&gclid=EAIaIQobChMIpPXR7LiO8gIVbMqzCh2ahg6cEAMYASAAEgIvxvD_BwE

http://www.pbs.org/wgbh/americanexperience/features/general-article/grant-panic

https://www.ssa.gov/history/lifeexpect.html

http://www.williamwhitepapers.com/pr/AddictionTreatment&RecoveryInAmerica.pdf

retrosheet.org

# Index

Abbey, Charles 40
Abell, Ferdinand (Gus) 103
Achorn, Edward 41, 138, 140, 247
Active Club (Reading, PA) 193–94
Albany (NY) Club 79
alcoholism 77–81
Alert Club (Washington, DC) 209
Allen, Maude 88
Allen, Ned 140
Allentown (PA) Club 85, 192–93, 195, 227, 250
Alpine Club 210, 251
Altoona (UA) 7, 16, 80, 126–27, 170–71, 180, 190, 246, 249
American Association 4, 5, 33, 40, 53, 65, 70, 86–87, 102, 110, 119–23, 150, 153, 167, 175, 179–80, 191, 213, 216, 219, 222, 224–27, 229–30
Amherst College 204
Andover Preparatory School 23
Androscoggin (ME) Club 58, 110
Anson, Adrian (Cap) 22, 24–27, 30, 36, 42, 53, 62, 67–68, 72–73, 83–84, 92–93, 101, 105, 125, 131–35, 147, 149, 237, 240, 243, 247
Anthracite Club 37
Arcidiacono, David 244
Arthur, Chester A. 152
Arundel, Tug 69, 88
Athletic Club (San Francisco) 138
Athletic Park (Kansas City) 171
Atkinson, Al 157, 188, 248
Atlanta Braves 29
Atlantic League 61
Augusta (GA State League) 202

Bailey, Bob 245
Baker, Phil 19
Bakley, Enoch (Jersey) 87, 237
Baldwin, Charles (Lady) 238
Baldwin, Clarence (Kid) 198, 230

Baltimore Athletics 210
Baltimore Monumentals 135, 191–92, 194, 250, 253
Baltimore Orioles 10, 31, 68–70, 80, 84–90, 98–99, 104, 116–17, 150, 158, 166–67, 174, 224, 227, 246
Baltimore (UA) 19–20, 36, 74, 85, 125, 174–76, 178–80, 218, 250
Bancroft, Frank 43, 48, 55–59, 62, 95–96, 99, 116, 118, 138, 140–41, 147–48, 175, 211, 213, 215–16, 224, 241
Bancroft House Hotel 56–57
Barkley, Sam 105
Barnie, Billy 68–70, 74, 85, 87–89, 116–17, 153, 158–59, 174, 191, 227–28, 231, 253
Barnum, P.T. 228
Barr, Bob 151–53
Barrett, Lawrence 72
Bassett, Charley 216
Bastian, Charley 23, 238
Bath, New York 52
Battin, Joe 107, 118, 156, 237
Bauer, Dr. Rob 33, 86
Bay City Club (CA) 79
Bay City Club (NWL) 151, 159–60, 172, 196–97, 199
Beacon Club (Boston) 147, 205
Becannon, Buck 215
Beck, Frank 155
Begley, Ed 131
Bell, Arthur 215
Bellan, Estaban 211, 240
Benedict, Lew 244
Bennett, Charlie 99, 125, 223
Bennett, H.B. 121, 246
Bennett, James Gordon 59
Billings, J.B. 44
Bingham House 121, 123, 228
Binghamton Bingos 31
Binghamton Crickets 52
Bird, A.L. 219
Black, Bob 198
black baseball 209–10
Black Stockings (St. Louis, MO) 209

Blaine, James 152
Blaisdell, Dick 172
Block, David 206
Blodgett, Judge 236
Blong, Joe 107
Bomeisler, Theodore 63
Bond, Tommy 139, 151, 173
Booth, John Wilkes 104
Boston Pilgrims 216
Boston Red Stockings/Beaneaters 1–5, 9–11, 14–15, 31, 34, 35, 37–38, 44, 79, 91–92, 136, 141–43, 147, 205, 217, 232, 247–48
Boston Reserve Team 122, 202
Boston (UA) 16, 126, 137, 170, 172–75, 180, 218
Boyle, Henry 19, 189
Braden, George 69
Bradley, Amelia 209
Bradley, George 22, 55, 107, 129, 231
Bradley, George (Foghorn) 75
Brady, Steve 113
Brennan, Jack 238
Brennan, Jack (umpire) 69–71
Brick, Maurice 86
Bridgeport, CT (Eastern League) 228
Bridgewater, Henry 209
Bridgton Academy 206
Brine, John 103
Briody, Charles (Fatty) 96, 145, 146, 177, 178, 247
Brooklyn (AA) 18, 45, 102–3, 154–55, 190, 221–22, 225–26, 233, 252
Brooklyn Atlantics 5, 84, 99, 116, 131, 192–93
Brooklyn Eckfords 46
Brooklyn Excelsiors 14, 116
Brouthers, Dan 72, 97–98, 106, 110, 133, 143–44, 187, 211, 245
Brown, Freeman 66
Brown, Charles 157
Brown, Jim 249
Brown, Lew 86, 173, 249
Brown University 204

# Index

Browne, Paul  48
Browning, Pete  83, 115, 164, 245–46
Brush, John  231
Buckenberger, Al  197, 250
Buffalo Bisons  3, 10, 14, 36, 43, 68, 79, 97–98, 101, 143–44, 178, 186–87
Buffinton, Charlie  91, 142, 148, 184–86, 211
Bulkeley, Morgan  222
Bunning, Jim  95
Burdock, Jack  74, 92
Burns, Dick  189
Burns, John  69–70
Burns, Thomas (Oyster)  158
Burns, Tommy  23, 70, 132
Burr, Raymond  18
Busch, Adolph  121
Bushong, Albert (Doc)  96, 146, 225
Butler, O.P.  118
Byrne, Charles  45, 46, 73, 103, 220–22, 225, 229

Cammeyer, William  12, 39
Camp, Walter  94, 203
Campbell, George  242
Canadian Association of Base Ball Players  211
Canadian baseball  211
Carey, _____  112
Carey, Tom  65
Carroll, Cliff  142, 215–16
Carroll, Fred  183, 220
Cartwright, Alexander  25
Caruthers, Bob  159, 162, 201, 243, 249
Casey, Dennis  158
Cash, Jon  42
Cass Club (Detroit)  48
Cassidy, John  103
Casway, Jerrold  24, 45
Cattanach, John  139, 216
Caylor, Oliver P.  4, 34, 53, 72, 87, 111–12, 121, 126, 129, 153, 160–62, 181, 226–27, 245, 248, 253
Chadwick, Henry  34, 47, 61, 65, 92, 120, 183, 213, 215, 219–20, 224–26, 230, 244
Chandler, Howard  71
Chapman, John  99, 136–37, 215, 223–24
Chapman and Soden Company  44
Chase, Charles  110
Chicago (UA)  80, 117, 124–25, 139, 157, 174, 178, 180, 236
Chicago White Stockings  2–3, 7, 9, 10, 15–16, 36, 40, 50, 68, 81, 83–84, 91–94, 101, 131–35, 146–47, 149, 213–14, 217, 234–36

Chillicothe (Ohio League)  201
Chittenden, H.T.  18–19
Cincinnati Buckeyes  35
Cincinnati Red Stockings  2–3, 35–36, 47, 86, 111–14, 153, 160–63, 181, 213, 224, 226–27, 231
Cincinnati (UA)  15, 49, 74, 126, 139, 144–45, 161, 169, 174–75, 177–78, 181–82, 218, 224
Civil War  8, 43, 55, 98, 154, 239, 252
Clapp, John  59, 82, 94, 110, 113, 168
Clarkson, John  147, 201
Cleveland, Grover  152
Cleveland (NL)  3, 10, 15, 17, 57, 82, 96–97, 101, 124, 144–46, 177–78, 217–19, 223–26, 247, 252
Clinton, Jim  116
Cody, Buffalo Bill  42
college baseball  203–5
Collins, _____  70
Colored League of Base Ball Clubs  210
Columbia Club (Cincinnati)  35
Columbia National Bank  43
Columbus (AA)  17–19, 36, 54, 86, 91, 103, 114, 164–67, 219–20, 239, 249
Columbus Buckeyes  80–81
Comiskey, Charles  42–43, 60, 62, 67, 108–9, 159, 162, 181, 242
Conant, William  44
Coney Island  221
Conley, Ed  140, 148, 216
Connecticut League  202
Connell, Terrence  68, 242
Conner, Roger  94, 106
Connor, John  122
Conway, Kate  245
Cooke, Jay  8
Coolidge, William  205
Corcoran, Larry  84, 94, 123–25, 129, 134, 139, 147, 185, 189, 203, 244, 247, 250
Corcoran, Mike  147
Cornell University  24, 205
Cox, _____  201
Crane, Ed  238
Crane, Newton  37, 225, 229–30
Craver, Bill  90, 252
Crawford House  129
Creamer, George  118, 156
Crowley, Bill  247
Cuban baseball  211–12
Cuban Giants  32
Culver, W.I.  235–36
Curry, Wes  68, 76, 191
Curtis, Ed  171
Cushman, Charles  75
Cushman, Ed  189, 196
Cuthbert, Ned  21, 41–42, 60, 237

Daily, E.  251
Daily, Hugh (One Arm)  97, 124, 130, 144, 177, 189, 217, 224, 230, 246, 251
Dalrymple, Abner  132–33
Daly, Tom  238
Dan, Stephen  70
Daniels, Charley  68, 75–76, 243
Day, John  4, 12, 40–41, 46, 59, 94, 100, 109, 131, 146, 226, 229
Dayton (Ohio League)  201
Deagle, Ren  161
Deasley, Thomas (Pat)  60, 88–89, 108, 124, 159, 244–45
Decker, Harry  88
Decker, Stewart  67–69, 72, 140
Dehlman, Herman  231
Dennison, _____  121
Denny, Jerry  30, 114, 139, 215–16
Detroit Stamping Company  195
Detroit Wolverines  14, 57, 77, 79, 98–99, 101, 105, 136–38, 178, 187, 189, 198, 217–18, 221, 223–24, 236
Devinney, Dan  64, 67, 70, 75
Devlin, Jim  86, 90, 129, 245, 252
Dickerson, Lew  89–90
Diddlebock, Henry  71, 192–94, 228, 253
DiSalvatore, Bryan  184
Dolan, Tom  88, 228
Dolly Varden Club  208–9
Domestic Club  79, 194, 217, 221
Dorgan, Michael  150
Dorr, Bert  78
Doubleday, Abner  25
Doyle, John  113
Doyle, John Hadley  70, 123
Dubuque Rabbits  60
Duffy, Hugh  173
Dundon, Ed  114, 164–65
Dunlap, Fred  19, 24, 52, 56, 97, 123–24, 127, 129, 144, 172, 176, 180–81, 224, 228, 230–31, 238, 246, 249
Dutton, Patrick  75
Duval, Clarence  25
Dyler, John  70, 75

East Liberty (Iron and Oil League)  201
Eastern League  6, 71, 76, 117, 122, 176, 190–92, 194–96, 221, 227–28, 253
economic conditions  7–10
Eden, Charlie  23
Egan, James  86
Eggler, Dave  98, 231, 237
Eliot, Charles  204–5, 251
Emory College  205
Emslie, Bob  88, 116, 158, 185, 211
Endler, Charles  192

## Index

English Blondes and American Brunettes 208
Esterbrook, Thomas (Dude) 74–75, 110, 226
Evans, Jake 146
Evansville (NWL) 197, 199–200
Ewing, John 238
Ewing, William (Buck) 72, 94–95
Exposition Park (Pittsburgh) 178

Failing, Frank 54
Fall River (MA) Club 58
Farrar, Sid 231
Farrell, Jack 215–16
Farrell, Joe 23
Farrow, John 103
Fearless Club (Utica, NY) 209
Federal League 119
Feller, Bob 173
Fennelly, Frank 153, 163
Ferguson, Bob 53, 63, 84, 121, 131, 155–56, 228, 237
Ferguson, Charlie 100, 136, 208
Findlay Colored Western Giants 32
Fitzgerald, _____ 70
Fleitz, David 25
Flint, Frank (Silver) 81, 83–84, 93–94, 134, 244
Flint, Mrs. Frank 83–84, 244
Flynn, Charles 198
Foley Club 176
football 204
Force, Davy 98, 237
Ford, Harry Clay 153
Foreman, Frank 238
Fort Dearborn 234
Fort Wayne (NWL) 75, 196–97, 199, 251
Fort Worth (Texas League) 202
Foster, Andrew (Rube) 26–27
Foutz, David 159–60, 162, 201
Fowler, John (Bud) 31–32, 197, 201, 209, 240
Fralinger, Joseph 135
Franco-Prussian War 8
Frank, George 68
Franklin (Iron and Oil League) 201
Franklin, Benjamin 77
Frantz, Dr. Abraham 75
Freeman, Harry (aka Sylvester Wilson) 206–8
Fulmer, Charles (Chick) 45, 53, 55, 112, 118, 129, 237

Gable, Clark 240
Gaffney, John 74–75, 243
Galveston (TX League) 202
Galvin, Jim (Pud) 97, 117, 143–44, 184, 186–87, 189, 243–44

gambling 13
Gandil, Charles (Chick) 62
Gardner, Franklin (Gid) 88–89, 158
Gassette, Norman 3
Geer, Bill 23, 103
Geggus, Charlie 189
Genesee House 74
Gerhardt, Joe 161
Gerlach, Larry 66
Getzien Charles 137, 189
Gibson House 129
Gifford, James 49, 103, 150–52, 248
Gilligan, Andrew (Barney) 31, 94, 96, 140, 216
Girard House 55
Glasscock, Jack 75, 96, 144–45, 177–78, 230–31, 247, 250
Gleason, Bill 24, 42, 60, 109
Gleason, Jack 60, 231
Goldsmith, Fred 84, 94, 134, 185, 211, 244
Gordon Club (Chicago, IL) 209, 251
Gore, George 68, 84, 93, 132, 218
Gould, Jay 10
Grady, John 90
Grand Avenue Grounds 41
Grand Rapids, Michigan (NWL) 54, 55, 137, 156, 196–200, 250
Grant, Frank 32
Grant, Ulysses S 6, 10
Grant and Ward Investment Firm 10
Griffith, E.A. 73
Gross, Emil 185
Grubbs, D.W. 152
Gunkle, Frederick 68
Gunning, Tom 74, 122
Gurney, _____ 236

Hackett, Charlie 26, 145, 225, 252
Hackett, Mert 92, 211, 231
Haggerty, Tim 45
Hague, Bill 71
Hall, George 245
Hamilton (Ohio League) 201
Hamilton Clippers 211
Hamilton College 205
Hammill, James 151
Hankinson, Frank 113
Hanlon, Edward (Ned) 99, 136
Harkins, John 96, 225
Harrisburg (Eastern League) 191–92, 194
Harrison, Carter, Sr. 234–36, 253
Harrison, William Henry 235
Harry Miner's Comedy Four Company 241

Harsh, Fenton 209
Hart, Frank 209, 251
Hart, John 87
Harte, Bret 242
Hartford Dark Blues 3, 84, 103, 116
Harvard College 204–5, 251
Haverly's Minstrels 114
Hayes, Rutherford B. 162
Haywood, Horace 240
Healy, Tom 250
Hecker, Guy 13, 115, 158, 163–66, 175, 182, 184–85, 187–89
Heifert, Frank 193
Henderson, A.H. 19–20, 117, 119, 121, 124–26, 174, 178–79
Henderson, Hardie 88–89, 116, 158, 244
Henry, John 146
Hershberger, Richard 204, 239, 251
Hetrick, J. Thomas 42
Hibbard, John 147, 248
HIgham, Harry 66
Higham, Richard 65–66
Hines, Paul 96, 215–16, 218
Hodnett, Charley 169
Holbert, Bill 94, 109–11, 117, 166, 215
Hollingshead, John 102, 104, 129, 153
Holyoke (MA Assoc.) 202
Hoover, William 70, 75, 242
Hornell, New York 51–52
Hornsby, Rogers 133
Hornung, Joe 92
Hotaling, Pete 225
Houck, Al 104
Houck, Sadie 87
Houston (Texas League) 202
Howe, George 124
Hoy, William (Dummy) 62, 249
Hulbert, William 3–5, 9, 16, 33–34, 39–40, 44, 64, 83, 91–92, 120, 160, 222
Hulbert Ground (Cincinnati) 111
Hutchison, Bill 203

Illinois Central Railroad 234–35
Indianapolis (AA) 15, 17, 49, 102–3, 150–52, 217–18, 221, 249, 252
Indianapolis (independent) 48, 80–82
Indianapolis (NL) 3, 81, 231
International Association 4, 27, 31, 64, 113, 117, 186, 211
Interstate Association 126, 154, 190–91
Iron and Oil League 201

# Index

Ironsides of Lancaster 192–93, 195
Irwin, Arthur 143, 216
Irwin, John 238
Ivor-Campbell, Frederick 148

Jackson, James 228
James, Bill 96
Jennings, Al 70
Jersey City, NJ (Eastern League) 228
Jewett, Josiah 43, 222, 228
Jewett, Nathan 43
Jewett City, CT 241
John Davis Company 248
Johnstown (Iron and Oil League) 201
Jones, Annie 208
Jones, Charley 34–35, 36, 112–13, 163, 240
Jones, Daniel Albion (Jumping Jack) 106, 203, 245
Jones, Henry 209

Kaiser, Anna 43
Kansas City (UA) 7, 15, 59, 61, 91, 171–72, 175, 177, 179–81, 189, 198, 217–19
Kappel, Joe 135
Keefe, Tim 109–10, 165–66, 183–84, 203, 215–16, 226
Keeley, Dr. Leslie 78
Keenan, Jim 23, 150, 152, 248
Kellinger, Jessie 52
Kelly, John 75
Kelly, John (Honest John) 64, 66–67, 74–75, 215, 242
Kelly, Michael 22–23, 68, 73, 80, 84, 93, 123, 149, 242–43
Kennedy, Ed 113
Keokuk Westerns 116
Kerr, Anita 88
Kerr, Roy 51, 246
Keystone Association 201
Kimber, Sam 103, 188
Kirby, Welcome 199
Kirkbride's Asylum 66
Kling, Johnny 62
Knight, Lon 89, 102
Koufax, Sandy 189
Krieg, Bill 225
Kuehne, Bill 164, 249

Lafayette College 117
Lake Front Park (Chicago) 94, 132–33, 234–36
Lancaster (Eastern League and Keystone Association) 192, 202
Landis, Kennesaw Mountain 26–27
Lang, John F. 210
Larkin, Kate 85

Larkin, Frank (Terry) 84–85, 113
Latham, Arlie 23, 108, 162, 245
Latham, Emma 108, 245
Latham, George 23, 211
Law and Order League 18
Lawrence (MA Assoc.) 202
Leadville, Colorado 160
Leary, Jack 77, 79–83, 87
Leland Giants 27
Levine, Peter 39
Lewis, Fred 60, 88–89, 108, 159, 162, 244
Littlestown (Keystone Assoc.) 202
Live Oak Club (Lynn, MA) 31
Louisville Eclipse 35, 69, 80, 86–87, 91, 105, 115, 150, 161–66, 181–82, 226–27
Louisville (NL) 3, 7, 13, 33, 81, 99, 110–11, 114
Lovering, Rueben 251
Lowry, Phillip 249
Lucas, Henry 31, 46, 60, 89–90, 119–30, 134, 140, 157–58, 162, 169–72, 175, 177–82, 199, 218–19, 221–25, 228–31, 246, 250, 25–53
Lucas, John 120
Luff, Henry 90
Lynch, Jack 13, 109–10, 113, 165–66, 216, 249
Lynch, Tom 147
Lynn (MA Assoc.) 202

Mack, Connie 29, 202
Mack, Denny 231
Mack, Red 201
Macon (GA State League) 202
Macullar, Jimmy 116, 246
Malone, Ferguson 21, 73, 176, 237
management 47
Manchester (NH) Club 79
Manlove, Charlie 249
Mann, Fred 164
Mansell, Mike 118
Mansell, Tom 88, 113
Maple Leafs of Guelph 31, 211
Mapledorum, Blake 67
Martin, Billy 50
Martin, Brian (Chip) 186
Martinez, Professor Carlos 12
Marylands (Baltimore, MD) 116
Maskery, Leech 115–16, 245
Mason, Charley 44–45, 53
Massachusetts Association 202
Massamore, George 191, 253
Mathews, Bobby 106, 116, 158, 185, 203, 237
Matter, Elias 104, 122, 195
Maul, Al 238

McAvoy, Michael 45
McBride, Dick 106
McCarthy, Tommy 173, 249
McClellan, Bill 225
McCormick, Jerry 19
McCormick, Jim 56, 80, 96, 144–46, 177–78, 231, 247
McElroy, Jim 86, 135
McGinnis, George (Jumbo) 42, 60, 108, 159, 184
McGlennen, Harry 126
McGuinness, John 249
McGuire, James 105
McKenna, Brian 30, 44
McKeon, Larry 151, 184, 189, 248
McKim, A. V. 171
McKinley, William 50
McKnight, Harmar Denny 4, 34, 87, 117–18, 122, 124, 145, 155, 160, 191, 195, 213, 220, 225, 230
McLaughlin, Frank 80, 177, 201
McLean, John 126
McLean, William 63, 66–67, 69, 71–72, 243
McNichol, Bob 75
McPhee, Bid 112, 163
Meriden (CT League) 202
Merkle, Fred 29, 116
Merrill, _____ 199
Merrill, Ed 151
Messer Park (Providence) 142
Metropolitan Exhibition Company 40–41, 165–66, 215, 217, 221–22, 226, 245, 249, 252
Metropolitan Park 109, 166, 245
Meyerle, Levi 176, 237
Michigan Central Railroad 234–35
Miller, Joseph (Cyclone) 139–40, 149
Mills, Abraham 5, 36, 38, 40, 43, 46, 122–25, 145, 181–82, 192, 195, 218, 222–23, 227
Millville Club 210
Milwaukee (NL) 3
Milwaukee (NWL/UA) 179, 196–97, 199, 200, 210, 218–19, 224, 251
Minneapolis Browns 48
Minneapolis (NWL) 159, 196, 199–200, 251
minor leagues 190–202
Mitchell, Bobby 22
Monitor Club 86
Moore, Jerry 146
Morrill, John 73, 92, 149, 186
Morris, Ed 22, 114, 164–65, 183, 188, 220
Morris, Peter 55, 88, 239–40
Morse, Jacob 141
Morton, Charlie 26, 29, 127–28, 224

# Index

Morton, Samuel 36, 160
Mountain, Frank 114, 164–65, 188
Moxley, Lloyd 104, 152–53, 179, 218, 248
Muckenfuss, Benjamin 43
Muldoon, Mike 224
Mullane, Tony 28–29, 60, 69, 105, 108, 115, 127–28, 129, 154, 226–27, 231, 247, 252–53
Mullin, Henry 248
Munce, John 23
Muncie Londons 32
Murnane, Tim 44, 173
Murphy, William 33
Murphy and Mack Comedy Four Company 241
Murray, Miah 216
Murray, Patrick (Curly) 30
Muskegon (NWL) 195–200
Mutrie, Jim 40, 48, 55–56, 58–59, 62, 110, 165, 214, 222, 226, 242, 249
Myers, George 211

Nash, Billy 208
Nassau Club (Brooklyn, NY) 116
National Association (minor league) 4, 79
National Association of Base Ball Players 1
National Association of Professional Base Ball Players (NA) 1–3, 33, 53, 96, 98, 103, 106, 222
National Hotel (Washington, DC) 179
National League of Professional Base Ball Clubs (National League) 3, 9, 33, 39, 64, 119, 121–22, 129, 149, 175, 178–80, 191, 216, 218–19, 222–24, 229,
Nava, Sandy (aka Vincent Irwin and Sandy Irwin) 30–32, 72, 139, 216
Nelson, Jack 109, 110, 113, 117
Nelson, Matter and Company 195
Nemec, David 59, 105, 160, 239, 245–46, 252
New Bedford (MA) Club 58
New Brighton (Iron and Oil League) 201
New Castle (Iron and Oil League) 201
New Haven Elm Cities 90
New York Female Base Ball Club 207
New York Gothams (NL) 7, 11, 15, 41, 94, 101, 109, 131, 146, 165, 214, 217, 222, 226, 252
New York Metropolitans (AA)

4, 21, 40–41, 58–59, 77, 79, 84, 86–87, 91, 94, 109, 111, 113, 149–50, 163, 165–68, 179, 213–14, 216–17, 221–22, 226, 245, 252
New York Mets 180,
New York Mutuals 3, 5, 98, 106, 165
New York State Intercollegiate Baseball Association 205
New York State League 228
Newark, NJ (Eastern League) 228
Nichols, Al 90
Nirdlinger, Max 195
Nolan, Edward (The Only) 80–84, 87, 116, 118, 175, 243
Norfolk, VA (Eastern League) 228
Northwestern League 6, 16, 28, 55, 60, 67, 90, 104–5, 137, 146, 154, 172, 178, 190, 194–95, 198–201, 228, 251
Norton, _____ 64
Norton, Charles Eliot 251

Oberlin College 28
O'Brien, Jack 23
O'Day, Hank 29, 154, 240
Ohio Institute for the Education of the Deaf and Dumb 164
Ohio League 190, 201
Oil City, Pennsylvania 115, 201
O'Leary, Dan 48–53, 55–56, 58, 60, 62, 90, 103, 129, 150–52, 157, 241
Olin, Frank 24, 248
Olin Corporation (aka W.W. Olin Company and Olin-Matheson Chemical Corporation) 24, 248
Olympic Park (Buffalo) 12, 144
O'Malley, Walter 155
O'Neil, James (Tip) 88, 109, 113, 159, 162, 211
O'Neill, John 227, 230
Oran, Tom 210
Orion Club (Philadelphia, PA) 210
O'Rourke, Jim 38, 97, 133, 144, 187, 248
Orr, Dave 23, 110, 166, 245
Overbeck, Henry 37, 241
Oxley, Henry 172

Page Fence Giants 32
Pank, Henry 13
Paterson (NJ) Keystones 80
Pearce, Dick 63, 65–66, 215
pedestrianism 58–59
Pennsylvania State University 23
Peoples, Jimmy 112

Peoria (NWL) 28, 37, 196–99
Peterboro, New York 206
Pfeffer, Fred 22, 93, 115, 132–33
Philadelphia Athletics 1, 3, 5–6, 9–10, 13, 16, 23, 44–46, 53, 86–87, 91, 105–8, 135, 157–58, 165–66, 176, 178, 213
Philadelphia Hospital for the Insane 55
Philadelphia Keystones 87, 90, 106, 115, 125, 174–76, 180, 193, 218
Philadelphia Mutuals 210
Philadelphia (NL) 5, 7, 10, 15–16, 21, 35–36, 46, 99–101, 135–36
Phillips, Horace 4, 45, 48, 51–56, 60, 62, 75, 113, 129, 156, 164, 196, 198–200, 220, 239, 241, 249
Phillips, William 152, 225
Phillips, William (promoter of women's baseball) 207
Pike, Lipman 107
Pinkney, George 37, 225
pitching 183–89
Pittsburgh Alleghenies 19, 55, 80, 82, 86–87, 117, 150, 155–57, 178, 189, 199, 217, 220, 227, 239
Pittsburgh Pirates 216
Pittsburgh (UA) 7, 178–79
Players' League 40–41, 119, 232
Polo Grounds 13, 40, 59, 109, 166–67, 214, 249
Portsmouth (Ohio League) 201
Portsmouth, Virginia 19
Powell, William 208
Pratt, Al 4, 80, 82, 119, 183
Pratt, Tom 119, 121, 125–26, 176, 249
Price, James 15, 94, 131, 146, 203
Princeton University 204
Providence Grays 3, 11, 15, 30–31, 38, 48, 57–59, 87, 94–96, 100–1, 131, 138–43, 147–48, 166, 172, 189, 213 16, 221, 247, 252
Pythian Club (Philadelphia, PA) 209

Quest, Joe 83, 88, 117
Quigley, John 245
Quincy (NWL) 172, 196–99
Quinn, Billy 69
Quinn, Joe 129–30, 238

Radbourn, Charles (Hoss) 22, 31, 94–96, 138–43, 147–49, 165, 184–89, 215–16, 247
Radford, Paul 142, 216
Rankin, William 40, 59
Reach, Al 19, 24, 46, 53, 57, 100, 123

# Index

Reading (Eastern League) 192
Reccius, Phil 166–67
Reccius, T.W. 115
Reeder, Julius (Icicle) 73
Reilly, John 112–14, 163, 166
Reipschlager, Charley 113, 215
Remsen, John 103, 215, 251
Remsen Club 210, 251
Renfroe, William 31
reserve rule 37–38, 44, 120, 144, 240, 244
reserve teams 122
Richardson, Hardy 68, 143
Richmond, John 21
Richmond, John Lee 22, 95, 188, 203
Richmond Virginians 7, 16, 29, 60–61, 85, 153–54, 191–94, 221, 228, 248
Richter, Francis 208–9, 220, 229, 252
Ringo, Frank 86, 136
Robert E. Lee Club 81
Robinson, Jackie 25, 28–29
Robinson, Yank 238
Rocap, Adam 117
Rochester Hop Bitters 53
Rogers, John 242
Rogers, J.S. 247
Rohner, Frank 245
Root, _____ 229
Rorabaugh, W.J. 78–79
Roseman, James (Chief) 166, 249
Ross, Robert 161–62
Rough and Ready Club 209
Rowe, Dave 172, 228, 230–31
Rowen, Ed 13, 79
Rozelle, Pete 213
Rush, Dr. Benjamin 77, 243
Rust, John 195
Ruth, Babe 106, 133
Ryan, Nolan 105

Sadie Thompsons 208
Saginaw (NWL) 105, 147, 196–97, 199
St. Francis Xavier College 45
St. John's College 211
St. Louis Brown Stockings 3–4, 7, 9, 12, 41–43, 86, 88–89, 107–8, 120, 127–28, 159–60, 162, 181, 214, 226–27
St. Louis Maroons 19, 31, 61, 96, 125, 127, 129, 162, 169–72, 174–76, 178–82, 199, 206, 215, 217–18, 224–25, 231
St. Louis Red Stockings 210
St. Mary's College 108
St. Paul (NWL/UA) 7, 179, 196–97, 199–200, 218, 251
Savannah (GA State League) 202

Scanlon, Michael 104, 125, 179, 221, 228–29, 253
Scarlett, Michael 87
Schmelz, Gus 18, 114, 164–65
Schoeneck, Louis 22
Seddon, W.C. 193
Seery, Emmett 19, 238
Serad, Billy 211
Seward, George 68, 70, 74–75
Shaffer, George 83, 97, 129, 144, 172, 176, 180, 224, 228, 231
Sharsig, William 44–45, 53, 87
Shattuck, Deborah 208
Shaughnessy, Sir Thomas 242
Shaw, Fred (Dupee) 22, 99, 136–37, 174, 177, 217, 223, 230–31, 249
Sherman, General William T. 65
Simental, Josefa 30
Simmons, Joe 65, 82, 176–77
Simmons, Lew 13, 44–45, 158, 176, 248–50
Sitting Bull 42
Slattery, Mike 173, 238
Sleeman, George 211, 252
Smiley, William 248
Smith, George (Germany) 171, 225
Smith, Thomas 157
Snyder, Charles (Pop) 111, 153, 163
Soden, Arthur 34, 38, 43–46, 91, 123, 229
Sommer, Joe 69, 116, 246
South End Grounds (Boston) 143, 173
Southeastern League 228
Southern League 61, 228
Southwestern League 61
Spalding, Albert 19, 24–27, 33, 39–41, 43, 46, 68, 73, 83, 92–93, 106, 125, 133–34, 147, 183, 217, 228, 235–36, 241, 244, 250, 253
Spalding, Walter 39
Spink, Alfred 2, 41, 59, 160, 214, 248
Spink, William 41, 107
Sportsman's Park (St. Louis) 42
spring training 24, 244
Springer, Jon 176
Springfield (Ohio League) 201
stadiums 12
Stafford, Captain John F. 234–36, 253,
Start, Joe 21, 95–96, 140, 215–16, 237
Stearns, Frederick 224
Steinbrenner, George 41, 242
Stenhauer, Mrs. _____ 88
Stern, Bill 50–51
Stern, Jacob 128

Stillwater (NWL) 32, 196–97, 199
Stonebridge Lithographing Company 112–13
Stovey, George 26
Stovey, Harry 36, 106–7, 166, 245
Sullivan, Dave 19, 67, 74
Sullivan, Ted 37, 42–43, 48, 59–62, 108–10, 127–29, 171–72, 195, 197, 217–19, 242, 246, 253
Sunday, Billy 84, 93
Sunday baseball 16–19, 198, 220, 240, 252
Super Bowl 213
Sutton, Ezra 65–66, 92, 237
Swartwood, Ed 118, 229
Sweeney, Bill 37, 85, 174, 180
Sweeney, Charlie 30–31, 95, 138–42, 148, 157, 177, 189, 216, 228, 231, 247
Sweeney, Rooney 85–86
Syracuse (NL) 3

Taylor, Billy 118, 157–58, 169, 248
Taylor, George 155
Taylor, George (Live Oak) 155
Tebeau, Patsy 71
Tecumseh International Association Club 4, 79, 94, 117, 211, 252
Temple Cup 216
Terre Haute (NWL) 36, 80, 196–98, 251
Terry, William (Adonis) 68, 103
Texas League 61
Thompson, William 46, 66–67, 98–99, 137, 223–24
Thoomwin, Thomas 86
Thorner, Justus 111–12, 121, 126, 144
Todd, James 66
Toledo (AA) 25–27, 29, 102, 104–5, 127–28, 150, 154, 167, 195, 217, 219, 226–27, 247, 252
Toronto Club 211
Traffley, Bill 74
travel 14, 196
Trenton (Eastern League) 194–95, 227–28
Tri-State League 228
Trott, Sam 70
Troy (NL) 3–5, 7, 52–53, 84, 86, 110, 239

umpires 63–76, 243
Union Association 6, 16, 33, 38, 40, 65, 75, 89, 94, 97, 102, 105, 111, 117, 119, 120–27, 129, 134, 140, 169–77, 180–82, 191, 193–94, 199, 217–19, 226, 229–31, 239

Union College 114
Union Colored Base Ball League 210
Union Grounds (Brooklyn) 12, 39, 103
Union League (aka Eastern League) 119
Unique Club (Chicago, IL) 209
University of Georgia 205
University of Michigan 28–29, 147, 224

Valentine, John 67
Van Court, Eugene 69, 72–73, 134
Van Dyke, _____ 36
Vassar College 206
Vinton, William 23, 136
Virginia-North Carolina League 61
Virginia State League 61
Voigt, David 130
Von Borries, Phillip 245–46
Von der Ahe, Chris 4, 13, 37, 41–43, 46, 60–61, 69, 89, 107–8, 127, 159–60, 181–82, 219, 226–27, 229–31, 241–42, 244, 252
Von der Ahe, Emma (Hoffman) 41, 43

Waco (Texas League) 202
Wainwright, Ellis 121
Walker, Moses Fleetwood 25–30, 32, 105, 154, 209, 240, 250
Walker, Welday 25, 28–30, 209
Walsh, Mike 65, 166
Waltham (MA Assoc.) 202
War of 1812 234, 252
Ward, John Montgomery 14–15, 23, 30, 46, 52, 74–75, 94–95, 131, 135, 142, 146, 177, 203, 230, 243–44
Washington (AA) 7, 91, 102, 104, 129, 150, 152–53, 189
Washington Nationals (UA) 19, 125, 174–75, 179–80, 189, 217–18, 221–22, 228
Washington (NL) 61
Washington Park (Brooklyn) 103, 154, 205, 210, 251
Waterbury (CT League) 202
Watkins, William 151–52, 221, 248
Weaver, George (Buck) 62
Weaver, Sam 115
Webster, Chet 17
Webster, Dr. Helen 206
Weidman, George (Stump) 137, 223
Welch, Mickey 94, 131, 146, 184
Weldon, Harry 112, 161
Wells, Della 43
West, John 177, 193–94, 250
Western Interstate League 126, 127, 201
Western League 61, 202
Weston, T.M. 198
Wheeler, Harry 171
White, James (Deacon) 97–98, 112, 143–44, 187, 237, 248
White, John M. 145
White, Warren 119, 121–23, 125, 178, 193, 218, 229, 237, 250
White, Will 24, 112, 149, 163, 184
White, William 240
White Sewing Machine Baseball Club 28
Whitfield, James 198
Whitmore, W.D. 199
Whitney, Jim 30, 52, 91–92, 116, 142–43, 147–48, 183–86, 250

Williams, Jimmy 109, 128, 159, 250
Williamson, Ned 22, 84, 93, 117, 132, 134, 149, 218
Wilmington Quicksteps 7, 23, 80, 82, 111, 153, 175–77, 179–80, 191–94, 200
Wilson, Sylvester (aka Harry Freeman) 207–8, 251
Winona (NWL) 199–200
Winship, H.B. 95
Wise, Sam 33, 149
Wolf, William (Chicken) 115, 164, 245
women's baseball 206–209
Wood, George 132
Worcester (NL) 3–5, 7, 56, 106
Worcester (MA Assoc.) 139, 202
World Series 213–16, 252
Wright, Frank 139, 144, 175
Wright, George 24, 38, 46, 95, 126, 141–42, 239
Wright, Harry 1–2, 21, 30, 35, 43, 46–48, 56–57, 62, 72, 87, 99–101, 111, 118, 121, 126, 130, 135, 139, 140–42, 175, 224, 241
Wright and Ditson 19, 121

Yale University 23, 136, 157, 203–4
York (Eastern League) 192, 195, 227
York (Keystone Assoc.) 202
York, Tom 87, 116, 237
Young, _____ 68
Young, Nicholas 71, 222, 225, 228–29
Youngstown (Iron and Oil League) 201

Zang, David 29

www.ingramcontent.com/pod-product-compliance
Lightning Source LLC
Chambersburg PA
CBHW060338010526
44117CB00017B/2875